DISBELIEF

THE ORIGINS OF ATHEISM IN A RELIGIOUS SPECIES

WILL M. GERVAIS, PhD

Essex, Connecticut

Prometheus Books
An imprint of Globe Pequot, the trade division of The Rowman & Littlefield Publishing Group, Inc.
4501 Forbes Blvd., Ste. 200
Lanham, MD 20706
www.rowman.com

Distributed by NATIONAL BOOK NETWORK

British Library Cataloguing in Publication Information Available

Library of Congress Cataloging-in-Publication Data

Names: Gervais, Will M., 1982– author.
Title: Disbelief : the origins of atheism in a religious species / Will M. Gervais, PhD.
Description: Lanham, MD : Prometheus, [2024] | Includes bibliographical references. | Summary: "A revelatory book, Disbelief is not about defining the relationship between science and religion; it's about using science to better understand religion in order to better understand human nature"—Provided by publisher.
Identifiers: LCCN 2023053912 (print) | LCCN 2023053913 (ebook) | ISBN 9781633889248 (hardback) | ISBN 9781633889255 (epub)
Subjects: LCSH: Atheism. | Faith. | Religion and science.
Classification: LCC BL2747.3 G45 2024 (print) | LCC BL2747.3 (ebook) | DDC 211/.8—dc23/eng/20240126
LC record available at https://lccn.loc.gov/2023053912
LC ebook record available at https://lccn.loc.gov/2023053913

™ The paper used in this publication meets the minimum requirements of American National Standard for Information Sciences—Permanence of Paper for Printed Library Materials, ANSI/NISO Z39.48-1992

First and foremost, this book is for Drew. Your love and support kept this book possible long before I started writing it.

For Mina and Huxley: your dreams, wit, and empathy are among the most potent superpowers you can carry into this world. Anyone who tells you otherwise ain't worth your focus. I wish for my generation to make good choices today so that you'll have the best possible chapter 14.

And finally for Lucy, whose zoomies embody the excitement of new scientific ideas, and whose world-weary HARRUMPHs embody then having to execute them.

CONTENTS

PREFACE

This Book's Journey

atheist

noun. someone who does not believe in any God or gods

DISCOVERING ATHEISM

I first truly appreciated the fact that atheists exist at approximately the same moment I realized that I was an atheist: freshman year of college at the University of Denver. That moment, sitting in a philosophy class discussing religion, I realized that I did not actually believe in God or gods, making me—by definition—an atheist. There was no fanfare. There was no scientific epiphany, no sudden breakthrough in logic and rationality, and no earth-shattering philosophical revelation. Richard Dawkins did not burst through the wall like Kool-Aid Man yelling "Oh yeah, God's dead!" I just sat there pondering whether I believed in God and realized that my answer was "no, not really."

Growing up, I was always curious about religion. My childhood religion could be described as **C**&**E**se, in that we tended to only go to church on **C**hristmas and **E**aster (or, in a probably unconvincing show of piety, when grandparents were coming through town). Our broader community had churches, but not a great deal of overt religion. I'd guess that most folks were religious, just not visibly so. My parents tried putting my older brother and me in Sunday school a couple of times, and we attempted regular church attendance in fits and starts. So we were nominally Christian in a vague sense, and I guess I believed in God without really thinking too much about it. But I was certainly no adherent. That doesn't mean I was disinterested in the supernatural—quite the contrary. I was a voracious reader of fantasy novels and an eager consumer of every book I could find on world mythology and religion. Norse? Check. Greek? Got it. First Nations/ Native American? Loved it. I was in some sense aware of the fact that people around the world held very different beliefs about the supernatural. But I did not personally have much stake in the question. Did I believe in God? Sure, why not? Now what's for dinner and when are the Rockies on?

Yet in university I was enrolled in a liberal arts program in which we explored a broad curriculum spanning the arts, sciences, and humanities. The first-year honors program taught us ancient Greek philosophy alongside classic Greek literature; modern religious thought alongside nineteenth- and twentieth-century European history; biology alongside anthropology, literature, and calculus. In the midst of this wide survey of Western thought, I had enrolled—spurred by my long-standing yet idle curiosity about world religions—in a class called Modern Religious Thought. Somewhat to my dismay, the course was largely a tour in Judeo-Christian theology, with but a single week's nod to non-Western religions. Kant and Kierkegaard. Hume and humanism. Apologetics and apotheosis. Problems of evil, free will, teleology, and ontology. By far, the liveliest portion of the class to an introverted and adolescently standoffish me was the online discussion board. Each week, the professor posed a focal question to the class, and we tackled it with gusto.

The final week of the class, our guiding question was "Does God Exist?" I spent some time really thinking about this, for the first time. As a class, we had weighed deep Western philosophical and theological arguments for and against the existence of God. I had treated them all as no more than academic exercises to work through. Having not yet developed a passion for evolutionary biology, I found questions about design at least superficially compelling. I found Anselm's ontological argument* silly.† But really, I didn't consider any of these arguments in terms of my own beliefs. My head was there, but I had no soul in the game. Though when I really knuckled down and thought about it, I realized that I did not believe in God or gods. I didn't feel any personal connection to some Divine Presence.

---

* In a nutshell: (1) God is the greatest being that can be imagined. (2) Beings that exist are greater than those that don't. (3) If we can imagine this greatest being but it doesn't exist, then we can imagine a greater one that does exist. (4) See the first point. (5) So God exists.

† If you're a first-year university student and you don't occasionally laugh at historical titans of thought, you're doing it wrong.

None of the theological arguments in favor of God's existence were persuasive from a neutral stance, and I don't think that's how faith is supposed to work anyways. Was I an atheist? Yes, I was, I suppose. I hesitantly registered my religious skepticism in the discussion thread.

Many readers will have encountered popular arguments from pundits like Haidt, Lukianoff, Sunstein, and seemingly countless op-eds that universities are raging bastions of ultra-liberal secularism. According to this view, one might expect that the vast majority of my fellow students atheistically aligned with me. Maybe you're even picturing the smug professor belittling and berating the few theistic holdouts, à la the 2014 Christian drama movie *God's Not Dead*.‡

Not exactly. At this regionally prestigious liberal arts university, only two students outed themselves as atheists. I did so with some trepidation and not much conviction. But as the online conversation progressed throughout the week, I became increasingly convinced. Or perhaps I realized that I had never really been much of a believer. Ironically, it was this course in Modern Religious Thought that, for the first time, galvanized both my own atheism and my interest in why other people do or do not believe in gods.

My anti-epiphany that I was, in fact, an atheist, and had been for some time led to a casual interest in all things atheism. I faithfully listened to atheist and rationalist podcasts. I read just about every book on atheism I could get my hands on. I spent far too much time arguing about science and religion in various online message boards. I didn't have a damn clue what I wanted to do with my life, but I had a keen side interest in atheism.

BEGINNING TO STUDY ATHEISM

Fast forward a few years. I was set to graduate from the University of Denver with a psychology major, although my heavy interests were rooted in evolutionary biology (I minored in biology and anthropology to complete the set). I was fascinated by the diversity of life, the theoretical unity and depth of evolution, and the peculiarities of *Homo sapiens sapiens*. I had been drawn to evolutionary biology through wonderful books like Richard

‡ $2 million budget, $62 million gross earnings, 13 percent approval via Rotten Tomato's Tomatometer.

Dawkins's *The Selfish Gene* and the late Steven J. Gould's *Full House*, which I had grabbed more or less at random from a library shelf. I knew I wanted to study psychology, but with an emphasis on our evolutionary inheritance.

I decided to try my hand at graduate school and focused on potential graduate programs that focused on evolutionary and cultural approaches to human behavior. I enrolled in the PhD program at the University of British Columbia, eager to work with eminent cultural and evolutionary scientists like Mark Schaller, Steve Heine, and Joe Henrich, alongside my primary adviser Ara Norenzayan. A cultural psychologist by training and rising star in the field, Ara had recently begun a productive line of research into the evolutionary and cultural origins of religious cognition. Why is it that almost every member of our species believes in supernatural beings? Why do we devote time and energy engaging in costly and painful rituals to prove our faith in the unseen? As an aspiring cultural and evolutionary psychologist with a long-standing interest in religions, UBC was an ideal academic home for me. The fact that it would also be possible to apply evolutionary thinking to religion—which I'd long been casually interested in—was a bonus too good to pass up.[§]

I knew broadly what I wanted to research (something about religion?) but didn't have a dedicated concentration. I remember perusing the news and seeing a Gallup poll about the electability of various candidates. This was a few years post-9-11 and the culture wars were in full swing. Anti-Muslim bigotry was sky-high, the United States was engaged in not one but two wars in the Middle East. So which group did US citizens view as the least electable? Muslims? No, it was atheists. Similar polls also painted atheists as the least welcome marriage partners, and the group of people with the most discordant view of America. I remember being dumbfounded: why would so many people evidently have such strong negative views about a group with no real collective presence in American life? I turned to the scientific literature and found . . . very little. It was a bit of a dead zone. There was very little research asking questions about atheists, especially within my nominal home field of social psychology. It seemed like the type of topic we should know more about, and I wanted to be one of the people helping us learn. I distinctly remember one conversation

---

[§] Vancouver's natural surroundings didn't hurt UBC's sales pitch.

my wife, Drew, and I had in our tiny apartment in Vancouver about how little science there was on atheists—it was wide open scientific territory. I half-jokingly said that I should change my focus and just become the go-to expert on the psychology of atheism.

But this jest turned out to be an exciting realization—that I could take my casual interest in atheism and my academic passion for evolutionary research and unite them. I immersed myself in my scholarly research while still maintaining a side interest in the cultural emergence of atheism and atheist advocacy. I was in many ways an easy target for the New Atheists when 2006 came along and books like *The God Delusion* were released. Here was one of my intellectual heroes, at the time—Richard Dawkins, who'd kindled my interest in evolutionary thinking—writing an entire book all about atheism at the exact same time I'd decided to pour myself into research on atheism!

My excitement over the New Atheism was short-lived, however. I was learning more and more about the science of how religion works. And the world described by the New Atheists—one in which childlike irrationality and parasitic memes combined to cause a brain-rot called religion, with grave and dire consequences for humankind—was increasingly not a world reflected in the scientific literature. In paper after paper, study after study, the science was clearly showing me that the New Atheists were shortsighted, light on evidence, and often just plain wrong. Year after year, we scientists were learning more and more about how religion and atheism work; the New Atheists, however, remained rooted firmly in the same odd and shallow culture war they'd kindled. Over the years, I followed the science as it emerged. In doing so, I moved intellectually further and further away from the New Atheists. I stopped judging religions, and started asking scientific questions about them, and then listening to the answers.

The science we were pursuing in Ara's lab was increasingly about the evolutionary and cognitive workings of religion. Why do people tend to believe in gods? Why are gods of world religions similar in predictable ways? How do some religions spread? We were doing a lot of work in the tradition of what's called the cognitive science of religion—a theoretical approach to religion that we'll meet in chapter 4. Cognitive science of religion was a promising start, but it in my opinion rather neglected the central question I was consumed by: why do most people believe in gods, while a large and potentially rising number of people reject theistic beliefs? What factors influence individual and cultural differences in religious belief?

In short, what's the deal with atheists?

Since then, I've been trying to answer that question.

A MATURING SCIENCE OF ATHEISM

Fast forward thirteen years. I was joining dozens of my colleagues in Rome for an interdisciplinary conference focused entirely on issues of religious disbelief and atheism. This conference was the culmination of a years-long project called Understanding Unbelief, and it brought together scholars from diverse disciplines who all recognized the import of taking atheism seriously. To me, it felt like a turning point—or, rather, a recognition that things had turned over the previous half decade or so.

Over the years, in fits and starts, I had pursued my goal of cracking the puzzle of atheism through science. I, along with a number of colleagues, had eventually managed to convince our scientific peers and betters that atheism was indeed a suitable topic of psychological inquiry worthy of publication in our mainstream journals. This wasn't always the case. The psychology of religion has never quite cracked the mainstream within psychology, and atheism wasn't even a core topic within the psychology of religion. Just a handful of years back, I remember my first paper submissions on the psychology of atheism being knocked back from mainstream psychology journals on unspecified grounds of "fit"—religion itself was a fringe psychology topic, you see, and atheism even weirder. When I was on the market for academic jobs, I'd get frequent queries from hiring panels and faculty at schools that had invited me to interview: why is an atheism and religion researcher applying for social psychology jobs? Or psychology jobs at all? Aren't weirdos like me housed way over there in Religious Studies? This was the baseline level of bemused apathy toward research on atheism.[¶] Many people thought the topic was quirky and interesting, a fun topic to see an isolated talk about—but not really something a Serious Social Psychologist ought to build a career on. Heck, I once

---

¶ I also got a lot of questions about whether I believed in God. And one faculty member who earnestly asked me if, in my professional capacity, I thought that Jesus has forgiven Satan.

had a department chair at a university where I'd been employed for some years suggest that I change my research focus to better fit in with his vision for the department—mere months after I'd accepted a major international prize for my work.**

And yet here we were, presenting our shared work on atheism, in a conference about atheism. The conference felt like a sort of mainstream arrival. Atheism researchers like me had worked our way from a fringe and neglected scientific topic to one that at least grudgingly was allowed at the big kids' table of scientific discourse. The scientific study of atheism had found a home. Not a large one or a prestigious one, admittedly, but dang it, we belonged. We shared an understanding—and had evidently persuaded enough of our peers—that atheism wasn't just an intrinsically interesting topic, a curiosity for a few of us. It was in fact a scientifically important topic. You see, every known society seems to have religion of one sort or another. Thus, religion is a core part of human nature. Yet no scientific understanding of religion is complete without accounting for the huge and potentially rising numbers of nonbelievers. Atheism is a vital testing ground for theories of religion.

The Rome conference featured talks on stigma against atheism, the cognitive and evolutionary forces that predispose people toward or against religious belief, the "coming out" process for nonbelievers, the potential existence of closeted atheist clergy, and a diverse range of different topics. There were no longer just a few pockets of people occasionally asking scientific questions about atheists; there was now an actual community and an ever-more-coherent body of scientific knowledge about atheists. We could now answer a lot of questions people had been asking about atheists for decades (if not centuries). The scientific study of atheism had rapidly matured in just a dozen or so years, and was casting light on puzzles far beyond those of just disbelief. We were answering important questions, and helping to reshape basic theory on human nature.

Outside the Ivory Tower, however, not much had changed. The same unsubstantiated claims about atheists were still making the rounds, often pushed by the world's loudest atheists. There were still annual kerfuffles about prominent atheist groups posting snarky Christmastime ads about

** Did I change my research? No. But I did enthusiastically change jobs shortly thereafter.

how Jesus was a myth just like Santa. Politicians like Ted Cruz still chest-thumped about how "any president who doesn't begin every day on his knees isn't fit to be commander-in-chief of this nation." Prominent atheists like Richard Dawkins were still parroting scientifically naive theories of religion and atheism—that religion was borne of childish credulity and atheism of a mature rationality—that simply ignored decades of scientific research that showed a different picture of reality. How had we scientists learned so much about atheists, while popular discussion on atheism was stuck in the same pointless discursive rut left by *The God Delusion* and commentaries in response? Why was the actual progress on the scientific understanding of atheism completely disassociated from the stale popular discourse on it?

During this period, I was living in Lexington, Kentucky, where I worked as an assistant, and then associate, professor of psychology at the University of Kentucky. I was the only member of my department with an active interest in the psychology of religion. Heck, I was pretty much the only one working from a broad evolutionary and cultural perspective. I was a bit of a departmental outlier in many ways. But living in the Bible Belt, doing work on atheism and religion that occasionally got media attention, my work was noticed. When I first moved to Kentucky, I was nervous that conservative religious elements would target me for my work.[††] That didn't happen at all. Maybe it was hubris on my part to think they'd notice the likes of me—I was thoroughly ignored by religious groups. But my work did find an appreciative audience in local atheist and secular groups.

I was invited to give talks about my research to small local meetings around the state. There was also the state-wide Kentucky Freethought Convention, which I was invited to the first year I arrived, and where I gave another talk a couple years later. I was surprised to find vibrant secular communities, even in a very red state in one of the most religious regions in the country. If anything, there were more strongly identified atheists, and atheist communities, in Lexington than we'd seen in Vancouver. In hindsight, this makes some sense. There's little need for a nonreligious community in a largely secular locale like Vancouver. But in Kentucky, in what

[††] Before I was on the job market, I had a paper get some media buzz. As sometimes accompanies media buzz, I got some emails from enthusiastically critical strangers. One told me that if he ever saw me in Kentucky, he'd show me with his fists how wrong I was. "Haha," I thought, "I live in Canada, not Kentucky, so he'll never see me." Then we moved to Kentucky the next year.

can be religiously hostile territory for the secularly inclined—for example, Kentucky is home to a choir of Bible-thumping right-wing politicians, as well as tourism sites like the Creation Museum and Ark Park, museums devoted to young-earth creationism—atheist community makes more sense.

Giving talks to atheist groups, chatting with our friends at the humanist forum, people were really curious about my work. I tried to convey how much more we were learning about how both religion and atheism work. I tried to explain how a lot of the bestselling atheism books out there ignored vast swathes of relevant science, or simply distorted what it cited—including my own work!

Friends would ask for book recommendations on what got it right, and I was a bit stumped. I could recommend good books about evolution and culture, but that didn't say much about religion. Good books about religion, but that didn't say much concrete about atheism. The atheism books I was most familiar with tended to be more polemical than scientific.

I couldn't come up with a single recommendation that would really pin down what I'd felt at the Rome conference—the sense that we were starting to have a pretty good scientific picture of how both religious belief and atheism work. And that the scientific study of atheism had spurred lots of progress in understanding both religion and human nature more broadly.

I hope that you're now holding exactly this sort of book.

THIS BOOK

I set out to write a book about what we'd learned about atheism, and what it, in turn, had taught us about human nature. As my agent Giles Anderson can no doubt attest, the earliest book proposal drafts were a mess. Chapters were things I'd studied, but there was no narrative arc or cohesion. There were dots, unconnected; tools, but no toolbox to organize them. Giles patiently reminded me that books aren't the same as lists of things the authors know about.

In crafting the proposal, I realized that a book about atheism would be necessarily incomplete. You see, if I wanted to explain where atheism comes from, or why people have such peculiarly negative perceptions of atheists, I'd have to also explain a bit about how religion works. And if I wanted to explain about how religion works, we'd need a deeper dive into how culture works. Which necessitates some background scaffolding about how evolution works. But to make that understanding work, we'd first have to deconstruct misconceptions that people might have. The book idea got a lot more coherent, but it also got *much bigger*.

From the first stumbling attempts to write a book proposal to the present moment, a lot has changed. My first book progress came in Lexington, Kentucky. In 2019, I had the opportunity to take a sabbatical year with my family in New Zealand, to work with my friend and collaborator Joe Bulbulia, as well as folks I met there like Danny Osborne and Quentin Atkinson. Kia ora, gents! Much of the proposal work, and deeper background reading for this book, took place on the placid beaches of Waiheke Island, a forty-minute ferry ride from downtown Auckland. This charming little island had the endearing idea of placing driftwood constructed tables and benches at various beaches and viewpoints about the island. So I'd set out, coffee thermos in hand, with a book and a laptop in a bag, to hike and think, then stop to write and read. This is, without a doubt, the ideal way to churn an inchoate book idea into a concrete proposal. Drafts got better. Giles's feedback on successive proposals was increasingly warming up—this was starting to sound like a substantive book.

Then, some upheaval. COVID struck. Lockdowns. Closed borders. On the professional front, I'd decided—for intersecting professional and ethical reasons—that it was time to leave the psychology department at the University of Kentucky. So I was also applying to jobs elsewhere, but uncertain where I'd land. Overlapping global and personal turbulence aren't exactly conducive to writing, so progress stalled a bit. Family, mental health, avoiding pathogens, and securing a job I'd want to keep were rather important aims.

Fortunately, things cleared. My friend and colleague for over fifteen years, Aiyana Willard, tipped me off that her department was hiring. Brunel University, in London, had a rapidly growing research center devoted to culture and evolution. The Centre for Culture and Evolution had about a dozen members, all professor types studying psychology from a cultural or evolutionary perspective. They were hiring. I'd never been to London, save a layover at Heathrow some years prior. But the family were keen for an adventure.[‡‡] I applied, interviewed, and was thrilled to get a job offer from the CCE, where I've now been working for about four years.

---

‡‡ Lest it sound like the family just follows my career around, there has definitely been some truth to that. But for my wife's career as a marine biologist, London is decidedly better than Lexington.

The Centre for Culture and Evolution is a unicorn. We evolutionary and cultural psychologists tend to, by necessity, work alone. That's not to say that we don't collaborate with each other—we do that all the time. But there are very few departments out there that seem to want more than one of us at a time. Departments can hire a token evolutionary or cultural person and call it a day. At the CCE? We have between a dozen and fifteen of us, depending on the year. And it's not just about quantity—the people here all kick serious ass. It's the best group of people I've worked with, anywhere, case closed. Smart, generous with their time, fun, collegial, collaborative. Name a superlative, we've got it.

The intellectual climate furnished by the Centre for Culture and Evolution is exactly what this book idea needed to crystallize. After about a year here, I had a proposal for a coherent book, one that Giles was confident in. He began shopping it around, and I was happy that Prometheus showed interest. I'd recognized the publisher's name from a lot of the books I'd read as I was just starting my initial forays into thinking about atheism, back when I was still in Denver. Publishing my own book with the publisher that'd helped launch me on this journey felt a rather fitting echo.

A couple years of preparation for the book, from Kentucky to New Zealand. And now it's been about a year of writing the book, here in London. From Waiheke's beaches to the Natural History Museum in London, this book has been a journey, to conceive and to write.

I hope by the time you put it down, you share my curiosity about our peculiarly religious species, and the atheists it also contains. About how we came to be religious through evolution, cultural and genetic, and the origins of atheism within that. And about how both faith and atheism teach us about our shared human nature.

CHAPTER ONE

THE EVOLUTIONARY PUZZLES OF FAITH AND ATHEISM

My atheism, like that of Spinoza, is true piety towards the universe.
—GEORGE SANTAYANA

I write these words in the Anning Rooms, a quiet lounge in the Natural History Museum in London where I've written much of the book you hold. The Anning Rooms are named after Mary Anning, a pioneering British paleontologist who—despite fierce nineteenth-century resistance to the notion that *a mere woman* could contribute to science—discovered the first complete plesiosaurus fossils in Britain and gained a measure of acceptance. I come here once a week to write, and the entire journey through the museum to the Anning Rooms is a celebration of life, and of science.

The museum's first director, Sir Richard Owen, said he wanted the building's structure to be a "cathedral to nature," and in every detail it is exactly that. The museum is a grand Gothic structure, not out of place among London's finest churches and other architectural marvels. But instead of gargoyles, the roofline is guarded by animals—extinct species on the east wing, living ones to the west.* The ceiling of the main hall depicts not God, as a cathedral might, but gorgeous botanical paintings, each representing a different species of flora. The columns in the hall are scaled by myriad climbing stone primates; each surface depicts some new biological marvel. Nature is built into the very fabric of this place, adorning every surface and structure. A cathedral to nature, indeed.

* For the moment, that is. We'll see what the next century brings.

My walk to the Anning rooms begins at the eastern entrances. I amble through the comprehensive human evolution exhibit, replete with fossil Neanderthals and australopithecines and even a specimen of *Homo floresiensis*, the recently discovered hominids whose small stature led to them being nicknamed "hobbits." After eyeing the hominids and hand axes, I pop in to see Dippy the Diplodocus, England's most beloved dinosaur. Past Dippy's room is a magnificent display of fossil dinosaurs including the very plesiosaur specimens that Anning herself unearthed. These fossil-lined hallways open into Hintz Hall, the primary and most picturesque gallery in the museum. An entire blue whale skeleton hangs above the hall, and the main corridor is lined with fossilized dinosaurs and mastodons. I was fortunate enough to see Jane Goodall accept a Lifetime Achievement Award under the blue whale skeleton in Hintz Hall, and she talked about how this museum held her origin story as a biologist—after all, before departing for research in Africa she'd cut her teeth as a biologist not in a university classroom but in these very galleries.

I walk up the stairs, past a larger-than-life statue of Charles Darwin that sits poised above the main gallery, gazing down upon the grand diversity of life he'd helped explain. Every trip up the stairs, I give Charles a quick fist bump as part of my little writing ritual. Just past the Darwin sculpture, and before you get to the statue of Darwin's friend and champion Thomas Henry Huxley, lie some of the museum's most precious and historically significant holdings, kept in the Treasures room. There are Darwin's own pigeons, butterflies collected by his evolution co-discoverer and eventual pallbearer Alfred Russell Wallace, and a beautifully preserved *Archaeopteryx*—perhaps the world's most famous transitional fossil that scientists, dating back to at least Huxley, saw as a "missing link" between dinosaurs and birds. This particular *Archaeopteryx* fossil is the type specimen for the species, the benchmark by which new *Archaeopteryx* finds are judged and classified. This isn't *an Archaeopteryx*; it is literally *THE Archaeopteryx*. The ceiling above these finds is a beautiful art installation of a tree depicting Darwin's famous sketches of the evolutionary tree of life.

Exiting the Treasures room, I walk up a final flight of stairs past a slice of a giant sequoia with key dates in the history of science and humanity labelled on its rings. For example, about two thirds out from the center: AD 1200, Italian mathematician Leonardo of Pisa, more commonly known as

Fibonacci nowadays, publishes *Liber Abaci*, earth population 432 million. Slightly further out, AD 1485, Leonardo da Vinci draws his ideas for a flying machine, human population 374 million (the intermediate marker notes the Black Death, explaining the substantial population dip). Nearer the edge now, in the 1600s, Isaac Newton publishes his *Principia*, population 579 million. The outermost marker, at the trunk's substantial bark layer: 1891, the sequoia is felled by pesky European colonists at the age of 1,335. Just to the right of this sobering display, a nondescript door opens into the Anning rooms, and my writing day begins.

This entire massive museum complex is one giant celebration of nature and our place within it. It might be my favorite building on earth. The specimens in this magnificent building show where we came from, what we're made of, and where we're headed.

Above all, *this building holds awe*. Not awe in a deity, or awe in some human creation. Awe in nature, refined and honed not by mysticism but by science.

In this book, I'm hoping to capture just a sliver of that scientific awe for nature and turn it in a perhaps unfamiliar direction: toward religion. Some people view science and religion as intrinsic opponents, mutually incompatible and inevitably in conflict. Others see them as contradictory explanatory frameworks from different eras of human history. In a more conciliatory spirit, some like to see science and religion as "non-overlapping magisteria,"[1] as separate and perhaps equal domains of the human experience.

This book is not about defining the relationship between science and religion—it's about using science to better understand religion, in order to better understand human nature. I have little interest in pitting science and religion against each other. Atheists and believers have been sparring for as long as there have been atheists and believers. From eighteenth-, nineteenth-, and twentieth-century predictions that religion would fade away within decades to early twenty-first-century New Atheist rhetoric on the irrationality and harms of religion, discourse about religion and atheism has been almost wholly devoid of actual scientific insights about how religion and atheism work. So much bluster, so little science. Heat without light.

Instead, I want to turn science on religion and tell you what we've learned about how religion works, why people believe in gods and—my own personal specialty—how atheism fits within it all. Specifically, I turn to evolutionary and cognitive science and ask how we came to be an overwhelmingly religious species, and what our evolution into a religious species can teach us about the origins of both belief and disbelief in gods.

Why evolution, you might be asking yourself—what on earth does evolution have to do with religion or atheism? At the end of the day, religion is both uniquely and universally human. Every known human society has had a religion of some form. Our ancestors have worshipped countless gods, in countless ways. We've erected monuments in their honor, and been willing to fight or die on their behalf. Even today, most humans are religious believers. Yet as far as we can tell, only humans have religion. On my trip to the Anning rooms this morning, I strolled through the human evolution exhibit downstairs, wondering which (if any!) of these hominids had religion, or something approximating it. Religious belief doesn't fossilize, but some evidence of religious thinking might. Occasional finds indicate burial rites and grave goods among early *Homo sapiens*, and perhaps Neanderthals. But most of the hominids on display were probably atheists. Not in the sense that they'd weighed the existence of various deities and decided against the possibility; in the sense that they simply didn't have the right kinds of evolved minds for religious beliefs to find purchase. Somewhere in our extended human family tree, much nearer our distant branch than the sturdy roots, there was a first species to have the kind of mind in which religions flourish.

Make no mistake: religion is as much a product of evolution as are ribosomes or rhinoceroses or ribonucleic acids or rhododendrons, and it merits just as much scientific and evolutionary curiosity. Religion merits our scientific awe. If we want to understand human nature—who we've evolved to be, at the level of our entire species—we must account for religion. Our evolutionary inheritance includes at the very least the *capacity* for religion, and we're the only species (currently) that can say that.

A MOST PECULIAR SPECIES

You are a member of a very peculiar species. Most species occupy a narrow niche and specific environment; humans colonize the globe, from desert to tundra and jungle to mountain. Most species cooperate narrowly with only close kith and kin (if even them); humans give their blood to perfect strangers and unite into symbolic bands comprising millions. Most species' communications are brief, targeted, and immediate; humans write sonnets and symphonies that can evoke powerful emotions in people centuries and continents distant.

Few things about our species, however, are more peculiar than religion. Human art, warfare, or architecture are vastly exaggerated relative to analogues in other species, but analogues can be sensibly drawn. We build skyscrapers? Big whoop, bowerbirds construct ornate decorative nests, and they have brains the size of almonds. We live in really big groups? Great, so do ants whose brains are even tinier. We can do math problems? Wonderful, but so can slime molds and they don't even have brains![2] Where humans often appear unique in some regard, a closer look usually shows us to be a mere outlier, rather than a genuine exception. This does not seem to be the case for religion. Most people who have ever lived believe in some sort of god; they are as certain of their gods as of their breath. But as far as we know not a single organism outside our immediate evolutionary lineage has ever contemplated the existence of a god.[3]

Pause and grapple with that thought for a moment: as far as we know every single sentient being in the universe that's ever believed in a god is a member of our odd little species, and almost every member of our species has believed in a god. To scientists interested in evolution and human nature, religion is a puzzle that absolutely screams to be solved.

In this book, I'll argue that religion is not *an evolutionary puzzle* so much as *two evolutionary puzzles* that can only be solved together. First is the Puzzle of Faith: the puzzle of how *Homo sapiens*—and *Homo sapiens* alone—came to be a religious species. Second, there is the Puzzle of Atheism: how disbelief in gods can exist within our uniquely religious species.

THE PUZZLE OF FAITH

Migration is nothing all that special within the animal kingdom. Plenty of species engage in an annual trek from one clime to another, usually chasing seasonal resources, or seeking communal breeding grounds. European eels travel four thousand miles to breed in the Sargasso Sea. Salmon, born in the freshwater streams of the Pacific Northwest and western Canada, spend years at sea maturing before returning en masse to the spawning grounds where they themselves hatched. Growing up in the Colorado mountains, we welcomed tiny ruby-throated hummingbirds every summer. Little did I know as a child that they seasonally braved an epic journey. These tiny birds, weighing just a fraction of an ounce apiece, held aloft by wings beating fifty times a second, fly for twenty straight hours over the open waters of the Gulf of Mexico to their winter grounds in Central America—at least those that make it the full distance, without splashing fatally fatigued into the cerulean waves.

Animal migration is relatively commonplace, and usually tracks tangible resources. As far as we can tell, however, our species is the only one to engage in migration centering on abstract beliefs. Consider Hajj. One of the five pillars of Islam, all Muslims physically and financially able to are encouraged to embark on Hajj pilgrimage at least once. Muslims make annual pilgrimage to Mecca, where they join together and circle the Kaaba, the iconic and sacred cube to which Muslims worldwide direct their prayers daily, at the center of one of Islam's holiest sites.

Hajj is in effect a mass human migration, centering not on food or mating sites (as migrations throughout the animal kingdom tend to center), but a chance for believers to mingle with others of their faith from around the world, in focused worship of a shared god. Each year, Hajj draws millions of adherents worldwide, for whom it is a truly life-altering experience. Such is the magnitude of the pilgrimage that not all who wish to attend are permitted to. In Pakistan, for example, a lottery system is used to allocate visas for would-be Hajj attendants. For crafty social scientists,[4] this system is an ideal way to look at the causal impacts that Hajj has on those lucky enough to be granted visas to attend. In comparing Pakistani Hajj attendants with those who had unsuccessfully applied in the visa lottery during the same year, researchers can pinpoint the downstream consequences that Hajj can have. Those attending Hajj subsequently show increased levels of Islamic practices (as one might easily expect), but also a whole cascade of other shifts. Attendees show greater acceptance of female education, and more generally favorable attitudes toward women, people of different religions, and even more belief in peace. Hajj attendance is transformative, both making Muslims feel stronger in their faith and in bringing a general shift in their attitudes. Against the backdrop of salmon runs and hummingbird flight, religious pilgrimages like Hajj stand apart as particularly impressive, albeit biologically peculiar, migrations.

Hajj is just one poignant example of how we humans can do something that looks superficially like the behavior we might see in other species, but done for entirely different sorts of reasons. An alien biologist visiting earth, until they figure out the interlocking sets of abstract beliefs that make up religions, might be totally at a loss to explain a great deal about the behavior of this blue-and-green planet's atypical apex species. Once these alien observers figure out a few general principles of what we call "religion," then human behavior becomes more explicable. Let's follow our hypothetical aliens as they tour the globe, to see what they see through their nonhuman eyes, or sensory equivalent appendage thereof.

In the island nation of Mauritius, off the coast of Madagascar in the Indian Ocean, we see people gathered on a beach. In the water, large clay sculptures of a many-armed hominid with an elephant head gradually dissolve into the waves, against a backdrop of feasting and dancing.

Across the sea in Malaysia, we'll see men piercing their skin with dozens of long needles, which are attached to chains, which are themselves attached to various structures and carts. The men pull their weighted loads with skewered flesh, hauling idols as throngs of people cheer them on.

Hopping to the Philippines, we see men nailing their hands to wooden crosses. They crawl, bleeding, through the streets, with thorns piercing their scalps. Once they reach the crest of a hill, their comrades help raise the crosses fully upright, before driving nails through the feet to hold the bleeding men aloft. This crucifixion is reenacted annually.

Moving across the seas to the United States, we see tents full of people who, whipped to an enthusiastic frenzy, begin to pass around venomous snakes, speaking in what seems to be an unfamiliar-to-the-region language of some sort. Among them, some will be bitten; some very few will, faith proven, succumb to the venom and perish.

Now off to Nepal, where we see monks sitting in silent contemplation, refusing to even speak for weeks or months at a time (to be fair, we could see affluent suburbanites spending good money to do the same back in Vancouver or Vermont).

Now, our alien visitors move from observing the present-day actions of humanity to looking at the things people have created over the millennia.

In Egypt, our visitors gaze upon the Great Pyramid of Giza. Standing almost five hundred feet above the desert floor, the Great Pyramid stood as the tallest human-made structure on earth for more than 3,800 years, until it was surpassed by the Lincoln Cathedral in England in 1311. The primary contents of the monumental pyramid? A desiccated and gussied up corpse, surrounded by riches—at least until looters removed both.

At the confluence of two rivers in the Sichuan region of China, a seventy-plus-meter-tall figure is carved into the sandstone cliffs. It is of a man, sitting serenely. Hundreds of miles distant, another monument to the same man, sitting cross-legged atop a pedestal with his eyes closed. The gold he is made of glimmers in the sunlight. Giant statues of this same man—Buddha—are spread throughout the region, and their construction ages from ancient to recent, their forms from simple to ornate.

In Cambodia lies a temple structure made up of more stone than all the Egyptian pyramids combined. Angkor Wat is a roughly four-hundred-acre temple city, with astonishingly beautiful towers made from sandstone quarried more than twenty-five miles distant, some thousand years ago. Iconography within the temples shows that, at various periods over the past millennium, the structures had been used in devotion to both a kindred god of the many-armed elephant figure we met in Mauritius, and the serene gentleman whose statues we encountered in China.

On a hilltop above a modern city, the ancient ruins known as the Acropolis look down over Athens, Greece. Some of these structures have stood for nearly twenty-five-hundred years. The friezes and carvings on some buildings, such as the Parthenon,[†] depict fantastical creatures and what seem to be humanlike supernatural agents.

In a region now encompassed by Mexico, Belize, and Guatemala, our visitors may be able to spot ruins of giant temples—many engulfed by the jungle, many since recovered from it. Tikal, Cabo, Chichén Itzá, Tulum: temples, with their hundreds of steel-gray stone steps leading up to a central platform, hovering above the dense green jungle canopy. Atop the central platforms of many of these temples sit altars which once hosted ritual sacrifice.

Monumental construction of idols and temples is no relic from antiquity, our alien scientists may observe. They could gaze upon the iconic Lotus

---

[†] Those bits that haven't been whisked off to the British Museum in London, that is.

Temple in New Delhi, India, completed just a few dozen years ago. Or the one-hundred-thousand-seat Glory Dome, completed in Abuja, Nigeria, in 2018.

These examples, and countless others like them, may be positively bewildering to our visiting biologists. What evolutionary force compels these strange hominids to invest such energy in rites that range from seemingly pointless (in a strict utilitarian sense) to positively dangerous, or to expend vast amounts of energy and indeed life to erect monuments to house the dead? If our alien biologists have a theory of evolution (and there's every reason to suppose that any species clever enough to sort out interstellar travel will have worked out the mindlessly creative mechanisms of natural selection, by which inheritable variability over generations leads to functional complexity and apparent design), they may quickly survey other animal species to see what they're missing. Do other apes act like this? Nope. How about other intelligent species, like the cetaceans of the seas? Nope, not them either. Neither close evolutionary relatedness nor overall intelligence seems to be generally associated with these bizarre behavioral outbursts, which themselves seem to have no visible goal or target in the observable world.

A keen extraterrestrial observer may notice that these peculiar behavioral outbursts tend to draw large numbers of people together. They'll likely also notice tight geographic clustering. People in *this part of the globe* do *these sorts of weird things*, aimed at statuary depicting *this rather than that figure*. People over there also have large gatherings the purpose of which is impenetrable to outside observers, but all the details are different. Sometimes, individuals who do the same sorts of odd acts seem to cooperate with each other, much better than one might expect based on this species' kin structures. Occasionally, fights break out between groups of hominids who do their costly rituals in different ways. Once again, these patterns of behavior appear unique to just one odd hominid. Neither close evolutionary relatives nor other highly intelligent species show these patterns of peculiar behavior.

Without concepts of *supernatural belief* or *religion*, much of human behavior and history would appear utterly mystifying. People harming each other—or themselves—with no apparent immediate environmental goal? Bands of these hominids worldwide engaging in similarly bizarre rites, but with little real consistency in the precise details of those rites? Vast sums of energy and life expended to create giant buildings and icons and statues, all with no apparent material benefit?

And all of this mysterious, painful, beautiful, musical, warlike, or peaceful pageantry worldwide, confined to just a single species.

Armed as we intuitively are, as humans, with an understanding of religion, it's relatively easy to make sense of even foreign-to-us religious beliefs and practices. Even avowed atheists have some sense of *how religion works*—we have ample experience, after all, of at least those religions that are commonplace wherever we've grown up. And if we've read or traveled widely, we're likely familiar with the dazzling diversity of religious expression worldwide.

Believers and atheists alike can recognize religion in our species, although their familiarity does not always engender similar reactions when different religions are encountered. To some religious believers, who view themselves as fortunate enough to have been born into the "one true faith," all of the other world religions are mistakes or deceptions, meant to distract people from the truth. People belonging to those failed or fallen religions must be converted, else they'll face eternal consequences. Other believers take a more ecumenical approach, willing to let others live with their faiths, perhaps thinking that all religions are but different manifestations of a universal spiritual yearning of some sort. Some atheists view all the world's religions as equally foolish delusions, relics from our primitive past, something we should collectively grow out of as a species. Other atheists simply view religions as something that's not for them—not appealing, but not a moral plague that must be eradicated either. Religious belief motivates people worldwide like few things throughout history have been able to. Beliefs in and about gods can draw people together, and bring them meaning in challenging times. They can also drive groups of people apart, motivate people to support repressive regimes, to cover for corrupt church leaders. Believers and atheists alike seem to share a common temptation to judge religions (ours or that of others) as good or bad, wise or foolish.

I'd like us, in this book, to resist that temptation. In this book, I'll refrain from labeling religious beliefs or practices as morally good or bad (as discourse in this area tends to often do). I'd just like to understand, as dispassionately as possible, how religion works. Within these covers, we need to set aside our own preconceptions about religions (be they seen as true faiths, godly delusions, or whatever your personal proclivity may be), and to try to view them as our extraterrestrials might. Not as objects of personal truth or falsehood, or societal good or ill, but as intriguing phenomena that we seek to understand. We will take a scientific approach to the Puzzle of Faith, trying to figure out why our species alone became religious. We won't be able to solve that puzzle, however, without grappling with disbelief.

THE PUZZLE OF ATHEISM

More than half of this book is about atheism, so right at the outset let's define the term, as it will be used throughout. *Atheism is no more than disbelief in gods. It is the state of not believing in any God or gods.* It is the absence of theistic belief: *a-theism.* Atheism is not dogmatic certainty that there are no gods. It is not moral opposition to religion. Between these covers, atheists are just beings that don't believe in gods—that's all. And atheists, at least those of the human variety, are deeply puzzling.

Almost every animal is an atheist, and there's nothing noteworthy about that. In our species of animal, there are atheists aplenty. That merits discussion.

Atheists throughout the animal kingdom are unsurprising, and hardly need explanation. Their evolutionary histories haven't endowed them with the sorts of mental adaptations and cognitive gadgets that are conducive to thinking religious thoughts, as far as we can tell. Nonhuman animals are atheists because they can't imagine gods.

Human atheists are an entirely different breed of atheist. We have no trouble understanding religion; we can imagine gods aplenty. Many of us may have believed in them at one time or another. We *understand* gods but do not believe in them. This self-reflective atheism sets us apart from the rest of the animal kingdom's atheists. Unlike, say, echidnas and elephant seals, we aren't atheists because our minds haven't evolved to have the requisite cognitive gadgets that make it easy to think about gods. Human atheists have the exact same capacity for faith as the rest of our species, but somehow don't find it compelling.

Our species' predilection for religion is among our most remarkable evolutionary quirks. And yet, within our religious species, we have atheists. This may seem an odd observation—bordering on trite or trivial, to people in lots of cultures where atheism is commonplace if not normative—but it's one I return to often, if nothing else to remind myself that atheism (like religion) is a human quirk demanding serious scientific explanation. Why is our species the only one that includes *reflective and self-aware atheists*, individuals who can imagine, but don't believe in, gods?

Increasingly, I see the scientific study of atheism—solving the Puzzle of Atheism, if you will—as central to the broader scientific study of religion, and by extension human nature. Full disclosure: I didn't set out studying atheism with any such theoretical grandiosity. I just found it interesting. I was a young graduate student cutting my teeth in a lab that was beginning to tackle the evolutionary study of religion, but I was also a young and impressionable atheist, eagerly consuming a media diet of books and podcasts devoted to atheism and skepticism. I ran across poll results showing that atheists were at the time among the least popular people in the United States,[5] and found them odd and fascinating. I started studying atheism because it struck my fancy, and it wasn't until years later that I really started connecting the dots with larger scientific puzzles.

Nowadays, I like to think of atheism as a testing ground for our theories of religion. Different theories of religion tend to make similar predictions about religious belief (that pretty much everyone believes, for example), but make wildly different predictions about atheism.[6] Some theories of religion—that is, some proposed solutions to the Puzzle of Faith—talk about atheism as an aberration, or as stemming from some fundamental cognitive deficit or dysfunction. Because we are a religious species, you see, atheists must be missing something. Otherwise, they'd be religious like "regular" members of our species. Other theories acknowledge that atheism might not stem from a deficit, but it mightn't be more than psychologically superficial. Sure, people might call themselves atheists, and verbally espouse disbelief. But if we could go beneath the cognitive surface with tricky experimental tasks, we might find a lingering intuitive theism.

I didn't recognize the atheism I'd experienced and witnessed in the prevailing theories of religion.

So I turned to the (at that time pretty limited) psychological literature on atheism, and again was unsatisfied. There were papers about the experiences of atheists, or looking at how atheists and believers might react differently to one experimental task or another. There were some approaches that tried to explain the origins of atheism—and we'll meet them in later chapters—but they all seemed to start from an assumption that people were, at baseline, religious believers. Again, there was an aura of *difference* or *deficit* when atheism was discussed in the literature, a striving to find the unique psychological obstacles that might derail our default march to belief in gods.

Given the numerical superiority of belief over atheism through our species' history, it does make some sense to think about atheism primarily in terms of *what went wrong* to disrupt faith, in thinking about the peculiar circumstances that disrupted default belief. But I think this focus led to a fragmented set of scientific ideas. Some scientists were concocting theories of belief, positing one set of mechanisms; others were trying to explain atheism, and positing different forces altogether. But the more I thought about it the more mistaken this approach seemed to be.

Belief and atheism are simply two destinations at which our evolved cognition could drop us, given prevailing cultural conditions. We didn't need one set of theories for religion, and a different set of theories that could explain atheism; we needed theories that could simultaneously answer both the Puzzle of Faith and the Puzzle of Atheism. If a theory of religious belief makes predictions about atheism that turn out to be untenable, it fails as *both* an explanation for atheism and an explanation of religion. Theories that explain atheism well also need to connect with theories of how religion works. To the extent that a theory can provide a satisfactory answer to the Puzzle of Faith, it would also need to answer the Puzzle of Atheism.

In the early 2000s, there was a lot more work aimed at religion than at atheism, at least in my scientific homes of psychology and culture and evolution. People were making lots of exciting advances at understanding how the predictable peculiarities of religion worldwide might be grounded in the regularities of our evolved cognition (a topic we'll cover in more detail in a few chapters). But there was relatively less emphasis on understanding atheism. Popular books and summaries about religion might offer a chapter of speculation on atheism, or no coverage at all. Religion was seen as the default. Predictions about atheism, however, could sensibly be derived from the prevailing theories of religion. Over the years, I started testing some of these predictions, and rather quickly it became apparent that some then-popular accounts of religion were simply wrong about atheism. Data kept rolling in, and as is often the case, theories needed to adapt or be discarded. Studying atheism forced a rethinking on how religion works.

Over the years, my attention was grabbed by one intriguing research project or another, most of them dealing with atheism in some way. Why are atheists so unpopular? How many atheists are there? Are there cognitive quirks that predict atheism? Cultural ones? At first, these projects felt a bit scattershot: I just threw my scientific attention at whatever seemed interesting at the time. Over the years, however, I realized that all my seemingly varied topics were in fact circling around the same basic questions about how atheism could work in a species as religious as ours.

There's nothing special about atheism in the animal kingdom. But within our religious species, it is puzzling. Learning about how atheism works is important business in its own right, but it also helps us understand religion as well. The Puzzles of Faith and Atheism can, I hope, be solved together. The chapters to come present my attempt at a unified theory of both faith and atheism, grounded in what we know about evolution, culture, and cognition.

A NOTE ON THE INHERENT PROVISIONALITY OF SCIENCE

Sometimes science is more art than science.

—RICK SANCHEZ, *RICK AND MORTY*

In the Treasures room at the Natural History Museum, a couple cases down from Darwin's pigeons and Wallace's butterflies, sits a large egg in its own glass case. The egg, it turns out, is from an emperor penguin, and was recovered from the South Pole in Robert Scott's ill-fated final Terra Nova Expedition. The explorers sought the South Pole, motivated to bring both glory and new scientific knowledge home to Mother Britannia.[7] One goal was to retrieve emperor penguin eggs, to test then-prevailing theories about evolution. The explorers traveled hundreds of kilometers through temperatures averaging -30 to -40 degrees Celsius (although at that range there's little difference between C and F), hoping to bring home eggs, on the assumption that studying penguin eggs was a good way to demonstrate a hypothesized evolutionary link between reptiles and birds. We now know that no such direct evolutionary link between birds and reptiles exists (save through eons-ago common ancestors). We also know that penguin eggs would not even in principle be able to furnish evidence of such a familial connection. Even by the time the eggs made their way back to London for study, the theory of a bird-reptile linkage had been largely abandoned and the penguin egg test understood to be futile. Explorers lost their lives trying to bring home these eggs. Eggs that couldn't test a theory, a theory that had been abandoned by the time the eggs arrived. The bottom line here? Even theories that gain popularity at one time can turn out to be foolish mere years later, and scientists aren't always good at picking appropriate tests for their theories.

Science is very much *not* a static document—a stone tablet of enshrined scientific findings that reflect truth. Science isn't a set of facts. Nor is it a cookie cutter, step-by-step process, like the overly simplified Scientific Method we're taught in grade school.[8] Science fundamentally won't be distilled to rote proceduralism, of the sort that could be automatized or bureaucratized; it's far too human to be so reduced—and for this I'm grateful! The poetry underlying science comes from its inevitable human imperfections.[‡] Science is a messy process of discovery, revision, and (at its best) enlightenment. It is far more like a complex tapestry that is being woven on one end while being torn apart at other ends, all with threads that we are learning to spin from raw materials on the fly. We are constantly learning that past methods and theoretical assumptions were mistaken, undermining conclusions drawn from them. Findings once taken as foundational have been shown to be empirically hollow. And this is exactly how it's supposed to work![§] From the mess, the discord, and the disagreement, at times reliable understandings emerge.

In this book, I'll talk about some prominent scientific findings that have proven to be flimsy, results that look to be false positives that cannot be independently verified. This includes findings I've published (and then disavowed) and findings where I've been in the critic's corner instead. Many scientific fields, including the ones I call home, are going through a period of methodological reinvigoration, spurred by the realization that many of our canonized findings are not robust, and the methods used to support them in the first place are flimsy.

---

‡ See also Schwartz, M. A. (2008). The importance of stupidity in scientific research. *Journal of Cell Science*, *121*(11), 1771.

§ Which is not to say that we can't intelligently design or accidentally evolve better cultural ecosystems for scientific progress.

In the decade or so that I've been a professor, I've seen finding after finding fail upon reexamination. This ought to instill a healthy dose of scientific humility: things we once assumed to be facts have been fairly rapidly discarded. One upshot is that this book would look very different had I written it just a decade ago, because many of the findings within would have seemed more solid back then. Throughout, I'll make every effort to flag apparent findings that I see as on shaky ground. But I am also quite confident that some of the work that this book frames as strong and stable will one day be discarded as well, hopefully in favor of stronger work.

Being a scientist comes with the realization that most of the work you do will one day be either forgotten or looked back on as interesting, yet wrong. Indeed, "interesting yet wrong" is about as high a target as we rank-and-file scientists can reasonably aspire to! Even a cursory read of the history of science leads almost inevitably to this conclusion. So if you're looking back on this book with a decade or so's worth of hard-won hindsight, and some of the work herein looks foolish from where you're sitting, rest assured: I predicted that this would be the case. In science, we're usually wrong (eventually), because science is goddamned hard to do!

I love the Terra Nova Expedition penguin egg's placement alongside treasures of science in the museum. I stroll past it often, on my way to writing. It serves as a necessary reminder: Theories are wrong, more often than not. And scientists, being human, can test theories poorly (with hindsight, of course). In this book, I'm presenting a theory, and evidence from experiments. It's entirely possible that one day this theory will seem silly, and the experiments testing it laughable. This book is my best attempt to create a solid theory of religious belief and disbelief, coming from a cultural and evolutionary perspective—based on the evidence and theory I have before me now, in the early 2020s. I hope it holds up well, while realizing that it probably won't. This is just playing the numbers as a scientist who's also read up on our own history. May this theory at least fail in a way that spurs progress in its refutation.

THE ROADMAP

For hundreds of millions of years, animals have wandered earth, and at night they may have gazed up to the sky. To most of these animals, the stars and planets above were probably not even worth noticing; it served no reproductive or survival purpose for them to ponder the twinkling lights. Some few animals extract more from the heavens, using them as navigation aids. The work of biologists[9] who discovered the mechanisms by which some birds use the stars for guidance is fascinating, and well worth reading about. But even those animals who found the stars *useful* haven't really pondered the mysteries that our night sky presents.

Over the past few hundred thousand years, just one evolutionary lineage that we know of has looked to the stars and planets and really wondered what they are: humans. To many members of our lineage, the heavens took on supernatural significance, and mythologies were erected to explain how the roving stars (read: planets) were driven through the sky by various gods. The patterns of celestial movement were taken as signs of supernatural intellects acting upon our world. More recently, some among our species discovered the natural regularities governing the movement of objects large and small, distilling the same basic forces that produce predictable movements of falling apples, planets, stars, and entire galaxies. These natural discoveries vastly expanded the size and scale of our cosmos—gone was a sublunary and superlunary distinction, separating the cosmos into what happens below and above the moon. Our species alone looked to the stars and asked what they were, first inventing gods to explain them and then dethroning their gods when naturalistic mechanisms were shown to suffice. Human minds alone put gods in the stars, and then evicted them.

Hopefully, this book presents a theory that can help us solve both the Puzzle of Faith and the Puzzle of Atheism. Before developing such a theory, it's important to consider some popular ideas about where either religion or atheism comes from. Both topics have inspired a lot of ink over the years, both within the ivory towers of academia and in the popular press. Religion is something that pervades our lives, it's something most folks have firsthand experience with. As a result, it's a topic where pretty much everyone seems to have strong opinions, and lay theories about how it works. Most of the popular notions out there, about how faith or atheism works, are quite bad. At best, they're incomplete, missing some key detail in need of explanation. At worst, these lay theories are woefully misguided, inconsistent with our best scientific evidence, and closer to popular myth than scientific theory.

The next two chapters address some popular misconceptions about the origins of faith and atheism. Conceptual clutter thus cleared, the next two major sections (a handful of chapters apiece) serve as the main scientific backbone of the book. Chapters 4–7 cover the Puzzle of Faith, building a nuanced interdisciplinary scientific understanding of how religion works. We'll consider whether religion is an evolved adaptation in our species, or a by-product of other adaptations. We'll meet the emerging science of cultural evolution. Finally, we'll ask how we come to believe in the gods we believe in, and why some religions prosper on a global scale. Chapters 8–13 pivot from the Puzzle of Faith to my own scientific wheelhouse, the Puzzle of Atheism. We'll look at perceptions and realities of atheists: are they the moral wildcards they're popularly seen as? We'll ask how many atheists there might be in the world—and find that our most reputable polls probably underestimate just how prevalent atheists actually are. Finally, we'll ask how individual people become atheists, and how some societies secularize over time. To close, I'll hazard a prediction about where faith and atheism are headed in the coming century, and then close with big-picture contemplation of how our vision of atheism has changed in light of new scientific approaches over the last decade or so. We will, it is my hope, develop a comprehensive theory that can satisfyingly answer both the Puzzle of Faith and the Puzzle of Atheism.

In the animal kingdom, belief in gods is vanishingly rare. It's only evident in a single lineage of hominids. Yet among those hominids, belief in gods is overwhelmingly—but incompletely—the norm. Zoom all the way out with a broad biological lens and religious belief is an aberration *between species*. Zoom in a bit further and it's atheism instead that stands out as exceptional *within our species*. Any comprehensive theory of human nature must account for religion. But any comprehensive theory of religion must also account for atheism.

Let's roll up our sleeves and try to build just such a theory!

CHAPTER TWO

POPULAR NONANSWERS TO THE PUZZLE OF FAITH

Ignorance more frequently begets confidence than does knowledge.
—CHARLES DARWIN, *THE DESCENT OF MAN*[1]

For a scientist, religion can be sort of a funny thing to study. Not because religion isn't a perfectly valid target for scientific inquiry—most emphatically, it is!—but because when I casually talk about my work, people assume that it's basically a puzzle we'd sorted out long ago. Religion has thoroughly permeated our societies, and everyone has at least passing familiarity with it. Many people have deep expertise in at least their own religion. Countless books have been written about religion, from the perspective of apologists and antitheist critics alike, and these works have spurred endless debate and discussion. Through experience or through reading popular treatises, people intuitively feel like they've got a pretty good grasp of religion.

So when I tell people that, professionally speaking, I'm obsessed with figuring out how religion works, I often get quizzical looks. Their puzzled eyes ask, "Don't we already know how religion works?" What insights am I going to offer about religion that aren't trivially obvious to people who are religious, or that haven't already been well-covered by greater minds than mine over the centuries? I might as well tell them that I study the wheel, how it rolls.

There are lots of narratives about how religion works. Many of the most popular accounts of religion fall well short of being scientifically satisfying—they are nonanswers to the important questions about religion. In this chapter, I want to present three accounts of how religion works, and discuss their scientific shortcomings. Some of the most popular explanations offered for religion don't actually answer the right questions, or they rely on unconvincing evidence. Simply put, some of the most common answers people give to the Puzzle of Faith don't actually solve the Puzzle of Faith.

Before we can build a stronger theory of religion that answers both the Puzzle of Faith and the Puzzle of Atheism, we need to clear our mental workspaces. This chapter dismisses a few popular accounts of religion; the next tackles what is perhaps the most common misconception I encounter about atheism. Workspace clear of clutter, we can then start theory building in a couple of chapters.

ON CREATIVE CRITICISM

Early on in graduate school, I remember sitting in a lab meeting where we'd all read a recent publication in our field. When it came time to discuss the paper, we graduate students—eager to prove how keen our scientific minds were—began listing the many shortcomings of the piece. We tore it to shreds; our intellects were just that sharp!

- Sample size too small.
- Geographically homogeneous sample.
- Didn't acknowledge our prior work on the topic.
- Is that statistical analysis legitimate?

Eventually the professor in the room, I believe it was Joe Henrich, stopped us and said that it was easy to poke holes in a scientific paper. There's no intellectual challenge in merely tearing something apart. A bigger intellectual challenge is seeing what it did well, what new knowledge or insight it brought, or how it could be improved. That incident stuck with me, and I've tried to build it into my own approach to criticism.

Make no mistake, critique is fundamental to science. We stress-test each other's ideas and methods, trying to put some intellectual pressure on theories to see which can withstand it. By discarding failed theories, by avoiding wrong turns, we gradually approach truth. Often in a roundabout way, with false starts and retread steps.

I like to think of scientific ideas as pieces of technology. They're mental prostheses that help us make sense of our world. There's no real challenge in breaking any piece of technology. Give me an iPhone and, knowing nothing of how it works, I can render it completely nonfunctional in minutes, with no tool more sophisticated than a rock. In the process, have I learned anything about the technology? Have I improved it? Have I inspired better iPhones? Have I demonstrated my own intelligence? No, I've merely taken something that, through someone else's hard intellectual labor, did something reasonably well, and I've crudely rendered it useless.

Unchecked, a lot of scientific critique can descend into banging rocks on iPhones. That day in the lab, we young graduate students were so focused on ways we could break the paper that we didn't step back and ask hard questions about what aspects of the paper worked well, and how it could help us design better science of our own.

That's the spirit I want to bring to the debunkings to come. These are ideas about religion (in this chapter) or atheism (next) that don't quite work. But in seeing how specifically they don't work, hopefully we can learn about what successful solutions to the Puzzles of Faith and Atheism would have to look like.

On that note, let's meet our nonanswers for the Puzzle of Faith. First comes the famous Marx aphorism that religion is the "opiate of the masses"—that the universal appeal of religion might lie in its existentially palliative properties. Second comes the idea that we have some God center of our brains, or a God gene that makes our species almost inescapably religious. Basically, this is the idea that we're a religious species because we have specific arrangements of neurons or nucleic acid that simply make us that way. Our final nonanswer swings from the strongly nativist view of religion presented by the brains/genes accounts, to one that focuses much more on nurture, on how we teach (or indoctrinate, depending on who you ask) and learn religion. We'll discuss a pet hypothesis that Richard Dawkins has popularized in his two books on religion: the idea that religion persists in our species because kids have evolved to just gullibly believe whatever their parents tell them. Each of these three ideas falls short in different and illuminating ways. In surgically taking them apart—with scalpels rather than rocks—hopefully, we can see the ways in which they work and the ways that they more fundamentally don't. In the process, we'll earn some hints about what a satisfying answer to the Puzzle of Faith must look like.

THE OPIATE OF THE MASSES

According to Marx, "Religion is the sigh of the oppressed creature, the heart of a heartless world, and the soul of soulless conditions. It is the opium of the people."[2] In this, Marx was offering not a diagnosis of religion's origins, but a description of its role in keeping oppressed peoples placid in their oppression. Despite this original usage, Marx's catchy line about religion being the opiate of the masses does reflect a popular account of religion's origins and persistence.

The world is, at times, not great. It doesn't take great observational powers or a keen understanding of history to see that. Famines, plagues, wars of our own making. Petty selfishness and greed. Ticks and leeches. From mild annoyances to the deaths of millions, there sure seem to be a lot of ways that this world ain't ideal. One frequently posited origin story for religion lies in its ability to explain suffering, and sometimes to help people cope with it.

If our station in life is mean and poor, characterized by suffering and inequities, there will be considerable appeal to any narratives about the cosmos that promise us that *everything happens for a reason* and, one day, *it'll be better for you*. Today might bring the injustice of greedy landlords, dishonesty from unethical bosses, cruelty from despots, or just nuisances like bed bugs. But what if I told you that one day, if you play your cards right, eternal bliss will be yours? That's an intriguing sales pitch!

So, does religion persist because it offers us meaning in suffering and a promise of eventual and eternal release from it? The religion-as-opiate account suggests that the ultimate origins of religion lie in its motivational properties, helping people struggle against and rise above our world's many imperfections.

To start, we must acknowledge some scientific strengths of the idea (remember, we're not bashing an iPhone with a rock here, we want to understand both how this idea works and also its limitations). First off, it's not entirely far-fetched to posit a link between our motivations and our beliefs. There's a whole subfield of psychology and behavioral economics focusing on motivated cognition. The general idea is that we don't just rationally process the world as it is. Instead, our cognitive systems are active in filtering and curating our information ecosphere. Our wants and desires (read: motivations) can affect what we focus on, remember, and ultimately believe. So, on a first pass, a motivation-heavy account of religion is at least plausible.[3]

Second, there are established links between motivations and religious cognition in the lab. Consider work from terror management theory in social psychology.[4] This is an approach focused on how our awareness of death affects our psychological life. One recurring theme is that we try to compensate for reminders of death by reaching out for immortality of one sort or another. If reminded of death, we might symbolically try to live on through allegiance to our surrounding culture, for example. Symbolic afterlives are neat and all, but aren't literal ones even better? The grim realization that we've all punched a one-way ticket on a ride terminating at a station six feet underground isn't fun. But what if the terminal station opens into a loving afterlife, where we live on, forever, with those we've loved? In lots of social psychology studies, reminders of mortality change people's responses, including by seemingly making people more receptive to afterlife narratives.[5] Now, I don't want to oversell terror management theory here. I think as an evolutionary account of human cognition (as it's often pitched), it falls well short of engaging with the relevant evolutionary literature. And I'm not convinced that an existential fear of death is something that the blind watchmaker of natural selection cares about one way or another. Also, if I'm being perfectly honest, the terror management literature is full of the small-sample studies testing whiz-bang counterintuitive predictions that we've seen fail on reexamination, time and again over the last decade. But nonetheless, there may be something to the idea that reminders of death can make afterlives seem more appealing. It wouldn't surprise me at all if something like this prediction ended up bearing reliable empirical fruit, whatever the current state of evidence and theory in this domain.

Third, there are some large-scale geographical trends where religious fervor burns hottest. Around the globe, there's a lot of variability in strength of religious commitment. Some societies are highly devout, others comparatively secular. Which living conditions predict the highest rates of religion? Conditions of scarcity, unpredictability, insecurity, and higher mortality risk. Where conditions are existentially rough, religion looks to be an attractive release.[6] Here is the largest kernel of truth to Marx's opiate of the masses line: just as desperation motivates release through opiates, so too does it predict religious faith. Where life is reliably tough and unpredictable, religions thrive.

So, if the palliative and motivational account of religion gets some important things right—motivation does affect cognition, we prefer immortality to mortality, and religion flourishes in harsh conditions—what then does the opiate account miss?

I think the biggest shortcomings of the opiate account are threefold. First, it doesn't include a theoretically plausible mechanism of belief. Second, it doesn't do a good job of explaining most religions, or the universal aspects of them. Third, the account is missing an explanation of why alleviating existential angst is of evolutionary import, to outweigh religion's potential costs. Let's take these in turn.

In order to answer the Puzzle of Faith, a theory needs to describe where belief comes from—what psychological processes link harsh living conditions or reminders of mortality to religious belief? It's nice enough if a theory can predict that belief will be higher under some conditions than others, situationally or geographically. Terror management predicts that immortality beliefs will be higher when people are reminded of death; secularism theory in sociology tells us that religion flourishes under hard everyday conditions (an idea we'll encounter in more depth in a later chapter). But neither tells us *how people come to believe*. Predicting variability in something is not the same thing as explaining how that thing happens. Without a mechanism of belief acquisition, the opiate approach will be fundamentally limited in answering the Puzzle of Faith. Which is fine! Not every scientific tool needs to work at every task we set it to.

I think a more serious shortcoming in the opiate approach is that it fails to explain the phenomena it set out to explain. It might be an okay explanation for why some sorts of religions proliferate—after all, many religions do include features that seem well-suited to existential palliative care. But this account fundamentally doesn't engage with the global diversity of religious thought. As such, it can't tell us much about the origins of religion in the first place. The opiate account works, to the extent that religions universally or at least generally include features that are good at alleviating suffering or unease. But not all religions do this! Heaven is a frequent example used to show religion's palliative properties. Yes, eternal bliss in heaven is a very enticing belief if one is living in less-than-ideal conditions. But do you know what's worse than living in less-than-ideal earthly conditions? Hell![7] Eternal torment as just deserts for a life poorly lived (or a life lived with insufficient deference to one deity or another). It makes little sense to posit that relief of existential unease is central to religion's evolution when many religions don't clearly have features well-suited to alleviating existential concerns, and many religions include elements that, if anything, would exacerbate existential unease.[8]

Surveying the global diversity of religions, we see that not all offer a particularly blissful afterlife. Many do not even attempt to offer much in the way of answers to big existential questions. Lots of religions offer afterlives that sound worse than our current circumstances, at least for many people. If religion's origin story lies in its ability to ease existential angst, then why do so many religions offer little in terms of existential relief? The postulated mechanism (religion as existential salve) is not at all a cross-culturally generalizable feature of world religions, and many religions don't really do what the opiate account says religion evolved to do.

A related issue here is that there are many genuinely universal features of world religions that seem to have nothing to do with existential concerns. Most religions heavily feature supernatural agents with quirky and counterintuitive skill sets. (See chapter 4 for an account of why this might be the case.) Why? The opiate account does not offer a solution here.

Finally, the evolutionary logic of religion-as-opiate is unclear. Evolution via natural selection trades in the currencies of survival and reproduction. In trying times, where survival is hard or uncertain, organisms don't need comfort, they need solutions. Opiates can relieve pain and induce euphoria, but they do not mend broken bones or seal open wounds. Religion, similarly, might be profoundly comforting to people in trying times. But how does this help people better pursue their adaptive goals? One could posit secondary benefits of religion, for instance that those comforted by religion are less paralyzed in the face of their challenges, more prone to solve them. But it is unclear how the specific features of religion are specialized solutions to this problem—and this, as we'll see, is a hallmark of good adaptationist thinking. Saying that religion makes people more optimistic, or helps them persevere, is interesting. But it is several scientific steps short of a coherent or compelling evolutionary thesis.

In failing to describe a mechanism for how people come to believe, in failing to grapple with what features religions actually include, in failing to ask which properties of religions are truly universal enough to merit explanation, and in failing to clearly articulate the evolutionary benefits that a religion-as-opiate would bring, the opiate approach comes up well short of answering the Puzzle of Faith. But in critiquing this idea, we've hopefully gleaned some insights about the sorts of questions a better theory of religion needs to answer.

GOD, GENES, AND BRAINS

In 2004, Dean Hamer published *The God Gene: How Faith Is Hardwired into Our Genes.*[9] This book outlined the emerging behavioral genetics of religion. His team and others had investigated the heritability of religion, finding for example that degrees of religious and spiritual commitment ran in families—in other words, that close relatives are more similar in degrees of religiosity than you might expect based on other similarities they share, suggesting some genetic component to the religious impulse. In the book, Hamer further tried to identify the precise gene sequence and affected neurotransmitters underlying the genetic correlations. This caused quite a media stir, including gracing the cover of *Time* magazine.

What was so intriguing about this book? Above all, it seemed to ground the spiritual in something as fundamentally biological and mechanistic as our genetics—perhaps a radical notion for those used to thinking about religious claims in terms of metaphysical truth rather than physical mechanism.

In the same vein, work claiming to have identified which parts of the brain underpin religion pop up and gain prominence from time to time, either in popular books or (less frequently) the peer-reviewed literature. A smattering of books like this: *The "God" Part of the Brain*;[10] *The God-Shaped Brain*;[11] *The Spiritual Brain*;[12] *Why We Believe What We Believe: Uncovering Our Biological Need for Meaning, Spirituality, and Truth*;[13] *The Believing Brain.*[14] Books on the neuroscience of faith and spirituality are plentiful enough that one can even find a curated Goodreads list of the top entries in the genre, which has come to be known as "neurotheology."

Then there's the so-called God helmet, discussed in Richard Dawkins's religion books and demonstrated in one of his documentaries. It's a brain stimulation gizmo that developers Koren and Persinger describe as capable of inducing spiritual awe and felt presences in many people, akin to how some people describe transcendent spiritual and religious experiences.

God genes. Believing brains. God helmets. None of these can solve the Puzzle of Faith.

Genetics seems to offer a deep biological explanation for social and spiritual phenomena, grounding the ethereal in the details of our deep biological inheritance. Something being genetically influenced or determined makes it feel "real" or perhaps even inevitable. These impressions that genetics are deeply biological or immutable are mistaken! Steven Heine, Ilan Dar-Nimrod, and colleagues over the years have studied the psychology of genetic essentialism, the tendency for people to ascribe far too much explanatory power, far too much immutability, to genes.[15]

And brains. Fictional zombies are known for their ravenous hunger for brains. If there's an entity with a more unquenchable appetite for brains, it's science popularizers who want to give their topic a veneer of "hard science." Brain science relies on fancy machinery, expensive equipment, and deep specialist knowledge. Social science questionnaires and ethnographies seem so soft and wishy washy; brain scan images emerging from a $10 million fMRI machine, on the other hand, feel substantial. A keen lay fascination for brains is demonstrated time and time again in breathless press releases about how this or that complex societal outcome is reflected in brain activity.

To be perfectly clear: I think that genetic and neuroscientific investigations of religious cognition are valuable and important. But in terms of explaining why we have religion *in the first place, as a species*, genetics and neuroscience are probably not answering the right sorts of questions.

To see why, let's consider a counterfactual. If genes and brains are not somehow the biological basis of religion, then what would be? If there aren't parts of the brain that are more active when we're thinking religious thoughts (as opposed to other kinds of thoughts), then what organ would be involved? The God gallbladder? The spiritual spleen? Of course things that enable religion will be encoded in genes and brains—there's simply nowhere else it would plausibly happen! Genetics and neuroscience may have much to tell us about the mechanisms that underpin religion, but neither seem to be the right tools for answering the Puzzle of Faith.

I think that there is a lot of potential for work on mechanism (like genetics and neuroscience offer) to inform work on function (as we're seeking in answering the Puzzle of Faith). For example, in a couple chapters we will encounter work suggesting that our capacity for religious cognition—our ability to conceive of gods—is grounded in our everyday capacity to think about other people's minds, to intuitively mindread our way through our social ecosystems. Here there is intriguing work showing, for example, that thinking about or praying to God recruits the same neural circuitry as does social interaction. Here work on mechanism is matching the predictions made from a more functional theoretical approach to religion.

But identifying this or that brain region, that or this gene, will ultimately not offer a solution to the Puzzle of Faith, primarily because neuroscience and genetic questions are operating at a different explanatory level than we are interested in. By my reading, this is made abundantly clear in the primary scientific literature on the neuroscience or genetics of religion. But by the time findings trickle up to the popular press, claims get distilled to a potency far beyond what the underlying science could ever support. Genes and brains are heavily involved in religious thought—this is an inevitability! But that doesn't mean that "God genes" or "God centers" in the brain will be solutions to our puzzle.

At best, genetics and neuroscience can give us important information about the physical and biological mechanisms influencing religion. They might offer answers about *how religion works*, to some degree, but not *why religion evolved in our species alone.*

CHILDHOOD CREDULITY

Finally, we turn to a hypothesis about religion's evolution that has been most developed in the popular writings of Richard Dawkins over the years. This account posits that religions largely persist through the gullibility of children—that children will believe whatever their parents tell them. Given Dawkins's outsized influence in the popularization of evolutionary theory, and his prominent role in the public discussion of religion and atheism over the years, I want to devote a bit more time to understanding Dawkins's proposal, and then carefully noting its limitations. Like the other nonanswers to the Puzzle of Faith, the refutation of this one points the way forward, highlighting aspects of the puzzle that we'll need to seriously consider.

The Argument

In *The God Delusion*,[16] Richard Dawkins offers a brief review of some (then-) recent research on what makes religion tick. Along the way, he offers his own speculative evolutionary account of religion. He suggests that one key to religion might be a human psychological adaptation that makes us basically believe whatever our parents tell us:

> More than any other species, we survive by the accumulated experience of previous generations, and that experience needs to be passed along to children. . . . There will be a selective advantage to child brains that possess the rule of thumb: believe, without question, whatever your grown-ups tell you.

To Dawkins, this leaves kids susceptible to religious indoctrination: "The flip side of trusting obedience is a slavish gullibility. The inevitable by-product is vulnerability to infection by mind-viruses."

Dawkins is appropriately cautious about the tentative nature of his conjectures in *The God Delusion*—he's quite upfront that he's spitballing here. But some fifteen years later, in *Outgrowing God*,[17] Dawkins again repeats his pet hypothesis:

> Our earliest ancestors lived in a dangerous place. . . . There were pythons and leopards lurking in the trees, lions behind bushes, crocodiles in the river. Adults knew of these dangers, but children needed to be told. . . . And natural selection would have favoured genes that built into child brains a tendency to believe their parents.

Returning to religion, gullibility is again central to Dawkins's story:

> If adults ever gave bad advice alongside good advice, the child brain would have no way to distinguish bad advice from good. . . . So if, for some reason, a parent were to give a child useless advice—like "you have to pray five times a day"—the child would have no way of knowing that it was useless.

> Natural selection simply builds into the child brain the rule "Believe whatever your parents tell you." And the rule will come into force even when "what your parents tell you" is actually silly or untrue.

First, let's acknowledge some strengths of the Dawkins childhood gullibility model.

The argument is straightforward, and intuitively compelling. Kids really do need to learn how to get along in the world. Some threats really are too serious to rely on trial-and-error learning. Kids who were skeptical of their parents' claims that there are jaguars in that bit of forest did not leave many descendants—they became lunch! So maybe it's a good idea to just believe whatever your parents tell you. Maybe our species evolved in such a way that we are generally gullible as kids, at least when it comes to stuff our elders tell us.

Broad-spectrum childhood gullibility of the sort posited by Dawkins seemingly accords well with some other observations about religion. Kids usually grow up to have more-or-less the same religious beliefs as their parents. Baptist parents tend to have Baptist kids; Mormon parents, Mormon kids; Sunni parents, Sunni kids; and so on.

On these two counts—intuitive plausibility and a general fit to observations about religion—the childhood gullibility model of religion appears okay. But let's take these ideas seriously. Seriously enough to ask whether the childhood credulity account of religion is consistent with our best theories of how culture works, or with our best evidence from developmental psychology on how kids learn and think about religions.

Theoretical Challenges

As intuitively satisfying as the childhood credulity story seems, it doesn't really hold together at a basic theoretical level. Over the past forty years, the science of cultural evolution has rapidly matured (we'll meet it in great detail in a few chapters). We've come to learn a great deal about how cultural information gets passed from person to person, and the specific learning strategies that we use to glean useful information from our fellow humans. This work—summarized in excellent books like Joe Henrich's *The Secret of Our Success*[18] and Pete Richerson and Rob Boyd's *Not by Genes*

Alone[19]—makes a compelling case that our species has become so phenomenally successful largely because we are good at learning from each other. We pick up techniques and technologies from our elders or peers, tweak them with our own innovations, and in turn pass them along to others. This capacity for cumulative culture is what let our species colonize the entire globe, from our humble origins as a peculiar African primate.

As Dawkins correctly notes, we do rely on each other for a substantial amount of our know-how. And we really do need to learn a lot from our caregivers—relative to the young of most species, kids are pretty useless and burdensome.* But Dawkins is wrong to assert that at our cores, humans evolved to be gullible and credulous. We do not passively accept the information that others try to feed us. Quite the opposite: we need to be vigilant against trickery, shenanigans, and exploitation. Indeed, one of the more interesting puzzles in cultural evolution is figuring out what information learners need to believe. In this regard, gullibility and credulity are self-defeating. Dawkins points out that there are lots of survival threats in our environment—crocodiles in the river, jaguars in the trees. But one of the biggest threats we face is each other. A gullible learner leaves themselves open to exploitation by unscrupulous teachers. Someone who believes whatever they're told—even by a parent or elder—isn't a survivor who avoids predators, they're a sucker who can be manipulated; a rube who would quickly be outcompeted by more epistemically vigilant peers. And like all interesting evolutionary puzzles it comes down to tradeoffs: we need to learn, but we also need to avoid exploitation. What's the right balance? This is such a thorny theoretical issue that Maciek Chudek, a quirkily brilliant graduate school contemporary of mine, dubbed it the "evil teacher problem," and it remains as a central challenge in the cultural evolution literature.

Cultural evolutionary theory relies heavily on building mathematical models of selective learning[20]—who do we learn from, under which conditions? An honest perusal of this body of theory gives no hints that we'd expect our species (or any other!) to use blind gullibility as its general learning

* Per a headline from the *Onion*, much beloved by developmental psychologists: "Study reveals: Babies are stupid."

strategy. Instead, we find ample theory and evidence suggesting that we are keenly strategic in our cultural learning, relying on a wide variety of specific learning strategies as situations demand. We pick and choose between different sources of information—we don't just believe whatever we're told, from anyone. We also vet what we're told, and preferentially adopt beliefs that are backed by credible behaviors attesting to their value. Relying on these *credibility enhancing displays*[21] (in the terminology of Joe Henrich, the Harvard human evolutionary biologist who first developed models of this sort of learning) is a key part of our cultural toolkit that helps cultural learners pick up on useful information while avoiding exploitation. No rigorous theoretical model that I'm aware of supports the plausibility of our species having evolved to just believe whatever our parents tell us. But a fairly vast body of theory tells us that broad-spectrum gullibility is an incredibly unlikely evolutionary outcome.

The reasons that broad-spectrum gullibility fails as an evolutionary solution are somewhat analogous to another failed evolutionary idea that Dawkins ably skewered in *The Selfish Gene*. Naive notions of group selection—the idea that some animals will make costly sacrifices "for the good of the species"—were once popular in biology, but fell apart once biologists in the 1960s and 1970s started to really model the details. People rigorously worked out the implications of the "good of the species" style group selection. And key to the dismantling of naive group selection is the notion that uncritical cooperators will pretty much always be outcompeted by individuals who exploit them. Someone who always helps others is at a huge competitive disadvantage relative to the moochers and the cheats. Truly, Dawkins's rhetorical takedown of shoddy group selectionist thinking in *The Selfish Gene*[22] is masterful. This makes it all the more puzzling that his pet hypothesis of religion relies on a cultural evolutionary analogue of unconditional cooperation: unconditional credulity. Both cases (a group selectionist universal cooperator and a generally gullible cultural learner) posit an evolved psychology that is incredibly vulnerable to exploitation, and we shouldn't expect either type to have ever really become an evolutionary success.

From the perspective of cultural evolution—as rigorously mathematically modelled over the years, and as observed in the world—broad-spectrum childhood gullibility is a theoretical nonstarter.

Empirical Challenges

Aside from being theoretically untenable, the childhood gullibility model also runs afoul of a wide range of evidence coming from developmental psychology—the subdiscipline of psychology that studies how kids learn about the world, represent ideas, and such. Just to highlight a few of these mismatches, let's consider three sorts of questions:

- Do kids always prefer to learn from their parents?
- Do kids think about religion in the same way they think about more mundane facts?
- How do kids learn about things they can't see?
- Does mommy know best?

Parents (and other elders) hold a special position in the Dawkins childhood gullibility model. According to Dawkins, one's parents have a vested interest in one's own well-being, and it might behoove learners to just believe whatever their parents tell them (or so the story goes). And as a parent to two children, believe me: I truly wish it were the case that kids believe whatever they're told. But kids don't seem to be built that way.[†]

Consider developmental psychological research on source credibility. The Dawkins model posits that kids just passively and uncritically accept information from certain people. But it turns out that kids are savvy and active in their information consumption. They recognize early on in life that some people are better to learn from than others, and rely on a bunch of cues to assess source credibility, including cues like a source's history of accuracy, or the degree to which they project confidence and certainty in their claims.[23]

And they also seem to realize that different types of information require different cultural models. For a lot of information, kids seem to use age as a cue to credibility—they often prefer to listen to their elders, especially elders who seem reliable. But for other types of information, such as information about hip new toys, they recognize that similar-aged peers are actually better sources of knowledge.[24] Kids can treat different information

---

[†] Interested readers may want to peruse the literature on another fascinating evolutionary puzzle that Dawkins discusses briefly in *The Selfish Gene* and more extensively elsewhere: parent-offspring conflict, the notion that kids and parents have interests that can often diverge sharply from each other, with all sorts of intriguing evolutionary implications.

sources as more credible than others, and know when to shift their attention to different sources depending on what type of information they're after.[25] This is quite at odds with a model positing that kids just blindly believe their elders.

The bottom line here is that kids aren't blindly gullible when it comes to their parents—or anyone else! They're keenly attentive to who might know best, under which conditions. Kids love to see evidence. They love asking "why." They are curious little critters, and active in their curation of knowledge. They are little scientists, rather than passive receptacles whose heads will fill up with whatever their parents pour in. Bottom line: if there's a general psychological predisposition for kids to just believe their parents or elders, developmental psychologists have yet to find it. I'm not holding my breath that they will any time soon.

Religion versus Facts

Dawkins posits that kids can't differentiate between the good factual advice their parents give them about predators and the iffy information their parents give them about gods: "If adults ever gave bad advice alongside good advice, the child brain would have no way to distinguish bad advice from good." This implies a child psychology whereby kids are not very good at distinguishing factual claims from other sorts of claims. Once again, this isn't how child psychology works!

First off, it's important to recognize that kids are quite adept at separating fact from fiction.[26] There are substantial scientific literatures devoted to figuring out how kids think about things that actually exist versus things that only exist in pretense. Kids positively excel at entertaining fictional worlds, without any confusion about whether or not it is fact. They have imaginary friends, and even imaginary enemies, that they recognize are not real.[27] One of my favorite papers in this area even looks at how children can mentally represent overlaps between different fictional worlds—they can think about what Batman might think about SpongeBob, without any confusion about the fact that neither character is real.[28] The bottom line here is that kids are pretty good at sifting different sorts of claims into different mental bins: some bins hold facts, others fictions.

Beyond the fact/fiction divide, there's some excellent research showing that children are pretty good at sorting factual claims from opinion claims.[29]

They realize that "the Colorado Avalanche won the Stanley Cup in 2022" is a verifiable factual claim about a hockey team, but that "the Colorado Avalanche are the best hockey team ever" is just someone's opinion.[‡] Kids are quite sensitive to this fact/opinion distinction, and they readily apply it.

How then do kids represent religious claims: as fact, or as opinion? (Remember: the Dawkins gullibility model specifically says that kids will believe religious claims in exactly the same way as they believe factual claims about predators, because they can't distinguish "good advice" from bad.) Some excellent work by Larisa Heiphetz Solomon and her colleagues over the years has revealed that kids think about religious claims as sort of an intermediate category, hanging in the balance somewhere between fact and opinion.[30] Some religious claims contain factual elements. But kids readily recognize that people can have different religious beliefs without just one person being absolutely correct with theirs—in this way religions are viewed a bit more like opinions.[§]

Kids seem adept at separating factual claims from claims of opinion, and they place religious claims somewhat in the middle. This rather strikingly contradicts Dawkins's assertion that kids are susceptible to religion and superstition because they need to learn facts about dangers in the world. In fact, kids don't even represent fact claims and religion claims as being the same as each other.

Learning about the Invisible

There are most definitely some things in the world that we can only learn about from others. Think of some of the invisible threats we must beware of. In the wake of a global pandemic that has killed millions,[¶] this shouldn't be a difficult task. There are innumerable tiny entities out there that can kill you, but have you ever directly seen these pathogens? No. Instead, we rely on the testimony of others to inform us about the unseen.

---

‡ Mine, specifically.

§ Perhaps important caveat: kids recruited into developmental psychology studies like this are often from the areas surrounding the major universities where the research takes place, for reasons of logistical necessity. Kids from affluent pockets of Boston or New York may have a lot of familiarity with folks from different religious backgrounds, and have more familiarity with religious diversity than kids elsewhere. Religion may seem less opinion-like, more factual, in a setting with more consistency in religious cues around kiddos as they grow.

¶ And it continues to kill and cause long-term disability in many, even though governments have seemingly moved on.

Testimony turns out to be an immensely important topic in the child development and learning literature.[31] How do we decide whose testimony to trust, and for which types of information? As with above, it turns out that kids are quite savvy about this! They're pretty good at figuring out that there are some things they'll never be able to directly observe, but that are nonetheless important. Reliance on testimony is necessary, but blind gullibility is not at all the expected outcome.

In what you may recognize as a recurring theme by now, kids have a nuanced appreciation for the types of things that they can only learn about via testimony. For example, both germs and gods are things that we learn about from others telling us about them. But are we just as convinced by testimony about both germs and gods? No. Learners are actually more convinced by testimony about natural unseens (germs) than about supernatural unseens (gods, ghosts, and the like).[32] They seem to have some intuitive skepticism of testimony about the supernatural—after all, this testimony directly contradicts their core expectations about and experience with the world. As a result, kids seem to flag testimony about the supernatural as requiring special attention.

There's a great deal of excellent developmental psychological work that specifically looks at how kids learn and think about supernatural agents, like gods. Interested readers should look up pioneering researchers in this area: folks like Drs. Kathleen Corriveau, Paul Harris, Rebekah Richert, Larisa Heiphetz Solomon, Paul Bloom, Telli Davoodi, and others. These fine scientists, who directly study how kids learn about religion, present a psychological profile of children that is directly at odds with the childhood gullibility model Dawkins has presented over the past two decades.

The Verdict

In *The God Delusion*, and again fifteen years later in *Outgrowing God*, Richard Dawkins presented his pet hypothesis about religion that depends on the notion that kids blindly believe whatever their parents tell them. Millions of readers may assume that this idea holds some scientific validity, or at least plausibility. After all, it's a claim made repeatedly over more than a decade by an incredibly prominent thinker who is a public advocate for science and skepticism.

Unfortunately, the idea doesn't hold up. It was theoretically and empirically unsupported at the time of its first presentation, and the intervening decade and a half before second presentation only rendered it less scientifically tenable. The childhood gullibility model of religion fails some basic tests of theoretical coherence—our most rigorous cultural evolutionary models suggest that a psychological predisposition for blind gullibility is unlikely to have ever evolved. Individuals predisposed to gullibility would be suckers, easily taken advantage of and outcompeted by more skeptical peers. The childhood gullibility model also conflicts with our best science on how kids actually learn and think about the world. This science portrays children not as passive receptacles of whatever hooey their parents dump into their heads, but rather as savvy and skeptical consumers who actively seek out and test cultural information.

If religion isn't borne of gullibility, does this mean that I'm saying kids don't need to learn religion? Of course not! Religion is most definitely learned, and subsequent chapters will tell us exactly how this works. The failure of the gullibility model is also somewhat at odds with another idea about religion popular in New Atheist-aligned circles, the notion that religion is a product of childhood indoctrination. I've always found it odd that both childhood gullibility and strict parental indoctrination have been posited as fundamental to religion, often by the same voices. In a sense, they are describing opposite psychological proclivities underlying the cultural transmission of faith. Boundlessly credulous kids wouldn't require any sustained indoctrination efforts, after all—indoctrination efforts are redundant if kids naturally believe what they're told.

A hallmark of science is its capacity for self-correction. We scientists try to break our ideas against reality, and are proud of our (occasional) ability to discard ideas that don't work. Here, I'm asking readers to move on from the notion that religion is rooted in childhood gullibility. It's time to discard this one and instead listen to the scientists who actually study these topics. They've done some truly excellent research over the years, and it's well worth engaging with their work on this topic. The psychological world they've uncovered is fascinating—a world where children aren't passive receptacles but are rather little skeptics and proto-scientists.

WHAT BETTER ANSWERS MUST LOOK LIKE

In considering three popular ideas about how religion works—that it's an "opiate of the masses," that it's simply built-in to our genes and brains, that it persists because our species evolved to have mindlessly gullible children—we've learned important ways in which explanations for religion can fall short. This points us toward better answers, by sharpening the questions we ask of religion.

Each of these three accounts can tell us things that are interesting, and probably true about religion. Many religions do include elements that may satiate our existential yearnings. Religions have the potential to tell us why we suffer, and can promise relief from it someday. The cognitive processes underlying religion will inevitably occur in the brain, and will inevitably involve genes—that's simply how these things work. Identifying which genes, and which brain regions, underpin different aspects of religion is important work! And finally, religion is learned, as the Dawkins gullibility model does predict in the broadest sense. One reason for the popularity of these explanations is that they each get some aspect of religion right.

Ultimately, they each fall flat as answers to the Puzzle of Faith, and they do so in different but interesting ways.

The opiate account fails because it does a poor job of explaining the diversity of religious thought across different religious traditions. Yes, many religions include elements that would be existentially satisfying to those in need. But many do not! Yet others include elements, like beliefs about hell or tormenting demons, that if anything seem to exacerbate existential concerns. The opiate account also fails to explain why the expression of religion—which varies so much from culture to culture—has predictable regularities. We need an explanation of religion that both describes the variety of religious beliefs we actually see in the world and also accounts for regularities among that diversity.

The genes or brains accounts have the potential to tell us about the physical encoding of religion, be it in genetic or neuronal stuff. But it answers a "how" question instead of our "why" question: why does our species alone have religion? The Puzzle of Faith is ultimately an evolutionary question. And while evolution acts on brains, and through genes, pinpointing neurons and nucleotides involved does not tell us, ultimately, what made our species religious. We need an explanation of religion that operates at the ultimate "why" level, tracing the evolutionary pressures that produced a religious species in the first place.

Finally, the childhood credulity model of religion moves in the right direction by first noting that religious beliefs are transmitted socially, and asking how our species could've evolved to socially transmit religious information in the way we clearly do. But it failed because, as we saw, it did not seriously engage with what we know about either cultural evolution or developmental psychology. It was an armchair guess, made in ignorance of relevant scientific work on precisely the topics it needed to consult, and we can do much better. We need an explanation of religion that seriously engages with what we know about cultural evolution and human psychology.

We will later attempt to find an explanation that can succeed where these have proven incomplete, or incompatible with our best science. Widespread and popular accounts of religion, as we saw in this chapter, have not been successful. But they've shown us what a better theory would need. Now, what does it look like when we take this same magnifying glass to the Puzzle of Atheism?

CHAPTER THREE

THE (MORE OR LESS) MYTH OF RATIONAL ATHEISM

Can we actually win a war of ideas with people? Judging from my email, we can. I'm constantly getting email from people who have lost their faith and were, in effect, argued out of it. And the straw that broke the camel's back was either one of our books, or some other process of reasoning.

—SAM HARRIS, *THE FOUR HORSEMEN*[1]

Over the years, I've been invited by atheist and secular groups to give talks about my research. These chats range from local "skeptics in the pub"–type gatherings, all the way up to national and international events. During the talks, and in the ensuing question and chitchat periods, I like to ask audience members how they think they became atheists. Is it just something they grew up with? Was it due to some especially impactful experience?

By far, the most common attributions are to some sort of rational struggle against religious indoctrination. Many folks describe growing up in a strongly religious, perhaps even fundamentalist family. But one day, something happens to get them thinking more rationally about their beliefs. Maybe they started getting really into science, and began asking hard questions about the fit between their textbooks and their tracts. Maybe they stumbled across a book or podcast that posed hard questions of religion. A not insignificant number of people have told me that rigorous Bible study or seminary school prodded them to think deeply and critically about religious claims, and they couldn't square things.

In short, people describe their atheism as resulting from rational, often effortful, thinking. They tried to approach both religious claims and the world they'd experienced and learned about in science classes, and they found the religious claims in some way wanting on intellectual merits.

This is what I have come to think of as the Rational Atheism Thesis—the idea that rational thinking is a key contributor to atheism. Put simply, here is the rational atheism thesis: *Rational thinking is a primary, and perhaps even necessary, cause of atheism.*

As we'll soon see, the rational atheism thesis is popular among lay atheists and celebrity atheists alike. It is probably the most common view of atheism that I've encountered, both when chatting with audiences and when reading some influential pockets of the scientific literature on atheism. It's been promoted far and wide by the world's loudest and most famous atheists.

However, it is almost certainly incorrect in its important details. It is, more or less, a myth. And given its popularity, it is a myth that we need to address head-on, from the outset. However, it is a myth that we also need to discuss seriously, because it does have a compelling logic to it, and it garnered some suggestive scientific backing, at least for a time. At times in my career, I've published studies that were celebrated as vindicating the rational atheism thesis; later in my career, I supported follow-up efforts on these studies that overturned them, leading to my open disavowal of the rational atheism thesis and my own work on it.

In this chapter, I'll open by demonstrating the ubiquity of the rational atheism thesis, both in popular portrayals of atheism and in people's own attributions for their atheism. Next, I'll discuss why the rational atheism thesis seems potentially compelling, on scientific grounds. I'll discuss early experimental work that seemed to vindicate the idea—including one of my most prominent publications—before discussing how those early successes have crumbled over the years. Finally, I want to present our best current evidence on the state of the rational atheism thesis, asking whether rational thinking seems to be a viable explanation for large-scale patterns of atheism in the world today (spoiler alert: it does not).

RATIONAL ATHEISM

Might atheism be rooted in rational thinking? If one peruses some of the most popular books on atheism, claims that rationality and science undercut religious faith abound. Richard Dawkins writes about growing up religious, but turning toward atheism after reading Darwin. Michael Shermer attributes his own shift toward atheism to philosophy classes. In the quote at the outset of this chapter, Sam Harris claims (based on his email inbox) that New Atheist books have nudged lots of people to rationally consider their faith and turn to atheism instead. Harris's inbox isn't dissimilar to what I hear at atheist meetings when I present my research—there's an overwhelming theme of people feeling like they've somehow thought themselves out of religion, using their rational faculties.

Now, all of the above are anecdotes. Dawkins's and Shermer's retrospective introspection might obscure other important factors. Harris's inbox and my post-presentation chats might tell us more about the sorts of people who are emailing Harris or joining the sorts of groups that invite me to present my research than they do about any broad trend. It's entirely possible that most atheists don't subscribe to the rational atheism thesis—but the people who end up contacting Harris or listening to my public talks are the sorts of atheists who do.

So instead of relying on anecdata, I was fielding a longer survey on atheism, and I included some questions probing people's attributions for their own beliefs—or lack thereof—when it came to gods. The survey was distributed in the United States and oversampled people who don't believe in God or gods in order to get a richer view of atheists.

The survey asked two questions about where people thought their beliefs come from. Did they feel that their current beliefs about God's (or gods') existence or nonexistence stemmed primarily from their upbringing? Or primarily from rational thinking? The plots in figures 3.1 and 3.2 show the attributions of atheists and believers.

As you can see, believers tend to attribute their specific beliefs largely to upbringing. Their attributions to rationality are all over the map. Most believers put a lot of weight on how they were raised; some, more than others, add a dose of rationality into the mix.

For atheists, however, the attributions are consistent and clear. They think that rationality is the prime cause of their atheism, with upbringing playing little role at all. In short, atheists on the whole endorse the rational atheism thesis, casting their own religious doubts as the outcome of rational thinking.

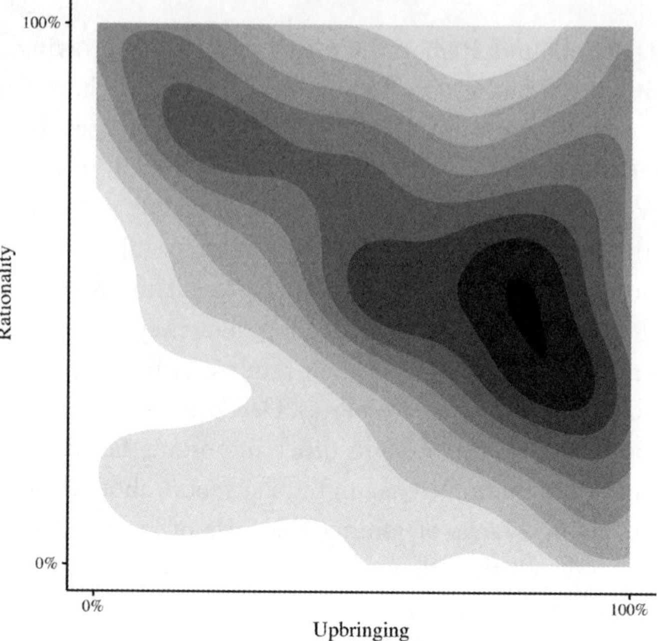

Figure 3.1. Religious believers (United States) attribute their faith largely to upbringing, with mixed attributions regarding rationality.

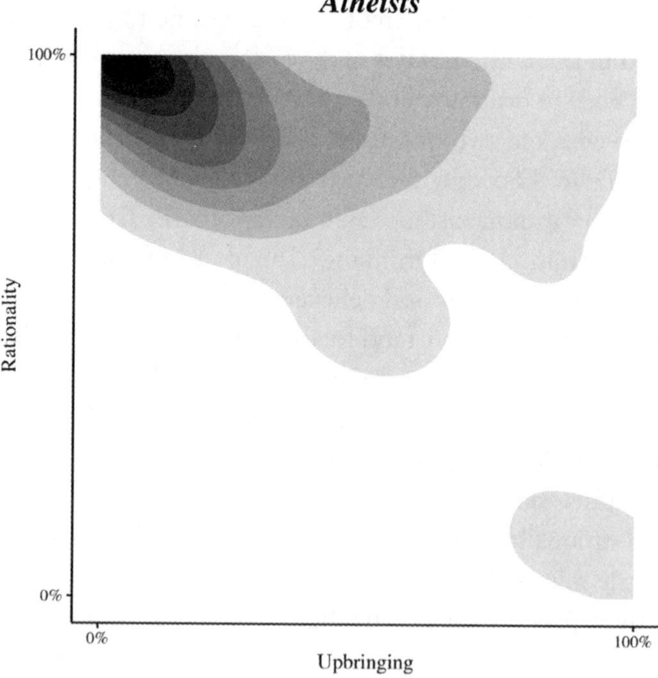

Figure 3.2. Atheists (United States) attribute their disbelief to rationality, rather than upbringing.

The notion that atheism stems primarily from rationality is widespread. It is common to narratives from celebrity atheists to everyday atheists I speak to at secular meetups and events, and to respondents in my surveys. The rational atheism thesis provides a satisfying narrative for lots of people, who get to view their religious doubts as in some sense chosen. And not just chosen, but *rationally chosen*. Arriving at one's precise beliefs about religion because one has simply thought things through carefully and deliberately? What's not to love about that view?

As an added bonus, the rational atheism thesis isn't entirely implausible, given some popular strains of research on both religious cognition and human reasoning.

THE PLAUSIBILITY OF RATIONAL ATHEISM

Some attributions people give for their stations in life are popular and widespread, but implausible on even the most cursory of scrutiny. For instance, every so often finance websites run stories with advice from some smiling twenty-seven-year-old who just bought a mansion and retired, giving advice to the masses on how their can-do attitude, mindfulness practices, and fiscal responsibility in youth let them get ahead. Typically buried somewhere in the story is the reveal: they inherited millions from a wealthy parent, who also put up the down payment on the mansion, and hired them into their finance firm fresh out of college at a mid-six-figure salary. But who knows, maybe it was the early wake up time for mindfulness meditation and skipping avocado toast that was the real impetus to lifetime financial security.

The rational atheism thesis isn't one of these flimsy and self-serving narratives. It has enough intellectual heft to it that it gained some degree of support in scientific circles, at least for a time. And the theoretical backstory to it is consistent with prominent and successful lines of research in psychology and decision-making.

One of the oldest and most successful ideas in the history of psychology is that our minds have at least a couple of different systems for thinking about the world. William James, the father figure of American empirical psychology, posited two different cognitive systems that we all use to make sense of the world. One system is what we might think of as hunches or intuitions. The other system is our capacity for effortful rational thought. Uncreatively, psychologists call these System 1 and System 2.[2] To keep them straight, it's easier to talk about an intuitive system and a rational or reflective system.

Our intuitive system (read: System 1 thinking) relies on fast and cognitively easy mental shortcuts. Hunches, intuitions, and gut feelings all fall under the banner of System 1. Intuitive processing is relatively quick, and relatively unconscious. Sometimes answers just pop into our head, or we feel a gut-level pull to respond in one way rather than another.

Our reflective or rational system (read: System 2) is quite different. Whereas our intuitive system operates under the surface, the operation of our rational system *feels like* thinking. Rational thinking takes work. It takes time. It feels effortful.

We all have both systems. And the System 1–System 2 divide isn't some hare-brained left brain/right brain flimflam. Both systems are relatively well-established. A decent popular presentation of dual process thinking—the fancy name for our intuitive and rational systems—can be found in Daniel Kahneman's *Thinking, Fast and Slow*.[3]

Psychologists and behavioral economists have invented some trick questions that let us see the parallel operation of our intuitive and rational systems at work. Take, for example, syllogisms. Syllogisms are logic puzzles in which you are given a set of premises and a conclusion, and your job is to ascertain whether the conclusion logically follows from the premise. For example:

Premise 1: All cats are evil.
Premise 2: Jethro is a cat.
Conclusion: Jethro is evil.

Is the conclusion valid? In other words, can we logically derive the conclusion if we assume the truth of the premises? In this case, yes, we can. Jethro's evilness can be logically inferred from the general evilness of cats (assumed in Premise 1) and the fact that Jethro is, indeed, a cat (Premise 2). If the premises are true, so must be the conclusion. The key to syllogisms is ignoring the baseline plausibility of the premises and simply asking whether the truth of the conclusion logically flows from the premises. Let's try again, to illustrate:

Premise 1: All moons are made of green cheese.
Premise 2: Earth has a moon.
Conclusion: Earth's moon is made of green cheese.

Is the conclusion valid? We know for a fact that the conclusion is untrue, but that isn't what we're asked to judge. In this case, the conclusion can be logically derived from the premises, if we assume them to be true. This conclusion is valid. It just isn't true.

Mismatches between the plausibility of premises and the logic used to derive conclusions can reveal a tug-of-war between System 1 and System 2 thinking. Our intuitive (System 1) system cares about whether or not the conclusion sounds like it's probably true. Our reflective (System 2) system cares about the underlying logic leading from premise to conclusion. Consider these two examples:

Premise 1: All plants are healthy.
Premise 2: Cocaine is a plant.
Conclusion: Cocaine is healthy.

Premise 1: US presidents must be US citizens.
Premise 2: Abraham Lincoln was a US citizen.
Conclusion: Abraham Lincoln was once president of the United States.

In the first example, the conclusion is logically derived—the syllogism is valid. Although we know that cocaine is not especially healthy, if we grant the premises then we could logically derive the conclusion. This is what our reflective system tells us. Meanwhile, our intuitive system screams "*But this isn't true, I know coke ain't good for you!*" The systems are in conflict.

In the second example, the conclusion does not even remotely follow from the premises—the syllogism is invalid. But our intuitive system again is upset! Every premise is true! The conclusion is also true! "*How can this not be valid when everything is true?*" screams System 1. But our reflective System 2 processing requires us to dispassionately set aside what we know of the claims in the premises and conclusion, and merely evaluate the logical structure of things. Again, the systems are in conflict.

The conflict introduced by syllogisms makes a nice reminder that we all have both systems. We can all feel the intuitive tug toward plausible conclusions; we can all sit down and rationally work through the logic to see which syllogisms are, in fact, valid. But the fact that everyone has both systems doesn't imply that we all use them to equal degrees. There are individual differences in both engagement and aptitude with both systems. Some folks trust their hunches a lot; others tend toward rational engagement instead. Some people enjoy rationally working through logic puzzles, others find it a bore. We can think of people's engagement and aptitude for each system as their cognitive style. And simplistically, we could picture cognitive style as a single continuum running from gut-trusting intuitive thinkers to staunchly rational reflective thinkers.

What does all of this have to do with rational atheism?

As we'll see in the coming chapters, there's been a consistent view among many scientists who study religious cognition that religions are supported by our intuitions. We have intuitions about how intentional agents (things like people and voles and lions) act in the world; intuitions that minds are distinct from bodies; intuitions about apparent order and meaning in the universe; intuitions about where living things come from. These intuitions, sown together, reap religious belief. The next chapter presents this argument in much greater detail, with more nuance.

If intuitive processing forms the basis for religious belief, then perhaps our rational system is what produces atheism. Just as our two systems might be in conflict in well-crafted syllogisms, so too might they conflict when it comes to religion. In its briefest form, here's the general scientific argument that might support the rational atheism thesis: intuitions support religious belief, rational thinking undermines it. If this is true, then cognitive style ought to predict religious belief or disbelief.

SMASHING EMPIRICAL SUCCESSES

In 2012, three different research teams independently published papers testing the basic logic outlined above. I led one of those teams.[4] We all independently hit on the same way to measure people's reliance on intuitive or rational systems of thinking, in the hopes that it would predict their levels of religious belief.

We all measured cognitive style with versions of what's called the cognitive reflection task, originally developed by Shane Frederick.[5] In this task, people get a few quick math problems. Each problem is computationally quite trivial, but has a bit of a trick in its presentation that leads people astray. One answer intuitively leaps to mind . . . but is incorrect. Only by reflectively overriding this initial intuitive impulse can people get the right answer. Here's an example problem:

> In a lake, there is a patch of lily pads. Every day, the patch doubles in size. If it takes forty-eight days to cover the entire lake, how long does it take for the patch to cover half of the lake?

Intuitively, "twenty-four" springs to mind. The pond is full on the forty-eighth day. Half of forty-eight is twenty-four, so it must've been half full on the twenty-fourth day (whispers our intuition). But rationally, if the lily pads double each day, then the lake must've been half full on day forty-seven, not day twenty-four. On day forty-six it was a quarter full, on day forty-five an eighth full. The math isn't difficult here, but our intuitions don't really care!

By giving people a series of questions like this, each with an intuitively compelling answer and a rationally correct one, each research team could gauge people's cognitive style, on a continuum from intuitive thinkers to rational and reflective ones. This task is far from perfect, but it can be quite useful. In measuring performance, we could somewhat measure how people actually think. This is a step up from other measures of cognitive style that ask people to self-report how rational or intuitive they think they are. Gimmicky math problems aren't a perfect measure of cognitive style, but they're probably an improvement over just asking people how rational they think they are.

As I mentioned, each research team correlated cognitive style—as measured by the cognitive reflection test—with measures of religious belief. The results? We all found a negative correlation between rationality and religiosity. People who scored as more rational in their cognitive style were more atheistic; people who scored on the intuitive end of the cognitive style spectrum reported being more religious.

One of the papers, led by Gordon Pennycook,[6] nicely illustrates the relation between rational cognitive style and religious belief. People who get zero cognitive reflection test items correct—our strongly intuitive thinkers—are most likely to believe in a personal God of some sort. In contrast, people who get two or three items correct—our more rational thinkers—are more prone to atheism. This team found an almost linear pattern in which more personalized and supernatural-seeming religious beliefs (personal God beliefs and pantheism) are more attractive to intuitive thinkers, and more abstract beliefs or full disbelief are more attractive to those participants with the most rational cognitive styles.

These correlations between analytic cognitive style and atheism are intriguing, but as you've probably heard, correlation doesn't necessarily imply causation.* We're left knowing that rational thinking is associated with atheism, but does rationality cause atheism? Of the three teams who published correlational studies on rational atheism, two went further and offered experiments that suggested causal relationships. One team (Amitai Shenhav, David Rand, and Josh Greene, hailing from Harvard)[7] had their participants think about times they'd relied on either intuitions or rationality, trying to nudge people toward one pole or another of the cognitive style continuum. People who were pushed toward rationality reported lower levels of religious belief than did people nudged toward intuitive thinking. Nifty! My team (well, it was just me and Ara Norenzayan) did basically the same thing, but with quirkier and more bizarre tasks that tried to nudge people toward rationality in ever-more-subtle ways. In one study we had people look at artwork connoting deep thinking (Rodin's *The Thinker*), or at other statuary with superficially similar features (the *Discobolus* of Myron). In one small-sample experiment, we found that people who'd looked at *The Thinker* for a bit subsequently reported being a bit less religious than their *Discobolus*-gazing control condition compatriots. If it sounds silly to you, well, it should. It was a silly study.

Combined, the three papers made quite a splash. I think that each team of authors was appropriately circumspect in their presentations at the time. None of us were claiming that our papers showed that rational thinking was the main or even an especially major contributor to atheism. But the media ran with it. When it comes to science journalism, newsworthiness and nuance tend to go together like nuts and gum—not at all. My paper, in particular, seemed to get a lot of media attention. It had been published in *Science*, a

* Correlation correlates with causation, and causation causes correlation. Clear?

high-profile general science outlet, one of the most prestigious science journals out there. It also used the, well, cutest experiments. Our manipulations had a bit of panache, even though they didn't offer any more scientific value than the other teams' works. (If I'm being honest, our paper was the worst of the bunch.) To illustrate the scale of media reach the findings eventually got, Altmetrics is a service that tracks media and social media attention paid to scientific publications. Ara Norenzayan's and my *Science* paper on analytic thinking and religious disbelief to this day is among the top 0.05 percent or so of science papers they've scored, out of nearly twenty-five million; it sits in the top thirty of more than one hundred thousand scientific outputs from the same time period. In short, our goofy little paper ended up getting a lot of coverage. Some good, some not so good.

Although none of the research teams would've claimed that rationality was the key ingredient in atheism, headlines took a salacious turn. For example:

Religious Faithfuls Lack Logic, Study Implies

By **Katie Moisse** April 26, 2012

Christophe Lehenaff/Getty Images

A rare and controversial study merging science and faith suggests that analytic thinking, a process that favors reason over intuition, promotes religious disbelief.

Figure 3.3. Headline sensationalizing the results of Gervais and Norenzayan (2012). *Source:* Screenshot from https://abcnews.go.com/blogs/health/2012/04/26/logic-linked-to-religious-disbelief-study-implies.

Neither the study in question, nor the researchers themselves, would have ever claimed that "religious faithfuls lack logic." Nonetheless, headlines went there. Incidentally, ABC News initially ran a slightly more sober and serious headline: "Logic Linked to Religious Disbelief, Study Implies." By fortune, I stumbled across the initial headline and was able to grab a screenshot before the switcheroo. It makes a lovely teaching example of how perverse media incentives can distort science communication.

Headlines like these, cringeworthy as they were, met receptive audiences among atheist and secular groups. I had a slew of podcast invitations to discuss the work. Popularly, our paper was seen as a key piece of evidence linking rationality to atheism, and ended up being favorably cited in New Atheist tracts. What was my paper, after all, if not scientific proof for the idea that rationality was a key to atheism—vindication, if you will, for the rational atheism thesis? To take one unfortunate and poignant example of this rhetoric, *A Manual for Creating Atheists* encourages its fledgling followers (termed "Street Epistemologists") to seek believers out in public and try to disabuse them of faith. He advises atheists to rationally confront the faithful at work, at school, in grocery stores, and on airline flights. He even claims that the science backs up his proposed strategy, citing our 2012 paper as proof positive that rationality undercuts faith: "In other words, if one gains a proficiency in certain methods of critical reasoning there is an increased likelihood that one will not hold religious beliefs."

To be perfectly clear: atheists, please don't harass your fellow travelers about their beliefs in public places like airplanes,[†] and don't cite my old paper as justification if for some reason you do. I cannot overstate my objections to this book's project, or the motivation behind it.

Let's pause here and take stock. Lots of atheists—famous and everyday—attribute their atheism to feats of rationality. There are decent enough reasons to expect that there might be a link between religious disbelief and a more rational cognitive style. And finally, there is evidence coming from three independent teams that seems to directly support the rational atheism thesis—evidence met with much media acclaim. Case closed.

Or was it?

[†] Or in private! Live and let live! And leave my name out of your mouth if you choose, against the science, to go down this path.

PAINFULLY, SCIENCE SELF-CORRECTS

As our papers gained widespread attention in the media, they also attracted attention within academia. My studies, in particular, began garnering interest from colleagues who wanted to see how robust the findings were. You see, right around the time our papers came out, psychological science had begun undergoing some painful introspection about our methods. Some influential papers and popular findings have proven to be impossible to replicate; those who tried ended up finding results that contradicted the originals. Especially cute and clever experimental designs, paired with small sample sizes, were proving elusive upon reexamination. Cute and clever studies, with small sample sizes . . . just like my own rational atheism studies, like the *Thinker* one. Truly, within a year or so of publishing the paper, my increasing awareness of the fragility of a lot of experimental psychology methods led me to suspect that my own work on rationality and atheism was probably not solid. My methodological awakening in psychology—the realization that we as a field needed to do better—came, inconveniently, just after I'd published a likely shaky result in the world's most prominent science journal, to much media attention. I was uncomfortable having a paper that I was increasingly uncertain about in the limelight. To my eventual relief, scientific reckoning came.

First to reappraise my paper was Bob Calin-Jageman. Calin-Jageman and his team had been seeking out papers to replicate, as a way of running quality control on the literature. They got in touch with me, indicating that they wanted to attempt to replicate the *Thinker* study, but with tighter controls and larger samples. I welcomed their replication and helped them with methodology as much as I could. Although I suspected the findings wouldn't replicate, I didn't want to leave myself the easy escape of claiming that they'd missed some important detail.[‡]

The results of Calin-Jageman's replication were eventually published in 2017.[8] They rather conclusively showed that looking at *The Thinker* did exactly nothing to people's religious beliefs. In the paper, Calin-Jageman also

‡ Reactions to failed replications around this time are chock-full of retrospective accounts of what must've gone wrong, and what the replication team must've done wrong to break an original author's sturdy effect. I generally find these post-hoc pleas unconvincing. You think your effect is robust and the replicators messed it up? That's cool. Run a study to support that supposition. Call forth data to testify on your behalf.

levelled heavy criticism at the other cute and flashy experiments in our paper, and rightly so! Our experiments gave no reason to suspect that subtle experimental prods to think more analytically caused people to report less religious belief. The experiments were just a collection of small-sample studies, using ad hoc and unvalidated methods—precisely the combination of problematic study features that our field was rapidly coming to realize spelled disaster. Small samples, unvalidated methods, flashy and counterintuitive findings: a recipe for irreproducible science. Our results were false positives, flukes, capitalizations on chance, false steps. Insert whatever euphemism you prefer; it won't bother me.

As Calin-Jageman's paper was published, I published a blog post[§] in which I pointed out that my work was exactly the sort that we'd expect not to replicate well, and commended Calin-Jageman's team for their attention to the paper. When shaky scientific work rises to prominence, it deserves to be reexamined, and if it falls apart on reexamination, that merits both reflection (on the part of original authors) and praise (to the replicators).

Now, that's the high-minded retrospective version. I confess that at the time, I found the whole ordeal incredibly stressful. Not stressful because I faulted Calin-Jageman in any way, his team was exemplary throughout, and I've been grateful that we maintained communication during and after publication. It was stressful because there I was, early in my first academic job, watching my most attention-grabbing result publicly go up in flames. It was stressful because *I knew it deserved to go up in flames, but had waited for someone else to strike the match first*. Some further excerpts of that blog post, to highlight the experience:

> Facts aside: Is it fun to find out that a study you published in a high-profile outlet back in the day does not hold up well to more rigorous scrutiny? Oh, hell no. I highly recommend you avoid the experience.
>
> How do you avoid the experience? Make sure you're more rigorous up front. More power. Open science, etc.... Embrace methodological reform. It isn't going away. We can look at old papers and say "sure, but we didn't know better then."... Maybe we will be able to pick a year and say "LOOK everyone, we get it, before YEAR XXXX we didn't always know better. But after YEAR XXXX nobody has an excuse for not changing yet. Nobody

§ http://willgervais.com/blog/2017/3/2/post-publication-peer-review.

> can claim ignorance on these issues after YEAR XXXX." I have no idea which year counts as that YEAR XXXX. But I am quite confident that it is already in the past rather than still in the future.
>
> I think my Methodological Awakening (tm) started in ~2012 and continues to this day. I'm optimistic about the direction our field is headed (though occasionally dismayed to see studies at least as weak as mine published in 2016 in places like *Psychological Science*, *JPSP*, *PNAS*, and everywhere. Progress ain't linear). And I'm super proud of the steps I've taken to both 1) educate grad students about methods, and 2) upgrade my own science. My best 2–3 papers HANDS DOWN are currently under review. I hope I can say the same thing again next year (assuming, of course, that I'm not talking about the same papers still being under review).

Enough pity-wallowing. That was the first inkling that our experiments were shaky, but I reckon the first refutations were conclusive enough. Mentally, I moved on to other projects over these years, looking for topics that seemed more likely to yield robust results. In the meantime, the challenges to the rational atheism thesis kept piling up. It was far more than just a single refutation of my cute little study.

In 2018, a team of researchers published a paper reporting replication efforts of social science studies that had been published in the prestigious journals *Science* and *Nature*. As you'll recall, our *Thinker* study had appeared in *Science*, so it was one of the studies included for replication. And again, even though I'd also helped this team get the methods right, rigorous replication showed that our initial results were a fluke—as, likely, were lots of the other replicated studies.[9] We were in good company, albeit for bad results. This large-scale replication project attracted lots of media attention, so this time around instead of lamenting my previous failures in my private blog, I got to do so in an NPR interview.[¶] My catchiest quote from that interview: "Our study, in hindsight, was outright silly."

Recall that three teams published papers relevant to the analytic atheism thesis right around the same time, two including experiments claiming evidence of causation. My experiments didn't hold water, but what about the other teams'? One of those, too, has proven elusive on replication.[10]

¶ https://www.npr.org/sections/health-shots/2018/08/27/642218377/in-psychology-and-other-social-sciences-many-studies-fail-the-reproducibility-te.

Beyond replicating the initial teams' studies, other researchers sought independent proof-of-concept tests. These were original experiments testing other applications of the general rational atheism thesis. A team led by Miguel Farias, for example, tried an opposite approach to the one we'd used. Instead of trying to experimentally boost analytic thinking, Farias and colleagues used an experimental manipulation to deplete it. The rational atheism thesis would predict that inhibiting analytic thought would boost religiosity. The results? Nada, zip, zilch. Three more studies failing to support the analytic atheism thesis.[11]

At this juncture it's important to note that the failures that were piling up were all attempts to experimentally manipulate analytic thinking, to see if it would affect reported religious beliefs. Maybe the issue isn't so much the conceptual linkage between rational thinking and atheism, but instead failures in experimental manipulations. Maybe analytic thinking and atheism just aren't the sorts of things we can experimentally push around in the lab. But recall that the first three papers didn't just present experimental manipulations—they'd all begun with more straightforward correlational tests of a general association between cognitive style and religious beliefs. As experimental support for the rational atheism thesis crumbled, did the correlations remain solid? Yes and no.

RATIONAL ATHEISM: WEAK AND FICKLE

The three 2012 papers relevant to the rational atheism thesis each reported a straightforward correlation between a more reflective or rational cognitive style and religious disbelief. All correlations were in the expected direction, and statistically significant. Unlike the flashier experiments, the correlations looked robust. They were based, generally, on larger sample sizes. The measures employed were either previously validated or so direct in what they measured as to appear valid on the face. (There are only so many ways to ask people how much they believe in God, after all.) Because each team used slightly different measures of religiosity as outcome variables, it looked like the correlation was at least somewhat robust across conditions, and not down to a chance pattern emerging from some idiosyncratic measure.

Over the ensuing years, lots of studies appeared showing the same basic correlation: people who tended toward a more rational cognitive style also tended to report being a bit less religious. Mind you, these patterns didn't always emerge from studies that set out to test for a relationship between cognitive style and religion; it's just that both cognitive style and religion are common enough measures in studies that the results could be pulled out. Curious about the generality of the rational cognitive style–religious disbelief correlations, Gordon Pennycook set out to assess the overall evidence.[12] He conducted a meta-analysis, which is just a fancy statistical way to smoosh a bunch of independent studies together to see what the average effect is. A meta-analysis is only as good as the studies that go into it, and meta-analysis is far from a perfect tool. Nonetheless, they're a decent enough way to quantitatively summarize a literature. Pennycook's meta-analysis included thirty-one studies, totaling more than fifteen thousand participants. The average overall pattern? A solid, statistically significant correlation between a more rational cognitive style and lower reported religious belief. Unlike our experiments on rational atheism, the correlations looked solid, emerging again and again in repeated studies by independent teams.

The correlations looked robust in Pennycook's meta-analysis, but they weren't especially large. Correlations can be summarized by a single value, r, running from r = -1 (a perfect negative correlation) to r = 0 (no correlation whatsoever, two randomly paired variables) to r = 1 (a perfect positive correlation). The correlation between rational cognitive style and religious belief? r = -0.18. More rational thinkers were, on average, just a little less religious than more intuitive thinkers, but a correlation of -0.18 means that cognitive style isn't giving us much information about people's religious beliefs.

It's possible to transform correlations into a crude measure of how much of the variability between two variables is shared. Height and weight tend to be strongly correlated. People who are taller also tend to weigh more. Variability in one variable (people are taller or shorter) is shared with variability in weight (taller people also tend to be heavier; shorter people also tend to be lighter). How much variability is shared between rational cognitive style and religiosity? A correlation of r = -.018 translates into about 3 percent overlap between the two.

How impressive is that r = -.018 correlation, that 3 percent overlap? Over the years I've enjoyed sparring with Pennycook about how to interpret the strength of this correlation. We agree on the basic values, you see, but not on whether to be especially impressed by them. He points out that if you just look at the difference in cognitive reflection test scores between the staunchest atheists and the most pious believers, it looks statistically substantial. Gord is also coming at these correlations as someone who primarily studies reasoning. From that perspective, it's impressive that a quirky measure of reasoning like the CRT predicts sociocultural beliefs like religion at all. I'm coming at these correlations from the other side, as someone interested in predicting atheism. From that angle, explaining 3 percent of the variability in religious belief and disbelief is a bit of a yawn. We've found lots of other variables with more explanatory power than this. Who's right? Depends, I suspect, on which set of variables you care more about: reasoning or religion.**

The studies that made it into Pennycook's meta-analysis were, as is common in the behavioral sciences, predominantly from the United States and other Western countries. How robust is the rationality-atheism correlation across cultures? Around the same time as Pennycook's meta-analysis came out, I was finalizing a cross-cultural investigation of people's moral perceptions of atheists. (We'll meet the main study in a later chapter.) We had data from thirteen countries, spanning the whole spectrum from strongly religious locales (United Arab Emirates, India, United States) to more secular societies (Czech Republic, Netherlands, China). The study also included our trusty friend the cognitive reflection test, as well as a measure of people's self-rated belief in God (or gods). This furnished an opportunity to gauge the cross-cultural stability of the correlation between rational cognitive style and religious disbelief.

Our resulting paper used some nifty statistical tools to look at the correlation within each country, as well as the overall correlation across all the countries, accounting for how data were clustered within countries. Looking at the overall correlation, it came out even more modest than Pennycook's meta-analysis. The aggregate relationship translates to just $r = -0.05$, which would mean a mere 0.2 percent overlap. At a global level, pooling across

** It's been genuinely fun over the years to have a friendly on-and-off debate in which we agree with the basic facts and approach each other's perspective with mutual respect. If you're reading this, Gord, I hope we never agree! That would close what's been a very fun intermittent conversation.

thirteen countries, cognitive style is telling us almost nothing about people's religious belief or disbelief.[13]

Drilling down to the country-by-country inferences, the overall pattern was one of substantial variability. As we might expect, given Pennycook's meta-analytic results, the expected pattern showed up in the US data. But beyond the United States, the correlation between rational cognitive style and disbelief was overwhelmingly evident in just two other countries (Singapore and Australia), with reasonably stable patterns also cropping up in a handful of other sites. In four countries, there wasn't a whiff of a correlation supporting the rational atheism thesis (New Zealand, Czech Republic, the United Kingdom, Netherlands). Across all the sites, it looked like the correlation between rational cognitive style and religious disbelief was most strongly evident in the more religious countries, and waned to meaningless in more secular places.

So much for the cross-cultural stability of the rational atheism thesis. Evidence was sparse in some of the most secular countries sampled, and was strong in precisely none of them. Aggregate results showed that cognitive style was, at best, a bit player in explaining variability in religious belief and disbelief across these thirteen countries.

Other results out of my lab allow a more nuanced test of the rational atheism thesis, just within the United States. Recall that the United States is one of the study sites where the cognitive style–disbelief correlation seems most solid. In a nationally representative sample of more than a thousand survey respondents, Maxine Najle, Nava Caluori,[††] and I were able to look at the relationship between a rational cognitive style and religious disbelief, to see if the correlation was general across other interesting individual differences within the country.[14] We were especially interested in looking at the relationship between rational cognitive style and disbelief across people who either were or were not raised in strongly religious households. This analysis was in part driven by the many conversations I'd had at secular gatherings, where people told me that science and rationality had been key to their move from fundamentalist upbringings to their current rational atheism. Recall the figure earlier in the chapter: atheists tend

[††] You'll see these names scattered throughout this book; they're brilliant students I've been fortunate enough to work with over the years.

to attribute their atheism to rationality, not upbringing. Paired with the numerous anecdotes I'd been told, it might suggest that rationality wasn't generally corrosive to religion, but might predict people turning to atheism from particularly strong religious upbringings. In short, that the rational atheism thesis might be a poor explanation for global atheism, but a better explanation for how people become atheists in more religious places like the United States.

With this in mind, we did some statistical sleuthing to see how strong the correlation between rational cognitive style and religious disbelief was, at different levels of religious upbringing.

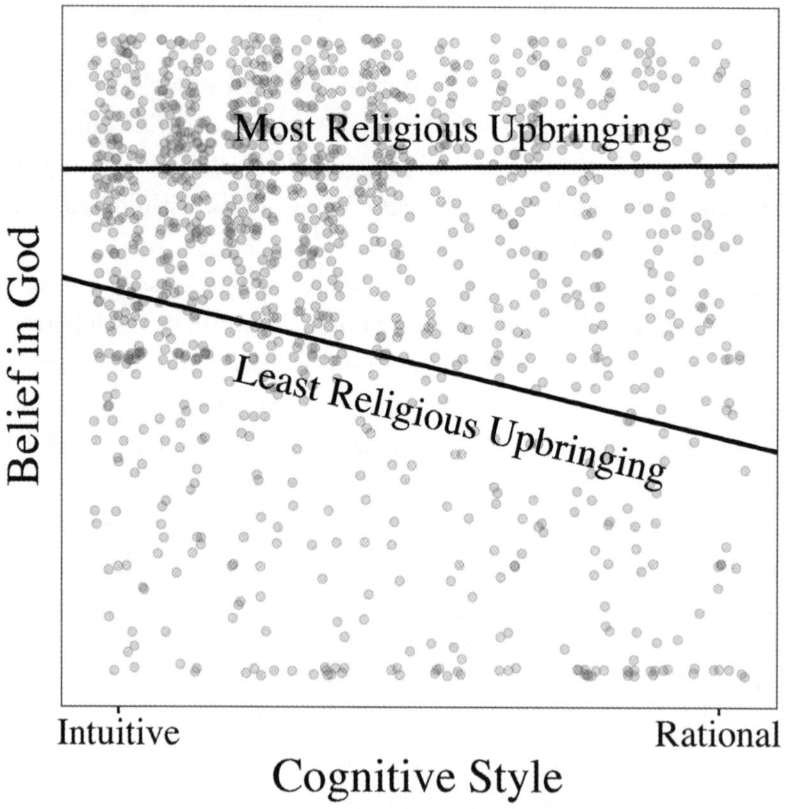

Figure 3.4. Rational cognitive style is entirely unassociated with religious disbelief among people with strong religious upbringings. *Source:* W. M. Gervais, M. B. Najle, and N. Caluori, "The Origins of Religious Disbelief: A Dual Inheritance Approach," *Social Psychological and Personality Science*, 12, no. 7 (2021): 1369–79.

Was the rationality-atheism correlation stronger among people who'd been raised to be religious? To our surprise, not at all. The overall correlation between rational cognitive style and religious disbelief looked to be entirely driven by people who hadn't been raised with a strong religious influence. Among the people who'd had the most strongly religious upbringings, there was no correlation whatsoever between cognitive style and disbelief. None. Zero. Far from rationality being the key force leading people to atheism from religious upbringings, it turned out to be entirely unrelated to religiosity among those with more strongly religious childhoods.

This is worth unpacking further because it seems a little counterintuitive. And it also conflicts with so many people's narratives about thinking their way out of religious indoctrination. But recall that a correlation of zero (like this one essentially was) just means that knowing someone's score on one variable tells you nothing about the other variable of interest. In this case, once we select people with strong religious upbringings, knowing their cognitive style tells us nothing about their religious belief or disbelief. So it doesn't mean that there aren't highly rational atheists who had strong religious upbringings. Instead, it means that among people with strong religious upbringings, rational cognitive style is distributed equally across the spectrum of religious belief and disbelief. No doubt there are highly rational atheists who had religious upbringings; but there are also lots of people who were raised religious and are now both highly religious and highly rational. This shouldn't surprise us! Theologians, philosophers of religion, thoughtful preachers—these are all highly rational people who turn their analytic prowess specifically to their faith. Even churchgoing doctors, lawyers, accountants, and all the rest. Again, these are people highly engaged with rationality and logic, but who are religious. Contra the rational atheism thesis, a highly rational cognitive style isn't *generally* corrosive to religious belief among people with a strong religious upbringing.

TAKING STOCK

So, what can we make of the rational atheism thesis? It has some scientific plausibility, what with religion being potentially rooted in intuition (as we'll see in the next chapter) and our dual process systems for processing information either intuitively or rationally. And it saw some early empirical success, with high-profile papers hitting the headlines in rapid order back in 2012.

Alas, the flashiest experiments linking rationality to religious disbelief proved to be scientific mirages, false positives emerging from subpar (though commonplace at the time) methods. Replication work by rigorous scientists like Bob Calin-Jageman sank that boat in short order, and a rapidly growing body of work chipped away at the never-especially-strong experimental foundations of the rational atheism thesis.

Although experimental work on rational atheism crumbled, there were still intriguing correlations between cognitive style and religious beliefs. One meta-analysis summarizing dozens of studies on thousands of people showed a reliable correlation between rational cognitive style and religious disbelief. But in full context, that correlation too appears fairly unimpressive as an explanation for atheism.

Putting the Pennycook meta-analysis alongside the cross-cultural results and alongside these most recent analyses across levels of religious upbringing, we can reach some conclusions about the rational atheism thesis. I'd say that the correlation between rational cognitive style and religious disbelief is (in the title of a paper we wrote on the topic) both weak and fickle. It shows up in some samples, but is never overwhelmingly strong. It disappears entirely in some countries. It also disappears entirely among participants in the United States who had a strong religious upbringing.

Recall that the rational atheism thesis doesn't just predict a smallish and unstable correlation between rationality and atheism, it predicts that rationality is a key driver of atheism. New Atheist popularizers claimed that their own atheism emerged from rationality and science, and that their books could spur people to rationally escape from the clutches of religious foolishness. To outgrow God, as one Dawkins book title alludes. It's not just celebrity atheists attributing atheism to rationality either: when I've surveyed people about where they think their beliefs come from, atheists reliably report that it was rationality, not upbringing, that led them to atheism.

Alas, our best scientific evidence gathered over the last decade or so tells us that the rational atheism thesis falls well short of explaining atheism. This is not because there was a lack of effort to find supportive evidence—I myself tried pretty hard to find evidence supporting the rational atheism thesis, following the narratives of atheists I'd spoken to. It was a pattern I set out expecting to find. But at the end of the scientific day, rationality being a driver of atheism is, more or less, a myth. I encourage rational-thinking and science-minded readers to move on from the simplistic narrative of the rational atheism thesis.

Where, then, does atheism come from? To answer that question, we first need to understand how religion itself works. The last two chapters disabused us of some faulty notions about both religion and atheism. Slate thus cleared, we can now proceed with building a theory of religious belief and disbelief, answering first the Puzzle of Faith, then the Puzzle of Atheism.

INTERLUDE

The Puzzle of Faith

As we grapple with the Puzzle of Faith, we need to answer a few key questions:

- ➢ What are the origins of religion in our species?
- ➢ Is religion an evolutionary adaptation? Or a by-product?
- ➢ How does our cognition shape religions?
- ➢ How does culture work? Does culture evolve?
- ➢ Why do people come to believe in the gods they believe in?
- ➢ Why do some religions persist and spread while most quickly fade?

CHAPTER FOUR

DARWINIZING FAITH

The Cognitive Science of Religion

Unlike any science-literate generation that has come before, we now possess the intellectual tools to observe our own minds at work and to understand how God has come to be there.
—JESSE BERING, *THE BELIEF INSTINCT*[1]

Believing in God is a natural, almost inevitable consequence of the types of minds we have living in the sort of world we inhabit.
—JUSTIN L. BARRETT, *WHY WOULD ANYONE BELIEVE IN GOD?*[2]

Career turning points can happen at odd times. I once had one while teaching second graders. During my university years, I earned some spare cash by working as a substitute teacher back in the school district where I'd grown up—highlights were elementary school PE classes, full of dodgeball and other assorted games. The work was tiring and poorly paid, but fun. Substitute teachers usually get handed a cursory plan for the day, largely full of filler tasks to keep the kids engaged.* But during lunchtime

* Most lessons were quite fun, but some occasionally got awkward. First example: in response to a question about what the students had done while school was canceled for a snowstorm the previous day, a girl earnestly told the class that she went to her friend's house because "my parents were praying for me to get a younger brother or sister." Second example: I had to show my girlfriend's younger brother's (now-brother-in-law's) class NOVA's *Miracle of Life* video, a precursor lesson for sex ed.

and planning sessions we had downtime, a chance to decompress. As a fully dedicated nerd I'd spend this time reading either popular science books or comics.

On this day, I'd brought a book I'd recently picked up, Pascal Boyer's *Religion Explained: The Evolutionary Origins of Religious Thought.*[3] I blew through lunch, reading as much as I could of this eye-opening book. I got home and finished the book that night, leaving me tired for the next day's substitute teaching. What about this book caught me so? After a couple of years as a shiftless undergrad who bounced between majors, I'd begun to actually get serious and had decided I wanted to get into evolutionary psychology, to understand our species' unique evolution. But on the side, I'd always been casually interested in religion. Not as an adherent, so much, but as an interested observer in the phenomenon of religion. I'd read about various world religions and mythologies, and took "Complete Idiot's Guide"–caliber forays into Norse Paganism, the I Ching, and just about any other belief system I could dig into. But Boyer's book was the first time I'd concretely realized that religion was something that could be productively studied from an evolutionary and scientific perspective. Something clicked for me then—my two main academic interests were possible to combine! This book spurred me to start seriously considering going to grad school, to find a program where I'd be able to combine my interests in evolutionary psychology and religion. It was the first time I'd ever really started to think about what in this book I'm calling the Puzzle of Faith, the unique evolution of our peculiarly religious species.

THE PUZZLE OF FAITH

The opening chapters posed two puzzles for us to ponder. The Puzzle of Faith asks how come our species alone came to believe in gods, and the Puzzle of Atheism asks how our species can be peculiarly but incompletely religious. This next stretch of the book dives into the first puzzle and tries to cobble together a coherent scientific story about how our species evolved to have religion, and why the world's religious landscape looks as it does today.

In chapter 2 we met some popular answers to the Puzzle of Faith, and found them wanting. Although religion can bring comfort to people in times of need, it doesn't seem that religion exists primarily because of its palliative properties. Opiate of the masses or not, religions both soothe and scare. There's heaven to hope for, but also hell to fear. The motivational aspects of religion are complex, but they fall well short of explaining our species' odd religious evolution. Second, we considered the possibility that humans are just innately religious. We've evolved to have a part of the brain (or the genome) that makes us religious. It's just built in. We found that this answer is either wrong in the particulars or isn't specific enough to give us much scientific leverage. Saying that something exists because it evolved to exist is rather tautological and doesn't buy us much in terms of explaining what specifically about religion evolved in response to which specific pressures. Finally, we considered the idea that religion results from childhood credulity. This hypothesis—popularized by Richard Dawkins in two books—says that religion is a side effect of kids just believing whatever they're told by their elders. But, as intuitively attractive as the idea may be on a first pass, neither kids nor cultures, it turns out, work like that. Kids just aren't built to be mindlessly compliant and credulous, and culture is a lot more complicated than the passive information absorption Dawkins described. Each of these answers fell flat, but in illuminating ways, ways that might help us ask better questions.

How and *why* did we evolve in a way that makes religions likely? These are the sorts of questions that serious scientists pose about religion. In this chapter, we'll explore the cognitive science of religion, an interdisciplinary scientific effort that sought to answer good evolutionary and cognitive questions about religions. The cast of key players in the cognitive science of religion included anthropologists, developmental psychologists, cultural psychologists, philosophers, and people from many other allied disciplines. There are some foundational assumptions that hold, but also quite a lot of variability in terms of what ideas were fashionable and which theories were pets of which researchers. I'll do my best to summarize some of the more popular ideas but am sure to miss important work along the way—a practical inevitability when one tries to do justice to more than a decade's worth of scholarship in a single book chapter.

So, with that throat clearing out of the way, let's dive in. A loose gang of researchers had begun to tackle religion head on, and in effect tried to solve the Puzzle of Faith, asking why it is that our species alone is a religious one.

To solve this puzzle, the cognitive science of religion progressed along two main fronts. One was evolutionary. Scientists needed to figure out plausible scenarios whereby a weird upright primate like us could've started to ponder the supernatural. The other thrust was cognitive. What sorts of cognitive apparatus does religion require and draw upon? What kind of a brain could produce supernatural beliefs? The dual evolutionary and the cognitive foci reinforced each other. At the end of the day, evolutionary questions about religion are questions about the evolution of cognitive systems. Nobody was suggesting that we're religious because of the functioning of our spleens or kidneys—obviously, the key to our religious evolution would be found in considering our mental evolution. And the cognitive questions being posed would obviously be constrained by what we know about our species' evolution. Cognition and evolution, hand in hand. So, throughout this chapter when I talk about the cognitive science of religion (as the movement came to call itself), definitely keep in mind that we're talking about both the cognitive and evolutionary science of religions.

WHAT NEEDS EXPLAINING?

From the outset, the cognitive science of religion focused on explaining *religion in general*, rather than in understanding the quirks of specific religious traditions. Cognitive scientists of religion were interested in how we'd evolved to have the sorts of brains that let us have religion. Doctrinal differences and details about karma, or the Trinity, or other theological minutiae unique to this-or-that faith were seen as surface variation that likely obscured deeper universalities in religious cognition. Presumably, there's a core religious cognition that underpins diverse manifestations of faith. It's this core universality that really drew the attention of cognitive scientists of religion. And if scientists could crack those universals open, they'd have gone a long way toward solving the Puzzle of Faith.

That's not to say that cognitive scientists of religion were disinterested in the particulars of any individual religion. Quite the opposite! Details about specific faiths were immensely important. Books and articles on the cognitive science of religion would often open with anecdotes about seemingly bizarre (bizarre to Westerners, at least) beliefs or practices specific to one specific religion or another. Anecdotes about the fickle and local ancestor spirits of many a small-scale society's religion might be juxtaposed against more culturally familiar (again, to Western audiences) examples from Christendom, for instance.

Cognitive scientists of religion searched for the deep universalities underlying all this surface-level religious diversity, if only researchers could view religions with a sufficient level of abstraction. For instance, a small-scale ancestor spirit might be mainly concerned about whether the band's youths were quiet at night, whereas a Judeo-Christian deity would be portrayed as caring deeply about which pieces of land his chosen people would control. The ancestor spirit might be geographically constrained, able to act only in a small area—say by hassling people who make mischief on one specific beach—whereas the Judeo-Christian deity could smite those who thwart his chosen people wherever they lay. These are massive differences in scope of concern (whether a few kids need to shut up, versus matters of broad geopolitical import) and also scale of action (hassling some beach-goers, versus sanctioning some Old Testament genocides). But drill down and you'll find some underlying commonalities to both. Specifically, both the local spirit and the universal God are represented as having more or less human minds. They've got *desires* and *concerns*. They *want* some outcomes rather than others. They have *preferences*. People work to *please*, or at least *appease*, their deities.

This is the sort of universality hiding behind difference that's the bread and butter of the cognitive science of religion. From the dizzying diversity of world religious thought, they sought to discover and distill a few abstract commonalities that might be scientifically explicable. As a book by a prominent cognitive scientist of religion puts it: "Children are born believers of what I call natural religion—parallel to the natural language that many linguists say children's minds are naturally inclined toward understanding. . . . Christianity, Hinduism, Islam, Jainism, Judaism, Mormonism, Sikhism, and other tribal and world religions are derivations and elaborations of natural religion."[4] Identifying these sorts of universals—these features of "natural religion"—gave cognitive scientists of religion traction. They helped set the research agenda and suggested fruitful avenues of inquiry. As the research program progressed over the years, much progress was made, and a few fault lines emerged. As is often the case, different theories can account for the same set of observations, and nuanced differences between different researchers' approaches emerged. But at its core, I think it's safe to say that the cognitive science of religion settled on one core idea: *religion comes naturally*.[5]

People might differ in their specific religious beliefs. But to a first approximation, human beings are religious (if by chance you're an atheist and this assertion makes you feel a bit squirmy, don't fret: the second half of the book is all about making the case that atheism is natural too). All else equal, people tend to believe in gods. The believed-in gods might be localized ancestor spirits; they might be all-powerful sky kings or sea queens or what have you; they might be fickle tricksters or moral barristers; they might explain lots or nothing about the natural world. But people everywhere believe that our world is populated not just by us humans but also by various supernatural agents. We're often taught details about these supernatural agents as we grow up. But, at least per standard cognitive science of religion work, we don't necessarily have to be taught *to believe* in the supernatural. That capacity for belief comes naturally.

HOW TO THINK LIKE A COGNITIVE SCIENTIST OF RELIGION

When science progresses, it often does so by breaking some large and seemingly unanswerable question into smaller chunks that can be analyzed individually. Cognitive scientists of religion want to take the question of why and how our species is religious—a genuinely *big* puzzle—and generate lots of smaller but more productive questions that can be productively answered on their own. If we start by recognizing that for some reason religion just comes naturally to our species, we can start to break the Puzzle of Faith into smaller sub-questions that are more scientifically tractable. For example, we could start asking specific scientific questions about our gods, including questions about how we mentally represent them and how supernatural agent concepts spread throughout our cultures. A good approach here is to start with an observation about religions, and then let that observation spawn specific and productive scientific questions. Let's illustrate this by highlighting a couple observations-then-questions an aspiring cognitive scientist of religion might want to answer.

Example 1: Gods on Minds

People everywhere seem to have a really easy time imagining gods and ghosts and djinn and all sorts of supernatural critters. ***Observation***: Something about the way our minds work just makes it easy for us to entertain thoughts of supernatural agents. ***Questions***: Why are supernatural agents so easy to think about? What are the specific cognitive mechanisms that enable us to think about gods? How did these mechanisms evolve—did they evolve in order to help us think about gods, or is the gods bit just a side effect of a cognitive system that evolved for some other purpose?

Example 2: Why We Love Gods

There are plenty of concepts that we find easy to think about, but they're too mundane to generate much interest. For example, it's pretty easy to imagine rocks or wind. But for the most part we don't obsess over them. They're just stuff that's in the world and are often not super interesting to nonspecialists. In contrast, religious ideas tend to grab the attention of most folks. It's not just the case that we find it easy to idly imagine supernatural agents. Instead, these agents are remarkably popular and evocative. ***Observation***: Gods and ghosts seem to capture people's interests, and stories about them spread far and wide. ***Questions***: What features of supernatural agent concepts might make them spread easily? What types of cognitive systems might help or hinder the spread of supernatural agent concepts?

Example 3: Costly Commitments

Religions are more than just popular folk tales. People don't just spread and re-tell their religious stories—they often kill and die for them. ***Observation***: Religions recruit passionate commitment, including costly and painful behaviors that people use to prove their faith. ***Questions***: Why do individual people subject themselves to costly and painful rituals to prove their faith? Given how costly religious rites and rituals can be, is there some offsetting benefit that helps them persist over cultural evolutionary time? If there are benefits to costly religious commitments, are they benefits that accrue to the individuals who perform the rites, or to religious groups that enforce them?

Here, we've taken three broad observations and carved them into at least eight useful scientific questions. Not bad! These are just examples of the types of questions that cognitive scientists of religion might ask in their research. Some of these questions have attracted lots of research attention, others comparatively less. But they help to show what the process behind cognitive science of religion can look like. Start with an observation about religion, and then try to carve out pragmatically and scientifically tractable scientific questions about what's going on under the (cognitive and evolutionary) hood.

Armed now with a handful of better questions about religious cognition, let's see what answers might look like to cognitive scientists of religion. Along the way, we'll learn about different types of evolutionary pathways for traits to become widespread.

ADAPTATIONS AND BY-PRODUCTS

Religion seems to come easily to people, and the superficial differences between religions might conceal some deeper universality among them. Where did these universals come from? Coming at the question from the evolutionary side of things, there are at least a couple of ways to make sense of this. Here, it's worth stepping briefly back from religion specifically and thinking more broadly about the evolution of traits in general. Namely, a trait could be more or less universal in a given species either because it's an adaptation in its own right, or because it is a by-product of some other adaptation or cluster of adaptations.[†] Both adaptation and by-product are viable as candidate explanations for species-typical traits.[6] By "species-typical trait" I just mean something that most typically developing members of the species will have. Like noses, or bipedalism, or (for most of our history) belief in supernatural agents.

To clarify the distinction between adaptation and by-product, think about your teeth. You've got some pointy teeth up front, you've got some knobbly teeth at the back, and all your teeth are basically white. Are these traits adaptations or by-products? Let's tackle tooth shape and tooth color separately.

[†] For completeness, adaptations and by-products aren't the only tools in the evolutionary toolkit. But they're the ones that get the most airtime in the cognitive science of religion.

Differently shaped teeth are physical adaptations for different types of mastication. The pointy teeth up front are adapted for biting and cutting; the knobbly teeth in back are adapted for crushing and grinding. Over generations, individuals whose teeth were shaped in a way that made them better at these tasks left more offspring, and you now have teeth shaped the way they are because those tooth shapes are specific adaptations that were naturally selected for in order to accomplish specific food-processing functions. Each tooth shape is functionally good at a rather narrow task—adaptations tend to be like this, functionally excelling at a specific something. They are tools, finely crafted by natural selection and well designed for the narrow and specific task at hand.

What about tooth color? Are white teeth an adaptation, like pointy cutting teeth and knobbly grinding teeth? Did ancestors having pearlier whites survive and reproduce at higher rates than individuals with teeth that are less pearly? Probably not. Instead, it turns out that teeth evolved to be hard and durable. Specifically, our teeth have an enamel layer made of calcium phosphate, a rock-hard mineral compound. This mineral compound just so happens to be white. Natural selection gave us teeth with calcium phosphate enamel because calcium phosphate enamel is hard and durable. Calcium phosphate is useful because it's hard, and it just happens to be whitish in color. The adaptation here is the hardness of the enamel, the whiteness of the enamel is just a side effect. Selecting for strength and durability led to a calcium phosphate enamel, which just so happens to be white. The whiteness of our teeth has nothing to do with any adaptive benefit to whiteness in teeth—the whiteness is purely a by-product.

Our teeth nicely illustrate two ways that species-typical traits can evolve: either as adaptations in their own right, or as by-products of other adaptations. Where does that leave religion: adaptation or by-product? Some combination of both?

IS RELIGION AN ADAPTATION? AND FOR WHAT?

First, let's consider the possibility that some core religious capacity is an adaptation that helped members of our species survive and thrive. It's in principle possible that we have some core religious faculty that was directly selected for in our lineage, an adaptation that helped our ancestors better accomplish one important task or another. Maybe humans tend toward religion because somehow in our evolutionary past religions (and ancestral proto-religions along the way) conferred direct benefits on our ancestors. Maybe religions and proto-religions aided ancestral survival or reproduction.

Various researchers have made the case for various religion-as-adaptation accounts over the years, each positing a different functional adaptive challenge that religion might've helped us solve. Maybe religion is a psychological adaptation that helped us solve cooperative dilemmas,[7] for example. Or maybe we evolved to have religion because it gives people a motivational push to persevere when the going gets rough. Maybe we've evolved to be religious in order to overcome a crippling fear of death.[‡] Lots of scenarios are possible.

Without delving too much into each possibility individually, however, I'll cut to the chase and reveal that the cognitive science of religion has tended more toward viewing religion as a by-product. In general, when cognitive scientists of religion state that religion is natural, they're saying that it comes easily to most humans, not that it's some directly selected mental adaptation that helped our ancestors survive. The reasons for caution regarding any specific claim that religion is an adaptation are as diverse as the religion-as-adaptation claims themselves. But these adaptationist accounts all tend to scientifically struggle in one of two ways.

First, little about religious cognition appears especially well-designed for tackling a specific adaptive goal. Remember, this is a hallmark of good adaptations—they're really good at solving some specific adaptive challenge. By my reading, genetic adaptationist accounts of religion tend to fail because they either fail to outline a clear adaptive challenge, or because they don't clearly outline how the specific features of religion are well suited as solutions. Religions might be able to promote cooperation in some contexts, or they might be able to motivate people to push on when the going gets rough. But religions don't look to be *specifically, uniquely, and directly*

[‡] As we saw a couple chapters back, it's not especially clear to me that some existential "fear of death" is really trading in the currencies that natural selection cares about—survival and reproduction. But the case has been made for religion being a human universal because it helps us deal with existential angst of this sort.

good at doing these things. There's just not a tight fit between the forms of religions and the functions they're postulated to serve in adaptationist theories of religion's evolution.

Second, a lot of claims that religion is an adaptation for one thing or another take an unfortunately narrow view of religion, as it is actually expressed across our incredibly diverse species. Humans occupy lots of niches around the world, and have incredible diversity in their religions. Many adaptationist accounts of religion are consistent with how some large-scale global religions like Christianity operate, but do a poor job accounting for religious diversity. A few religions have spread globally, but most religions throughout history don't look much like the big religions that have conquered the globe (chapter 7 has more to say on this point). Positing an evolutionary trajectory that explains Christianity but not the myriad smaller-scale religions that more representatively typify human religion is putting the scientific cart before the horse. We need to explain both the emergence of typical human religions—small-scale, localized deities and all—and also the current global religious landscape. Any explanation that ignores the former and focuses solely on incidental features of the religions that "won" the cultural battle for hearts and minds has failed before it left the station.

Adaptationism can be a powerful scientific tool for understanding lots of species-typical traits, but cognitive science of religion tends to view it as a poor tool for explaining religion.

RELIGION AS A BY-PRODUCT?

The by-product view asks us to consider the possibility that religion emerged as a universal in our lineage (despite some superficial variability) not because religion itself was especially good for our ancestors, not because it's exquisitely tailored to solving some adaptive riddle, but because religion just sort of tagged along for the ride. The by-product view says that we evolved to have cognitive systems that are really good at solving a bunch of different problems—finding mates, avoiding danger, tracking complex alliances, avoiding cheaters and liars—and that somehow, it just happens to be the case that brains good at solving these problems in a species like ours will also be brains that are good at thinking religious thoughts.

This is an exciting view! A by-product account of religion could explain why religion is a human universal, and it could explain why world religions all tend to share so many commonalities. But there's no need to posit or identify the specific adaptive challenge that religions solve. If we've evolved to have mental gadgets that are good at solving lots of specific adaptive challenges (as evolutionary psychologists point out we probably have), it's possible that these mental tools interact in such a way that it makes religions easy to think. If religion is an evolutionary by-product, it would mean that we didn't evolve to have religion, per se, but that religions are just good fits for the minds we've evolved to have.

To make this concrete, imagine a mind that had five different cognitive systems in it, each tailored to a specific task. Maybe one's our food-finding system, one's a mate-attractor system, one's a fight-or-flighter, one's a story rememberer, and one's all about avoiding predators. Each system might have its own presets and in-built biases to help it better perform the task it evolved to solve. Some systems might come with attentional biases, noticing some things rather than others in the environment. Some systems might have perceptual biases, leading us to make some predictable mistakes in how we see the world. Some systems might have memory biases, making it easier for us to remember some sorts of information. You get the point. You can imagine that each bias might predispose people to believe some things rather than others, even just by a tiny bit. But if all the systems have biases that point in similar directions, all of a sudden, you've got the potential for phenomenal cultural success for concepts that fit well with lots of our cognitive systems. Now, nobody's saying this is exactly how it works—five discrete systems, with discrete biases in attention or memory or perception. But something a bit like it might in fact be how our minds work, and this could help us understand the evolution of religion. Maybe we have lots of cognitive systems, each with its own preferences and biases that operate below our conscious awareness. And these biases all interact in a way that makes religious thoughts easy to think, transmit, and believe. That's the core conceptual story of the cognitive science of religion.

A by-productist approach like this can be just as scientifically productive as would an adaptationist approach, but it suggests a different set of scientific priorities. We don't have to pin down a specific adaptive challenge that religion solved. Instead, we need to identify which other specific mental adaptations might have led us to find religions so compelling. And cognitive scientists of religion have identified lots of features of religion that look like they might've emerged as cognitive by-products.

EVOLUTIONARY PSYCHOLOGY, MENTAL ADAPTATIONS, AND HUMAN NATURE

A trait like religiosity might become a species-typical, cross-cultural universal because it's an evolutionary by-product, rather than an adaptation in its own right. But any scientist worth their tenure can't just hand-wave and declare that something's a cognitive by-product. A convincing argument that a trait is an evolutionary by-product requires us to highlight exactly which cognitive systems the trait's a by-product of. And to find the cognitive systems that religion might be piggybacking on, it's worth reflecting on why we might expect there to be a bunch of different evolved cognitive systems in the first place. Before tackling religion head-on, it's worth stepping back briefly to make a more general case that we have a number of semi-independent evolved cognitive mechanisms that come with their own default settings and biases, and then we can try to piece them together to see if a religion-as-by-product story is a good fit.

Evolutionary psychology is a branch of psychology that turns to evolutionary theory[§] as a mental prosthesis to help us figure out how our minds work. Evolution by natural selection is among the most successful theories in the history of science. Indeed, if I had to pick a single "best theory ever," it would have my vote. From simple and verifiable premises, the theory of evolution by natural selection can explain the dizzying diversity of life. It can explain why different organisms appear to be so perfectly adapted to their specific ways of life, without positing any actual intelligence behind all the apparent design. As theories go, it's as much of a game-changer as the world has seen, well worth the moniker that Daniel Dennett gave it in his book of the same name: *Darwin's Dangerous Idea*.

[§] Here I'm using "evolutionary theory" as a lazy but convenient bit of shorthand. There are actually lots of different quite specific theories that fall under the broad umbrella of "evolutionary theory." When it comes to evolutionary psychology, "evolutionary theory" might be broadly invoked when researchers are actually referring (with varying degrees of accuracy or nuance) to a specific smaller theory—for example, reciprocal altruism, life history theory, or other specific instantiations of the broader insights derived from Darwin's ideas about evolution via natural selection.

Because we have this tremendously powerful theory for understanding living things, say the evolutionary psychologists, why don't we use it to guide our research on human psychology? After all, it would be really weird to say that evolution shaped our bodies but left the mush between our ears alone. Because our ancestors faced recurrent ancestral challenges that required specific behavioral solutions, it makes sense to assume that we might have some mental adaptations that helped our ancestors solve them.[8] And if you assume that mental evolution has happened, then we can productively study human cognition by using evolutionary theory as a guide to which hypotheses to test. We can use the theory to identify potential mental adaptations, and then use standard psychology research methods to figure out how they work. There are a lot of books out there outlining the general approach, so I don't want to dwell on it overly much here. But for the purposes of this chapter, let's just move forward with the (probably overly simplistic) assumption that we've got specific cognitive mechanisms that are adaptive solutions to recurrent evolutionary challenges.

Mental adaptations are expected to be narrowly good at specific tasks. Remember the tooth example: some teeth are narrowly good at cutting, others at grinding. With this in mind, we can consider a few different cognitive systems that might be "for" reasoning about different types of things. These systems come with their own semi-built-in assumptions about the world, and are each good at reasoning within their own domains. To many evolutionary psychologists, what we call "human nature" is just the idiosyncratic set of mental adaptations that our species has evolved over the millennia, as they operate in our current environments.

FROM MENTAL ADAPTATIONS TO RELIGIONS

Following evolutionary psychologists, cognitive scientists of religion argue that we probably have distinct cognitive systems that are each good at reasoning about different stuff we encounter in the world. And in the world, we can broadly classify things into *agents* and *objects*—the *who* and the *what* of our worlds. Agents are capable of intentionally acting on the world. They move of their own volition. They make choices. In short, they behave. Inanimate objects, on the other hand, lack volition. They either are acted upon (perhaps by an agent) or else they remain in place. Agents are the cast of characters in our lives, objects are the scenery.

Agents and objects offer different opportunities and affordances and challenges, and as organisms we need to think about them in different ways. To make things slightly more complicated than a strict agent/object binary, it turns out that lots of the objects out there are actually alive. They require sustenance, they grow, they reproduce, they die. This adds a third category of cognitive system for tracking and thinking about living things, be they animate or not. Putting all of these ideas together, it implies the potential existence of at least a few distinct cognitive systems that are specialized for thinking about (1) inanimate nonliving objects, (2) living things, and (3) full-blown intentional agents. We could call these our core ontological systems. Why "ontological?" Ontology is the branch of philosophy dealing with the nature of being, with the relations between categories. Our intuitive ontology is basically putting the stuff of the world into different categories and building in some assumptions about their basic natures.[9] Rocks go in this bin and act like that; trees in this bin, acting like that; people in their own bin, acting in all their deliciously complex and frustrating ways. Let's unpack these core ontological systems a bit.

A lot of the world is just inanimate stuff—solid objects and the like. To navigate the challenges posed by this stuff, we seem to come equipped with a mental system tracking basic physical properties of things, a cognitive system devoted to folk physics. Our folk physics system isn't tracking quantum entanglement and isn't much concerned with the speed of light. It deals in folk physics rather than physics as, say, a theoretical physicist might. Our folk physics system helps us understand how objects work, and comes with some crude and basic, but usually good-enough, assumptions. For instance, our folk physics tells us that solid objects can't pass through each other, and that thanks to gravity objects will tend to fall unless supported below or held from above. We can see the operation of this folk physics system even in young children, who show surprise when objects fail to act as expected in clever psychology experiments. We expect physical objects to move according to certain rules, and to interact with each other in certain ways. People—even quite young ones—are quite surprised when the assumptions made by their folk physics system are violated.[10]

Beyond the inanimate junk in our world, there's also lots of junk that's special because it's alive. Trees, mushrooms, gnats, sawfish, bowerbirds, you name it. These are objects that can grow and die and reproduce. Living things matter a great deal to us, so it would make sense to assume that we have systems that track folk biology.[11] And our folk biology comes with some rudimentary understanding of living systems.[12] We know that living things grow and die. We know that lots of living things like animals are capable of independent goal-directed movement. A rock will roll down a hill in a straight line until its movement is somehow impinged; a rockhopper penguin can zig this way and that by its own volition. There's agency and animacy to contend with. We recognize animacy as an important characteristic of lots of living things, and it's important for us to be able to think about how and why animals might move as they do.

Finally, some of the living and animate objects we encounter also seem to have a lot more cognitive sophistication, and thus require even more specialized cognition on our end to decode it. Our fellow humans are hugely important for our survival. Other humans are our allies, our lovers, our frenemies and nemeses. We need to understand, interpret, and predict the behavior of other humans. As a result, we've probably evolved systems of folk psychology to in effect read each other's minds—albeit imperfectly. This folk psychology system relies heavily on a cognitive capacity termed *theory of mind*[13] or (my preferred term) *mentalizing*.[¶][14] If you're already familiar with the term *theory of mind* but less familiar with the term *mentalizing*, remember that they're mostly different terms for the same social cognitive skill. Basically, it's the ability to track what's going on in other people's heads, to interpret human behavior in terms of mental states. Mentalizing is so central to religious cognition that it deserves a bit more depth of discussion.

¶ I prefer the term *mentalizing* to *theory of mind* for a couple of reasons. First, it turns out that there are different research traditions when it comes the study of our social cognition and folk psychology. One tradition—so-called theory theory—describes our intuitive mindreading as a sort of proto-theory that we form about people's minds. Other approaches to folk psychology don't posit any sort of intuitive theorizing, and instead describe folk psychology through other metaphors than proto-scientific theorizing. "Theory of mind" somewhat implies allegiance with "theory theory," whereas "mentalizing" just describes the fact that we can view things through the lens of mental states—we "mentalize" them. The second reason I prefer *mentalizing* to *theory of mind* is it's shorter, one word vs. three words. Feel free to use the terms interchangeably in your own mental states.

MENTALIZING

It is immensely important for us to be able to understand and predict each other's behavior. It is much easier to do this if we can figure out why people act as they do at a level of explanation that goes deeper than physics. We don't want to just say that a man walked into a coffee shop because his hand is a solid physical object that was able to move the solid door into an open position. We want to be able to say that the man walked into the coffee shop because he wanted some food and caffeine to prepare for a busy workday. Look at how much more inferential potential there is there when we add in some mental states! The key here is representing behavior in terms of those mental states—the wants and desires of our caffeine-deprived protagonist. It's a bit like a soft form of mindreading. We can figure out a bit of what's going on in other people's minds not through magic, but through the action of a devoted cognitive system that's pretty good at representing other minds—at mind perception.[15]

Mentalizing is the system that lets us view actions through the lens of mental states. Mentalizing is what lets us figure out that our friend might be *upset* because her boyfriend *lied* about going out with friends when he was actually on a date with another woman, trying to use his charms to *convince* her to be more *attracted* to him. We can easily imagine the scenario depicted in the last sentence, but only because we can relatively easily decode the various mental states of the characters involved (which I've italicized). But imagine trying to parse what was going on in that last sentence with no sense of the mental states involved. Our friend was ??? because another man ??? in order to ??? a third person to ???. Not so easy to figure out what's going on there once the mental state terms are removed.

Our mentalizing abilities seem to have been key innovations in our evolutionary history.[16] Tracking mental states is a key lubricant for social living, it helps us interpret and predict each other's behavior. It really helps get the ball rolling with cooperation (which after all requires a level of aligning our interests with others—much easier to do if one has an implicit understanding of the concept of people's *interests*, another mental-state term). It also helps us keep an eye on rivals and enemies who might wish us ill. Representing the mental states of others is a game changer when it comes to understanding and predicting behavior: wants and desires buy us much richer behavioral inferences than do mere velocities and vectors. Yes, humans are physical objects and our folk physics assumptions still hold. But we're additionally guided by inner psychological states and our mentalizing abilities give us some leverage at understanding how the big lumbering bipeds in our environment are propelled by more than just physics. Our folk physics might tell us to avoid the large humanoid object that seems to be moving rapidly toward us because the humanoid object is big and pointy in some spots; our folk psychology is what tells us that the object is especially worth avoiding because it's a human who happens to be pissed off at us!

Mentalizing isn't just a neat trick that helps us thrive as a social species—it might be the single most important evolved faculty that has enabled out species to become religious.[17] Our evolved ability to read and interpret the minds of other people might be what cognitively underpins our ability to think about gods.**

HOW MENTALIZING BIRTHS GODS

Cognitive scientists of religion tend to generally agree that mentalizing is a key ingredient in religious cognition. Let's consider a few different ways that religious cognition might be built up from a foundation of mentalizing (alongside our systems for folk physics and folk biology). From the outset, it's important to note that I'm recounting ideas that have held various degrees of influence within the cognitive science of religion research tradition. But that doesn't mean I'm endorsing each of these ideas. Some few of them have held up well; others have, despite their influence in popular summaries, not really been well-supported by evidence over the years. Nonetheless, let's meet our cast of cognitive biases that might predispose us to belief—and I'll try to signal which ones are strong, and which weaker.

A few paragraphs ago, I sketched a hypothetical example where different cognitive systems might come with their own built-in presets and biases, and these biases might combine in a way that makes religions work. The next section is basically extending that argument and concretely showing how some postulated cognitive systems might actually have the sorts of

** For an engaging book-length treatment of this idea, I'd first recommend Jesse Bering's *The Belief Instinct*.

in-built biases that make religions so natural. Each of these subsections in effect describes one or more potential mental shortcuts or cognitive biases that might make religion a little bit more natural; all of them working in concert could make religion quite natural indeed.

MINDS AND BODIES

In the Tom Hanks movie *Big*, Hanks begins as a child and after wishing to be "big" he awakens in an adult's body, but he's retained his child's mind. Shenanigans ensue. A similar motif underlies *Freaky Friday*, in which a daughter and mother (played by Lindsay Lohan and Jamie Lee Curtis) switch bodies—the kid gets to wear the mom's skin for a while, and vice versa. Or Kafka's "Metamorphosis," in which a man awakens as a giant insect.

Or imagine you're living in a future like that depicted in *Star Trek*. If you want to travel from one place to another, instantaneously, all you have to do is step into a transporter and, zip, your body is dissolved on one end and reconstituted on the other. You, somehow, have been taken apart and reassembled somewhere else.

We have no problem thinking about minds persisting, through changes to the body—even minds swapping bodies. Minds, bodies: they feel fundamentally distinct, even though our modern understanding of neuroscience tells us that the mind is basically what happens in the brain, one part of our physical body. We can intellectually understand this fact, but it still doesn't *feel* correct.

There's a lot of research documenting how very easily mind-body dualism comes to us. It seems to be a sort of intuitive default view of the world in our species. Children reliably develop an intuitive sense that minds and bodies are distinct, and that the mind is the seat of who we are.[18] Adults and kids have no problem tracking body swaps or body duplications, like those depicted in films and literature, and those presented in clever psychology studies.[19] Even cognitively minded coding of ancient Chinese scripts reveals traces of mind-body dualism, in texts both temporally and culturally remote from Western science and media.[20]

Philosophers have concocted lots of variants of thought experiments to probe our intuitions about minds and bodies. For example, what happens if you step into a *Star Trek* transporter, and instead of your Point A body disintegrating before being reconstituted at Point B, it remains, leaving "you" simultaneously at both Points A and B. Who gets the mind? Do both "yous" retain your mental stuff, your identity? Just the original? If we suppose that the original is somehow more real than the Point B version, then does that mean that every transporter trip is in fact murder, rapidly yielding a clone somewhere else? People reading these thought experiments might disagree about the implications of them, but few people truly have a hard time intuitively following them. All these philosophical issues stem from the stubborn intuition that minds and bodies are fundamentally distinct.

In lots of religious traditions, this mind-body dualism—the intuitive feeling that mind stuff is different from, and in many ways more metaphysically interesting than, physical body stuff—is resolved by positing the existence of a soul.[21] The soul is the nonphysical stuff of the mind, the seat of your personhood, personality, intellect, and unique identity.

Mind-body dualism seems to come naturally to humans. It may be the psychological origin of beliefs in souls. And if we're able to think of minds and bodies as being fundamentally distinct, it's not so hard to think about minds existing without bodies. Ghosts. Gods. What are these except for minds without bodies (plus some additional abilities, in the case of gods)? Mind-body dualism makes it quite easy for us to entertain thoughts of incorporeal supernatural agents. Among the ideas we'll meet in this chapter linking cognition to religion, this one may be the most solid in terms of evidence.

AGENCY DETECTION

Next, some cognitive scientists of religion have argued that the very origin story for religions might lie in our detection of agency in the world, in our ability to identify, detect, infer, and track the contents of minds of other intentional agents. People and other animals exert their agency on the world. They make choices. They have behavior. And the behavior of agents is of utmost importance to us. Other human agents are our social peers, offering myriad benefits and threats. Nonhuman agents are our food sources and our predators—they both feed and feed on us. So, given the importance of agents in our environments, it stands to reason that we might have evolved some cognitive faculties for detecting and dealing with them.

There's a catch, however. We can't always directly detect agents and instead we have to rely on indirect cues to agency in the world. We listen for the sound of footsteps in the woods. We look carefully for objects that seem to be furtively lurking in the shadows. Given the asymmetrical risks of failing to detect agents relative to over-detecting agents, perhaps we evolved an agent detection system that's got a bit of a hair trigger. After all, it's far more costly to miss a jaguar lurking in the shadows than to have a brief jump-scare over a shadow that turns out to be nothing. When in doubt, we assume agency. Some cognitive scientists of religion dubbed this hypothesized cognitive gadget our *Hyperactive Agency Detection Device* (oft shortened to just HADD).[22] Like a smoke alarm is overly sensitive to potential smoke, HADD is wired to cry "AGENT!" given only minimal or spurious evidence of agents in our surroundings. This, more often than not, leads us to avoid dangerous agents in our environment. But it also often goes off when no real threat is there (again, like the smoke detectors). We interpret snapping sticks as evidence of lurking bears, and shadows in the night as intruders. This helps us avoid actual bears and intruders, but at the (relatively modest) cost of the occasional harmless false-alarm fright.

So we have a supposed cognitive adaptation that evolved to protect us from environmental threats posed by predators and other agents, and it's trip-wired to over-detect agency. This leaves us chronically overperceiving agency in the world. And if we're chronically overperceiving agents, it's not so unrealistic to think that people will start thinking that some of these illusory agents are in fact supernatural agents. Sure, we'll quickly dismiss most of HADD's "detections" as false alarms, but maybe every now and then we find one hard to dismiss. Sure, most of the bumps in the night are just the wind, but maybe some of them are more than that! Maybe they're actual agents that just aren't visible by ordinary means. Herein, we have the putative origins of belief in spirits and ghosts—a system primed to over-detect agency leads us to suspect supernatural agents. Boom! Hyperactive agency detection is the birth of spiritualism or animism, a common form of religion.[††]

[††] Or so the story goes. In a subsequent section we'll assess the strength of evidence for the existence of HADD and its potential link to religion. For now, let's just recognize HADD as an influential hypothesis about which cognitive systems might have birthed gods.

MINIMALLY COUNTERINTUITIVE AGENTS

We have different intuitive cognitive systems that are triggered by different categories of stuff in our world. Inanimate objects recruit our folk physics. Living things activate our folk biology. Sophisticated intentional agents like humans call our folk psychology and mentalizing systems online. Each of these systems comes with its own built-in assumptions. Folk physics has assumptions about object movements in relation to basic forces, folk biology adds assumptions about life and death, and folk psychology brings assumptions about goal-directed behavior and such. I like to think of the assumptions that each system makes as nice little mental shortcuts that give us good-enough rules to get us through the world without too much effort.

If you think about the supernatural agents that predominate world religions, you might notice that they tend to violate some of the assumptions our core ontological systems are making. As an example, let's consider ghosts. A ghost is psychologically basically just a person. They have wants, desires, memories, and the like. Our folk psychology system can track this. But ghosts violate our assumptions about physics—a ghost might travel through a wall or disappear in the light, for example. So the concept "ghost" is basically fine as far as folk psychology goes, but it violates our expectations when it comes to folk physics. Many an ancestor or natural elemental spirit fits this same basic template: a humanlike mind with some quirky physical attributes.

As another example, a lot of world religions and folklore include things like talking trees or rocks. Maybe even a burning bush that talks, or something of that nature—inanimate objects that communicate The Divine to us. Here we have an object that does all the usual physical object stuff—lying around unless moved, falling when unsupported. But it also seems to have some bonus humanlike psychology; it can communicate with us! So here we again have a supernatural agent concept that ticks all the boxes from one category (all systems go when it comes to folk physics), but also checks some unexpected boxes from other categories. (Wait—this physical object also has and communicates desires?)

There's something quite interesting about concepts like our talking tree and our ghost. They're pretty mundane, ontologically speaking. For the most part, they fit right into one ontological category or another and do most of the stuff we intuitively assume them to do, based on their ontological category. But they have one salient tweak that makes them more interesting. The talking tree is basically just a tree—with the added ability of speech! A ghost is basically just a person—with the ability to violate physics! These supernatural agents trick our core intuitions, but only a little bit. In a nice bit of jargon from the cognitive science of religion, these agents are *minimally counterintuitive*.

Clever researchers have dug into the phenomenon of minimally counterintuitive agents a bit more, wanting to see if there's something about minimal counterintuition that might give these concepts a cultural boost. And it turns out that minimally counterintuitive concepts—talking trees, invisible people, vengeful seas, and the like—are more memorable than both mundane, as-expected objects and more maximally counterintuitive objects.[23] There's a bit of a cognitive sweet spot, where minimally counterintuitive concepts are different enough from expectations to draw attention, but not so different as to be confusing.

A concrete example might drive this point home, so let's think about a tree that's either ordinary, minimally counterintuitive, or maximally counterintuitive. The ordinary tree is just a tree, nothing special. The minimally counterintuitive tree is a tree that can talk. The maximally counterintuitive tree is a tree that can talk on Wednesdays but turn invisible under the full moon and can fly but only when nobody's looking. Our ordinary tree is too boring to be memorable. If you tell me an ordinary story about an ordinary tree that does your basic tree stuff, I'll forget it by next week. The talking tree is more interesting than the basic tree, and the fact that it can talk will grab my attention. But it's still pretty easy to keep straight in my head. This is that sweet spot of interest factor and processing ease. The maximally counterintuitive tree is a conceptual mess. I might be a bit interested in it, but who can keep all those details straight? It's just too hard to think about, and I've already forgotten about its details as I write about it two minutes later.

In a couple of key studies, researchers found evidence of a memory boost for minimally counterintuitive concepts. Again, minimally counterintuitive concepts are interesting enough to grab our attention but not so complex as to confuse us. People are better able to remember minimally counterintuitive concepts hours or days later. When it comes to cultural success, a memory advantage can be crucial! If a concept is more memorable, it'll linger in people's minds a bit longer and be easier to transmit to the next person. All else being equal, a more memorable concept would be favored in cultural transmission. One of my favorite studies on minimal counterintuition makes this point quite plainly.[24] It turns out that fairy tales differ in how much they rely on mundane versus minimally or maximally counterintuitive concepts, and they also vary in their sustained popularity over time. For example, from the Brothers Grimm, I'll bet you can recite details of "Cinderella" with ease but have little if any familiarity with "The Donkey Lettuce." And which centuries-old folk tales do we remember and retell today? Ones that have just a few minimally counterintuitive agents sprinkled throughout! Pigs that can construct humanlike homes from various building materials? Memorable. A wolf that can talk and impersonate a grandmother? Memorable. These sorts of minimally counterintuitive elements make stories more memorable and, thus, likely to be passed on to others. It's the cultural transmission jackpot.[‡‡]

HADD might give people the imaginative fodder to initially think about various supernatural agents. But a memory bias favoring minimally counterintuitive concepts could help explain why some supernatural agent concepts are so culturally successful. At this stage in the story, though, we're still falling a fair bit short of explaining religion. We've explained why people might start playing with ideas of supernatural agents, and why some stories about them might become popular. But religions offer more than just catchy concepts. They often offer meaning.

TELEOLOGY AND THE SEARCH FOR MEANING

Why is a shovel blade pointy? It's not a trick question, don't overthink it. A shovel is for digging. The ground can be hard. It's easier to dig through the

‡‡ In the interests of full disclosure: I think the evidence on this front is considerably weaker than lots of summaries like this would suggest. The laboratory studies on minimal counterintuitiveness are not numerous, and they more often involve lists of unfamiliar concepts, rather than the more naturalistically compelling narratives that the folk tale studies depict. There's a mismatch between studies run and claims made on their behalf. I'd be surprised if the minimal counterintuition story retains its priority in explanations of religion in a decade's time. As an additional counterpoint, consider "Cinderella." Aiyana Willard astutely points out that "Cinderella" is more popular because it is a good human interaction story, not because of the counterintuitive content. There are numerous versions of this story, and the evil stepmother is common to all of them, but the counterintuitive content changes or disappears in many.

hard ground with pointy things. A shovel blade is pointy because digging is the function that shovels fulfil, and that function is more easily accomplished via pointiness than via dullness. Easy, right?

Okay, so why is a pointy rock pointy? And I'm not talking about an Acheulean hand axe or other stone tool that was cleverly crafted for pointiness; I'm just asking about any plain old pointy rock that you might find in the garden. Odds are, you're right now thinking of lots of causal stories for how a rock became pointy, but you're not trying to ascribe some deeper function to the rock's pointiness.

If we want to know why an object is the way it is, sometimes it's useful to think about the function it serves. Some objects have their specific forms because there's a specific function that the form fulfils. In philosophy, thinking about function in this way is called teleology. And lots of times, a teleological answer makes sense when asked why something is the way it is. For artificial and human-designed things, the form is often teleological. Hammers are shaped like that to be good at knocking in nails. Atlatls are shaped the way they are to fulfil the function of throwing a spear a long way. My ten-speed bike has lots of components with lots of specific shapes because each component has a function, a job that it needs to do. The chainring has teeth spaced just right to fit into the holes in the chain. The derailleur needs to be shaped just right to help the chain bounce up and down the chainrings in accordance with the pressure exerted by a tiny cable that runs up to my shifter. All of these precise forms combine in service to the bike's function—the pedals and chain and chainring functionally convert the force of my legs into the rotation of the wheel, the shifter cable and derailleur functionally alter the rate at which this conversion happens. Here, when we're talking about human tools, teleological explanations make a lot of sense. Each component fulfils some specific function and purpose in a grander design.

What about the natural world, though? I think that evolution via natural selection, properly understood, gives us solid footing to view lots of biological features through a somewhat teleological lens, albeit not a telos set by any intelligent force. Mindless forces of natural selection can create almost miraculously complex and beautiful adaptations that exquisitely fulfil their functions, with precisely no intelligence behind it. But still, like with human-made tools, teleological thinking can be usefully brought to bear on many biological adaptations, at least as a handy heuristic. It's perfectly scientifically sensible to talk about a bird's wing in terms of the function of that wing—helping the bird to fly.

Clearly, however, not every feature of the natural world has a function or a purpose, not even a function produced by the mindless creative logic of natural selection. Imagine you walk outside and go for a walk. You pick up the pointiest little chunk of gravel you can find on the path. This rock, for example, isn't pointy because it was crafted (by a human or by natural selection) to serve some pointy-needing end. Instead, the crude forces of nature just broke a bigger rock apart in a way that rendered our little piece of gravel kind of pointy. And as adults, we recognize that there's no deeper meaning to our pointy little stone. It's the shape it is, but not for any particular reason. Some things just are.

It turns out that not everyone is content to say that our piece of gravel is purposelessly pointy. If clever developmental psychologists ask kids about why rocks are pointy, kids tend to invent teleological responses.[25] Maybe that rock's pointy because bears need to scratch their backs sometimes, for example. Can't have itchy bears, can we? So of course the world has pointy rocks! Given lots of questions about inanimate stuff in the world, kids seem to have a general tendency to jump to teleology and function. Why are rocks pointy? To scratch an itch. Why is it raining? So that flowers can grow. Why do flowers grow? So that bees can make honey.

Boston University psychologist Deborah Kelemen has done lots of research on this kind of teleological thinking over the years, in both kids and adults. Her general conclusion is that people are a bit biased to read more function into things than is scientifically warranted. In a clever turn of phrase, Kelemen dubs us *promiscuous teleologists*.[26] We slap function on form a bit willy nilly, and especially if we aren't thinking rigorously about it. The proclivity for promiscuous teleology is present in kids. But it's also present in adults who are suffering from dementia. It seems that as adults tragically lose some higher cognitive faculties, they may be less able to effortfully override a deeper teleological bias in their thinking.[27] Consistent with this possibility, Kelemen and colleagues have also found that people tend to endorse promiscuously teleological statements (e.g., statements like "clouds are for raining") when they're put under pressure to respond quickly.[28] These studies together suggest that we might have a general intuitive preference for viewing nature teleologically. We readily see function where it might not actually exist.

Teleological thinking, at least according to a lot of clever laboratory studies by Kelemen and others, seems to come quite easily to us. And we overapply our teleological thinking far beyond the domains where it's most relevant. We read function into all sorts of functionless stuff. As with HADD and with minimally counterintuitive agents, folk psychology and mentalizing may again be key. Promiscuous teleology is a psychological tendency to read function into form in the natural world. But because we are so used to thinking about *function* in terms of *intent*, we've looped again back to intentionality and agency, the purview of our mentalizing gadgets.

People might readily "see" functions in all sorts of natural creations, but where does the function come from? It's not such a large leap from "clouds are for raining" to "someone made clouds for raining." If we're primed to (over-) perceive function in the world, we might rather easily postulate designers behind all the apparent functionality, making us intuitive theists of a sort.[29] In a sense, our mentalizing system might be projecting (rather than detecting) agency, to explain the functions that we've misperceived thanks to our tendency toward promiscuous teleology.

INTUITIVE CREATIONISM

Kids (and adults in some circumstances) seemingly intuit that natural things have functions. This promiscuous teleology has been likened to intuitive theism, the basic idea being that if we're inferring purpose and function to things, it's a small step to inferring an agent who imbues things with that purpose and function. Indeed, Kelemen explicitly links teleological thinking to religion. One of her most prominent papers on the topic of promiscuous teleology is even titled "Are Children Intuitive Theists?" Our folk psychology misreads function from form, intentionality behind natural creations. In short, this work suggests that we might be sort of intuitive creationists as a default.

There's some intriguing evidence in support of this idea! In a nifty series of developmental psychology studies, Newman and colleagues presented young children with a little puppet play of sorts on a computer screen.[30] This play was meant to get at the question of whether kids intuitively assume that only agents can create apparent order in the world. In one study, for example, kids would see what appeared to be blocks. These blocks could either move from a disordered and jumbled state to an ordered state, or the opposite. Across experimental conditions, the change appeared to be caused by one of two objects: either an ordinary inanimate ball or a ball-like figure that had cues of agency (eyes and goal-directed behavior). Kids seemed surprised if an ordinary ball produced order from disorder but were relatively nonplussed when the agent-decorated ball did the same. To the kids, a non-agent producing order from chaos is quite surprising. But they were not surprised that an agent could produce order. It's almost as if the kids saw order being produced from disorder and spontaneously inferred that only an agent could do this. This isn't quite creationism, but inferring agency behind order might be an early developmental building block that helps creationist beliefs flourish.

Other studies are cited as providing a more direct test of whether kids are intuitive creationists, who see intentional (and maybe supernatural) agents behind the order we see in the natural world. In a couple high-profile papers, Margaret Evans asked kids in the United States where they thought new animal species came from.[31] The highlight results from these studies are that kids in the eight-to-ten-year-old age range tended to prefer creationist explanations for the origins of species, and only older kids tend to consistently offer even rudimentary evolutionary accounts for the origins of species. A follow-up study compared kids across cultural and religious context[§§] and showed a preference for creationist explanations when they're in that eight-to-ten age range, perhaps implying that intuitive creationism cuts across the lines of family religiosity and broader background.[32] These results are widely cited and discussed as evidence that kids intuitively prefer creationist explanations, and that religious upbringing might not be the sole culprit. Some even go so far as to claim that these results show that *regardless of upbringing or cultural input*, kids are intuitive creationists.[¶¶] At least according to these few studies, it's possible that kids intuitively lean

§§ It specifically compared kids in public school to kids who are in fundamentalist religious schools, or homeschooled for religious reasons—a fairly limited cultural difference, but one nonetheless.

¶¶ If this sounds like a rather strident and implausible claim, buckle up. In a couple of pages, we'll deconstruct the underlying evidence and see just how overblown claims like this are.

toward creationism, inferring that our ordered and (apparently) teleological world was intentionally created by a supernatural agent of some sort.

At this point, let's try to put some of these pieces together to see how cognitive scientists of religion can move from studying individual psychological quirks like HADD and mentalizing and promiscuous teleology to concluding that religion naturally emerges as a cognitive by-product.

RELIGION AS NATURAL

Dualism, HADD, a memory boost for minimally counterintuitive concepts, promiscuous teleology, and intuitive creationism are individually each just psychological proclivities that clever scientists have either hypothesized or observed. On their own, each is just a quirky little bias in how we perceive or remember or reason about the world, stemming from the operation of different cognitive systems. Individually, none of them really seem to say much about religion. But together, they might tell us a lot.

Dualism, HADD, and minimal counterintuition might explain how we start thinking of supernatural agents in the first place, and why some agents are memorable and thus culturally transmissible. They're the cognitive biases that might underpin our fascination with supernatural agents. Promiscuous teleology, in turn, starts explaining how these supernatural agents start to seem, well, religious in nature. Promiscuous teleology is what gets us from imagining memorable forest spirits to imagining the sorts of supernatural agents who can deliver meaning and purpose to our lives. Inferred supernatural agents can serve as the intellects behind the apparent design we see in the world, the intent behind the functionality we've (mis) perceived, creators even of our ordered world. Here, it is not the operation of any individual cognitive system that enables religion to flourish, but the coordinated action of many different cognitive systems.

Our species seems to have a bunch of semi-distinct cognitive systems that have evolved to help us solve specific adaptive problems. Some of these cognitive systems come with default settings and biases that predispose us to find some things more interesting or memorable or evocative. Sometimes these biases interact synergistically with each other, boosting their respective outputs. They might even fit together in a way that makes certain types of cultural creations quite catchy. Supernatural agents, for example, seem to tick a lot of boxes from a bunch of different cognitive systems. A convenient way to explain some of HADD's misfires? Check. Minimally counterintuitive and thus memorable? Check. A handy fit to our promiscuous teleology, explaining where order and function might've originated? Check. When a given concept—like say a god or ancestor spirit—jibes with lots of our cognitive biases, that gives it a cultural boost. It becomes more likely to spread from person to person and persist over time because it just fits how our minds work. Religious concepts are sticky and persistent; the contents of these ideas fit well with our evolved psychology.

Most of this is going on well below our conscious awareness. We needn't deliberatively and reflectively sit down and think, "Okay, I'd like to think that rock's pointiness serves a purpose, but whose purpose? Well I remember hearing a story about a forest spirit, and I found that story memorable, so maybe it's the purpose of a forest spirit; and also sometimes I hear noises in the woods so maybe that's also forest spirits, so I guess now I believe in forest spirits." That's just not how it operates. But under the hood, in the deeper unconscious recesses of our minds, concepts that suit lots of our hidden biases might be more likely to stick around and be culturally successful. Cognitive science of religion pioneer Justin L. Barrett puts it thusly in his short book *Why Would Anyone Believe in God?*:

> Belief in gods requires no special parts of the brain. . . . Belief in gods requires no coercion or special persuasive techniques. Rather, belief in gods arises because of the natural functioning of completely normal mental tools working in common natural and social contexts. . . . The more mental tools with which an idea fits, the more likely it is to become a (reflective) belief. . . . Belief in gods is common precisely because such beliefs resonate with and receive support from a large number of mental tools.

This is the meat of the argument from the cognitive science of religion. We don't have religions because religions do cool adaptive stuff for us (although as we'll see in a later chapter, some of them certainly might). Instead, some concepts are culturally successful because they fit well with our evolved cognitive biases, and religious concepts like disembodied supernatural agents are really good at tickling a lot of these nonreflective systems.

Here's the cognitive science of religion in a nutshell: We didn't evolve to have religions, but religions are great fits for the minds we've evolved.

IS THAT REALLY ALL?

When I started grad school in 2006, cognitive science of religion was in full swing. My primary grad advisor had authored some influential papers on minimally counterintuitive agents and also a big theory paper trying to weave the different cognitive science of religion threads together into a cohesive theoretical account of how religion worked at a cognitive and evolutionary level. Around this time, several books came out to really develop the ideas with more nuance and detail. They had titles like *Religion Explained* and *The Belief Instinct* and *Born Believers*. The general argument of all of them was that religion had emerged as a by-product stemming from lots of different cognitive biases (though with a heavy emphasis on mentalizing) working together to make belief in supernatural agents all but inevitable.

Different scientists had different spins on the core theme. Jesse Bering's *The Belief Instinct* really leaned into the ways that mentalizing was central to it all.*** Justin L. Barrett in *Why Would Anyone Believe in God?* pushed HADD as a key player, and also argued that we might find gods like the Judeo-Christian one especially easy to think about and believe in. Naturally, my chapter-length summary here can't cover all the nuanced differences between their positions. I remember reading all this work with excitement as I began applying to graduate schools and embarking on my own research career. Cognitive science of religion seemed like a semi-coordinated research effort that tried to understand religion from two sides: cognition and evolution. This seemed fundamentally like the right approach to me.

But as I continued my studies and research, I found myself having some reservations about the cognitive science of religion. The cognitive science of religion approach emphasized that lots of little cognitive biases might coalesce to make religions easy to think. This sounds compelling, but on close inspection I found that the arguments circulating in the scientific literature and popular press went well beyond what the evidence could reasonably justify. There appeared to be holes in some individual cognitive bias claims, and upon close inspection the individual pieces might not fit together quite as seamlessly as implied.

*** If you read one book in this genre, I'd recommend this one. It's lively, beautifully written, and thought provoking.

To illustrate, let's first consider the popular-yet-largely-speculative Hyperactive Agency Detection Device. Next, we'll dig deeper into the evidence supporting intuitive creationism. Finally, we'll ask the broader question of whether lots of little cognitive biases can, even in principle, explain what we're trying to explain.

HADD: A POPULAR HYPOTHESIS STILL AWAITING COMPELLING EVIDENCE

Remember that HADD describes a cognitive system that's trip-wired to over-detect agency in the world. We interpret noises in the dark as lurking agents. When lots of our HADD "alarms" appear to be false, we might begin to suspect the presence of unseen supernatural agents—or so the story goes.

Alas, in spite of being around since the 1990s, speculation linking religion to HADD has never really been supported by much direct evidence. Intrepid researchers, including myself and seemingly every other graduate student engaged in the cognitive study of religion for about a decade, tried in earnest to empirically flesh out a link between agency detection and religion. Early on in my graduate career, my advisor Ara Norenzayan called research on HADD and religion "low-hanging fruit," an idea that he was confident was true, but lacking that key empirical result that we all assumed would be easy to find.

One of my first graduate school projects was an attempt to empirically link HADD to religion somehow. Along with my friend, collaborator, and now Centre for Culture and Evolution colleague Aiyana Willard, we tried a handful of studies seeking to first detect this putative hyperactive agency detection device scientifically and then to see how it relates to religion. Early on, we thought the going would be easy. After all, prominent cognitive scientists of religion discussed HADD as if it were settled science, a strong foundation that was just in need of some light empirical finishing touches. And yet, in study after study after study, using as many different experimental techniques as we could think of, we turned up nothing. Nothing looking like HADD, no link between this putative device and religion. That seemingly solid foundation turned out to be flimsier than we'd imagined.

Dismayed, we eventually packed up the project and moved on to other lines of inquiry that seemed more likely to bear fruit.[†††] But before burying the project entirely, we presented our evidence at a scholarly conference with lots of cognitive scientists of religion in attendance. Aiyana Willard gave a brave talk outlining how we—despite sincere scientific efforts—hadn't been able to find any hint of HADD or its relationship with religion. As she gave the talk, I noticed a lot of nodding heads in the audience, but not every audience member was favorable toward her talk. As the talk wrapped up, one prominent cognitive scientist of religion who'd long advocated on behalf of HADD (without ever publishing his own empirical work validating the idea, I might add) monopolized the question-and-answer period to lambast Aiyana for her presentation. As the Q-and-A wrapped up, this senior scholar literally backed Aiyana into a corner to continue his scathing objections. If some uppity grad student attending her first academic conference couldn't find evidence supporting something he'd claimed in article after article and book after book, she must simply be some scientifically inept rube, apparently.

The entitlement and anti-scientific "How Dare You, Don't You Know Who I Am?" of it all was shocking. It was the most appalling display of a senior scholar weaponizing their prestige against a student that I've seen in twenty years as an academic. Despite all the poor behavior, however, he still could not point to a single piece of direct evidence validating the HADD notion he'd popularized for years.

After the conference talk brouhaha, a number of researchers in the audience approached Aiyana to signal their support. You see, many of them had also tried and failed to find HADD or its link to religion. One person even told us that they'd worked with the HADD advocate in question and had similarly been unable to find supporting evidence. We were apparently far from the only team who'd tried in vain to find HADD. Several colleagues (and now collaborators!) commented on Aiyana Willard's courage in giving the talk, publicly calling out an empirical gap that many had come to suspect, albeit in private.

[†††] Indeed, dropping this dead-end project made time for the atheism research that I continue to this day!

The HADD emperor remained empirically nude, and does to this day. Our so-called failed studies went unpublished,[‡‡‡] given scientific incentives to publish flashy positive results. Thus, there have not been smoking-gun publications demonstrating the failure of HADD as an idea, just an accumulation of dead-end projects as junior scientist after junior scientist tried to pick the "low-hanging fruit" of HADD. But it is quite telling that an idea openly flagged as speculative two decades ago has never gained any substantial empirical traction, even though it is often discussed in the literature as if it's an established scientific fact.[33] Yet even HADD's advocates tend to not cite actual direct scientific evidence when they discuss the idea.

Beyond repeated empirical failings, the HADD-religion idea has now come under pretty intense scrutiny for its conceptual limitations.[34] Simply put, there is no evidence that humans have any sort of a dedicated agency detection device. It turns out that brains don't really work like that, and neither does evolution! One scholarly journal that focuses specifically on cognitive and evolutionary approaches to religion, *Religion, Brain, and Behavior*, has now published multiple articles and even entire special issues in which the HADD-religion idea has been dissected, and researchers have opened their file drawers of failed studies.

Despite repeated empirical failures, you can still see HADD cited in the scientific literature. Nobody cites a compelling empirical result (presumably because there aren't any). Instead, people tend to cite older review and conceptual papers that discussed HADD as if it were settled science, rather than an idea still awaiting evidence. HADD has also reached escape velocity, appearing in popular writings on religion. Popular books by folks like Michael Shermer and Daniel Dennett and Richard Dawkins cite HADD as a key part of religion's evolution. Without compelling evidence, it somehow became canonized as a scientific fact—at least if you only read popular and one-step-removed summaries.

As far as I'm concerned, HADD is a zombie theory, ambling about despite having long lost any empirical animation. It was an exciting idea when it was first proposed. But as the years pass by and the evidence remains

---

[‡‡‡] Publication biases like this are a persistent problem in science and keep zombie theories posthumously perambulant far beyond their expiration dates. There is no simple, scalable, downside-free solution or silver bullet for fixing these sorts of biases, although there are some promising experiments and innovations that are (hopefully!) steps in the right direction.

stubbornly absent, it would be scientifically prudent to turn to better-supported hypotheses. Generally speaking, scientists who actually study this religious stuff for a living have moved on from HADD, even though popularizers still discuss the idea as if it's a part of scientific canon.

HADD never quite lived up to its promise, but that doesn't mean that we need to abandon all of the cognitive biases that cognitive scientists of religion focus on. Some of them accumulated supporting evidence over the years and appear to be on firm scientific footing. Cognitive science of religion doesn't sink or swim due to HADD alone, and the strength of evidence for other cognitive biases is generally stronger than what HADD's mustered over the past couple of decades.

INTUITIVE CREATIONISM: INTERESTING STUDIES, OVERBLOWN AND MISINTERPRETED

HADD proved to be an intriguing hypothesis that never really gained solid empirical support. Intuitive creationism, on the other hand, started with legitimately interesting findings, but I soon grew a bit disillusioned because the claims made on behalf of the very interesting Evans papers discussed a few sections ago—claims, it should be noted, that Evans herself was careful to avoid—just didn't match the studies themselves. Let's begin with some of the stronger claims made about Evans's interesting studies, and then look at the studies' actual methods to see if these studies even in principle could have supported the claims made on their behalf.

First, an influential review article summarizing the cognitive science of religion[35] states that "when children are directly asked about the origin of animals and people, they tend to prefer explanations that involve an intentional creator, even if the adults who raised them do not." That is similar to other discussion I've seen of the Evans studies in the scholarly literature, but the studies also get coverage in more public-facing summaries. For example, here is Justin L. Barrett's summary from his popular press book *Born Believers*:

> Children up until about ten years old . . . showed an affinity for creationist accounts over evolutionary accounts that cannot be accounted for by their parents' own position. Perhaps most striking, this study suggests that evolutionary accounts as endorsed by parents or as included in school textbooks

> and science curricula do not penetrate children's thinking effectively until around age ten. Parents believe in evolution and say they would teach it, the textbooks include it, but the children just do not affirm it as might be expected.

Based on descriptions like this, readers plausibly come to think that science has shown that kids firmly prefer creationism, even in the face of education and indoctrination to the contrary, that kids endorse creationism across cultural contexts and in spite of explicit parental efforts to nudge their kids toward a scientifically rigorous evolutionary worldview. You'd be forgiven for assuming that the studies in question were well designed to support strident conclusions like that, for assuming that the studies had rigorously tested creationist intuitions across a wide range of cultural and educational contexts. Alas, these assumptions would be unfounded. Upon close inspection, not only did these studies not support the strong claims like those that *Born Believers* made on their behalf, but these studies, even in principle, *could not have supported those claims.* The methods preclude strong inference about culture, and summaries about the results (Barrett's above quote in particular) make embellishments and assumptions about the cultural context of the studies that fall apart quickly upon even cursory critical inquiry.

Evans's studies asked kids about where they think new species come from, and researchers coded the kids' responses as endorsing evolution, creationism, or various nonsystematic responses or responses indicating a sort of spontaneous generation view—that species are just there, and the kids don't much know or care why. The studies looked at kids from different age brackets. It turns out that the youngest kids (aged five to seven or so) were largely random in their responses. They showed no obvious preference for evolution, creationism, or spontaneous origins. At the youngest age, in other words, the kids seemed to have no consistent intuitions about the origins of species—they were puzzled or disinterested, but nonsystematic in their intuitions.

Slightly older kids, those in the eight-to-ten bracket, tended to favor creationist explanations. Kids older than ten largely mirrored their parents' views. Summaries like Barrett's cling to the temporary spike in creationist views in the eight-to-ten range, but seem to overlook the fact that younger kids didn't have a clue.

Both of the above summaries also hint (or stronger!) that creationism is intuitively favored, even though parents and educators might explicitly wish otherwise. Where's the origin of that claim? In terms of cultural context, in Evans's second paper on intuitive creationism, she coded kids as either "fundamentalist" or "non-fundamentalist" based on where the kids went to school. If the kids went to regular old public school, they were viewed as "non-fundamentalist," whereas kids who were religiously homeschooled or who attended private religious schools were coded as "fundamentalist." There surely might be a cultural or educational difference between kids in public school and those pulled from public school for explicitly religious reasons, but merely attending public school doesn't at all imply that a child's upbringing is free from religious influence. Notably, all of the kids in this study came from the same area of rural Ohio,[§§§] a strongly Christian region in the United States. All the kids came from a strongly religious cultural context, and many of the kids coded as "non-fundamentalist" based on their public school attendance nonetheless attended the same fundamentalist churches as their "fundamentalist" peers in the study. In short, all of the kids in this study had lots of cultural exposure to religion, up to and including explicit religious teaching. That eight-to-ten-year-olds in this hugely religious cultural context temporarily endorse creationism might not tell us as much about their intuitions as it does about their upbringing, in other words—the actual design of the study precludes strong inference about the role of culture-versus-in-built-intuition.

Are these kids getting as much exposure to evolution as they are to Christianity? Color me suspicious about this assumption. Recall that Barrett explicitly claims that the kids are being exposed to evolution at home and at school: "evolutionary accounts *as endorsed by parents or as included in school textbooks and science curricula* do not penetrate" [emphasis added]. I grew up in the mountains of Colorado, in a religion that's far less overtly religious than the rural Ohio locale where these children were recruited for study. Nonetheless my high school honors biology teacher was a creationist who

[§§§] The paper notes that all children came from "26 rural and suburban towns and cities in one Midwestern state." Given the author's institution is in Ohio, that seems a likely inference, although I should note that neighboring states are also possibilities—possibilities that largely present the same inferential challenges regarding cultural exposure to Christianity and evolution, respectively.

quietly refused to teach us about evolution. I first learned about evolution in school when I was thirteen, only because my seventh-grade science teacher made a point to teach it;[¶¶¶] it was a single unit, a couple of weeks long, due to one teacher's initiative. It would be about five years before I was taught about evolution again, and university before I explored it in any depth. But Barrett would have us believe that K–5 students in rural Ohio were being taught Darwin regularly and rigorously? Sure.

It seemed highly implausible to me that kids in these studies were fed a steady diet of evolution, so I investigated whether there was any evidence to support the assertion that these kids were likely taught evolution in school. Here's what I found. The Evans papers came out in 2000 and 2001, so it's safe to assume that the research took place a year or two prior to this. When I dug around to find what was in Ohio's public-school curricula in the late 1990s and early 2000s, I found an article from the National Center for Science Education titled "The Evolutionary Wars in Ohio."[36] The NCSE, a respected science advocacy group, had at the time graded Ohio's public science education as an "F" for its treatment of evolution. The state standards lacked even a single mention of evolution in school curricula, from kindergarten through high school. In response to calls to add evolution to the state-mandated curricula, creationist advocates lobbied strongly for evolution to only be taught alongside "Intelligent Design Theory," a thoroughly debunked successor to young earth creationism. Intelligent Design Theory was slapped down by the courts as an obvious pseudoscientific Trojan Horse that tried to smuggle creationism into schools through a pathetically flimsy veneer of pseudoscientific jargon.[****] As of 2002, the issue remained unresolved, and evolution was still absent even from high school curricula in Ohio.

Returning to the Evans studies—which, again to be entirely clear, I find fascinating and well worthy of discussion, albeit without the hyperbolic embellishments that popular summaries have included—here's what we know. Children from one of the most strongly Christian regions in the United States, from a state with no mandated mention of evolution even in high

---

¶¶¶ Thanks mom! Yes, I had both Mrs. Gervais and Mr. Gervais for teachers in middle school.

**** My favorite bit of incrimination here is "cdesign proponentsists": https://ncse.ngo/cdesign-proponentsists.

school curricula and an active creationist lobby, were asked about where species come from. At the youngest age, the kids had no systematic pattern in their responses—they were clueless. Kids in the eight-to-ten bracket showed an interesting preference for creationism. By about ten, kids largely mirrored their parents. Commenters on this work tend to attribute that blip among the eight-to-ten-year-olds to an "intuitive" creationism that comes in spite of enculturation, but I genuinely do not think that this attribution is the most plausible explanation for the data, in light of the realities of these children's cultural backgrounds. It's highly unlikely that any of these kids had been taught about evolution in any rigorous way in school—indeed, Evans's 2000 paper explicitly notes, "No child had been formally taught evolutionary theory in school"—and it's unclear what they'd been taught at home. But the parents in these samples are themselves overwhelmingly religious and churchgoing, often attending the same fundamentalist churches as the kids who were sensibly coded as fundamentalist in the studies. In short, these kids received a steady cultural blast of Christianity and, most likely, creationism through their formative years. In contrast, it's not clear that any of them had ever been taught about evolution in school. Remember that the state didn't mandate any teaching of evolution at this time, even for high schoolers. Even in states that do teach evolution, it's usually not something covered by third grade, as Barrett's summary would require. A temporary blip toward creationism, in this cultural context, seems entirely unsurprising. Indeed, it's remarkable that kids older than ten showed any endorsement of evolution, given the broader religious and educational context that the kids in these studies were exposed to.

HADD appeared to be a nifty hypothesis whose evidence never really arrived. In contrast, the intuitive creationism claims do have their origins in published research. There's definitely something interesting going on in the Evans studies, with eight-to-ten-year-olds showing an appetite for creationist thinking. But whatever is going on in these studies, it's a huge stretch (to say the least) to get from the design and results of the studies to the claims made on their behalf. These studies don't—indeed can't—support strong claims about kids being intuitive creationists in spite of explicit enculturation and education to the contrary. Instead, the results are entirely consistent with the possibility that kids in a strongly religious region with scant-to-no exposure to evolution temporarily favor creationism simply because that's what they've been culturally exposed to. As with HADD, I had deep reservations about the scientific foundations of claims about intuitive creationism. Over time, my reservations about the standard cognitive science of religion framing grew deeper, and began to focus less on individual evidence shortfalls and more on basic and fundamental conceptual issues.

WHAT ABOUT FAITH?

HADD and intuitive creationism were central to a lot of arguments supporting the cognitive science of religion when I embarked on my graduate studies. Seeing how overblown these specific claims ended up being, relative to the actual underlying evidence, caused me some scientific angst. If I couldn't trust the empirical building blocks, why should I trust the broader structure? If popular summaries got the details so wrong, what other holes was I missing? However, beyond the individual empirical strength or weakness of any given cognitive bias, I think that there's an even more challenging set of conceptual issues. Namely, I grew suspicious of the general premise that religious faith rests solely or primarily on a foundation of low-level cognitive biases like those that cognitive scientists of religion had largely focused on. Cognitive biases can help explain many interesting quirks about religions—why they take similar forms across cultures, for example—but they seem to entirely miss one defining feature of religion.

Even if we grant that lots of cognitive biases might work together to shape religious cognition in some regard, something really important seemed to still be missing. Where was the passionate commitment to gods that makes religion, well, religion? What about faith? Where was belief?

Think here about minimal counterintuition. Concepts that slightly tweak our ontological expectations—like talking plants, ghosts, and the like—are more memorable than their mundane or bizarre counterparts. This will help the concepts spread and gain a measure of cultural success, but there's little reason to think that this will positively affect belief in those concepts. There are many highly successful cultural concepts out there that precisely nobody believes in. A cognitive bias like minimal counterintuition affects *popularity*, but not *faith*. By extension, the cumulative impact of different cognitive biases might be okay explanations for why a given concept might endure and spread through a culture, but that's an explanation for popular folk tales that people tell for entertainment, not an explanation for religions that people fight and die for.

Even more broadly, I developed reservations about some of the evolutionary theorizing at play. My original academic interests and reading started with evolutionary biology and only eventually strayed toward psychology. Although evolutionary claims abounded in the cognitive science of religion, the cast of leading researchers were all people trained first and foremost in fields like developmental or social psychology, rather than in fields like evolutionary and theoretical biology. How legit were the evolutionary claims the cognitive scientists of religion were making? Sure, it sounded intuitively plausible that we'd be trip-wired to detect agency, or that concepts like supernatural agents would spread throughout cultures if they were more memorable. But at the end of the day this is a sort of vague and hand-wavey bit of evolutionary hypothesizing. I was used to seeing more precise modeling and theory from evolution than the cognitive science of religion offered, and it seemed like there must be richer theory to be mined.

It turns out that there was a lot of excellent theory out there that would prove to be directly applicable to religion. It was coming from the study of cultural evolution—a vibrant scientific subfield that sought to use the rich modeling toolkit of evolutionary theory and apply it to cultural transmission. I think I first started thinking seriously about the world of cultural evolution during my graduate school interviews at UBC. A faculty member named Steve Heine mentioned that if I came to UBC I'd be coming in at the same time as a new faculty member they'd recruited, a guy by the name of Joe Henrich. He was evidently a big deal in the world of cultural evolution and if I wanted to learn more about the cultural evolutionists, I should check out a recent book by some of Joe's collaborators. This book was *Not by Genes Alone* by Pete Richerson and Rob Boyd, and reading it was a turning point for me, not unlike stumbling across Gould and Dawkins some years prior and getting launched on a path to study evolution. The next chapter introduces the science of cultural evolution, and along the way I'll try to show you why it's so important to understanding religion.

CHAPTER FIVE

HOW CULTURE EVOLVES

Though each individual mortal experiences life for but a score of years, they can draw upon a store of stories left by all their forbears. The race of humankind grows toward infinity, even as the nature of each individual is limited.
—KEN LIU, *THE VEILED THRONE*

The mechanisms for introducing variation—the cultural equivalent of mutations—are generators of "error" or of "innovation" in social learning.
—CECILIA HEYES, *COGNITIVE GADGETS*[1]

Imagine you wake up tomorrow in an entirely new environment. Gone is your flat or house, it's just you and the elements. Instead of being in a town or city or suburb, you find yourself in the Bolivian Altiplano, Brazil's Amazon, or perhaps the Arctic islands in the Bering Strait. How would you survive? You'll quickly need to procure food, shelter, and potable water. Whoever transported you here failed to drop off your high-end backpacking gear—you're on your own.

One survival strategy is trial-and-error. You take what you know about the world, and then see what you can find in your new surroundings. Scrounge some berries, try to find a cave to hide out in. Drink the cleanest water you can find. The most likely result of this strategy is a rapid and uncomfortable death. But don't worry, you'll be following in the footsteps of countless European explorers over the centuries who brought their familiar tools and ideas and ecological know-how to various "exotic" locations—and were utterly unprepared for what they found.

Take, for example, the Franklin expedition that sought to chart the Northwest Passage in the 1840s. More than a hundred crew members perished of various causes: hypothermia, malnutrition, starvation. There's even suggestive evidence that late-stage survivors resorted to cannibalism to stave off their eventual terminal fate. Was the environment simply too harsh for survival? Hardly. What is now called the Canadian Arctic is harsh, but it is certainly habitable with the right know-how. In the 1840s, the lands traversed by the Franklin expedition were populated by various First Nations peoples who had made the harsh, cold land their home. Time and patience had given them an intimate knowledge of how to not just survive but thrive in a difficult environment. Franklin's ships, the HMS *Erebus* and HMS *Terror*, were unfound for 160 years, until Westerners finally thought to ask local Inuit peoples about it—their oral histories rather quickly directed seekers to the wreckage.[2]

The Franklin expedition was fatally flawed not because the explorers were undersupplied but because they made no effort to learn from others how to survive. Our species positively excels at social learning. So much of what it takes for us to survive in all the various environments we've come to inhabit is ultimately cultural—it's not about the physical attributes we have or even our individual intelligence, it's about our collective intelligence as a cultural species. We're mid-sized bipedal mammals who aren't particularly strong or fast or agile. We're smart, it's true. But above all, we are cultural. Harvard's Joe Henrich calls culture "the secret of our success" in a recent book (of that name) that outlines how culture has led us to be the planet's dominant species.[3]

As you're stranded in your new environment, a far better strategy than trial and error would be to find some people who live in the environment and try to ingratiate yourself so you can learn how they survive. Eat what they eat, drink the water they drink. In short, your survival could very well depend on your ability to acquire new cultural practices. You need to adapt and learn from others, those who survive in this environment through the cultural practices and technologies they've learned from others before them, culturally honed.

You need culture to survive your new environment, just as you've always needed culture to survive in your old and familiar environment.[4] We're exceedingly good at ignoring all the familiar-to-us cultural innovations that we rely on every day and could never design or innovate on our own. Like fish in water, we seem not to notice our dependence on culture. But whether we're in our familiar environments or transported to a novel one, culture will largely determine our survival.

So, how does culture actually work? In this chapter, I'm hoping to briefly introduce you to the science of cultural evolution. Cultural evolution is a thriving and rapidly maturing scientific discipline organized around a straightforward idea: that culture operates via relatively well-understood principles of evolution. Evolution via natural selection is perhaps the best theory in the history of science. Cultural evolutionists apply the tools of evolution—rigorous mathematical models, computer simulations, and hard-won empirical observation—to cultural phenomena. The end goal is Darwinizing culture, understanding how sharing of information can both mimic and diverge from genetic evolution.

It's not an especially new notion that culture might operate via evolutionary processes conceptually akin to how we understand genetic evolution. Social Darwinists of bygone eras justified societal inequalities by appealing to evolutionary notions of "survival of the fittest." This proved to be transparently self-serving scientific dreck, but the notion was popular in many circles for a long time. It was far from the last attempt to Darwinize culture. Perhaps most famously, in the closing sections of *The Selfish Gene*, Richard Dawkins opined that cultural transmission might operate much like genetic transmission, with discrete information units hopping from mind to mind. Culture and genes are both about information, with some bits proving more successful than others. So perhaps culture evolves, much like we see genetic evolution in the biological realm, with some discrete units surviving better than others. Dawkins called these ostensibly discrete units of cultural information "memes" in direct analogy to genes. There's no small irony in the fact that the "meme" meme has itself mutated, changing over the decades from a serious scientific proposal about how culture works, to simply what we call goofy images and jokes circulating around social media. As we'll soon see, modern scientific approaches to cultural evolution are quite different from Dawkinsian memes, or Victorian Social Darwinists. These false starts illustrate the general appeal of applying evolution to culture, they just proved wrong in the important details.

I want to briefly build an understanding of a few key concepts in cultural evolution. A full treatment of this exciting discipline is well beyond the scope of this chapter. For that, I'd highly recommend books like Richerson and Boyd's *Not by Genes Alone* and Henrich's *The Secret of Our Success*.

Before getting into the nuts and bolts of how cultural evolution works, I first want to discuss the false dichotomy of culture "versus" evolution, and then try to sell you on the benefits of thinking about culture as an evolutionary process in general. These two sections are just tidying the workspace of conceptual clutter before we start putting the pieces of cultural evolution together. Genetic evolution and cultural evolution are different in lots of ways, but they share some deep underlying similarities as fundamentally evolutionary processes. After building some core intuitions about how evolutionary processes work in general, we'll move on and learn about the specific learning strategies that make culture work.

EVOLUTION "VERSUS" CULTURE

I first encountered the modern science of cultural evolution when I was applying to graduate schools, and I must confess I was wary. I got into psychology via evolutionary biology, and then a steady diet of popular evolutionary psychology books. Pinker's *The Blank Slate* informed me that wicked postmodernists appealed to culture as an answer for everything—and in doing so they'd answered nothing.[5] A frequent evolutionary psychology bogeyman was called the "standard social science model"—a disciplines-wide ideology masquerading as theory that quite incorrectly assumed that human nature was nonexistent and that everything came down to culture. I learned that appeals to culture were a form of "blank-slatism," an academic insult I still see hurled at cultural evolutionists from time to time. To call someone a blank-slatist is to accuse them of denying the biological reality of our evolved minds and ignoring harsh scientific realities in favor of leftist political ideologies with only a thin veneer of serious inquiry. The general attitude I'd inherited from the books I'd been reading was that "culture" was often a hollow academic platitude driven by postmodernist fads, not a serious and robust evolutionary science.

Against this backdrop, while I was visiting the University of British Columbia as a potential graduate student a faculty member recommended I read *Not by Genes Alone*,[6] a book recently published by cultural evolutionists Pete Richerson and Rob Boyd. They also mentioned that a hotshot cultural evolutionist named Joe Henrich was also soon to be joining the faculty. Stop. What was going on here? Was I in a warren full of blank-slatist, standard-social-science-model, culture-appealing know-nothings? I was here to study evolutionary psychology, not be indoctrinated into some left-wing postmodernist cult! I got back to Denver and reluctantly checked *Not by Genes Alone* out from the library, figuring I should at least learn what I was up against should I head to Vancouver for graduate study.

I soon discovered that I had been incredibly wrong about cultural evolution. Far from being some blank slate denial of the importance of evolved cognition, I soon discovered that cultural evolution was entirely compatible with a richly evolved psychology, replete with evolved mental gadgets that specifically enabled culture.[7] We weren't blank slates that culture could paint in any which way. Instead, we were a unique species whose members came into the world with a rich cognitive architecture that had evolved in part to capitalize on cultural information. We didn't just passively absorb culture, we sought it out and actively created and curated it. This whole process requires us to have finely tuned mental adaptations for learning culture from our conspecifics. In short, we'd evolved to have specific strategies for cultural learning. This opened up a rich and varied behavioral repertoire that a noncultural species couldn't tap into. Culture got us where we are, and the cognitive capacity for culture is a key mental adaptation that explains our species' evolutionary success.

Our species has two forms of inheritance. Like most, we have a genetic endowment. But unlike most, we also inherit all sorts of beliefs and practices and technologies and norms from each other, only it happens via cultural learning rather than via DNA. Far from being an evolutionary-theory-free bit of postmodern blank-slatism, I quickly discovered that modern cultural evolution took evolutionary theory at least as seriously as did the evolutionary psychologists I'd been reading. Indeed, a hallmark of the science of cultural evolution is its reliance on formal mathematical models and computer simulations of evolutionary processes. If anything, this sort of basic theoretical modeling work was to my great surprise more prevalent in cultural evolution than in most of the mainstream evolutionary psychology I'd been reading, where "theory" was far more likely to stem from verbal than mathematical argument.[8] Cultural evolutionists started with the same modeling and theoretical toolkit of evolutionary biologists—they just adapted these models to the unique quirks of cultural inheritance. The result is a rich body of theory and evidence, fully evolutionary in nature, that helps us explain how culture works.

My current view is that squabbles between evolutionary psychology and cultural evolution are pretty counterproductive. At the end of the day, evolutionary psychologists and cultural evolutionists are all interested in using evolutionary tools to understand our species, and turf battles do little to advance our shared interests. So, if you're a culture-wary evolutionary psychologist like a younger me and feel your hackles rise during this chapter, hang in there. Aside from some few but loud hyper-partisans, the sister disciplines* of evolutionary psychology and cultural evolution are mutually enriching, and it's entirely possible to intellectually drift between the two camps, much to your own benefit and enlightenment. As an aside, this is the central ethos of the Centre for Culture and Evolution. We're a group of anthropologists, evolutionary psychologists, cultural evolutionists, human behavioral ecologists, demographers, and cross-cultural psychologists who strive to get over petty academic disciplinary feuds and just get on with the fun and hard work of understanding evolution and culture in our weird species—truly a unique academic environment.

CULTURE AS AN EVOLUTIONARY PROCESS

How does evolution work? When we're talking about the origins of species, as Darwin did in his book of the same name, or how some organisms come to cooperate with each other, as Dawkins did in *The Selfish Gene*, we're usually talking about genetic evolution. Parents beget offspring by passing along a bit of their genetic material, their DNA. This genetic material helps shape the offspring's body and behavior—that is, the genotype influences the phenotype. Genes are nice little discrete packages of information that tend to be transmitted with quite high fidelity across the generations.

Culture isn't like that. As far as we can tell, there aren't discrete bits of information that hop from mind to mind the way genes travel intact across

---

* I suspect partisans on both sides will resent this framing. As the internet meme with sunglasses says, deal with it.

generations.[9] Cultural transmission is also incredibly messy compared to genetic transmission—although cultural innovations like teaching practices can help tidy up the transmission process.[10] My kids will get some genes that were passed largely intact to me by my parents and to them by their parents and to them by their parents, on back to our distant ancestors millennia ago. On the other hand, cultural information is fuzzier. I might learn something, then change it a bit (whether through intentional innovation or through my own fallible memory) before I pass it on. Transmission is quite low in fidelity, relative to genes. Whereas genetic transmission is vertical—from parent to offspring to their offspring, on down through successive generations—cultural transmission can be vertical, horizontal, or diagonal. Sure, I learn some things from my parents. But I also learn from friends, from my children, and from strangers on the internet. In short, genetic transmission is relatively tidy; cultural transmission is an entirely messier affair.

Given all these quite important differences between how genetic information is passed on and how culture gets passed on, does it even make sense to talk about cultural evolution? Has the analogy between genes and culture been strained beyond the breaking point?

Here I think it's worth zooming out a bit and asking how evolution works. Not just how genetic evolution works (that being the type of evolution we've studied the most), but how evolutionary processes work in the most general sense. Remember, Darwin described the process of evolution via natural selection even though he didn't have a clue how most of the particulars of genetics work. He came up with general evolutionary principles that didn't depend on any particular notions of genes or genetic transmission. So in that spirit, what are the general features of evolution?

At the most basic level, evolution requires three ingredients. First, evolution requires variation among individuals. Second, evolution requires there to be some consequences associated with available variation; some variants do better than others. Finally, evolution requires some mechanism of inheritance. If you have these three ingredients, you've got an evolutionary process on your hands.[†] Modern evolutionary biologists like Richard Lewontin

---

[†] Interested readers who want a more technical walkthrough are highly recommended to crack open Samir Okasha's lovely *Evolution and the Levels of Selection*, which presents a fascinating exploration of how evolution works at a deep theoretical and philosophical level.

have highlighted these as the necessary ingredients of evolution, but they are also clearly identified all the way back in Darwin's original formulation, who in a single page of text in *The Origin of Species* laid them bare. Here's that text, with italic text emphasizing the key ingredients:

> If during the long course of ages and under varying conditions of life, *organic beings vary at all in the several parts of their organization*, and I think this cannot be disputed; if there be, owing to the high geometrical powers of increase of each species, at some age, season, or year, a severe struggle for life, and this certainly cannot be disputed; then, considering the infinite complexity of the relations of all organic beings to each other and to their conditions of existence, causing an infinite diversity in structure, constitution, and habits, to be advantageous to them, *I think it would be a most extraordinary fact if no variation ever had occurred useful to each being's own welfare, in the same way as so many variations have occurred useful to man*. But if variations useful to any organic being do occur, assuredly individuals thus characterized will have the best chance of being preserved in the struggle for life; *and from the strong principle of inheritance they will tend to produce offspring similarly characterized*. This principle of preservation, I have called, for the sake of brevity, Natural Selection.

Putting this together and trimming the verbose fat, we have the following tidy theoretical construction:

IF:
organic beings vary, and
some variants are more useful, and
inheritance lets beneficial variants persist in offspring

THEN:
you've got natural selection

You may notice that this construction says precisely nothing about high-fidelity transmission, discrete units of inheritance, or any of the precise details that we've come to understand are vital for genetic evolution. Those are all incidental and contingent features of one particular evolutionary system—themselves products of an evolutionary process—not necessary or general features of evolutionary processes.[11]

When it comes to genetic evolution, this is all quite straightforward. There's obvious variability between individuals—some folks are tall, some short, some have curly hair, some straight, some people are stronger than others, you get the drift.[‡] These traits are influenced by genes, units of genetic inheritance encoded in chunks of DNA. These chunks of DNA can be passed on to future generations via (in our case at least) sexual reproduction. Genes are the vehicles of inheritance. If we imagine that of all the ways that individuals vary, some of these variations will be better suited to surviving and thriving in a given environment, this means that genes "for" different traits will have differential success. This is genetic evolution in a nutshell: we have variability in traits that are themselves influenced by different genes (variability); genes themselves are units of inheritance that get passed on to subsequent generations (inheritance); among a great tumultuous variety in phenotypes, some will do better than others (consequences). Genes that happen to be "for" variants in traits that do well in a given environment will outcompete genes "for" alternate variants, and as a result will be more prevalent in subsequent generations.

Evolution requires variability, consequences, and inheritance. It does not require genes or DNA—these are merely incidental features of genetic evolution. Genes happen to be particulate units of information, transmitted in high fidelity across generations. This is convenient (from the perspective of an evolutionary process), but far from necessary. It's important to not mistake the incidental and contingent features of genetic evolution (genes, DNA) for the deeper necessities. Genes and DNA are very useful for evolution, but that doesn't mean that every evolutionary system needs to have something like them. Here is perhaps one of the reasons why memetics sputtered out as a science of culture: it mistook incidental and contingent features of genetic transmission (particulate, high-fidelity inheritance) for a universal feature of evolution, and forced a direct and ultimately unnecessary analogy between genes and memes.[12] To satisfy an unnecessary analogy, it made assumptions about cultural learning that proved to be empirically and theoretically untenable—its conceptual foundation laid atop a foundational analogy that proved both unnecessary and unstable.

Culture lacks particulate units of information like genes, but when it comes to the deeper necessities of evolution—variety, inheritance,

---

[‡] No, not genetic drift. That's an immensely important topic in the evolutionary sciences but well beyond the scope of our present discussion.

consequences—culture fits the bill just fine. We pick up so much information from others around us via social learning, and this leads to huge amounts of obvious variability, both between individuals and between groups. Cultural information varies; there's one necessary ingredient down. Different bits of cultural information have different levels of fitness: some ideas do better than others. Some songs are catchier than others. Some bits of technology prove useful and spread rapidly. In a later chapter, we'll also see that different cultural variants can have profound implications for the success of groups. Here we see differential success, our second ingredient of an evolutionary process. The final piece of the puzzle is a mechanism of inheritance. Here, social learning provides ample power for inheritance. We learn, and then pass our learning on to others. Our capacity for social learning is what completes the evolutionary trifecta for cultural evolution.

Cultural information varies across individuals and groups, with consequences.[§] Learning is the mechanism of inheritance that drives cultural evolution. All three necessary criteria for evolution are clearly met, meaning that it can be useful to think about culture as an evolutionary process in its own right.

Hopefully, this section persuaded you that culture fulfils the necessary criteria for evolution to work (or at least made you consider the possibility in a new light). Culture is quite different from genes, but these contingent and superficial differences overlay a conceptual similarity in variability, consequences, and inheritance. The rest of the chapter now focuses on the details of how cultural evolution works. We'll pay special attention now to the mechanism of inheritance—after all, learning is the engine that drives cultural evolution. I'd like to introduce three metaphors that we might use to understand how cultural learning works.

CULTURE IN THREE METAPHORS

In essence, culture is just stuff we learn from each other. When this learning works well, the results are spectacular. Culture is what allowed a bipedal primate to move out from its original home in Africa and eventually

---

[§] It also varies across the lifespan, but this book is too long already and the developmental aspects of all this are a topic for another day.

colonize the globe. Culture is what gave us the technology to put people on the moon. It's what gave us the technology we're currently using to destroy our planet; with luck, it'll be culture that lets us stave off this impending disaster.

So, how does culture work? Fundamentally the question is a psychological one—how do our minds sift information in a way that makes culture go? How do we learn and communicate ideas and technologies? Some other species show social learning and some limited capacities for culture, but nobody else around this joint seems to show the capacity for cumulative culture the way we do—cumulative culture referring to how we can take in ideas, tweak and improve them, and then pass them on to others for their own tweaks and improvements.¶ Culture effectively links groups of individuals together to form a collective intelligence that's far better at solving problems than any isolated individual could on their own.[13] Lone geniuses are overrated; groups are where the most useful sorts of intelligence lie. It's clear that we have the mental capacity for culture, but what might this capacity look like?

There are different ways to think about brains that are capable of culture—different metaphors for how brains can work together to make culture work. Let's consider three: cultural learners as *sponges*, as *sieves*, and as *strategic seekers*. Each metaphor has proven popular within some scientific circles, so let's meet them in turn.

Sponges

One possibility is that we've evolved to just be passive culture sponges. There's no filtering to speak of—put us in contact with cultural information, and we just passively soak it up.

We've met this metaphor already in early chapters. Recall Dawkins's pet hypothesis that religions persist because kids just gullibly believe whatever their parents tell them. This gives children no agency in their learning. In the Dawkins gullibility model, children have no defenses against "bad" cultural information—they just absorb whatever information their parents immerse them in.

¶ Important caveat: the cumulative nature of human culture helps explain how we've thrived, but cumulative culture, per se, doesn't guarantee innovation. Some species have cumulative culture, but it's domain specific, such as dialects of birdsong. Cumulative? Yes. Innovative? Not as such.

The core premises of memetics also have a "cultural sponge" flavor. Memetics envisioned little discrete bits of cultural information—memes—floating about and colonizing susceptible minds. Memes are in a constant arms race with each other, and our mental energy and attention are the spoils of that literal war of ideas. The verbiage of memetics emphasizes our passivity to the ravages of hostile memes: hapless humans are vehicles, robots, hosts to mind viruses.[14]

You may also encounter a mind-as-sponge metaphor in some evolutionary psychology writings, albeit as a sort of cautionary bogeyman. Early popularizations of evolutionary psychology (most notably Pinker's *The Blank Slate*) describe evolutionary psychology as a necessary counterbalance to what they call the standard social science model, a view that humans are essentially blank slates who are filled out in any way imaginable by culture, with little constraint. Evolutionary psychologists dismiss this view of culture (correctly, in my view) on the grounds that our species does seem to have some universals in our cognition that go deeper than we'd assume if we all truly started out as blank canvasses to be painted to completion by whatever arbitrary whims our culture happens to paint with.

Childhood gullibility, memetics, and the dreaded standard social science model all view cultural learning as ultimately passive. Put us around some information, and we soak it up. Doesn't so much matter what the information is—we absorb all information equally, to our own benefit and detriment. This, ultimately, is a quite unsophisticated view of human learning.** Not only are we not active agents in our own learning, we aren't even able to avoid absorbing bad information. The mind-as-sponge metaphor casts us as victims of culture, hopelessly doomed to soak up whatever nonsense our peers have polluted the memosphere with.

Sieves

A slightly more sophisticated metaphor views our minds as cultural sieves. We encounter lots of ideas, and we sift through them like a sieve. Some

** It's also not a view that seems to actually be held by anyone, contra the bogeyman of the standard social science model—even advocates of pretty radical social constructivism take a more sophisticated view of culture and emphasize the co-construction and participation by kids/learners.

things stick, others pass right through. The process is still largely passive—nobody is actively out there trying to figure out what to learn. But at least it isn't wholly uncritical.

The basic idea of the mind-as-sieve metaphor is that we have minds that are built a certain way, thanks to our evolutionary inheritance or past experiences. One result of this is that some concepts are just natural fits for our mental architecture, and we retain these concepts; other concepts are poor fits, quickly lost and forgotten. Some concepts are simply sticky, given our evolved minds. We're likely to retain these concepts and pass them to others.

Sound familiar?

The mind-as-sieve metaphor nicely encapsulates canonical assumptions from the cognitive science of religion. At the end of the day, HADD and minimal counterintuition are about which concepts we are receptive to. We're drawn to ideas about agents, and we find minimal violations of our expectations memorable. This means that ideas like agents with supernatural powers are incredibly likely to be retained.

The mind-as-sieve metaphor is also a key player in a lot of evolutionary psychology work. If we view the human mind as a collection of mental adaptations for different sorts of tasks, it's quite easy to see that the mind might be more receptive to some kinds of ideas than to others. Here our evolved minds constrain which cultural concepts we're likely to adopt.

The mind-as-sieve metaphor imagines a more complex psychology than does the mind-as-sponge metaphor. In the mind-as-sponge metaphor, we just passively soak everything up—no cognitive sophistication required. In the mind-as-sieve metaphor, we readily pick up some stuff and readily discard other stuff. Minimally, this requires a psychology complex enough for a bit of filtering. It requires a cognitive architecture with some presets that make it a better fit for certain types of information. But it still doesn't require much agency on our part. Learners just keep the sticky concepts, but they don't really need to do much to actively learn. We're bombarded by ideas and concepts; incidental features of our evolved minds become nooks and crannies for some concepts to wedge themselves into. Cultural success is determined primarily by the conceptual fit between ideas and our evolved minds. Our final metaphor adds yet more complexity, and finally grants cultural learners some agency.

Strategic Seekers

Sponge and sieve metaphors depict culture as fundamentally something *that happens to us*. Our final metaphor imagines culture as what happens when agents like us are actively trying to learn important information. It views us as eager cultural explorers, out to find the best information we can.

Instead of sitting back and just passively soaking up whatever memes float past us (like sponges) or lightly filtering so that some are likely to stick (like sieves) I like to imagine us as strategic seekers who actively scour our worlds to find the best, most relevant information.

We are active learners, eager to figure out who knows best about what. We recognize that people around us have differing amounts of expertise in different domains, and we try to get the best information from the best sources. When we're uncertain, we can use lots of different cues to figure out who we want to learn from. And even then, we can be wary about what our teachers want us to learn—after all, they may have their own vested interests in us learning this rather than that. The challenge is to get the best information out of those around us, while simultaneously avoiding becoming suckers along the way. We try to be choosy cultural consumers.

By my read, the strategic seeker metaphor has become the dominant narrative in cultural evolution for understanding how we learn from each other. For the remainder of the chapter, I'll introduce you to some of the strategies that we use, and that have allowed us to culturally conquer the globe.

LEARNING STRATEGIES

Instead of genes and DNA and sex, cultural evolution depends on our capacity for social learning. We use specific strategies to actively extract social information from our environments. Social information isn't all created equal. Some concepts are more useful than others; some teachers better than others—more trustworthy, competent, knowledgeable, skillful. We want to survive in our world, and thrive if possible. Cultural information is thus a crucial currency, and it seems we've evolved to use lots of different strategies to profitably trade in it.

Imagine that you wanted to intelligently design an organism to most effectively extract and exploit cultural information. What might this look like? You can't just build in some blanket instruction to "go get some culture." Instead, you'd have to program in some specific learning programs. You'll need to instruct your organism to look for information in some places but not others. Do you want it to just copy what everyone else is doing? To try to identify the most successful people to imitate? To blend together the practices that it observes? Things quickly get complicated.

Over the years, cultural evolutionists have come to recognize lots of specific learning strategies that enable culture. To drive home the point that cultural learning isn't so much a single skill as a bundle of aptitudes and learning biases that coalesce to enable culture, consider figure 5.1, which is based on a prominent review paper on social learning by Rachel Kendal and colleagues.[15] Each node on this figure represents a distinct learning strategy that an agent might use to navigate its environment.

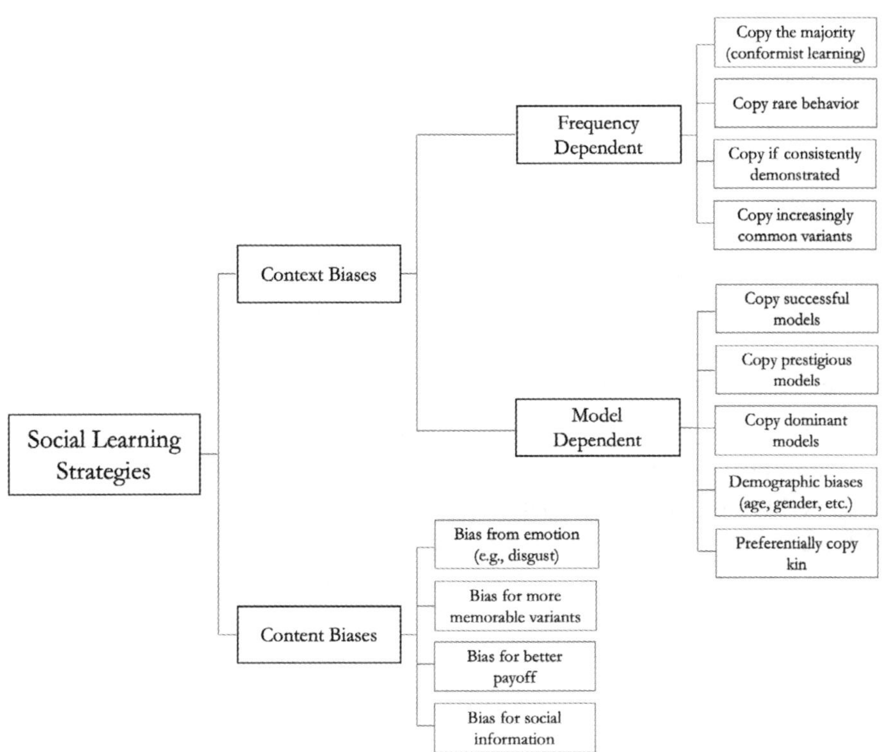

Figure 5.1. Social learning strategies. *Source:* R. L. Kendal, N. J. Boogert, L. Rendell, K. N. Lala, M. Webster, and P. L. Jones, "Social Learning Strategies: Bridge-Building between Fields," *Trends in Cognitive Sciences* 22, no. 7 (2018): 651–65.

Some strategies focus on the fit between an agent's mental apparatus and the information in question. This represents biases favoring social information, or for memorable variants, or for emotionally evocative information. We also see lots of learning biases that come down to selectively choosing from whom to learn. Agents might preferentially copy what seem to be majority stances; they might try to selectively copy the most successful person rather than aggregating majority opinions. These are effectively different strategies for choosing teachers.

To impose some conceptual order on this mess of learning strategies, cultural evolutionists have drawn a coarse distinction between *content biases* and *context biases* in cultural learning. Content biases are about the fit between information and our evolved minds; context biases are about picking the right models to learn from. Let's expand on this dichotomy.

What to Learn: Content Biases

Some ideas just seem to be sticky. "Sticky ideas" doesn't feel like an especially scientific way of talking about things, and we could gussy it up by adding a lot more jargon: given the constraints of our evolved cognitive architecture, some mental representations will be easier to acquire, retain, or transmit. But "sticky ideas" conveys the gist quite well.

Content biases in cultural learning merely mean that our evolved minds find some ideas stickier than others. Catchy jingles, memorable stories, juicy rumors you can't help but share—because of the ways our minds work, some concepts will be better fits and will end up experiencing greater success in cultural transmission. The crucial thing for content biases isn't something inherent to our minds, or to concepts, but to the interaction between them.

An important caveat here is that "stickiness" isn't an inherent feature of ideas, ultimately it boils down to the fit between an idea and our minds. What's sticky to us might be spectacularly slippery to a species with differently evolved cognition, and vice versa. Songbirds and cetaceans show cultural learning, for example in "dialects" of songs of birds and whales alike. But I'm guessing that what counts as a sticky tune for, say, a humpback whale will not be at all sticky for humans or birds. Stickiness is about the fit between a given bit of cultural information and a particular type of brain. The rest of this chapter will pretty much only talk about culture in people—it's always useful to remember that we aren't the only cultural species around, just the most obvious one (at least to members of our species).

Fundamentally, an idea's cultural success depends on the ease with which people can learn, remember, and transmit it. Ease of learning, memorability, and transmission are sort of like separate settings that an idea might have, that will in turn influence its cultural success. A memorable idea, for example, will be more likely to linger and persist across cultural learners whereas forgettable ideas are likely to die out much more quickly. Similarly, an idea that's easier to learn (say by being simpler, or more resonant with other available ideas) will get a huge boost in cultural transmission. Content biases are all about turning these settings up for certain concepts that have the right contents to fit well with our evolved minds.

To take one example, recall minimally counterintuitive concepts from the previous chapter. Researchers found that concepts that violate just a few of our ontological assumptions about the world are more memorable than those that violate none or many.[16] A talking chair, a person who walks through walls, a wholly disembodied spirit—these are all examples of minimally counterintuitive concepts that are more interesting and memorable precisely because they just slightly violate our expectations about the world. These minimally counterintuitive concepts have their memorability dial cranked up just a little bit. This means that over time we'd expect minimally counterintuitive ideas to hang around and remain popular, while more wholly intuitive (or maximally counterintuitive) concepts would die out. And this is precisely what we find. In a fascinating paper we met in the last chapter, Ara Norenzayan, Scott Atran, Jay Faulkner, and Mark Schaller looked at the cultural success of Brothers Grimm fairy tales over time.[17] The Grimm corpus is much bigger than lots of us realize, simply because only a few of them really caught on and sustained their popularity. You've probably heard of "Cinderella," for example. But do you know much about "The Donkey Lettuce"? Norenzayan and team coded fairy tales based on their composition, paying close attention to which ones contained notable minimally counterintuitive elements. It turns out that tales with a smattering of minimal counterintuition—say, a wolf who can talk here, or a person with magical abilities there—are the ones that rose to sustained prominence. The most successful stories from the Grimm corpus are generally those that contain just a few minimally counterintuitive elements. Stories with wholly intuitive occurrences, or those with more off-the-wall levels of bonkers maximal counterintuition just didn't make the cultural evolutionary cut.

Another nice example of content biases in cultural learning comes from philosopher Shaun Nichols's work on etiquette norms.[18] Nichols speculated that concepts that evoke a primal emotion like disgust might be especially memorable and, as a result, successful in cultural transmission. Because a lot of etiquette concerns food and dining, disgust seems an especially pertinent concern. After all, the evolutionary origin story for the emotion of disgust is all about pathogen avoidance—it's what helps us avoid putting the wrong stuff in our orifices.

Nichols coded centuries-old etiquette books to see which bits of etiquette have been preserved over time, with a special interest in whether etiquette norms that concern disgusting actions might be privileged in transmission. A lot of etiquette is just arbitrary convention—which fork goes where, how to hold a spoon. On the other hand, some of it is strongly evocative. And, just as Nichols hypothesized, some bits of disgust-evoking etiquette that once had to be explicitly codified—one oughtn't spit across a dinner table, for example, or vomit openly during a feast—have certainly stuck around, and to such a powerful degree that we probably wouldn't even consider implicit rules like "don't spit on shared food" etiquette anymore—it's just common sense.[††] But once upon a time it was a novel idea that was noteworthy enough to be recorded as a form of etiquette. Note here that what drives the cultural success of these bits of etiquette is their contents, and how they interface with our psychology. Etiquette like "excuse yourself from the table if you must vomit" is memorable, in part because it strongly evokes the disgusting image of someone vomiting on our meal.

Content biases, whether for minimally counterintuitive fairy tales or disgust-evoking etiquette, are all about how a concept fits with a learner's psychology. They are entirely silent when it comes to questions about to whom we turn to learn, the teachers and cultural models whose cultural expertise we'd like to absorb. For that, we turn to context biases in cultural learning.

[††] If you have or have spent time with young kids, you'll be familiar with the wide range of seemingly commonsense things you must teach kiddos about food. Don't put it in your ear. Don't wipe it on the couch. Don't lick the salt off the tortilla chips and put them back in the bowl. Animal droppings aren't food. The health necessity/commonsense/etiquette gradient is porous.

Learning from Whom: Context Biases

Content biases are rather like our sieve metaphor: we encounter lots of concepts and some of them are more likely to stick around, given the makeup of our minds. Context biases, on the other hand, exemplify the strategic seeker metaphor. Context biases encompass lots of learning biases that are all about whom we turn to as sources of learning. Content biases reflect the fact that our evolved minds don't treat all concepts as equal; context biases reflect the fact that not all teachers are equal. To illustrate, we'll consider a handful of context biases in social learning, including conformist transmission, various demographic-based learning strategies, success-biased learning, and prestige bias.

Returning to our original thought experiment about being transported to a new environment and trying to make our way in the world, think first about what you'd eat or drink. Imagine you find yourself in a jungle with ample fruits and vegetables around, and water aplenty. Can you just chow down on whatever you see and drink water wherever it's available? Hardly. Some foods will prove toxic, or at least nonnutritious. Some water may be fine, some may be tainted by upstream contamination of one sort or another. Assuming you find yourself in the company of other humans, you have a ready solution: just copy them and eat what they eat. Specifically, you could do much worse than just copying what most people seem to be doing. If lots of people drink from a certain spring or eat from a certain tree, you can directly infer that it is safe. Beyond food and water, you can probably glean lots of useful survival information just by copying the majority. If a given cultural tool—a bit of clothing, or a way to construct shelter, for example—seems to be working for most everyone, it'll probably work for you too. This copy-the-majority strategy is known as *conformist transmission*.[19] Conformist learning is a safe and reliable strategy for picking up useful and normative cultural goodies. In a later chapter, we'll also see that conformist transmission can help explain how groups of people maintain their groupish differences, as fads and trends can easily be maintained within groups simply by people tending to copy the majority. This maintenance of within-group practices will prove to be quite theoretically important.

Copying the majority is fine for lots of learning, but can be limited if we're in a group composed of lots of people in lots of different roles. We might, for example, see some specialization happening along age or gender lines. Lots of learning strategies and context biases require attending to demographic differences of one type or another. As a straightforward example, we might want to obey our elders and preferentially learn from older people. Why? Among other things, older people have shown that they are good at not dying; presumably if we follow in their footsteps, we can pick up some of their useful not-dying skills in the process. Age-biased social learning is a decent strategy (unless you're learning about, say, the new iPhone features or TikTok trends. These things are context-sensitive, not broad spectrum). Alternatively, we might tailor our learning so that we can pick up the right information for people like us in some dimension. Divisions of labor within a group might mean that people of certain demographics simply have more expertise in a given domain. *Age- and gender-biased learning strategies* can help learners pick up the right information for the roles they'll likely inhabit. It's tailoring learning to those whom we expect to be especially knowledgeable.

Conformist transmission might be a good trick for survival—if everyone does something, it probably isn't fatal after all. Demographic biases also help us learn specialized knowledge from those who are most likely to be specialists. But what if we want to do more than merely survive and fit in, what if we want to excel? Cultural learners who merely conform to the majority will never stand out or rise above their peers. If we really want to thrive, we'd be well-served to seek out information from the most successful individuals. If you want to be the best, learn from the best. *Success-biased* learning strategies try to directly figure out who will have the best information, based on tangible evidence that they are successful. We might preferentially learn from people who directly evince success in a given domain—the best hunters might have the most trophies; the best potter might have the most shapely and sturdy ceramics.

We want to learn from the most knowledgeable people, but knowledge and skill aren't always easy to directly observe. As a result we might turn to indirect cues about who's in the know. We might use social status as a cue to whom we'd like to learn from, but there's a catch. Status can be gained through at least two pathways. Some individuals are dominant—they're high status through force and coercion. Others are prestigious—they're the people who are admired and respected, and who people freely defer to in recognition of their genuine leadership and expertise. I'm guessing over the years you've had bosses who fit both molds, and have a clear preference for one over the other. Dominant individuals might attract some fearful toadies as followers, but prestigious individuals tend to attract cadres of willing followers who pay deference as a required cost to gain access for learning from the best. Cultural learners can thus see who others defer to as a cue of who is likely to be a prestigious and valuable source of information. *Prestige-biased cultural learning* is all about figuring out who's likely to be the most knowledgeable, and then doing what it takes to stay close enough to them to learn what makes them successful.[20] Interestingly, people are likely to over-imitate prestigious leaders. A learner doesn't know what exactly makes a prestigious leader so successful, so you might as well copy as many details as you can. The key to their success might be in their daily routine, their diet, their fashion choices, or their supernatural beliefs. Might as well copy the whole lot, just to make sure. This over-deference and over-imitation of prestigious individuals is what lies at the heart of the burgeoning celebrity endorsement industry. An underwear company or a political campaign will eagerly court endorsements from athletes or actors or other people who have little direct authority, simply because ad agencies know that people are so eager to follow in their idols' footsteps.

Prestige is a limited commodity, and everyone wants to learn from the best. Deference is an access cost that learners pay to gain access to prestigious leaders. Over-imitation and access costs create a potential conflict for learners: if learners need to pay some cost to curry favor with a prestigious individual and then don't know which specific things they should be learning, that prestigious individual might be tempted to exploit their followers to gain benefits for themselves. Here, imagine a cult or shady megachurch leader who holds their congregation in thrall, demanding resources and attention and favors in exchange for specially conferred "wisdom." How can followers protect themselves against exploitation? How do learners know that their cultural idols are sincere in their teachings, and not just stringing their followers along in order to finance that private jet?

WALKING THE WALK: CREDIBILITY ENHANCING DISPLAYS

Imagine a prestigious individual, let's call him Joe, advises you to eat some mushrooms they found. "Try one of these, it's delicious and nutritious," says Joe. Should you believe him and chow down? On the one hand, you've been following Joe around for a while, offering him praise and presents to maintain access, because he seems quite successful and prestigious. Others similarly pay deference to him in recognition of his great skills. Maybe he's sharing some insider fungal knowledge with you because he truly believes that the mushrooms are delicious and nutritious, and he'd like you to share in his bounty. On the other hand, maybe Joe is sick of your sycophantic bullshit and has decided to end it for good by tricking you into eating poisonous mushrooms. Naive cultural learners are open to exploitation like this, but we may have evolved some epistemological defenses.

If Joe refuses to eat any of the mushrooms himself, that's a massive red flag. If they're so delicious and nutritious, why doesn't he want any? On the other hand, if you see Joe eat the mushrooms, that gives you some behavioral proof of their edibility. Here, eating the mushroom serves as a credibility-enhancing display of Joe's sincere belief that the mushrooms are indeed delicious and nutritious (or at least safe). *Credibility-enhancing displays*[21]—a bit of jargon often shortened to simply CREDs—will play a crucial role in subsequent chapters, so let's take some time to develop the idea fully.

In economics and evolutionary game theory, costly signals are a fascinating topic. Sometimes a trait will become widespread not in spite of its great costliness, but because of its costliness. Consider a peacock's tail, for example. It's a beautiful bit of plumage that is simultaneously a massive liability when it comes to survival. Peacocks display their feathers to attract mates, but those same feathers can act as an anchor when fleeing from a predator. The costliness of the tail might serve as a signal of the peacock's other admirable qualities. It's effectively saying, "Look, if I wasn't pretty hot shit otherwise, how could I afford to lug this decorative flight impediment around all the time?"

Credibility-enhancing displays are superficially similar to these costly signals, and they can often be confused for each other. But a crucial distinction can be drawn by focusing on the cost. Costly signals are always genuinely costly. The cost of a peacock's tail doesn't change depending on the peacock's frame of mind—no matter what the peacock believes, the tail is an anchor when they're fleeing from a predator. CREDs aren't like that. A credibility-enhancing display could be quite costly for someone displaying it, but only if the displayer doesn't actually believe their claim. When Joe says, "The mushroom is delicious and nutritious" and then takes a bite, there is a huge cost to Joe if he knows the mushroom is actually poisonous. But if he's sincere and accurate in his proclamation about the mushroom's delectability, there is not only no cost but an actual benefit to Joe for eating the mushroom. CREDs are basically behavioral proof that others are sincere in their proclamations because *their actions would be costly if their words weren't sincere.*

The bottom line for CREDs is that learners are looking for cultural models who don't just talk the talk, but walk the walk. We only want to pick up sincere beliefs from others, and we infer sincerity from actions.

PUTTING THE PIECES TOGETHER

Our species is so phenomenally successful largely because of culture. We're able to connect our brains together and collectively solve problems that none of us alone could. We don't do this by passively absorbing cultural information or because our evolved minds just find some concepts sticky. Instead, we are active cultural consumers who strategically seek the best information available.

To do this, we rely on lots of different learning strategies. These strategies can be productively thought of as evolved learning biases that help us extract cultural information from our social worlds. We're choosy about cultural information in at least two ways. Some cultural information succeeds due to content biased learning—because some concepts are simply good fits for our evolved minds. Concepts that are more emotionally evocative or memorable stand a better chance of cultural success.

Beyond content biases, there are also many context biases in social learning: we selectively attend to some information sources rather than others. We might engage in conformist transmission, preferentially adopting beliefs and practices that seem to be normative and commonplace; we defer to the wisdom of the crowds. We might preferentially imitate people who are the same age and gender as us, or we might try to selectively learn from the elders who've excelled in our environment before us. These demographic-based learning biases are about picking models to learn from who are most likely to have the information we need. Finally, we might try to learn from the best among us, either by trying to copy people who directly show evidence of their success or by paying deference to prestigious individuals in order to gain access to their secrets of success.

Reliance on social learning leaves people open to exploitation—especially when it comes with associated deference and access costs. To buffer ourselves against exploitation, it seems we've evolved some epistemic defenses. By paying attention to credibility-enhancing displays of others' sincere beliefs—actions that would be costly if the models' beliefs didn't match their rhetoric—we preferentially learn from people who back their words with actions, talk that's backed by walk.

The modern vision of cultural evolution is one where learners are constantly bustling about trying to get the best information possible about the world. We turn to different sources for different information, and we're willing to pay some costs to curry favor with the best teachers. We don't drift through life passively absorbing culture, or even acting as a sieve and letting just some cultural bits stick around. We actively pursue and consume culture by selectively deploying different learning strategies to best extract cultural information from our environments. And, as folks like field pioneer Cecilia Heyes remind us, some of our mental tools that we use for extracting good cultural information are themselves the products of cultural evolution.[22]

The result is a fully evolutionary process. There is variability in our cultural constructions; there are consequences attached to this variability, with some variants proving more successful than others; finally, social learning provides a mechanism of inheritance. All of the three key ingredients of evolution—recognized as far back as Darwin—are evident in culture. Culture evolves, and our strategic social learning is a key to how that happens.

This chapter has been all about how we learn culture in general, with little-to-no direct application to our puzzles of faith and atheism. I'm hoping, however, that you've started to connect some of the dots on your own. In the next chapter we'll return to religion and ask some questions about why people come to believe in specific supernatural agents. We'll introduce a few related riddles—about Mickey Mouse and Santa Claus and Zeus specifically—that seem superficially silly but actually highlight pressing conceptual questions for our understanding of religion. We'll deploy the full cultural evolutionary arsenal to hopefully solve these riddles. In doing so, we'll cobble together a working model for understanding why people believe—or not—in different gods.

CHAPTER SIX

FAITH IN CONTEXT

Mickey, Santa, Zeus, and Yahweh

Because what gods need is belief, and what humans want is gods.
—TERRY PRATCHETT, *SMALL GODS*

When my kids lose teeth, we have a ritual and routine. The kid puts their lost tooth in a special bag and then under the pillow at bedtime. By morning, the tooth has magically been swapped for some cash by a supernatural agent called the Tooth Fairy. If the kids left out a little bowl of water for the thirsty tooth fairy, they'd wake to find that the water had changed color and now sparkled with magic fairy dust (by the by, it just so happens that fairy dust looks suspiciously like glitter, and fairies only come in the same colors as the food dye in the pantry). Sometimes there were little sparkly "footprints" nearby. From our kids' perspective, magic had occurred: they had been visited by a wee supernatural agent, a dental demigod of sorts, and they had both cash and evidence attesting to the visitation.

A couple years ago, my eldest child lost a tooth and disrupted the routine. You see, instead of leaving her tooth under her pillow, *she left a note.* The note made it clear that the gig was up. She'd seen through the Tooth Fairy bullshit and knew it was just mama and papa keeping the magic alive. She brought receipts. She noted the time we were moving house, and she found a bag holding tiny child-sized teeth. Either her mother had a creepy stash of random kids' teeth, or else the Tooth Fairy hadn't actually kept the teeth that had allegedly been taken over the years. She noted the time she'd overheard one of our adult friends asking us what we did with the kids' teeth. Damning, incriminating details of our subterfuge had been laid bare. The note also dripped with the implication that she'd seen through the ruse of other childhood gods: no more Tooth Fairy, but also no more Santa Claus or Easter Bunny for her. She is now an eager accomplice as we keep these childhood gods alive for her younger brother—at least for now. The cost of her secrecy? Lost teeth still have a price tag, and that stocking is still full come Christmas morning.

In this chapter, we ask why people believe in some gods and disbelieve in others. We ask why some supernatural agents are wildly popular, but universally acknowledged to be fictions. Why other gods can go from targets of worship for entire societies to targets of mere study in mythology classes. Why kids do—and then don't—believe in childhood gods like the Tooth Fairy and the Easter Bunny.

Thinking about *patterns of belief and disbelief* in this way proves to be of immense value for puzzling through different theories of religion. The previous two chapters outlined the cognitive science of religion and cultural evolution, respectively. It turns out that these two perspectives offer quite different answers to the questions of who believes in what gods, and when. Grappling with a few riddles about belief can really help illuminate both theoretical perspectives and highlight their points of contention. In doing so, it will help us build a coherent model of how specific religious beliefs emerge and are sustained.

OPENING RIDDLES

To get the ball rolling, let's begin with some riddles. Consider four supernatural agents: Mickey Mouse, Santa Claus, Zeus, and Yahweh. All four are minimally counterintuitive agents with more-or-less human psychology. All are memorable and evocative. In the parlance of the previous two chapters, Mickey, Santa, Zeus, and Yahweh are all supported by relevant content biases in cultural learning.

Content biases might explain why each of them enjoys some measure of cultural success and popularity. But each of these minimally counterintuitive supernatural agents is characterized by a very different pattern of belief. Mickey Mouse is a popular cartoon character that we all recognize as fiction. Santa Claus is a focus of intense devotion for children but not adults. Zeus used to be a focus of devotion and worship but is now limited to study in mythology and history classes. Finally, Yahweh (and alternately named variants in related religions) is probably the most believed-in supernatural agent in history, He's just God. Four very different fates when it comes to belief.

Why?

THE MICKEY MOUSE PROBLEM

For a cartoon character, Mickey Mouse gets brought up more than you might expect among academics in certain circles. Cognitive scientists of religion, for example, have discussed "The Mickey Mouse Problem" since at least the late 1990s. I can't cite a definitive source as the originator of the Mickey Mouse Problem because when I dug around to find its creator, nobody could really pin it down with any confidence. My hunch is that the Mickey Mouse Problem emerged where interesting scientific ideas often do: at the hotel lobby bar where everyone congregates at the end of the day at an academic conference.

The Mickey Mouse Problem goes something like this: Mickey Mouse is a minimally counterintuitive agent. He's got the usual properties we associate with mousehood, but he also has humanlike psychology. If we recall the ideas from chapter 4, this means that Mickey Mouse has at least some of what it takes to become a successful god concept. He's an intentional agent, with some interesting and exceptional powers (at least relative to other mice) that make him memorable and culturally successful. Like many successful animist gods and spirits, Mickey is a minimally counterintuitive supernatural agent.

Essentially nobody believes in Mickey Mouse. We all know that he's a popular cartoon character, no more. Why does the same representational content that supposedly underpins the mental representation and cultural success of gods—minimally counterintuitive features and all—not make Mickey Mouse into a successful god himself, to be worshipped with cheesy offerings?

Cognitive scientists of religion have traditionally sidestepped the Mickey Mouse Problem by pointing out that minimal counterintuition might be important when it comes to making culturally successful gods, but clearly it isn't sufficient. Other sorts of features probably separate the gods from the cartoon characters and other beloved fictions. Some supernatural agent concepts have just the right contents to become successful gods; others, like Mickey, almost but don't quite make the cut. Within the cognitive science of religion, the difference between godhood and fantasy comes down to slight differences in how they're described—in the content biases that they evoke.

To illustrate this argument, let's consider Santa Claus next.

WHY SANTA CLAUS IS NOT A GOD

We can all imagine a whole lot of supernatural agents. We've got gods like Vishnu and Yahweh. But we've also got characters like Mickey Mouse, Sparrowhawk of Earthsea, the Scarlet Witch, Count Chocula, and Santa Claus. They've all clearly got the types of features that are good fits for our content-biased social learning (hence their cultural popularity, in part). But why don't we come to worship them as deities?

Some cognitive science of religion advocates, most notably field pioneer Justin L. Barrett, proposed that the solution was even more content-biased learning. Sure, Mickey Mouse as a concept might have the right contents to trip a lot of our content biases and become widespread, but he's lacking some special sauce to inspire belief. Check a lot of content bias boxes to become widespread and popular, check even more to recruit belief and attain godhood. Barrett made this claim in an entertaining thought paper called "Why Santa Claus Is Not a God," in which he argued that some supernatural agent concepts almost *but don't quite* have the exact right contents to recruit belief.[1] In this paper, Barrett outlined five key bits of content that can elevate a given supernatural agent from memorable fiction to successful god.

First, successful gods are minimally counterintuitive. They violate a few of our ontological assumptions and are therefore memorable and culturally transmissible. Second, successful gods are intentional agents. A rock that hovers in the air is interesting and minimally counterintuitive, but it wouldn't become a god. A rock that can talk and engage in intentional actions with the world? Now we're cooking. Third, gods tend to be described as not just intentional agents, but as agents who can possess strategic information. A talking rock that can recite the digits of pi is intriguing; a talking rock that can tell us where we can successfully hunt is important. Fourth, successful god concepts usually describe agents who have detectable interactions with our world. People are committed to their gods in part because their gods can do stuff. The combination of strategic information and detectable action is a potent one—this describes the gods who might be able to help us with our lives. Finally, Barrett argues that successful gods have content that motivates ritual practice, which in turn bolsters belief. If there's a god out there who knows about the world and doesn't care if anyone interacts with them, that's nifty but unlikely to last. In contrast, successful gods tend to require check-ins from their adherents.

These features of successful gods aren't some sort of necessary checklist. A god might become successful without containing all the features. But, on the balance, to cognitive scientists of religion like Barrett, supernatural agents that check more of the boxes are more likely to become successful gods that attract widespread belief. As we saw in chapter 4, this is a pretty common view in the cognitive science of religion literature, to the effect that beliefs in gods emerge not from the operation of one or even a few little cognitive biases, but from the combined operations of lots of content biases that all nudge toward belief. If a given supernatural agent concept checks off more of our boxes, if it recruits more content biases in cultural learning, it's more likely to become a successful god.

According to Barrett's piece, Santa Claus is right on the cusp. He's an intentional agent with strategic information about the world (specifically about the properties of naughtiness and niceness). He acts in detectable ways, doling gifts and coal. He does inspire at least annual ritual devotion. But when Santa's features are all combined, he seems to lack some essential ingredient and as a result adults don't believe he's real. The paper's offered explanation for why Santa Claus isn't a god is that Santa almost but doesn't quite have the right content to inspire widespread belief. It's content biases all the way down, and Santa just barely misses some content-bias-laden cognitive sweet spot.

When I first read the paper, I remember nodding along at first, but then shaking my head by the end. All of the content features highlighted by Barrett did seem like they could be important for explaining why some concepts spread better than others and as a result become popular. But as an explanation for patterns of *belief* it just wasn't very satisfying. Joe Henrich and I discussed our shared dissatisfaction and ended up writing a short rebuttal piece. Some of our objections were relatively minor, but others seemed quite fatal to the argument that content biases alone could explain belief and disbelief.

On the minor side of things, we noted a few issues. First, the five-item checklist that Barrett proposed didn't seem to fit the gods and spirits that people actually do believe in, across cultures and time. There are plenty of ancestor gods whose knowledge isn't especially strategic, or whose interactions with the world aren't especially impactful. Lots of these ancestor spirits are no more strategically important than the ancestor in question was in life; Great Aunt Ida isn't suddenly powerful, it's just that she's still lingering around after death, potentially doing no more than pissing and moaning about noisy kids.

Second, the criteria for godhood that Barrett described do seem to capture some useful notions about which gods might become popular. But they don't provide a tidy explanation for what the paper set out to explain: why Santa Claus is not a god. The paper ends up concluding that Santa Claus must be missing some key ingredient that other gods have, but it stops well short of specifying that key missing ingredient. The reader is left with the impression that since content biases have been assumed to be the main drivers of belief and disbelief, supernatural agents who don't recruit belief must prima facie lack some required content. Content driving belief, however, is an assumption rather than a conclusion.

Third, some of the listed criteria for godhood seem to presuppose a measure of belief in order to work—hardly a satisfying ingredient in what's supposed to be a model of why people come to believe things. The Barrett model assumes that belief is more common for agents with strategic information or who have detectable interactions with our world. But this assumes either that people already believe in the god, or that people might somehow increase their degree of belief in an agent they wouldn't otherwise believe in, simply because the agent has been described as being more useful. How exactly would this work?

I think that some reworking of the content bias model might be able to address some of these superficial limitations that Joe and I were concerned about. Add new criteria, remove or tweak the problematic ones. Refine, revise, resubmit. But at the end of the day, we thought that any explanation for why people believe in some gods but not others that relied solely on content biases would fail a deeper conceptual challenge. Following in the august footsteps of the Mickey Mouse Problem, we dubbed our challenge the Zeus Problem.[2]

THE ZEUS PROBLEM

If the content of supernatural agent concepts is sufficient to explain why some of them recruit widespread belief and others don't, then how can we explain gods who used to be objects of faith and devotion, but today have been cast aside in the hearts and minds of would-be adherents? Consider Zeus. Once the mighty king of the Greek pantheon, he was the object of belief and worship, as attested to by monuments, sculptures, and tales that we'd call mythology today, but were once religion.

Zeus clearly has the content to make it as a successful god concept—after all, he was once a wildly popular god. Whatever content-based criteria we come up with to explain successful gods—be it Barrett's five-point list or some other formulation thereof—would have to be satisfied by Zeus. After all, he was worshipped. Over time, belief in Zeus has dwindled, even though his described content has not changed. Zeus's content alone, with its fit to our evolved minds, cannot account for patterns of belief—and then disbelief—in Zeus.

The Zeus Problem isn't just about why belief in gods can wax and wane over time. More broadly, the Zeus Problem forces us to consider why people don't come to believe in any gods that have the requisite content to inspire belief among their adherents. Supernatural agent concepts are psychologically sticky, but they don't seem to be so incredibly sticky that people adopt beliefs in culturally unfamiliar gods when they learn about those gods' described content. A Christian or Muslim today could learn everything there is to know about Zeus's described content—his minimal counterintuitive features, his strategic knowledge, his ability to interact with our world—and still not come to believe in Zeus.

Most people today are believers in one god or another. But crucially they tend to believe in only the gods of their group. People don't just willy nilly start believing in any old god they hear about that has the right sort of content to inspire belief. A traveler could learn about and witness rituals devoted to a huge variety of gods—Papa Gede, Vishnu, Mithra, Papatūānuku, Senawahv, Yahweh, or Zeus—without coming to believe in any of them.

The Zeus Problem asks why people generally don't come to believe in gods other than their own group's, even though those gods clearly have content compatible with belief. In answering the question of why Santa Claus isn't a god, Barrett hypothesized that Santa almost but doesn't quite have the right content to inspire belief. Appealing solely to features of Santa's described content, and by extension solely to content biases in learning, may or may not provide a satisfactory explanation for the specific case of Santa Claus. But leaning so heavily on content biases exposes, in my mind, a deeper problem in canonical cognitive science of religion approaches to religion. If the answer is content biases all the way down, then why do people show the specific patterns of belief and disbelief that they very obviously do? If some gods have content that on its own inspires belief, then why don't people rapidly adopt belief in these gods when they learn of their described content? When people from different religions run into each other, why don't they leave believing in both their original gods and the gods of their new friends? Content biases alone can't provide satisfying answers.

PAINT-BY-NUMBERS: AN INTERLUDE

So far, this chapter has been a bit silly. We've talked about Mickey Mouse and Santa Claus and Zeus. Far from being a mere distraction, thinking carefully about these peculiar supernatural agents lays some key conceptual issues bare. It also lets us assemble the pieces we've collected in previous chapters. What comes next shifts from lighthearted consideration of silly questions about Mickey and Santa to a key crux of this book: we're eventually going to build a full model of how religious belief works (the remainder of this chapter), and why the world's religious landscape looks as it does today (the topic of the next chapter). The themes we develop in the remainder of this chapter will also echo in the next major section of the book when we turn from the Puzzle of Faith to the Puzzle of Atheism.

A key consideration moving forward is figuring out how (and if) people learn to believe in their gods. This is a key point of contention between the cognitive by-product approach and the full cultural evolution-informed model I'd like to develop.

It may seem trite or obvious that *of course* religion is something we learn from those around us. And every cognitive scientist of religion I've met would acknowledge at least some minimal role for culture. But the canonical approach to cognitive science of religion that we met a couple of chapters ago is quite clear that cultural learning per se isn't the key driver of religious belief. Instead, the cognitive by-product approach that defines the cognitive science of religion describes religious belief as a nearly inevitable outcome regardless of culture—culture just furnishes some minor doctrinal details to a core religious belief that naturally emerges on its own, with little to no cultural prodding. Culture doesn't teach people to believe in gods; it merely teaches them the minutiae of how to worship a given god endorsed by their peers. In Barrett's words, "Cognitive biases and tendencies, born out of maturationally natural systems *and not cultural particularities*, make children born believers" [emphasis added]. Cognitive biases and tendencies (read: content biases) are apparently sufficient to explain religious belief. Mere "cultural particularities" offer little more than embellishment on a robust natural religion that will emerge on its own.

Cognitive science of religion views the role of culture in the development of faith kind of like one of those paint-by-numbers kits, where you get an already-drawn picture and specific instructions on which hues go where, with the end result being a fully colorful masterwork. The linework of the picture is complete before you pick up a brush to make your first stroke. Your role is to merely fill in the colors in a specific way. With the cognitive by-product approach, culture is sort of like the painter of a paint-by-number picture. Sure, they fill in some important details, but the artwork is fairly complete without them. In contrast, our evolved cognition and natural intuitions are rather like the image you get at the outset of the paint-by-numbers exercise: all the key patterns are already there. Just as the painter of a paint-by-number isn't really the key creative driver, culture isn't a terribly important factor in the emergence of religious belief in the cognitive by-product model. The religious pattern is there, culture just paints in some details.

Over the years, my colleagues and I have tried to build a better model of how religious belief works, a model that embraces the full arsenal of modern cultural evolutionary theory. Our model places much more emphasis on cultural learning than does the standard cognitive science of religion approach. Gone is the paint-by-numbers analogy, where culture just fills in a few blanks in an otherwise largely complete canvas of religious belief. Instead, we view the very capacity to believe in any specific gods as fundamentally a product of cultural learning. Specifically, we think that faith in specific gods is far more a product of context-biased learning than of content biases alone. In other words, faith emerges from context.

FAITH IN CONTEXT: A DUAL INHERITANCE MODEL

Time to roll up our sleeves and get to work.

Let's try to develop a model of how religious belief works that both incorporates insights from the previous two chapters, and also explains the puzzles posed in this one. If we incorporate the cognitive science of religion framework (with its heavy reliance on content biases) into our broader understanding of cultural evolution (which recognizes both content and context biases), we can gain some traction on understanding Mickey, Santa, Zeus, and Yahweh. In doing so, we can better understand how religious belief works in general—why people come to believe in their specific gods.

My colleagues and I have been calling this model of religion the dual inheritance approach. Here, dual inheritance just means that our species has two parallel and interacting streams of inheritance: one genetic, one cultural. Our genetic inheritance builds brains that work one specific way—that find some concepts more compelling or interesting or intuitive or memorable than others. This will help those concepts spread, all else equal. Our evolved cognition—the collection of more-or-less innate proclivities and intuitions and preferences that evolutionary psychologists would call "human nature"—cognitively underpins the content biases favored by the cognitive science of religion.

However, as we saw in the last chapter, there's more to cultural evolution than just the content biases described by cognitive scientists of religion. Ideas and beliefs don't spread merely because their contents are psychologically sticky—there are also massively important differences in cultural context, the people from whom we choose to learn. A content-bias-only approach has a really hard time telling us why people nowadays believe in Yahweh but not Santa Claus. It has a harder time yet telling us why

Christians or Sikhs today don't start believing in Zeus when they learn about his lightning-tossing ways. Myriad gods from diverse world cultures over time have the requisite content to attract belief. Yet the vast majority of us only believe in one or a few of these gods that have the right contents to recruit belief. Content can only explain so much.

Might context biases gain us some intellectual traction on the Zeus problem? Let's consider how a few different context biases might interact to produce the patterns of belief we find.

First, conformist transmission is the tendency to imitate the majority. When most people in your group prepare their cassava root in a certain way, you can probably infer that it's at the very least a safe way to prepare your cassava. It might even be a sort of optimum preparation method that the collective intelligence of your group has arrived at over the years. Conformist learning is a good strategy in lots of circumstances. As an added theoretical bonus, conformist learning also helps stabilize traits within groups, and maintain differences between groups.[3] Lots of between-group differences ultimately come down to people within each group simply going with the flow and copying local majorities. Coordination within groups can sustain differences between them—a theme we'll return to in the next chapter.

Returning to religion, the role of conformist learning seems fairly obvious. People tend to adopt the same religious beliefs as their surrounding communities. If a naive cultural learner grows up in a Sikh-majority community, they're likely to become a Sikh themselves; Buddhist communities have Buddhist children; in an area where Zeus is the god of choice, learners will probably grow up worshipping Zeus. Oftentimes the clustering of beliefs driven by conformist learning is incredibly obvious. I was recently visiting Belfast, Northern Ireland, where the sectarian conflagrations known as the Troubles saw Protestant and Catholic neighborhoods that were mere blocks from each other erupt into decades of violence that eventually resulted in walls being erected to separate the communities for everyone's safety. The peace process is ongoing, and was driven by far more than just slight doctrinal differences between rival Christian factions. But the incredible susceptibility to local majorities helps maintain between-group divisions, often with terrible consequence.

Second, recall that prestige-biased learning stems from our desire to extract the best possible information from the most successful individuals.[4]

We pay deference for access to elites, in the hopes that we can emulate whatever has made them so successful. In short, this gives elites tremendous influence over their communities. Trends in fashion and dialect can spread rapidly though communities, driven by cultural influencers central within them. Emulation of elites ends up being fairly content-neutral. We aren't great at figuring out what specifically makes elites so great, so we tend to over-imitate them. In terms of religious beliefs, elites have tremendous influence over the religious beliefs of their communities. The forces of prestige-biased cultural learning will often act in concert with conformist transmission. The elites of a Christian (or Zoroastrian, or Sunni, or Shia) community are probably Christian themselves (or Zoroastrian, or Sunni, or Shia, respectively).

Finally, successful religions offer their adherents plenty of opportunities to prove their faith with actions: costly and painful rituals; abstentions from specific food or sex; scarification, tattooing, and other forms of bodily mutilation; fasting; attendance at congregations; tithing, public volunteerism, and service. Religions include bundles of credibility-enhancing displays of faith in gods.[5] Indeed, the credibility-enhancing display model that's proven so important for the study of cultural evolution emerged in part to explain the prevalence of costly rituals and practices inherent in religions worldwide.[6] CREDs allow people to prove their faith with their behavior. To cultural learners, CREDs guarantee the sincerity of their cultural models' professions of faith, which in turn ratchets up observers' own commitment to the beliefs in question.

Interlocking forces of conformist- and prestige-biased learning combine with credibility-enhancing displays of faith to give each community of people its own god(s) that learners ought to worship. Context biases in cultural learning help create and then cement between-group differences in beliefs and norms. This is a potent combination. Imagine that you're a youngster growing up and trying to make your way in a community. You see most (maybe all) people professing faith in a given god. The leaders and elites that you look up to also show a sincere commitment to that god. And everyone—prole and elite alike—takes part in costly and painful rituals to prove their faith in that god. As a learner, you're getting wave after wave of consistent context-based cues that *you ought to believe in this god, and only this god.*

Our dual inheritance model incorporates insights from both the cognitive science of religion and the broader theoretical toolkit of cultural evolution. Content biases in cultural learning can help constrain and canalize the types of gods that are likely to feature heavily in world religions—a key insight of the cognitive science of religion. We have a fascination with agents, and minimally counterintuitive powers are catchy. But that doesn't mean we'll come to believe in just any old minimally counterintuitive supernatural agent just because it's got psychologically sticky content. Instead, context-biased cultural learning will ultimately determine which specific gods we're likely to believe in—an insight we've gleaned from the broader cultural evolution literature. Of all the minimally counterintuitive gods that we can imagine, we'll come to only believe in that tiny subset of minimally counterintuitive gods that receive converging support from context biases in cultural learning within our own group. For example, gods that enjoy support from most people in our group (conformist transmission), from elites (prestige-biased transmission), and especially gods for whom people credibly prove their faith through actions (credibility-enhancing displays) will become targets of belief for cultural learners.

The dual inheritance model of religious belief can be put pretty simply: Content biases help explain why gods everywhere have similar features; context biases are necessary to understand patterns in belief and disbelief in specific gods.[7]

MICKEY, SANTA, AND ZEUS REVISITED

Let's see if our dual inheritance model can do a better job of explaining Mickey, Santa, Zeus, and Yahweh. The cognitive by-product approach rather unsatisfyingly appealed to a constellation of content biases to try to explain why some of these supernatural agents enjoy belief and others don't. Can we gain more traction by adding in context biases?

Mickey Mouse is counterintuitive and grabs attention. He's beloved worldwide, and is clearly a successful concept in terms of popularity. But nobody believes in him. He's a universally acknowledged fiction. Neither elites nor majorities evidence belief in him, and outside of the Disneyland gift shop there's not much that we could sensibly classify as costly behavior directed at Mickey. He may or may not have the right content to inspire belief, but he has never enjoyed the context that breeds belief.

Santa Claus, like Mickey, is incredibly popular. I think a compelling case could be made that Santa Claus actually is a successful god concept among lots of children worldwide. They do sincerely believe in Santa and his gift-giving ways. In recent years, many families have also added a creepy new henchman to the Santa pantheon. I'm speaking, of course, of the Elf on a Shelf. Santa (and that pesky elf that's so easy to forget to move, leading to awkward questions) is a counterintuitive supernatural agent that lots of kids genuinely believe in. As kids grow older, Santa's content remains identical, yet belief in him dwindles to zero. All that changes is the surrounding contextual support.[8] As kids grow older, the conformist majority shifts. Maybe a parent or elder sibling spilled the story on Santa's true identity. Kids are more likely to encounter movies and television shows that reveal the secret. What was once a belief supported by consistent cues from peers and parents, and a belief backed by credible displays of faith, soon becomes an acknowledged fiction. Santa's content does not change from early to late childhood; all that changes is contextual cues supporting his existence as a real supernatural agent instead of a fun fairy tale. It's not that Santa lacks the content to be a god, it's that kids stop believing in him when they stop seeing consistent and credible cues that other people believe in Santa. Context, not content, explains trends of belief and disbelief in Santa Claus.

The Zeus Problem, which appeared intractable using only content biases as tools, has an almost trivially obvious solution under the dual inheritance model. People can learn about the gods of other groups and find them interesting and memorable—that's our content biases in action. But they won't come to believe in any gods that fail to receive consistent support from context biases in cultural learning. A Christian (or Muslim, or Zoroastrian, etc.) today will not see people worshipping Zeus. No conformist cues of widespread belief, no hint that prestigious elites have joined Zeus cults. Most importantly, they won't witness credibility-enhancing displays of faith in Zeus. Gone are the sacrifices. The temples are either crumbling or historical monuments, preserved precisely as monuments to beliefs that once were. As Zeus's content remained the same over the centuries, credibly proven cultural support for him dwindled, as eventually did belief.

Yahweh—under His various names—currently enjoys massive amounts of CRED support; also, belief.

People believe in only those gods who receive consistent support from relevant contextual cues in cultural learning, and especially from credible displays of faith. Supernatural agents can have content that makes them interesting and memorable, but without credible cues that others believe in them, learners are unlikely to believe themselves. These shifts from faith to disbelief can happen within an individual's own lifespan—as happens with Santa—or within cultures over time—as happened with Zeus. Like Santa (to children) and Zeus (to ancient-Greeks) gods that enjoy converging support from relevant context biases inspire belief. But like Santa (to adults) and Zeus (to non-ancient-Greeks), gods that don't enjoy these converging context-biased cues may be interesting, but they won't inspire belief no matter how well their described content fits some cognitive sweet spot or content bias checklist.

This is the core of the dual inheritance model: content biases constrain *what gods are about*, context biases determine *degrees of belief* in them. We'll return to this idea time and again in the book. Now, let's consider a few objections that may have already sprung to your mind.

CAVEATS AND CLARIFICATIONS

If you've been paying attention so far, you may wish at this point to call "bullshit" on a few things. Hopefully I can convince you not to dismiss the argument just yet.

ISN'T THIS JUST CHILDHOOD GULLIBILITY?

Back in chapter 2, we met Richard Dawkins's pet hypothesis about religion. In short, Dawkins across fifteen years has repeatedly hypothesized that religion results from children being blindly credulous to whatever things their parents tell them—be it good survival knowledge or religious foolishness. In grounding religious belief in context biases in cultural learning, in saying that cultural learners adopt beliefs credibly modeled by people in their communities, aren't I basically just gussying up the Dawkins gullibility model in fancy cultural evolution jargon about "conformist transmission" and "credibility-enhancing displays"?

Not at all.

The Dawkins gullibility model explicitly assumes that children blindly believe whatever they're told by adults, especially their parents. As we saw previously, this assumption is directly contradicted by developmental psychology research. It also proves to be theoretically incoherent from the perspective of cultural evolution: blindly credulous learners are suckers, quickly outcompeted by even mildly skeptical peers. Indeed, the whole concept of credibility-enhancing displays arose in part to solve the problem of how learners could avoid exploitation. The gullibility model ignores available evidence and theory from the two scientific disciplines with the most direct expertise on how kids are likely to learn, hardly an auspicious start for a supposedly novel theory of religion.

The dual inheritance framework developed in this chapter, like the gullibility model, assumes that religious beliefs are heavily learned from those around us. But that's where the similarity stops. The gullibility model ignores relevant theory and posits an incredibly unlikely-to-evolve learning strategy; the dual inheritance model starts by considering those learning strategies that have already been scientifically well-vetted by cultural evolutionists over the last forty years. The gullibility model makes a sweeping claim about the acquisition of beliefs that ignores what we know about how kids learn, and how they represent different sorts of claims; the dual inheritance model can specify precisely how religion is learned, appealing to our best available theory and evidence from the scientific fields who'd know best. The gullibility model is a science popularizer's pet hunch that seems to have not engaged with the most relevant science; the dual inheritance approach is a full-fledged scientific theory of religion, drawing on our best available scientific evidence. The two approaches are similar at only the most simplistic and superficial level.

SO RELIGION IS ALL ABOUT INDOCTRINATION?

In *Born Believers*, Barrett includes a lengthy section contrasting his favored cognitive by-product model of religion with what he terms the "indoctrination thesis." The indoctrination thesis is basically the notion—also popular in some New Atheist circles—that religion only persists because religious leaders and elders deliberately indoctrinate kids into faith. It is cynical-to-abusive religious leaders who exert great effort to make kids believe. Is the dual inheritance model just indoctrination?

I think that Barrett is right to dismiss the indoctrination thesis. His main counterarguments are that (1) indoctrination doesn't account for regularities in religious beliefs or the naturalness and ease with which they seem to emerge, and (2) the indoctrination thesis doesn't describe a religious upbringing that most believers would recognize.

On the first point, if the indoctrination thesis held, then people could presumably indoctrinate their kids to believe any old thing—so why do world religions have recurrent features? The dual inheritance approach easily answers this: content biases in cultural learning help constrain the concepts that are likely to become widespread and popular in religions, and context biases determine rates of belief. As we'll see in the next chapter, the dual inheritance model can also help us understand why some religions, rather than others, have conquered the globe.

On the second point, Barrett notes that when he talks to religious people (and, by the by, he is a religious person so has relevant expertise and life experience here), their accounts of their faith and upbringing are much lighter on indoctrination than popular New Atheists tropes might suggest. Yes, some religious sects go heavy on indoctrination, but that is far from the norm. Religious enculturation can involve direct and explicit teaching, but it also involves a lot of more passive and observational learning. CREDs, conformist transmission, and prestige biases can get learners to adopt traits from their learning models *without those models explicitly indoctrinating learners.*

Indoctrination is one quite extreme example of how explicit teaching can be a form of cultural learning. But it's far from the only—or even most common—way that kids learn religions. In highlighting the role of cultural learning in religious belief, the dual inheritance model is quite explicitly not an indoctrination-based model.

BELIEF PRODUCES BELIEF—ISN'T THIS CIRCULAR REASONING?

Our dual inheritance model says that people come to adopt their favored religious beliefs largely because the relevant cultural context supports those specific beliefs. People believe in a given god because other people in their society credibly evince belief in that god. Belief comes from . . . belief?

On the surface, the dual inheritance approach seems tautological. But on a deeper level the apparent tautology is easily resolved. For individual cultural learners, context biases in cultural learning will largely influence which (if any) gods are believed in. There's no tautology here, just a clear mechanistic explanation of how specific religious beliefs emerge from the confluence of specific cultural learning biases. The apparent tautology arises when we consider the problem at larger scales: if people believe in the gods that their communities evince belief in, then doesn't that just push our puzzle backwards in time and upwards in scale? What explains how some gods, over time, attract widespread and enduring belief?

As we'll see in coming chapters, the dual inheritance approach offers solutions to these larger-scale puzzles as well. In subsequent chapters we'll consider two such puzzles: why belief in specific gods waxes and wanes over time, and why rates of atheism vary so much as well.

If modern people tend not to believe in gods of antiquity like Zeus simply because nobody's around displaying Zeus CREDs today, then how might we explain the downfall of Zeus belief (and CREDs) over time, at a broad societal and historical level? In the next chapter, we'll see that the cultural evolutionary machinery underlying the dual inheritance approach can easily handle questions of which religions thrive and spread over time and which wither and die. The key here is imagining a world where religions are in evolutionary competition with each other, battling for the hearts and minds of adherents.

Second, if beliefs (well, CREDs) determine beliefs, then how can we explain the rise of atheism in many parts of the world today? Several subsequent chapters will tackle this puzzle head-on. Along the way, we'll learn about how CREDs interact with other factors to predict atheism (chapter 11), the stages of secularism (chapter 12), and how the dual inheritance approach shows us that atheism can come easily, as a natural outcome in lots of contexts (chapter 13).

This chapter began with some seemingly silly puzzles about why people do (or don't) believe in Mickey Mouse, Santa Claus, or Zeus. In playing with these puzzles, we developed a coherent theoretical account of religion that unites the cognitive science of religion work we met in chapter 4 with the cultural evolutionary framework we met in chapter 5.

The vast conceptual universe of possible gods is but sparsely populated: among all the possible gods we might imagine, the world's religions cohere around just a few consistent themes. Successful gods tend to be minimally counterintuitive agents, often with strategically important information about the world, and at least a passing concern for us mortals. The content biases favored by the cognitive science of religion offer a good explanation for the consistent themes that predominate the world's gods. But these content biases don't buy us much traction when it comes to explaining why a given person believes in *this god* rather than *that god*. To explain patterns of belief and disbelief, we turned to context biases in cultural learning. From all the gods we could imagine, that we find evocative and memorable, we come to believe in only those supported by credible displays of faith within our communities. Cultural milieu, rather than minimally counterintuitive content or hyperactive agency detection, explains belief.

This dual inheritance approach can help us explain why people believe in the gods they believe in; it tidily solves the Mickey Mouse problem and the Zeus problem. In short, folks believe in the gods that are supported by relevant context biases in cultural learning—conformist learning, prestige biases, and especially credibility-enhancing displays of faith. This approach explains how individual people might come to believe or disbelieve in specific gods, but seemingly offers little when it comes to explaining why belief in specific gods overall can vary so much, over time. The account we've developed so far can explain why Christians today are unlikely to believe in Zeus, but doesn't yet explain why once-popular Zeus now attracts little belief. Why have some religions conquered the globe while others flash and fade? The next chapter expands our dual inheritance framework to consider how the world's religious landscape came to look as it does today, with clear winners and losers in the cultural evolutionary arms race in which religions compete for adherents.

CHAPTER SEVEN

WHY SOME RELIGIONS PERSIST

A tribe including many members who, from possessing in a high degree the spirit of patriotism, fidelity, obedience, courage, and sympathy, were always ready to aid one another, and to sacrifice themselves for the common good, would be victorious over most other tribes; and this would be natural selection.

—CHARLES DARWIN, *DESCENT OF MAN*[1]

My wife and I once took a trip to Nicaragua. Our flight from Vancouver to Managua connected through Houston, where we had a few hours to burn. As we often do when there's time to kill, we turned to a favorite airport pastime: people watching.

We gradually noticed a fascinating trend. The international departures terminal we'd been housed in mainly had passengers bound for various South and Central American destinations. And at gate after gate after gate, we saw what were clearly gospel-driven Christian missionary groups. Initially we were quite confused by this. Didn't these Christian missionaries realize they were flying into some of the most heavily Christianized areas on the planet?

Then we were struck by what should've been the obvious answer. Yes, Latin America skews heavily Christian, but it is *overwhelmingly Catholic* in affiliation. The missionary groups we saw, replete with teens chastely goofing around in the terminal? Southern Baptists. Methodists. Pentecostals. The dynamic was overwhelmingly that of evangelical Protestant groups heading off to proselytize in Catholic hotbeds. No doubt there would be good works—school and hospitals built, sanitation projects completed. But each trip also came with the prospect of converting heathens from their Papist idolatry to one of the various evangelical One True Faiths represented in the concourse.

Religions rise and fall over the years, centuries, and millennia. Something like a thousand new religious movements get their start each year. It's really tough to pin down a precise number here, both because it's tough to define what counts as a religion and also because it's scientifically challenging to measure and record these movements accurately and quickly.[2] And quick measurement is a necessity! The vast majority of new religions fade in a year or less—the shelf life of new religious movements is spectacularly unimpressive, not unlike the track record for new restaurants in a busy urban area. But, again like trendy restaurants, some lucky few faiths have staying power and persist over time. Fewer still have not only staying power but *spreading power*. These winning religions might expand beyond their initial geographical roots and become truly global—they franchise, to continue torturing our restaurant analogy. But even today's global faiths have their local origins. Remember, at one point in history the religion we now call Christianity was in all likelihood just a few dudes following around one of the many messianic prophets popular in the region at the time.

Christianity, Islam, Hinduism, and Buddhism represent a tiny subset of the world's historical religious diversity. And yet, more than three in four people alive today subscribe to one of these global faiths. How is it that most religions fizzle and fade but a few endure and expand instead? Why have just a few of the world's faiths become truly global?

The last chapter developed a theoretical model of why individual people come to believe in the gods they believe in. This chapter, we'll zoom way out and ask why entire peoples—rather than individual people—come to believe in the gods they believe in, and why the world's religious landscape looks the way it does. In the global religious ballgame, there are winners and losers. Among the numerous religions that our species constantly spawns, a tiny few have staying power. How can our dual inheritance theoretical model of religion account for these broad trends in religions over time?

As we'll see in this chapter, the cultural evolutionary toolkit comes well-equipped for answering big-picture questions about how cultures themselves change over time. Here we extend our theoretical model and use cultural evolutionary theory to explain the wild cultural success of just a few isolated gods over history. The key to the success of these gods lies in the cultural consequences of some supernatural beliefs. To sketch out the best available theory on how some religions have come to dominate the global religious landscape, we'll have to introduce two important concepts: cultural group selection[3] and religious prosociality.[4]

CULTURAL GROUP SELECTION

To understand how some religions win in the global cultural evolutionary battle for adherents, we'll have to head into some fraught and tricky conceptual terrain. One of our key theoretical building blocks is the concept of cultural group selection. It's basically the idea that some cultural traits persist not because they're good for individuals who hold them, but because groups with lots of individuals who hold them outcompete groups without. As Darwin's quote at the outset of the chapter illustrates, this idea is neither complicated nor new. Being an old idea, however, does not make group selection uncontroversial. In this section, I'm hoping to tackle the controversy head-on, and then show how the idea of group selection isn't some fringe or discarded bit of scientific detritus, best forgotten by serious evolutionary thinkers. Instead, it's a valuable tool in any serious evolutionary thinker's toolbox. At worst, group selection is a different modeling or accounting system for tracking evolutionary change, one that's largely redundant with more orthodox accounting systems; at best, it's a theoretical approach that can bring novel insights to tricky scientific puzzles.

First, let's tackle the controversy. Next, we'll walk through some of the idea's fraught history. Then I want to present a couple of toy scenarios that illustrate the general plausibility of group selectionist thinking. We'll consider the conceptual reasons that led many to abandon group selectionist thinking a few decades back. Finally, I want to argue that cultural transmission helps resolve some outstanding issues with the concept of group selection—*cultural group selection* might be an easier sell than *genetic group selection*. People who've read just enough about evolution to be confident that group selection is impossible, stay tuned: the mechanisms of cultural inheritance help resolve the fundamental issues that made genetic group selection look unlikely when it was popularly dismissed back in the 1970s.

HERE BE (THEORETICAL) DRAGONS

If, like a younger me, you've gotten your ideas about evolution from biology popularizers like Dawkins, or from public-facing evolutionary psychologists like Steven Pinker, you might now be thinking I must be some sort of a crank. Didn't sociobiologists of the 1970s conclusively dispatch group selectionism, in favor of inclusive fitness? Haven't serious evolutionary thinkers moved on?

In some scientific circles today, group selectionist thinking is still viewed with skepticism if not scorn. In 2012, for example, developmental and evolutionary psychologist Steven Pinker penned an essay for the online forum Edge* titled "The False Allure of Group Selection." In the piece, Pinker argues that modern science should move on from group selectionist thinking once and for all.[5] Pinker writes,

> Group selection has become a scientific dust bunny, a hairy blob in which anything having to do with "groups" clings to anything having to do with "selection." The problem with scientific dust bunnies is not just that they sow confusion; . . . the apparent plausibility of one restricted version of "group selection" often bleeds outwards to a motley collection of other, long-discredited versions. The problem is that it also obfuscates evolutionary theory by blurring genes, individuals, and groups as equivalent levels in a hierarchy of selectional units; . . . this is not how natural selection, analyzed as a mechanistic process, really works.

There you have it: group selection isn't just wrong, per Pinker, it is *fundamentally anti-Darwinian*. This claim hearkens back to Dawkins, who in *The Selfish Gene* dismissed group selectionist thinking as a theory that was "assumed to be true by biologists not familiar with the details of evolutionary theory," and that "commands little support within the ranks of those professional biologists who understand evolution." Quite clear, that.

---

* Edge was for a time a sort of online salon where public intellectuals thought weighty thoughts for all to see. It currently enjoys a less-than-savory reputation. You see, Edge's primary financial backer was Jeffrey Epstein, with literary agent and Edge founder John Brockman acting as an intermediary between Epstein's wealth and the intelligentsia: https://www.buzzfeednews.com/article/peteraldhous/jeffrey-epstein-john-brockman-edge-foundation.

Apparently, group selectionism only has supporters among rubes who don't properly understand evolution.[†]

Here we have two heavyweight evolutionary popularizers in Dawkins and Pinker. Both argue that group selectionism is the sort of hand-wavey pseudo-theory that only people with little to no understanding of evolutionary theory would adopt. It was wrong, wrongheaded, and fundamentally anti-Darwinian.

If group selectionism is thoroughly dead, ignored by serious scientists, skewered by Dawkins in 1976 and again by Pinker in 2012, then why am I including sections about it in this book? One possibility—one I consider regularly—is that I'm simply not a very good scientist. Another possibility—one we'll consider below—is that knee-jerk dismissals of group selectionist thinking, like those of Dawkins and Pinker, fail to engage with the robust science supporting sophisticated theories that include group-level evolutionary processes.

As we'll see in subsequent sections, group selectionist thinking is a tool, a mental prosthesis. It's no more than another theoretical tool in the evolutionary thinker's toolbox. That's all. Like all tools, it will prove to be more useful for some tasks than others. Scientists may choose to discard a perfectly useful tool from their own toolkit, for reasons of idiosyncratic personal taste or disciplinary convention. But they should be very cautious in telling other scientists which tools they should or shouldn't use. The confident proscriptive dismissals offered by Pinker and Dawkins fail to engage with group selectionism in a deep or meaningful way, and fall short of accurately describing their current states of evidence and consensus within the world of evolutionary theory.

MODELS AS LANGUAGES

Despite my initial knee-jerk dismissal of group selectionist thinking as a grad student, nowadays I'm more-or-less copacetic about the theoretical

[†] What about the eminent evolutionary biologists who'd been actively modeling and working with group selection ideas at the time—including no less an evolutionary thinker than William Hamilton, who worked to help George Price get his theoretical work mathematically vindicating group selection published in *Nature*? Are we to believe that Hamilton was No True Darwinian?

approach—especially as applied to cultural phenomena and cultural transmission. Fifteen or twenty years ago, I would've been a vocal cheerleader in Dawkins's and Pinker's anti-group-selectionist campaigns. I would have been astonished if you told then-me that I'd go on to productively use the concept of cultural group selection in my work. Having read a lot of popular evolution and evolutionary psychology books, I was confident of two undisputed facts. First, that appeals to culture were a form of wickedly leftist standard social science model blank slatism. Second, that only fools and charlatans still took group selection seriously. Cultural group selection was, to a younger Will Gervais, even worse than just a bad idea; it was in fact two separate wrongheaded ideas that somehow engaged in heretical miscegenation to create what must be an even more wrongheaded—even more heretical!—pseudoscientific spawn of blank slatism and discarded group selectionism.

How did I shift from vehement opposition to group selection to now embracing it in my work, in the form of cultural group selection? Simply put, my views on group selection changed as I began to read the primary scientific work on the topic, instead of relying on dismissive popular accounts of group selection from bestselling authors. Scientists may have been right to largely disregard the sorts of group selection ideas floating around in the 1950s and 1960s (as we'll see shortly), but modern group selection was far less silly and heretical than I'd been warned it would be by celebrity evolution popularizers. There was simply a lot more meat to the idea than their dismissals acknowledged.

As I learned how to read and understand the mathematical models that have formalized evolutionary theory over the years—learned how to minimally "read modelese," if you will—I came to realize that there was nothing wrongheaded or dangerous about group selectionist thinking. It was just a separate way to model evolutionary processes, a sort of separate accounting system that lets us track evolutionary change over time. For lots of phenomena, like altruism, one could model its evolution using the conventions of kin selection or inclusive fitness (as Dawkins and Pinker would have us solely do), or one could model its evolution using group selection conventions instead. Sometimes the result would be analytically simpler or more elegant and parsimonious using one modeling convention or the other. Some phenomena will seem simpler when modeled as inclusive fitness rather than group selection; for other phenomena, the reverse is true. But for the most part, the results could be translated from one convention to the other and back. In this way, the modeling conventions of inclusive fitness or group selection are far less like mutually exclusive Kuhnian paradigms, and far more like mutually translatable languages.

The mutual translatability of inclusive fitness and group selection was made vividly clear during a mathematical modeling class I took in graduate school. We were introduced to basic mathematical models of social evolution, including inclusive fitness mainstays like Hamilton's rule (rb > c, the idea that helping kin pays off to the extent that the costs of helping [c] must be less than the benefits accrued [b], weighted by the degree of relatedness [r]). At one point, we re-derived Hamilton's Rule using the Price Equation—a formalism that underpins many group selection models.[6] If we could start with what is fundamentally a group selection model and use it to derive a workhorse of inclusive fitness and kin selection models, it seemed that the two approaches were far more consilient than group selection opponents had let on in their popular writings.[7]

Just as one can translate a sentence from English to Mandarin, one can usually translate an evolutionary model from inclusive fitness lingo to group selection lingo—and vice versa! Some sentences might be structurally simpler in Mandarin, others in English. Some languages might even have words that are unwieldy to translate into another tongue. My daughter's favorite current example of this is the German *schadenfreude*, the state of ecstasy one can experience at another's suffering.[‡] Her favorite schadenfreude elicitor nowadays is passing gridlocked rush hour traffic on our bikes—she extracts great joy from the palpable frustration of stalled motorists as we happily pedal past. We can recognize the state of schadenfreude, whether we are English or German speakers. The feeling of schadenfreude may be more easily expressed in German than in English—one word versus a sentence to capture the feeling. But that doesn't imply that German is correct or that English is faulty and should be abandoned. It just means that for one particular idea, German proved a bit simpler. The fact that a sentiment might be easier to express in one language does not at all imply that we

‡ My Brunel buddy Michelle Kline tells me that in Fiji where she does work, the term *maleka* is used, and roughly translates to "delicious."

should abandon other languages. If anything, it suggests that we should all strive to learn more, not fewer, languages!

To bring the analogy full circle and return to group selection thinking and gene's-eye-view inclusive fitness thinking, the situation is similar. Some phenomena may be more easily modeled using an inclusive fitness framework; other phenomena are more easily captured with a group selection framing like the Price equation. This doesn't make either modeling "language" right or wrong, just as a handy term like *schadenfreude* doesn't render English a failed language. It can be tremendously useful to have multiple modeling "languages" to describe and explore different phenomena. The existence of multiple modeling languages in no way implies that one of them is wrong or should be abandoned—instead it implies that translators, folks who are fluent in both modeling "languages," are incredibly valuable scientists.

This brings us back to Pinker's Edge essay dismissing group selection as "a scientific dust bunny, a hairy blob." The essay spawned some twenty commentaries. Many agreed with Pinker that group selectionism was dead. A handful rejected his premise, arguing that Pinker had fundamentally misunderstood the issue and had not accurately portrayed the state of evolutionary theory regarding group selection. Interestingly, those who agreed with Pinker that group selectionism was muddle-headed came from a diverse group of scientific backgrounds. There were philosophers, there were psychologists of various stripes. Represented among those rebutting Pinker? Theoretical biologists and other scientists who regularly worked with and published primary modeling papers in evolutionary biology. Among those commentators who didn't primarily work with mathematical models of evolution, most agreed with Pinker that group selection was bad. Most of those who had published modeling papers in the main theoretical biology journals countered Pinker's dismissal. Here's what a few of them said.

Joe Henrich, himself a modeler and now Chair of Harvard's Department of Human Evolution, wrote: "What Steven Pinker wants banished from our science is a modeling tool that has proved useful for breaking down and analyzing different components of a selective process." Henrich likens group selection and inclusive fitness to separate accounting systems or coordinate systems that an aerospace engineer might consider—merely separate ways to track the same information. "Rejecting group selection models is like banning spherical coordinates because you prefer to do your verbal reasoning in Cartesian coordinates," Henrich notes drily.[8]

Switching from accounting or coordinate systems to languages, esteemed evolutionary biologist and modeler David Queller[9] (himself an inclusive fitness aficionado) wrote: "Modern group selection theory is as mathematically rigorous as individual selection or inclusive fitness theory. . . . I think of these less as alternative theories that make different predictions than as two different languages describing the same world. They simply divide up fitness in slightly different ways."

David Sloan Wilson,[10] who's been leading modeling efforts around multilevel selection theory in evolutionary biology for five decades, followed on Queller's linguistic analogy and wrote: "Queller compares the two theoretical frameworks to two languages, such as English and Russian, and appreciates that both languages can be useful. The challenge is to become bilingual and to identify the important issues that can now be addressed within either framework."

If a monolingual English-speaking critic declared Mandarin incomprehensible and useless (over the objections of bilingual speakers of both tongues, no less!), calling for its banishment from scholarship, we'd rightly dismiss the critique as facile. To readers still skeptical of group selection on the grounds of dismissals like Pinker's, I'd urge you to listen to the bilingual translators in this debate. To a first approximation, scientists from fields that rarely or never work firsthand with evolutionary models agreed with Pinker that group selection was wrong. In contrast, those scientists who regularly rolled up their sleeves to develop formal evolutionary models pushed back against Pinker's dismissal of a perfectly rigorous and useful scientific tool. The more firsthand experience a scientist had with the mathematical models that form the foundation of modern evolutionary theory, the less likely they were to agree with Pinker. The modelers' collective response was somewhat akin to a group of multilingual translators bemusedly looking on as some monolingual English speakers argued that some foreign languages should be abandoned because the English-only speakers found them unnecessarily confusing. Just as comprehensibility to English speakers is not the best measure of Mandarin's worth as a language, confusion among nonspecialist onlookers is not the barometer of scientific utility for a modeling tool.

The Pinker Edge back-and-forth illustrated the fraught present surrounding group selection theory. Despite a general consensus among theoretical biologists that group selectionist modeling is a perfectly rigorous and useful tool, scientists who are a step or two removed from the primary theoretical biology literature, like Pinker and many of his supporting commentators, nonetheless view group selection as anathema. Let's consider the history that led to wholesale dismissal of group selectionism.

HISTORICAL TRAJECTORIES AND CONCEPTUAL TIDYING

Group selectionist thinking has waxed and waned over the decades. Understanding rejection of it today (and over the previous twenty or so years) requires some appreciation for the intellectual history of the idea. We can trace group selectionist thinking in a Darwinian framework all the way back to Darwin himself.

Darwin recognized that there are lots of traits that are not especially beneficial to individuals holding them, at least as those individuals are in competition with their immediate peers. For example, self-sacrifice and altruism place individuals at a competitive disadvantage relative to the cheats and the moochers.[11] However, groups made of altruistic and self-sacrificial individuals could probably outcompete groups of selfish individuals. Within groups, selfishness prevails; between groups, selfishness fails. The classic read on the evolution of cooperation remains *The Selfish Gene* by Dawkins, but for a modern treatment I'd highly recommend Nichola Raihani's recent book *The Social Instinct*.[12]

To make this concrete, consider some trench warfare soldiers facing a rogue grenade. Diving on a hand grenade in the trenches is detrimental to the individual soldier doing the diving—with explosive finality!—but is good for the rest of the unit. Units with soldiers willing to sacrifice themselves for their brethren will outcompete units without such altruistic individuals. Self-sacrifice is supremely bad for the individuals who sacrifice, but groups whose members are willing to sacrifice themselves win.

Darwin saw these group-level competitive arrangements as rather crucial for the social evolution of our species. The quote at the outset of the chapter arises in Darwin's writing not in a section about how groups function, but instead from a discussion of how Darwin thinks our species evolved to have prosocial and moral faculties in the first place, in how we became so peculiarly cooperative relative to our closest primate relatives. Here's the Darwin quote above, expanded for some additional context:

> Turning now to the social and moral faculties. In order that primeval men, or the apelike progenitors of man, should become social, they must have acquired the same instinctive feelings, which impel other animals to live in a body; and they no doubt exhibited the same general disposition. They would have felt uneasy when separated from their comrades, for whom they would have felt some degree of love; they would have warned each other of danger, and have given mutual aid in attack or defence. All this implies some degree of sympathy, fidelity, and courage. Such social qualities, the paramount importance of which to the lower animals is disputed by no one, were no doubt acquired by the progenitors of man in a similar manner, namely, through natural selection, aided by inherited habit. When two tribes of primeval man, living in the same country, came into competition, if (other circumstances being equal) the one tribe included a great number of courageous, sympathetic and faithful members, who were always ready to warn each other of danger, to aid and defend each other, this tribe would succeed better and conquer the other. Let it be borne in mind how all-important in the never-ceasing wars of savages, fidelity and courage must be. The advantage which disciplined soldiers have over undisciplined hordes follows chiefly from the confidence which each man feels in his comrades. . . . Selfish and contentious people will not cohere, and without coherence nothing can be effected. A tribe rich in the above qualities would spread and be victorious over other tribes: but in the course of time it would, judging from all past history, be in its turn overcome by some other tribe still more highly endowed. Thus the social and moral qualities would tend slowly to advance and be diffused throughout the world.
>
> But it may be asked, how within the limits of the same tribe did a large number of members first become endowed with these social and moral qualities, and how was the standard of excellence raised? It is extremely doubtful whether the offspring of the more sympathetic and benevolent parents, or of those who were the most faithful to their comrades, would be reared in greater numbers than the children of selfish and treacherous parents belonging to the same tribe. He who was ready to sacrifice his life, as many a savage has been, rather than betray his comrades, would often

> leave no offspring to inherit his noble nature. The bravest men, who were always willing to come to the front in war, and who freely risked their lives for others, would on an average perish in larger numbers than other men. Therefore, it hardly seems probable that the number of men gifted with such virtues, or that the standard of their excellence, could be increased through natural selection, that is, by the survival of the fittest; for we are not here speaking of one tribe being victorious over another. . . .
>
> It must not be forgotten that although a high standard of morality gives but a slight or no advantage to each individual man and his children over the other men of the same tribe, yet that an increase in the number of well-endowed men and an advancement in the standard of morality will certainly give an immense advantage to one tribe over another. A tribe including many members who, from possessing in a high degree the spirit of patriotism, fidelity, obedience, courage, and sympathy, were always ready to aid one another, and to sacrifice themselves for the common good, would be victorious over most other tribes; and this would be natural selection. At all times throughout the world tribes have supplanted other tribes; and as morality is one important element in their success, the standard of morality and the number of well-endowed men will thus everywhere tend to rise and increase.

Darwin's casual period-era misogyny and ethnocentrism aside ("tribes" of "savage" "men"), this passage provides a remarkably clear description of how something like group selection could work, and in a way that Darwin himself saw as fully compatible with his view of natural selection. To sum, liberally pulling and paraphrasing quotes from the above passage, here's what Darwin thought:

> Our species' "social and moral faculties" did not arise because they pay immediate survival or reproductive dividends for individuals. Indeed, "the bravest men . . . would on an average perish in larger numbers than other men." Rather, these social and moral faculties arose because of their group-level consequences, because "a tribe . . . possessing in a high degree the spirit of patriotism . . . would be victorious over most other tribes." This group-based evolutionary outcome is entirely consistent with Darwin's own view of how evolution works: ". . . and this would be natural selection."

Here Darwin recognizes some inherent tension between the individual-level fitness consequences of a trait and its group-level consequences. *Within groups*, selfishness wins. But *between groups*, cooperation wins. Darwin was unclear on the mechanism of how exactly groups could stabilize cooperation and root out selfish free riders (he offers a speculative account centered around reputation, praise, and blame). But, as is often the case with Darwin, he rather precisely identified the intricate dynamics and tradeoffs of this evolutionary puzzle. How can groups maintain high levels of cooperation and therefore outcompete groups with more selfish members? How can a group of people (or proto-people) ensure that it has a high cooperative makeup—of "sympathy, fidelity, and courage" in Darwin's own words? Darwin saw group-level processes, one group outcompeting a rival group because of the composite interactions of its constituent individual pieces, as entirely consistent with natural selection.

Fast forward a century or so to the 1950s and 1960s. Thanks to work of people like V. C. Wynne-Edwards,[13] group selection was seen as a viable explanation for lots of behavior in the animal kingdom. Group selection was invoked almost casually, to explain a wide variety of phenomena. How do organisms avoid overgrazing a resource? Group selection! How does cooperation evolve? Group selection!

The group selection ideas of the day were not much like their rigorously mathematically modeled counterparts of today. Instead, they resulted from intuitive-sounding verbal descriptions of how individuals would sacrifice themselves "for the good of the species." A poster child for group selection of the day is lemmings, a small rodent that—per popular accounts persisting to this day—would purportedly commit suicide to maintain population numbers and ease overgrazing risks. This suicidal story turns out to be apocryphal. Lemmings don't deliberately commit suicide. But you might object that you've seen video evidence of lemming suicide! If you've seen old grainy footage of lemmings plummeting off a cliff "for the good of the species" from Disney's *White Wilderness* documentary, you've witnessed a cruel fraud. The film crew staged this, forcing hapless lemmings to their death for the sake of a great shot.

Cruel fraud aside, lemming suicide ably shows how many people conceived of group selection at the time. Supposedly, individuals would sacrifice themselves for the good of their groups, or for the good of their entire species. The idea sounds intuitive enough—after all, self-sacrificial behavior was clearly bad for those being sacrificed, with benefits accruing to other group members. But evolution doesn't work like this at all! Individuals don't act "for the good of the species," and indeed the species is a scientific abstraction rather than a meaningful evolutionary unit.

Intuitive or not, this conception of group selection proved to be naive and unsupportable, hence its broad dismissal in the late 1960s and early 1970s. The next sections lay bare the precise conceptual issues that led to naive group selection's downfall, and paved the way for its modern resurgence, albeit in a vastly more rigorous form. To get there, let's first play with some basic evolutionary models.

PRISONERS AND STAGS: TWO TOY EXAMPLES

As an interlude, let's introduce a couple of games—toy models that can be useful intuition pumps for seeing how something like group selection might work—at least in some select circumstances. Games and models like this are hugely important. They let scientists transparently check their assumptions in simplistic and contrived situations; they're rigorous thought experiments that can help hone our intuitions.

Pretty Deadly, by Kelly Sue DeConnick and Emma Rios,[14] is one of my all-time favorite comic series. It's a visually stunning hybrid of western, noir, dark fantasy, and mythology, genuinely mind-blowing stuff. In one passage, one of the main characters, Sissy (who by the by happens to be a sort of incarnation of death, in charge of maintaining the boundary between living and dead worlds), is trying to decide on a course of action on a matter of great importance. To aid in her decision-making, she constructs a tiny model world in a glassy skull terrarium, hoping to use this model world to better understand the broader world. An onlooker explains, "Building a model of a thing is a wonderful way to study it . . . a model of a world. A particular world, or a possible world, or a terrible world." The model world is vastly simpler than the real world, it's far from a realistic re-creation of the world, and that's the point. Sissy's companion, trying to appreciate the import of the model, asks, "Seeing it there on a small scale . . . does it help you imagine what this world might look like if you could just see it from far away?"

This little comic book passage illustrates my view of scientific modeling as well as any I know of. In science, models are little toy worlds whose parameters we can simplify and control. They allow us to imagine a very simple *possible world*—usually a possible world that resembles our world in some crucial way, while removing additional messy complexities. Scientists can tweak the simplistic parameters and see how the possible world is affected. We all know that the models aren't fully realistic, but they are useful precisely because their simplicity can reveal previously hidden dynamics and interactions. Seeing it on a small scale helps us imagine what our world could look like. Done well, models help us cut through complexity and isolate just what we want to examine, after filtering out all the bumbling buzzing confusion the real world presents to scientists. As Paul Smaldino puts it in a recent paper, "Models are stupid, and we need more of them."[15] Models allow scientists to create their own toy worlds where they have full control, to see what happens when the settings are altered.

These models ideally capture some key aspects of the real world, but should never be confused for the real world. They are a scientist's attempt to distill some useful truth from a known oversimplification, a way to learn something new from a world they have full control over.

That's all we're doing here, playing with a couple of toy model worlds to see what sort of possible world might allow something like group selection to work. Crucially, in this section I'm not claiming that these toy examples actually capture how human groups work, or how cultural group selection might work. Instead, I'd just like to chip away at the intuitive resistance some folks might have toward even contemplating group selection. We'll turn to two theoretic games: the Prisoner's Dilemma and the Stag Hunt. Like the incarnation of death in *Pretty Deadly*, we're imagining possible worlds to better understand how things could work in our own world.

In the familiar Prisoner's Dilemma, we imagine two co-conspirators arrested for the same crime. The prosecutors have a weak case, not enough to pin a heavy sentence on either inmate. If both heisters keep their lips sealed, they'll each get a small sentence. The prosecutors need one inmate to flip—to provide incriminating evidence against the other. They offer a deal: testify against your co-conspirator and you'll get off free. The only downside? Your buddy goes to prison for a long time. If both flip, the deal's off, and both conspirators get a modest sentence. We might illustrate the payoffs as shown in figure 7.1, with one prisoner's choice represented by rows, the other by columns, and the numbers within depict the length of each prisoner's sentence. Within each cell, A's sentence is along the left, and B's sentence is along the top. So to read the table, if B cooperates and A defects, then A gets 0 years in prison and B gets 5; if both cooperate then each gets 1 year. If both rat the other out, they both go to jail for 3 years.

As you can see, each player's best outcome is to be the sole defector—they get off with no jail time whatsoever. Each player's worst outcome is to be the sole cooperator, earning 5 hard years. The best aggregate outcome (adding both players' payoffs) is for both to cooperate, and each gets just one year behind bars. But no matter what the other player chooses, defection pays better than cooperation. Check the math for yourself. If B cooperates, A is better defecting (0 years < 1 year); if B defects, A is still better at defecting (3 years < 5 years). Here's why the Prisoner's Dilemma is, well, a dilemma: the best overall outcome is mutual cooperation, but each player benefits from defection at every possible turn.

Imagine a world where everyone cooperates, and suddenly there arises a lone defector. This rebel will dominate! Our rebel will get off free every time, 0 years in prison, while the cooperative majority will net 1 year in prison for almost every of their interactions (the exception? The 5-year sentence when they're occasionally paired with the interloping rebel). Our selfish defector reaps the rewards of others' cooperation without having to pay any costs. To the extent that the payoffs influence reproductive rates (or something similar), then pretty quickly cooperation will break down

B's Choice

A's Choice	Cooperate	Defect
Cooperate	1 1	0 5
Defect	5 0	3 3

Figure 7.1. Prisoner's Dilemma payoff matrix.

and the group will consist of nothing but defectors, who after all do better no matter what their partners choose. Now imagine the opposite scenario, a world chock full of nothing but defectors. Would a cooperative strategy similarly invade and take over? Could a sole cooperator thrive in this selfish world? Not at all—this sucker will get obliterated at every turn! A sole cooperator in a defector's world will only ever get the maximum sentence.

In one world, the sole deviant prospers, and we'd expect their selfishness over time to spread and take over the whole group. In the other world, the sole deviant does worst of anyone, and we'd expect the deviant cooperation to be pruned from the population. In both worlds, the end result is that defection roots out cooperation. Because defectors could "invade" a cooperative world (that is, the first defector does better than the baseline cooperator payoff), but cooperators couldn't invade a defector's world, we can call defection in Prisoner's Dilemma a stable strategy.[§] Given just these two strategies, things pretty quickly run to nothing but defection. So even though the overall "group" payoff—just adding both prisoners' payoffs together—favors cooperation at that group level, the individual benefits of defection are more immediate. Here, the group-level optimum of cooperation just can't get off the ground, because individual defection is too potent a temptation.

Now let's turn to the Stag Hunt,[16] which, like the Prisoner's Dilemma, comes with a cute little backstory. Instead of imagining criminals, we now imagine hunters. In the toy world we construct now, our hunters can either hunt hares—a reliable if uninspiring prey—or stags—a much more impressive haul. The catch is that while everyone can catch a hare on their own, hunters can only take down stags in pairs. When two hunters take down a stag, they split the goodies equally. Instead of choosing whether to cooperate or defect, in this game our players merely choose what they'd like to hunt. Let's draw up a payoffs table, as before, only instead of imagining years in prison being tallied within, we'll imagine how many gold pieces each hunter could sell their haul for. Figure 7.2 shows how things look, using the same row/column table conventions as on page 166.

[§] It's stable, given just these two strategies. Things get complicated quickly once you start considering additional strategies. If you're under the impression that tit-for-tat always wins, that's again a drastic oversimplification that describes one result from one tournament and is very much not a general take-home message from the modeling work over the years.

A's Choice \ B's Choice	Stag	Hare
Stag	3 3	1 0
Hare	0 1	1 1

Figure 7.2. Stag Hunt payoff matrix.

Everyone can nab a hare on their own, which they could sell for 1 gold coin. Coordinated pairs can take down a stag, worth 6 gold coins, that get shared equally (3 apiece). But if one partner chooses to stag hunt while their partner hunts hares, the lone stag chaser returns empty handed and receives 0 gold coins.

As with our Prisoner's Dilemma example, let's see if there are stable strategies. Imagine a world where everyone hunts stags. Each individual returns with 3 gold coins on every outing. A lone hare hunter in this world doesn't utterly fail—they get a gold coin every round after all—but they always do worse than their stag-hunting majority peers. Now imagine a hare-hunting world, with everyone always returning from a hunt successfully with a 1-gold-coin hare. A solitary stag hunter moving into this world will quickly be outcompeted—they never have a stag-hunting partner, and thus always return empty handed. In a stag-hunting world, stag hunters outcompete hare hunters. In a hare-hunter's world, hare hunters beat stag hunters. In either world, deviance never pays. Thus in this game, we have two different stable equilibria: either everyone hunts stags or everyone hunts hares.

In this example we could imagine a whole bunch of independent groups that have stabilized into either a stag-hunting "culture" or a hare-hunting "culture." Both types of cultures are internally stable—solitary hare hunters are unwelcome and unprofitable in stag cultures, and solitary stag hunters are unwelcome and unprofitable in hare cultures. But the two sorts of "cultures" don't do equally well at the group level. Each round of hunting, the stag-hunting groups get higher overall payoffs than do the hare-hunting groups—they net 6 total gold coins instead of 2.

In the imaginary world we've created in the Stag Hunt game, we'd expect something like group selection to happen. It's practically inevitable, given the parameters we've modeled. Groups stabilize around different equilibria, but not all equilibria are created equal. Within groups, it pays to do what everyone else is doing. But between groups, there are huge payoff differences, where some internally stable strategies are clearly better than others.

If you've been reading a steady diet of popular evolution and evolutionary psychology books that talk about how group selection is impossible (or at least implausible or muddle-headed), I hope these little toy examples erode your confidence, at least a tiny bit. If we lived in a world well described by something like the Stag Hunt game, something like group selection would be almost inevitable. As always, though, the devil's in the details, and I don't want to push the Stag Hunt comparison too far or take it too literally. Many or even most interesting puzzles surrounding the evolution of cooperation will be better captured by a game like the Prisoner's Dilemma than by a coordination game like the Stag Hunt; I'm not at all trying to claim that Stag Hunt proves that group selection has been a potent force in our species' evolution, or any such grandiose claim. Once again, this section is only here to plant a seed that *something like group selection is not only theoretically possible, but actually quite probable, given some types of worlds we could imagine and model.*

The question now is not whether group selection could ever work—it can, in something like the Stag Hunt game, and under conditions we'll see in subsequent selections. The question is whether our world is one of those possible worlds where conditions arise that make group selection an evolutionary force worth reckoning with. In the next section, we'll see why a genetic inheritance system like ours might not be a good fit for group selection. In the section after that, we'll see why a *cultural inheritance system* like ours might be an excellent fit indeed.

WHY (GENETIC) GROUP SELECTION IS TRICKY

Dawkins's *The Selfish Gene* came out to great acclaim in 1976, and it quickly became the most successful public-facing popular account of developments in sociobiology and evolutionary theory from the 1960s and 1970s. In it, Dawkins dismissed group selection as a theory that was effectively dead, even if some of its loyal adherents were too dense and ill-informed about evolution to acknowledge the fatality with which it'd been dispatched. His treatment of group selection is not especially thorough—among other things, it fails to even mention developments like the Price equation, published in *Nature* just a few years prior and with great potential to mathematically bolster a new wave of group selectionist thinking.[17] But what his treatment lacked in comprehensiveness it made up for in rhetorical aplomb.

The book briefly describes the position attributed to Wynne-Edwards that group selection worked—even "for the good of the species" style group selection—because altruistic groups could outcompete groups that did not include fully altruistic members. That logic, so far as it goes, is inevitable: cooperative groups would self-evidently outcompete selfish groups. The catch is that it would be impossible for cooperative groups to remain cooperative, because selfish members of otherwise cooperative groups come out best of all! Being a member of a cooperative group is great, *especially if you don't have to cooperate yourself.* Here is his initial dismissal of group selection, front-ended on page 8 of the book:

> [Group selection as described by folks like Wynne-Edwards fails because . . .] Even in the group of altruists, there will almost certainly be a dissenting minority who refuse to make any sacrifice. If there is just one selfish rebel, prepared to exploit the altruism of the rest, then he, by definition, is more likely than they are to survive and have children. Each of these children will tend to inherit his selfish traits. After several generations of this natural selection, the "altruistic group" will be over-run by selfish individuals, and will be indistinguishable from the selfish group. Even if we grant the improbable chance existence initially of pure altruistic groups without any rebels, it is very difficult to see what is to stop selfish individuals migrating in from neighbouring selfish groups, and, by inter-marriage, contaminating the purity of the altruistic groups.

The argument seems impregnable. Yes, Dawkins acknowledges that a purely cooperative group would outcompete a noncooperative group. The catch is that within an otherwise cooperative group, selfish individuals prosper most of all. Without a mechanism for kicking out the freeloaders, for insulating cooperative groups against selfish intruders, group-level competition is rendered impotent as an evolutionary force. Dawkins and others seemed to acknowledge that some form of group selection might be plausible in principle, but that observable facts about our world render it highly improbable in practice.

Developments within theoretical biology around this same time seemed to provide a similar conclusion that group selection might be theoretically sound in principle, but was implausible in the world we actually live in. An eccentric autodidact polymath named George Price had recently presented a new mathematical formalism for modeling evolutionary change—what is now known as the Price Equation. As an outsider and an unconventional thinker, Price had a lot of trouble even publishing his work. In the end, he found an unlikely benefactor in William Hamilton, one of the world's most preeminent evolutionary thinkers, and a key proponent of the inclusive fitness approaches that were well on their way to dethroning group selection as a viable mainstream evolutionary concept. Price sent his work to Hamilton, who quickly saw that the math was sound, that Price had stumbled across a genuinely innovative way to mathematically model evolutionary processes. With help (and a bit of light academic sleight of hand) from Hamilton, the work was published in the top journal *Nature* in 1970. As an aside: Price became obsessed with altruism, gave away many of his possessions, let destitute folks squat in his home, and eventually committed suicide via a set of nail scissors to the carotid. For a fascinating dive into Price's life, and the import of his work on the eponymous Price Equation, I highly recommend the book *The Price of Altruism*[18] by Oren Harman.¶

The Price equation simultaneously put the concept of group selection on firm mathematical and theoretical footing, while also seemingly showing that it was unworkable in principle—at least for genetic systems like biologists of the day were trying to explain. Let's see how.

¶ If any film producers are reading this, a George Price biopic would make great viewing, and actor Jared Harris is a dead ringer for Price. Please contact me to arrange payment of my finder's fee for this brilliant cinematic idea.

In short, the Price Equation partitioned evolutionary change into a within-group and a between-group component. Overall rates of evolutionary change in some trait could be broken down into the following components:

- The fitness consequences for individuals, within groups
- The amount of variability among individuals within a group
- The fitness consequences for individuals between groups, based on group-level differences
- The amount of variability between groups

Crucially, the within-group fitness consequences were proportional to the available within-group variability. Similarly, the between-group fitness consequences were proportional to the amount of stable between-group variability. Natural selection can only act along the gradient of available variability (remember our three key ingredients of natural selection: variability, fitness consequences, heredity). In short, we could draw up evolutionary change described by the Price Equation with the following simplistic formula:

Overall evolutionary change = (bgF × bgV) + (wgF × wgV)

where:
bgF = between-group fitness consequences
bgV = between-group variability
wgF = within-group fitness consequences
wgV = within-group variability

Hearkening back to Dawkins's dismissal of group selection, quoted above, here's what we find. Groups of cooperators outcompete groups of selfish jerks (between-group fitness consequences are positive for cooperators, bgF > 0), but within groups individual cooperators suffer at the expense of the cheaters and the moochers (within-group fitness consequences are negative for cooperators, wgF < 0). Mutation and other chance processes can be assumed to generate a steady diet of variability within groups—variability being the raw fuel for natural selection (wgV > 0). Because the within-group dynamics drive down cooperation rates over time, and selfish individuals joining otherwise cooperative groups (via mutation or migration) prosper, it's not feasible to keep cooperative groups uniformly cooperative. Even modest rates of migration between groups would thus quickly drive between-group variability down to zero (bgV = 0). Without raw between-group variability to work with, the self-evident fitness benefits that wholly cooperative groups might enjoy become moot. Mutation and migration will give selfishness an easy foothold in cooperative groups, compromising their uniform cooperativeness and thus their between-group advantage.

The key challenge here is that the genetic transmission systems that Dawkins and others considered don't provide a good mechanism for firmly maintaining between-group boundaries. Even the modest between-group migration rates observed and inferred for humans are vastly too high to maintain stable genetic differences between groups. As species go, we're simply too mobile and amorously frisky to maintain solid reproductive boundaries between populations.[19] Thus variability between groups cannot be maintained, and the between-group fitness benefits are effectively multiplied by zero, reducing the Price Equation to one that purely focuses on individual selection within groups.

Overall evolutionary change = (bgF × bgV) + (wgF × wgV)

When between-group variability (bgV) becomes zero, we are left only with:

Overall evolutionary change = (bgF × 0) + (wgF × wgV)

Overall evolutionary change = (wgF × wgV)

Here we started with an equation that included both within- and between-groups components, and ended up with a result implying that only individual-level selection matters. Even starting with a formula that considers group selection, we've concluded that individual selection is all that really matters when push comes to shove. Lack of stable between-group variability makes the entire between-group component of the formula cancel out.

The Price Equation, like Dawkins's verbal logic rejecting group selection, paints a grim picture for genetic group selection in our lineage and others like it. Realistic migration rates drive between-group variability to zero, and the entire between-group component gets similarly driven to zero. In short, without a clear mechanism for maintaining stable variation between groups, we shouldn't expect to see much in terms of group-level selection, even if it proves both theoretically elegant and possible in principle.

To some, this insight killed group selection dead. To others, however, it seemed that this only killed the sorts of group selection processes that could be undermined by modest rates of migration between groups. But if we can imagine other inheritance systems that aren't as susceptible to having between-group variability diluted by migration, we might just be able to salvage some semblance of group selection.

CULTURE MAINTAINS GROUP BOUNDARIES

When organisms migrate to a new group, they bring their genes with them. Their genes don't change as they settle in. If they interbreed in the new group, their genes will be shuffled into the new group's genetic deck. If there's a steady rate of migration between groups, this constant genetic reshuffling will render the divides between groups effectively nonexistent—well-mixed groups effectively become one giant group, at the level of genes. If organisms migrate and interbreed at even modest levels, genetic differences between groups cease to meaningfully exist. This deprives group selection of its raw material—variability!—and means that evolutionary consequences will pretty much solely be felt at the level of competition between individuals, rather than groups.

The above observation is taken by many to be the conceptual deathknell of group selectionist thinking. Recall that this logic was the entirety of Dawkins's conceptual dismissal of group selection in *The Selfish Gene*. But it turns out not to be a general problem for all group selectionist ideas, merely those evolutionary systems that are underpinned by an inheritance system that cannot easily sustain between-group differences. Migration and genetic intermixing kill genetic group selection, but they don't nullify the potential for group selection acting on other inheritance systems.

Enter culture.

We're endowed with genes by our parents, and they remain with us pretty much unchanged for our entire lives. Culture ain't like this! We are constantly learning new cultural information via the various learning strategies we considered back in chapter 5. We copy majorities (conformist transmission), elites (prestige bias), and people who walk the talk rather than just talking the talk (CREDs). When we learn cultural information, it's not locked in for life like genes. Culture isn't about high-fidelity transmission of particulate bits of culture like memes. We change our beliefs and behaviors in line with new culturally acquired information. When we move, we can assimilate and adapt.

While our genes remain unchanged, our culturally acquired inheritance is constantly shifting. These fuzzy aspects of cultural transmission make it uniquely powerful for maintaining group lines. Take conformist transmission, for example. We like to copy what lots of others in our groups are doing. We model our beliefs and practices on those that are credibly evinced by lots of people in our surrounding cultural milieu. When people use conformist learning biases to copy local majorities, there's a lot of potential for forming and maintaining more or less discrete groups. This dynamic—local conformist copying generating stable groups—is pithily summarized in the title of a prominent paper by cultural evolution pioneers Joe Henrich and Robert Boyd: "The Evolution of Conformist Transmission and the Emergence of Between-Group Differences."[20] Conformist learning is a useful cultural learning strategy that helps individual people pick up handy information from others. As an emergent property, it creates and maintains stable between-group variability in cultural traits.

Conformist learning isn't the only cultural evolutionary factor that reinforces group boundaries. Cultural evolutionists like Maciek Chudek and Joe Henrich have argued that we have an evolved "norm psychology."[21] In essence, that we have a proclivity for inferring what's locally normative, and following that. Beyond simply learning local norms, we also seem highly motivated to actively enforce them. Deviance is often punished, formally or informally. Modeling work shows that this sort of norm punishment can stabilize just about any norm within groups. Think about fashion trends, patterns of speech, food preferences, cooperative norms, marriage customs, you name it! Where local deviance from norms is punished, we'll see stable differences between groups in their preferred norms.

In the Prisoner's Dilemma we considered previously, there was just one stable equilibrium: selfish defection. In the Stag Hunt, however, we saw two stable equilibria: locally stable hare hunting and locally stable stag hunting. Conformist learning, norm psychology, and punishment of deviance[22] can, at the level of cultural evolution, create a blizzard of different stable equilibria for different cultural norms. Instead of just having hare groups and stag groups, norm psychology and conformist transmission let us imagine a vast number of internally stable groups, cohering around different specific norms.

Picture a large global population of individual agents. They could be humans, simulated computer agents, Fraggles, Popples,** anything of this sort. Within the global population, there are smaller clustered groups of neighbors. The groups may initially be formed by geographic boundaries, chance migrations, or other happenstance events. Genetically speaking, if there are reasonable amounts of migration between the groups, there won't be stable between-group boundaries—the overall population has some lumpiness but is generally well-mixed when it comes to genes. Culturally speaking, however, we can picture each group finding its own stable equilibrium point on various cultural norms. These might be different norms on cooperation, on fashion, on food production and consumption, on reproduction, or on religious beliefs. Groups who like spicy food and worship a punitive god; groups who prefer bland food and animist spirits; groups who fight, feast, and f . . . reproduce, all in the name of some Dionysian deity. You get the drift. Cultural forces like conformist transmission and norm psychology ensure that the groups remain stably variable, that boundaries are maintained over time. Migrants from one group to another are likely to enculturate and assimilate, or keep moving on until they find a group with norms more befitting their proclivities. Within each group, it pays to conform; in this way groups diverge and remain culturally distinct.

Recall that this is basically how things worked in the Stag Hunt: we ended up with stable groups of stag hunters and stable groups of hare hunters. *But the stag hunters on average did better than the hare hunters.* This is precisely what we'd expect to happen in our culture example. If groups are locally conforming to any of a blizzard of stable norms, be they about reproduction or food or what-have-you, between-group differences will persist over time. Migrants from one group to another can conform to local norms—here is one key difference between genes and culture! But by chance or innovation, some group norms will be more helpful than others, more conducive to group thriving.[23] Cooperative-norm groups will outcompete selfish-norm groups. Fecund-norm groups will outbreed chaste-norm groups. Militaristic- or missionistic-norm groups will spread at the expense of privately pacifist-norm groups.

** Remember Popples? Those fuzzy be-pouched critters of TV and plush toy popularity?

This all sounds fine in principle, but does it work in practice? Let's look at a few examples that illustrate both how culture reinforces group distinctions when genes cannot, and also how those stable between-group differences can profoundly affect the long-term success of those groups.

GENETIC SHUFFLING ALONGSIDE CULTURAL CLUSTERING

Population geneticists can use a statistic called FST to describe the genetic differentiation between two groups. In a nutshell, FST tells us how much observed genetic variability in an overall population comes from differences *between groups* within that overall population, as opposed to from differences *between individuals* within groups. For example, in a sample consisting of both British and Canadian people, FST would index how much of the overall observed genetic variability could be described along the "British versus Canadian" axis, rather than among folks within each country. A higher FST merely means that more of the observed variability falls across group boundaries than within them.

One can compute cultural FST as well, looking at how much variability in attitudes, values, beliefs, or norms can be attributed to differences between groups, rather than to individual variability within those groups.[24] To make this concrete, think of a single sort of cultural trait that might vary both within and between groups. The word *pants*, for example. If we took our same sample of Brits and Canucks and indexed the various ways that everyone conceives of "pants" we might try to figure out how much of that variability comes down to Britishness or Canadianness, rather than personal idiosyncrasy within each country. It turns out that the word *pants* will evoke entirely different concepts for our two groups of people—Canadians will picture something that goes on the outside (blue jeans are a form of "pants") whereas Brits will picture an undergarment (boxers-versus-briefs is a "pants" debate in Britain). In this silly example, most of our observed variability in what "pants" are will come down to national origin, rather than personal whim. If you repeat this for lots of words and traits and values—what is "hockey" or "football" or "the prime minister"—you could calculate an overall cultural FST that tells us the degree to which these different values or traits differ across national clusters, rather than within them.

In a neat paper, Bell, Richerson, and McElreath[25] calculated both standard genetic FST and a novel index of cultural FST worldwide in human populations, allowing them to ask whether genes or culture show greater degrees of group-level clustering. Their analysis showed that (consistent with lots of previous work), our species is genetically quite homogeneous and well-mixed—we're one big human race, without a lot of notable genetic differences across groups, and those between-group genetic differences pale in comparison to the massive degree of genetic variability within groups. In contrast, cultural FST values were drastically higher. Genetic variability overwhelmingly exists within groups, with much similarity between groups. For example, there's much more genetic diversity within the continent of Africa than between the occupants of all the other continents, a remarkable pattern that joins now-overwhelming evidence pointing to our species' African origins and much-later global colonization. Variability in cultural traits, on the other hand, fell largely across group lines. Within groups, people share cultural values; most of the action for variability in cultural traits, however, falls across group lines.

Genetic transmission yields well-mixed global populations with little between-group clustering. Cultural transmission yields largely homogeneous groups that differ drastically from each other. Genes don't yield enough stable between-group variation to fuel genetic group selection. Culture, on the other hand, yields ample amounts of between-group variability as fodder for the engine of cultural group selection. The Bell paper we've been discussing explicitly links the high observed cultural FST rates to their potential for creating cultural group selection effects, specifically aimed at the evolution of cooperation (much as Darwin argued some seventeen decades ago). The paper's title? "Culture Rather Than Genes Provides Greater Scope for the Evolution of Large-Scale Human Prosociality."

The previous section laid out the conceptual and theoretical argument for how culture could salvage group selection. This section provided some quantitative evidence in support of the fact that culture provides stable group-level variability, which might help lead to cooperation via group selection—much as Darwin argued. Theory meets evidence, if you will, in pointing toward cultural group selection as a potentially vital part of our human origin story. Theory and evidence are nice and all, but this is a popular science book, so the argument in favor of cultural group selection isn't really complete until I sprinkle an evocative anecdote on top.

SHAKERS AND LATTER-DAY SAINTS

The Shakers and the Latter-Day Saints[††]—more formally called the United Society of Believers in Christ's Second Appearing, and the Church of Jesus Christ of Latter-Day Saints, respectively—are two Christian offshoot movements that rose to prominence in the United States in the nineteenth century. Both initially developed as religious communities who set themselves apart from the rest of society, including more mainstream-at-the-time Christianity. They share some common features, but for this anecdotal exploration we'll focus on a few key differences in their norms surrounding family and reproduction, and the very predictable consequences those norms wrought over the decades.

The Shakers originally formed in England in the late 1700s, but found a foothold in America—as many Christian and Christian-adjacent religious groups did at the time, following the religious liberty the fledgling nation promised (for Christians at least). They formed utopian communes, founded on principles of egalitarianism, pacifism, and simplicity. They practiced what was for the time a radical gender egalitarianism. Women held leadership positions in the church and communes. By the mid-1800s, there were a few thousand Shakers in a couple dozen communes scattered throughout the northeastern United States. They reached a population nadir of somewhere in the ballpark of five thousand to six thousand members.

The Latter-Day Saints also rose to prominence in the northeast United States in the early 1800s. Founded by self-proclaimed prophet Joseph Smith in upstate New York in the 1820s, they spread west under subsequent leaders, finding a physical and spiritual home in Utah, where they are the most prominent and powerful religious group today.

Both the Shakers and the Latter-Day Saints developed into groups with strong and coherent identities. They were communal in nature, and insular. This insularity presented as strong norms that stabilized within these groups, and that helped set these groups apart from their surrounding communities. In the parlance of this chapter, there was strong between-group variability maintained by the tight cultural norms in both communal religious movements.

[††] Also colloquially known as Mormons: *Mormon* is a commonly used term, but since 2018 the Church has noted that *Latter-Day Saint* is the preferred nomenclature, as *Mormon* arose as a pejorative term.

Despite having commonalities as utopian commune Christian offshoot new religious movements, the Shakers and Latter-Day Saints had hugely different group norms, especially when it came to reproduction and family life. You see, the Shakers practiced universal celibacy. No marriage, no sex. They viewed sex as the original and universal sin, and wanted no part of it. In contrast, the Latter-Day Saints to this day are seen as having incredibly strong pro-family norms.[‡‡] The early church enthusiastically practiced plural marriage—a polite euphemism for aggressive polygamy in which elite men would take many wives. To provide just one poignant example, the LDS church's second leader, Brigham Young, took sixteen wives and fathered more than fifty children. Many of his sons followed in his reproductive footsteps, and by twenty-five years after Young's death he had an estimated one thousand direct descendants. Do this calculus for any of your ancestors who've passed a couple of decades ago and you'll see just how staggering that number is.

Here we have two different new religious movements coming up in the same region, at roughly the same time. They similarly insulated themselves from mainstream American life, rigidly maintaining their cultural barriers. But they had vastly different culturally learned and enforced norms around sex and reproduction. Shakers practiced universal celibacy—no sex at all, for anyone. Latter-Day Saints, on the other hand, had norms that enabled them to be as fruitful and multiplicative as logistically possible.

It's not difficult to see how these norms could have profound impacts on the groups that held them, over cultural evolutionary time. The Latter-Day Saints have been among the fastest growing religions in the world, and boast some sixteen and a half million members spread across the globe. In contrast, the Shakers have not fared numerically well. In 2019 the Shaker newsletter *The Clarion* announced the church's full and complete membership list: Brother Andrew, Brother Arnold, and Sister June.

IN (SOME) GODS WE TRUST: BIG GODS AND RELIGIOUS PROSOCIALITY

The Shakers and Latter-Day Saints vividly illustrate how cultural norms and beliefs can impact the long-run success of groups that hold them. One

‡‡ Including the various conservative political positions that these days are called by their fans "pro-family" even though they tend to rigidly prescribe a very specific and narrow view of both marriage and family.

group has prospered and spread; the other has dwindled to near extinction. Their differing success is directly attributable to culturally learned beliefs held within each group, specifically about family and procreation. Moving forward, we'll extend this idea—that group norms and beliefs influence group success—and see if we can gain some insights into why the world's religious landscape looks as it does today.

The biggest global faiths of today—Christianity, Islam, Hinduism—feature deities that are, to varying degrees, highly powerful, knowledgeable, and concerned with human behavior. These gods are immensely powerful, have access to privileged information, and are morally concerned with the thoughts and actions of humankind. This makes them very strange gods, by the standard of all the gods in all the religions the world has seen. Most gods have been small and local. Their powers are limited. They might be able to access some privileged information, but are far from omniscient. Some are described as relatively amoral (think of the Greek pantheon's petty squabbling with each other that leaves humans trampled along the way) or parochially moral, looking out only for their chosen people above all others (the early Old Testament's Yahweh, like many other similar gods-of-one-tribe-or-another of the era and area, comes to mind here). Over the millennia, these myriad small, local, and morally ambiguous gods have been replaced in the minds of believers by just a few big, powerful, and morally universalizing gods. This represents a thorough and rapid demographic shift regarding which sorts of gods occupy the minds of humankind. Most people living today believe in gods that are, historically speaking, really quite peculiar.

How have just a select few and atypical gods gone on to effectively capture the global market of believers? The remainder of this chapter argues that the few successful gods have "won" the battle for adherents in large part because the religions that worship them have features that have helped their groups outcompete rivals. In short, that certain features of certain religions have proven to be incredibly useful in cultural evolutionary competition—that cultural group selection has favored some religious concepts over others. These concepts have been favored not because their contents are especially catchy or memorable or intuitive, but because their contents motivate actions that benefit cultural groups.

Our discussion here is brief, but if you find the arguments intriguing, you can find them developed in greater depth in books like Henrich's *The*

WEIRDest People in the World,[26] or—especially!—in Norenzayan's *Big Gods*.[27] D. S. Wilson's *Darwin's Cathedral*[28] is also a treasure trove of excellent insights, both about multilevel selection theory (which Wilson has backed since the 1970s) and religion. Haidt comes close in *The Righteous Mind*,[29] but his argument rests upon genetic group selection and thus ultimately fails for the reasons outlined a few sections back.[§§]

TWO CURIOUS TRENDS

Ara Norenzayan's book *Big Gods* invites readers to ponder two puzzling anthropological and historical trends. First, many cultures shifted from small-scale hunting and foraging lifestyles in small bands of perhaps a few dozen to a hundred members to a setup involving larger-scale cooperation, replete with cities and agriculture and hierarchies and all the other trappings of state-level societies composed of thousands to hundreds of thousands of individuals. This shift represents a key turning point for our species! The shift in scale of cooperation is astounding and unprecedented, with a species rather rapidly altering its default mode of social organization.

The second puzzling trend is an apparent shift in gods. You see, the shift to larger-scale cooperation roughly parallels the emergence of the big, powerful, and morally concerned gods that typify the world's dominant religions today.

---

§§ Shortly after *The Righteous Mind* came out, Haidt gave a book talk at UBC and then met with several of us graduate students. My then-co-student and now Brunel colleague Aiyana Willard asked Haidt if he was at all concerned that rigorous modeling work showed that the genetic group selection aspect of his book's favored verbal model wouldn't work—migration kills the between-group variability that such a model would depend on. Haidt replied that he didn't trust the mathematical models of theoretical biology and was confident that future work would vindicate his extended-well-past-the-theory assertions about genetic group selection in humans, as well as the potentially rapid pace of evolution. (See, for example, this essay in which he opines that group selective processes and rapid evolution could produce genetically derived ethnic differences in not only IQ but also morally laden traits like "aggressiveness, docility, or the ability to delay gratification," https://www.edge.org/response-detail/10376.) The publication timing of *The Righteous Mind* suggests that Haidt's genetic group selection musings might've spurred Pinker's dismissal of group selection in Edge, which was, to its credit, right about the shortcomings of Haidt's suggested rapid genetic group selection approach. Or perhaps the timing was coincidental.

To Norenzayan, the timing of these two shifts is no coincidence. Perhaps, he's hypothesized over the years, the shift in religious beliefs helped pave the way for shifts in cooperation and organization. Big gods may have bred big societies, via the cultural group selection dynamics we've considered so far in this chapter. To understand how this could've happened, let's step back and consider how cultural norms might be key instruments in cultural group selection.

NORMS AS WEAPONS: REPRODUCTION, OUTREACH, COOPERATION

Darwin recognized that, all else equal, more cooperative groups could outcompete less cooperative groups. A century and change later, Dawkins conceded this logic, but he balked at group selectionist explanations because he couldn't foresee a way to overcome the tendency for selfish individuals to erode group-level cooperation. Dawkins's rejection might make sense in the domain of genes, but as we've seen, cultural evolution has mechanisms that make group-level processes much more plausible.

If we envision cultural groups as existing in a state of competition with each other, the weapons in this cultural group selection battle will be the norms and beliefs that each group adopts. Our Shakers-versus-Latter-Day-Saints example highlighted one very poignant way that norms and beliefs influence societal success—via directly influencing reproduction rates. Groups with beliefs and norms more conducive to having and raising kids will have a considerable head start when it comes to cultural competition between groups. Fertile groups expand, split, and spread. Celibate groups quickly die out. Between these two poles, there is considerable room for more subtle gradations in reproductive norms.

Competition between rival cultural groups depends on far more than baby-making. Successful groups must cement cooperation. They need to tamp down internal strife. They might even have active outreach programs for bringing others into the fold. I like to think of these as separate settings that can be independently dialed up or down, like control knobs for cultural group selection.

Groups with constellations of norms and beliefs conducive to cooperation, reproduction, internal peace, and external outreach will—all else equal—thrive in intergroup competition. Groups with norms and beliefs that don't cement cooperation or outreach or reproduction will tend to be outcompeted. These groups will be replaced, converted, or conquered.

RELIGIONS AS NORM ACCELERATORS

In chemistry, catalysts are compounds that can increase the rate of a separate chemical reaction. Our bodies contain numerous enzymes that act as catalysts—they facilitate the numerous chemical reactions that sustain life.

I've come to think about religions as catalysts in cultural evolution and cultural group selection. Religions act as norm accelerators—they can take a given belief or norm and ratchet up commitment to it. A group might have norms conducive to reproduction or outreach, but if that group believes that those norms are divinely mandated and enforced, people will be that much more receptive to them. Religions both furnish groups with their norms (remember: both Shakers and early LDS saw their beliefs about reproduction as rooted in divine will) and also give people ample motivation to uphold their religious norms—after all, an afterlife often hangs in the balance.

Going back to the idea that there are different dials or "settings" that cultural groups have—reproduction dials, cooperation dials, outreach dials, and so forth—religions might act as catalysts that help each dial get cranked a little higher or lower. The Latter-Day Saints' religious beliefs dialed the reproductive knob up to 11; the Shakers' beliefs about sex as original sin turned the reproductive knob to a conclusive zero, with very predictable effect. Some religions (Latter-Day Saints again come to mind) vigorously encourage missionary activity, reaching out to convince persuadable outsiders to join the faith. It's easy to see how effective outreach programs like this would benefit their groups—all else equal, effective mission programs benefit fledgling religions. Going back a couple millennia, the early Christian church excelled at outreach, winning cultural competition primarily by enlisting new members.

One crucial assumption here is that religions will have distinct enough norms, maintained over time, to emerge as key players in cultural group competition. Remember, after all, that cultural group selection only works if between-group differences are somewhat stable and maintained over time. So, do religions have what it takes to drive this sort of cultural group competition?

Linking together a few different ideas from this chapter, we can start to think of religions as broad units of cultural groupishness. Each religion arises with its own unique history and cultural trajectory, but over time religions end up in competition with each other. The competition needn't involve battle or physical combat (although it obviously can!), and religions can rise and fall as much for their impacts on fertility or group cohesiveness as on any military outcome. The features of cultural evolution—things like conformist transmission, norm psychology, and CREDs—help keep religions distinct, preserving the between-group variability that serves as raw fuel for cultural group selection.

Over time, we'll even see successful religions acting as global cultural groups that can transcend national and broader geographic borders. In a fascinating recent result, Cindel White, Ara Norenzayan, and Michael Muthukrishna turned to the trusty cultural fixation index we recently discussed (cultural FST) and asked whether religions specifically show the type of cultural clustering that we can measure.[30] They found that across a whole host of attitudes and behaviors, people of the same religion tended to cluster together, and groups that were more closely historically related to each other (e.g., the Abrahamic faiths share cultural descent) hang together in cultural "families." The upshot of this is that global faiths tend to stabilize distinct patterns of norms and attitudes among their adherents, even across other national, cultural, or linguistic boundaries. For example, Protestant Christians in Ecuador would be expected to show a surprisingly high degree of similarity to Protestant Christians in Ethiopia or Estonia or elsewhere; Buddhists in Myanmar and Mongolia and Massachusetts all show some degree of cultural clustering, driven by their shared religion. Religions act as supranational cultural groupings, exemplified by within-faith similarities that transcend broader geopolitical divides. Religions act as norm accelerators, and global religions end up producing some global consistency among believers. This is one compelling piece of evidence supporting the assumption that religions have what it takes to maintain group boundaries and thus drive cultural group selection. If we again think of religions as having different control knobs that can be dialed up or down—knobs controlling norms about reproduction or evangelism or cooperation—coreligionists worldwide have similar "settings," if you will, for the various knobs. This group-level consistency in settings opens the door for those specific settings to have profound group-level consequences, like those we saw for the Shakers and Latter-Day Saints.

The remainder of this chapter takes a deeper dive into the cooperative dial, considering the possibility that certain religious beliefs catalyzed upgrades in large-scale human cooperation. We'll be focusing on cooperation in particular, but throughout I think it's worth remembering that religious beliefs might similarly serve as catalysts for other sorts of cultural norms, be they cooperative, reproductive, or missionistic. We're focusing on cooperation now, not because it's the only relevant dial that religions can ratchet up or down; it's just that cooperation has received comparatively more research attention than the other dials.

So, how might some religious beliefs catalyze cooperation?

BIG GODS AND RELIGIOUS PROSOCIALITY

Might beliefs in certain kinds of gods have been a key cultural innovation that helped our ancestors cement cooperative intent within groups? Specifically, is it possible that the emergence of big and powerful and morally concerned gods—we'll follow Norenzayan and just call them Big Gods for brevity—has helped stabilize cooperation within some groups?

The logic linking Big Gods to cooperation goes something like this: selfish free riders undermine cooperation within groups. It's possible to root out selfishness if free riders are reliably punished. But we humans can't possibly detect and punish all selfishness. It's just not feasible to universally police cooperation, especially as groups grow large. Punishing free riders is also itself a form of cooperation—altruistically punitive individuals have to give their time and energy toward finding and sanctioning the selfish. Sure, people might inhibit their basest noncooperative urges if they thought there was a reasonable chance that their misanthropy would be caught, but it just isn't realistic to expect that all selfishness will be reliably detected and handled. There might be norms encouraging cooperation, but enforcement rapidly becomes unwieldy as groups grow larger.

What if people's beliefs in all-powerful, all-knowing, and morally concerned Big Gods help fill this gap? To the extent that people believe that a Big God will know and care about their misdeeds, and have the capacity to punish bad behavior now or in an afterlife, might people curb their excesses? In short, is it possible that Big Gods help keep people honest and cooperative, and that Big Gods were thus a key weapon in the cultural group selection arms race in which cooperation was a key currency?[31] Groups who secured cooperation via Big God beliefs spread at the expense of those who didn't have supernatural beliefs equally conducive to large-scale cooperation. The idea that Big Gods might have helped create big groups, via beneficial effects on cooperation, has been termed the *religious prosociality* or *Big Gods* hypothesis.

I confess, when I first read this idea, I kind of hated it. I was an early graduate student with New Atheist leanings, and a popular-evolutionary-psychology–earned distrust of both cultural explanations and group selection. So a cultural group selection theory in which belief in gods was seen as functional in an evolutionary sense triggered all my alarm bells. Culture, group selection, and a view of gods as anything more than delusional mind viruses—blegh, no thanks!

As I read the science, my knee-jerk skepticism waned.¶¶ Researchers like Norenzayan and Henrich have by now amassed a pretty considerable body of evidence linking religious shifts to cooperative shifts—evidence laid out in Norenzayan's *Big Gods* book as well as in a more technical theory paper a bunch of us published in *Behavioural and Brain Sciences* in 2018.[32] I don't have space to consider all the evidence here (I'd recommend you check out that book and paper, especially if you share my younger self's knee-jerk skepticism), but I want to share some illustrative evidence. We'll start by considering some evidence coming from large-scale cross-cultural and historical work, and then move on to some evidence coming from in-lab experimental psychology investigations and related field research.

HISTORICAL AND CROSS-CULTURAL COMPARISONS

The Shakers and Latter-Day Saints are just one vivid example illustrating how differences in religious beliefs and norms can powerfully affect group-level outcomes. The Latter-Day Saints have fruitfully multiplied, and their

¶¶ Does this feel like a recurring theme yet?

religion is thriving globally. Meanwhile, the Shakers have chastely crept toward extinction.

The Big Gods thesis asks us to consider the possibility that some religions—and particularly those religions that have become successful and enduring—happen to include sets of beliefs and practices that are conducive to group functioning. Big Gods religions help groups ease internal friction, overcome cooperative dilemmas, and in return outcompete rival faiths. This sounds fine in principle, but is there compelling evidence? Let's consider a few key empirical results.

First, anthropologist Rich Sosis and colleagues have looked at the survival rates of communes.[33] This is a really nice real-world investigation, as what we now know as global religions got their starts as small communal endeavors. Communes—be they religious or secular—pop up regularly; they come and they go. Most don't last very long before their eventual dissolution, others have a bit more staying power. Sosis and team looked at different attempts at utopian communes that have cropped up over the years, and tried to statistically account for which ones lasted a while and which quickly winked out. In their analysis, religious communes outlived secular communes. Sosis and colleagues specifically linked this pattern to the religious communes' tendency to enact more strict prohibitions and costly signals of commitment. Religious communes, in other words, were able to outlive secular communes in part because they were better at stabilizing coherent norms and motivating adherence to them. The story in Sosis's data isn't about Big Gods, per se, but about the broader features of religious communes that might prove beneficial for their success. In the parlance of our chapters on cultural evolution, we might think of lots of the religious communes' costly requirements as credibility-enhancing displays, that in turn can ratchet up commitment among commune members. Here we see aspects of religions—specifically, their use of costly CREDs—acting as norm accelerators, and helping their groups survive longer.

The commune data are fascinating, but are silent about the specific flavor of supernatural beliefs that groups held. As such, they make at best an indirect example of how some religions might help stabilize big groups. For a more direct test, Roes and Raymond analyzed historical and cross-cultural data pertaining to the types of religious beliefs that groups held and their levels of societal complexity—which here we can think of as a crude proxy for the degree of diffuse cooperativeness within each group. In small groups, cooperation can be sustained among close kith or kin, but larger and more complex societal structures require higher degrees of cooperation than pure kin or reciprocal altruism can easily sustain. The question is whether those groups with greater degrees of hierarchical complexity show any distinctive patterns in their religious beliefs. And using a good historical cross-cultural database, Roes and Raymond found that bigger, more complex (and by inference more cooperative) groups tended to espouse beliefs in moralizing high gods—in other words, big groups tended to have Big Gods.[34]

Recently, Ben Purzycki has pushed back a bit on some of these ideas.[35] He points out that it isn't really correct to say that morally concerned gods are a peculiar innovation that's only seen in large groups. Instead, he finds that moralizing gods are actually fairly universal. There aren't cultures whose gods are wholly morally unconcerned. Nobody's gods are entirely morally fickle. What does seem to vary considerably is in how much gods know—what sorts of information they have access to. The gods of smaller-scale societies are moralizing, but limited in what they can observe. So it's possible, for example, to avoid a god's judgment by hiding your misdeeds, or doing them outside the village boundaries. But the gods still moralize aplenty! They just are limited in what they can do about it.[36]

Beyond finding that moralizing gods are more ubiquitous than previously assumed, Purzycki has also quite compellingly argued that we shouldn't necessarily trust the raw data used in the Roes and Raymond work we just discussed.[37] They relied on the Standard Cross-Cultural Sample, a nice archival data source culled from ethnographies over the years. It's an attempt to make a standard dataset of cultures, for use in quantitative comparisons. Purzycki notes that the coding on what types of religions each culture has or had is largely drawn from primary colonial contact reports back in the day. These reports aren't coming from trained ethnographers skilled in sensitively learning about and documenting cultures. Indeed, most of these reports are coming from missionaries reporting back after trying to convert a people to Christianity. The degree to which a culture's god was seen by a missionary some centuries ago as "moralizing" probably has more to do with that missionary's perception of closeness to Christianity than it does with any set of rigorous observations about what people actually believe. A missionary could return from an outing to sneeringly deride a group of "savages" as having no morality in their religion. Some decades and centuries later, researchers like us could open the Standard Cross-Cultural Sample dataset and see numbers in columns describing this culture as small scale, and its religion as having an absence of moralizing high gods. But unless you're confident in the cultural observations of century-ago missionaries—with their motivated recounting of how moral those to-their-eyes "filthy savages" were—you shouldn't be all that confident in the Standard Cross-Cultural Sample's records. The entire observed correlation between societal complexity and the presence of moralizing high gods in cultures might be attributable to reporting biases among a bygone era's missionaries.

Does this mean there's nothing to the Big Gods-cooperation link? Hardly! After a recent conference presentation on this work, I asked Purzycki whether we should abandon the Big Gods-cooperation story in light of his revelations, and he said that with some light tweaking, the general theoretical story is still sound. Gods might be more universally moralizing than a source like the Standard Cross-Cultural Sample would reflect, but there is still a lot of variability in gods' observational purviews. All gods are fairly moralizing, but the gods of smaller scale societies tend to be more localized and limited. In contrast, the Big Gods of world religions tend to be omniscient and universal. This is an important difference! A moralizing god with limited information isn't going to change people's behavior much. Folks will hide their misdeeds, or take them out of town. These gods are like a lazy but judgmental uncle—you know he doesn't like your worst habits, but what can he do about it? In contrast, a morally concerned and omniscient god is a much better cooperative motivator. To the extent that religions differ along this dimension—from our judgmental uncle gods to universally observant moralizers—there could be profound consequences on cooperation and other relevant outcomes.

To pin down the Big Gods–cooperation link even more securely, consider a couple of lines of research looking at how religious beliefs might impact how anonymously generous and cooperative people are. In a high-profile paper in *Science*, Joe Henrich and a huge team of researchers had people in fifteen small-scale societies play several different standard economic games that measure cooperative and fairness norms. They found that people who practiced one of the world's global Big God religions—Christianity, Islam, Hinduism, and the like—were more cooperative than people who didn't.[38]

Here, belief in Big Gods was a consistent predictor of increased cooperation in a rich cross-cultural investigation. A large follow-up project, with a star-studded cast of twenty coauthors, found that people exposed to the big world faiths aren't just more cooperative with folks in their own groups, they also show reduced parochial trends in their cooperative behavior.[39] Big Gods expand people's cooperative circles.

Religious beliefs don't just widen people's cooperative circles—first beyond kith and kin, then eroding more parochial barriers—they also change their broader moral concerns, with important implications for cooperation and other group-beneficial outcomes. Quentin Atkinson and Pierrick Bourrat analyzed data from a huge cross-cultural survey, the World Values Survey, and found that specific religious beliefs about whether God can monitor and punish misdeeds were linked to a wide range of moral views.[40] According to Atkinson and Bourrat, "Across cultural and religious backgrounds, beliefs about the permissibility of moral transgressions are tied to beliefs about supernatural monitoring and punishment, supporting arguments that these beliefs may be important promoters of cooperation in human groups."

These papers, and a rapidly growing literature like them, point to an important connection between religious beliefs, cooperation, and group-level outcomes. This hypothesis isn't without its complications—there is vigorous debate about the precise timing of Big Gods and big groups, for example.*** Given the challenges of inferring patterns of historical religious beliefs, and their effects on group outcomes, some scientific humility is in order all around. It is possible that we'll never be able to precisely pin down exactly how it all unfolded, and will have to take our best scientific guesses with clearly articulated uncertainty around them. But, for the time being, there's pretty decent evidence connecting religious beliefs to important outcomes for cultural groups: Big Gods make cooperative people, which in turn make and sustain big groups.

*** One prominent paper published in *Nature* claimed that Big Gods precede big groups, for example. Inspection of data analysis by an independent team of researchers found a bug in the analysis code that invalidated the key claims, however. After two years of back-and-forth critique and discussion, the paper was ultimately retracted. For those who love to view science as self-correcting, keep this timeline in mind: it took two years for a clearly faulty report to be expunged from the record, in which key analyses had been based not on observations but on data that had been imputed manually.

This section mostly dealt with comparative evidence for the Big Gods thesis, asking how specific religious beliefs might manifest in different broad patterns of behavior. A key assumption in this work is that it is something specifically about the religious beliefs in question that are motivating the cooperative outcomes. In particular, this model assumes that people are changing their behavior in part because of their Big God beliefs—that people curb their basest urges when they're mindful of their Big God who can monitor and police behavior. Next, we'll consider psychological evidence testing this particular claim, with admittedly mixed success.

GOD IS WATCHING: DO REMINDERS OF GOD INCREASE COOPERATION?

Big groups have tended to worship Big Gods, and people today tend to show more expansive norms of cooperation if they're believers in a global Big God religion. This is great, but where's the evidence that Big God beliefs themselves have a direct causal relationship to cooperation?

There are some experimental psychology data from in-lab studies that are often presented as strong evidence in favor of the religious prosociality/Big Gods thesis. Because these studies have taken an outsized role in both the scientific literature and in public presentations of it (including both Norenzayan's *Big Gods* and Henrich's *WEIRDest People* books), I want to unpack them in some detail, and walk through what these studies can and cannot demonstrate.

In short, the whole religious prosociality/Big Gods thesis is premised on the assumption that people will check their selfish urges if they're worried that a Big God might smite them for their selfishness. People are pretty sensitive to being watched—anonymity often brings out our worst, and watched people are trustworthy people. So it goes to reason that people might alter their behavior—and specifically in a more cooperative direction—to the extent that they think "God is watching!"

Even the most devout believers aren't chronically fixated on their gods. There are errands to run, kids to care for, jobs to do. The moment-to-moment salience of God waxes and wanes. As social psychology researchers, we're often interested in how people's behavior shifts across different situations—at how we might behave when religion is on our mind, versus when it fades to the background. A now-burgeoning research effort looks to examine religion's psychological effects in part by seeing how people change their behavior when their religious beliefs are made salient—when God is brought from background to foreground.

The highest-profile experimental result in the Big Gods world is a paper titled "God Is Watching You: Priming God Concepts Increases Prosocial Behavior in an Anonymous Economic Game," published in the journal *Psychological Science* by authors Azim Shariff and Ara Norenzayan.[41] The paper has been cited an eye-popping seventeen hundred times as of December 2023, and has spawned an entire cottage industry of religious priming research—"priming" being a bit of psychology jargon for "making people think about specific stuff." If a researcher "primes religion" that just means they've gotten participants to think religious thoughts; if she's claimed to "prime aggression" that means she's prodded people to think and act a little more aggressively.

In the Shariff priming paper, a few dozen participants were brought individually into the lab. They were randomly split into a control group and an experimental group. Everyone played a little word game that served as the priming manipulation, and then completed an experimental economic game that measures anonymous prosociality. This outcome measure is called the Dictator Game, and in it each participant is given a $10 stake and asked how much (if any) they'd like to allocate to a stranger, ostensibly another participant in the study. The donation is anonymous, the participants will never meet each other. So it's basically measuring anonymous cooperative intent—would participants split the windfall payment, or default to selfishness?

The word game preceding the Dictator Game was the main experimental manipulation. All participants had to rearrange words to form meaningful phrases. For example, the string "shoes brown were running the" could become "the shoes were brown." All participants played this scrambled-sentence game for ten trials, forming ten coherent phrases. For those participants in the control condition, all sentences and words were as mundane as the brown-shoed sample just provided. But for participants in the experimental condition, half of the scrambled sentences had religion-connoting content. For example, the string "felt she eradicate spirit the" could become "she felt the spirit." The string "fainted thank here God you're" could become "thank God you're here." In principle, this means that half of the participants were reminded of religious concepts, via five words planted in the scrambled sentences. Religious cognition was "primed"—the sneaky researchers had ostensibly planted a reminder of God in their participants' minds.

The original paper reported a remarkably strong effect whereby people who'd seen the subtle religious words gave more money away in the dictator game—baseline donation rates jumped from a meager $1.84 average gift in the control condition to nearly half ($4.22) in the experimental condition. A second follow-up study yielded the same exact pattern. The reported effect sizes were remarkably large, by experimental social psychology standards, ostensibly implying that the effects of subtle primes on economic behavior were really, really strong.[†††]

This paper garnered a lot of immediate attention, both scholarly and in the press. Over the years, dozens of additional papers emerged, using the same experimental setup to see what else happens, beyond prosociality and generosity, when researchers subtly prime religious concepts using the scrambled-sentence manipulation. And, according to the published literature, religious primes had lots of interesting effects! They led to increased social self-awareness, increased risk taking (but only for non-moral risks like skydiving), they helped people resist temptation. It seemed like a few times a year a new priming paper would come out, linking the Godly scrambled sentences to a flashy new outcome variable.

Over time, people began revisiting the original result, and it proved quite elusive to obtain on reexamination and replication. A couple of different teams tried to replicate the original Dictator Game study, and found no cooperation difference between the control and experimental conditions.[42] Other teams (including one I led) tried to replicate other religious priming studies, and experienced similar frustrations.[43] Time and again, published papers that had used the scrambled-sentence task to prime religion proved impossible to replicate, in more tightly controlled settings. Larger samples

[†††] For the most dedicated nerds out there, the paper's first study returned an effect size estimate of *Cohen's d* = 1.07. To benchmark this, the readily observable gender difference in height is about a *Cohen's d* = 1.7, the finding that people in a bad mood are more aggressive than people in a good mood clocks in at *Cohen's d* = 0.9 or so. So, the Shariff and Norenzayan paper is saying that the effect of subtle God primes on generosity is more evident than the effect of grumpiness on aggression, but not quite as evident as the gender difference in height.

and tighter experimental standards led effects that had been reported as large and robust to fade to insignificance. Robert Ross, giving a talk about religious priming studies at the annual meeting of the Cultural Evolution Society, noted that there was not a single successful replication study in the religious priming literature, in which an independent team using a preregistered study[‡‡‡] was able to confirm the results of a published religious priming study that had used the scrambled sentence manipulation. None, zero. Every published scrambled-sentence religious priming study has so far failed to replicate.

Does this mean that the religious priming results are wrong? Here I think it's worth breaking this into two separate questions. First, does this mean that specific results, like those reported in the original religious priming paper, are probably spurious? Second, does this mean that the underlying conceptual hypotheses are all wrong? I'd answer "yes" to the former and "not necessarily" to the latter.

Regarding the first question, I think it is eminently reasonable to dismiss the original Shariff results as an unfortunate false positive—to be perfectly clear, I have no scientific faith in those specific results. My skepticism for this finding is similar to my skepticism toward a lot of the flashy, small-sample studies in the literature around this time, including flashy small-sample studies I myself published, and have since publicly renounced. There's little reason to trust the original priming result, or most of the specific follow-ups using the scrambled-sentence primes.

Regarding the second question (does this mean the conceptual hypothesis should be abandoned?), things are a little more complicated. The core conceptual insight of the religious priming papers is that people ostensibly change their behavior when they are reminded of a watchful and moralizing God that they believe in. I find that conceptual hypothesis eminently plausible. The key empirical result presented by the Shariff paper, however, rests upon a specific methodology: the scrambled-sentence paradigm to prime god thoughts. And that's where I think the original result fails.

Aiyana Willard and I are in the midst of a project where we're revisiting the burgeoning religious priming literature, and hoping to do some

[‡‡‡] Preregistration is just the process whereby scientists lock in their planned methods and analysis before collecting data. If done well, it reduces the influence of subtle researcher biases. If done poorly, it merely looks like it has done so.

very basic proof-of-concept experiments. In short, we're trying to see if the priming methods themselves do what they've claimed to do: Do scrambled-sentence religious primes actually prime religious thoughts? To explore this, we paired the primes that Shariff pioneered with a really basic task to see whether people are actually thinking about religion—whether religious thoughts spring easily to people's minds after they've been primed. And it turns out that the scrambled-sentence religion primes do precisely nothing that we can detect. People who've just completed the God-condition scrambled sentences are no more likely to be thinking about religion than are people who've completed the control-condition task. The scrambled-sentence God primes don't prime God. That's the bad news: the original God-priming paper, and all the follow-ups that used the same experimental setup, likely report faulty results because that specific priming procedure doesn't work as advertised.

Does this mean that all those priming papers are wrong, at a deeper conceptual level? Relevant to our current discussion, does this mean that the Big Gods theoretical story has lost its key experimental support? Not so fast. The general idea that people might alter their behavior when their gods are on their minds seems solid. That's the core premise behind frequent religious reminders like those What Would Jesus Do bracelets, or behind recurrent religious iconography and repeated religious rituals. Think: five-times-daily call to prayer, prayers before bed, religious attendance multiple times per week, visually striking religious iconography, and all the other things that religions use as booster shots to remind people of their faith. Presumably successful religions do these things in the real world because, in some sense, they work.

The failure of the original religious priming studies might not be in concept so much as in execution. The priming manipulation doesn't seem to do what it's supposed to do: make people think about their gods. That doesn't mean that the hypotheses in published papers using the scrambled-sentence primes are wrong, but that *the hypotheses remain fundamentally untested.* The methods weren't sensitive enough to provide a meaningful test of the deeper scientific hypothesis.

To clarify this, let's try a tortured analogy involving my backyard. Let's say I have a hunch that there's an aquifer under my back garden. To test my hunch, I hire a dowser. He shows up, dowsing rod in hand, and probes about my back garden, doing specifically whatever it is that dowsers do with their rods. After much vigorous dowsing, the dowser tells me he couldn't detect any water. Based on this, should I conclude that there's no groundwater to be found? Hardly! We know that dowsing rods don't work. All I've done is waste some money running a trial based on a flawed methodology. I haven't disproven my hunch of groundwater; I've just tested it in a manner so spectacularly inefficient that I've learned precisely nothing despite my efforts. Based on the dowsing rod results, I don't need to abandon my hope of groundwater; I need a better tool for finding it.

That's precisely the situation religious priming researchers find themselves in: wanting a better tool for testing the hypotheses that they've previously dowsed for using the scrambled sentences. The Shariff paper used the scrambled-sentences task and a smallish sample; unsuccessful replications used bigger samples but the same priming apparatus. The issue here isn't the size of the sample (or dowsing rod), it's that the tool just doesn't work.

Fortunately for us, there is a fair amount of evidence on how the salience of religious concepts affects behavior that doesn't rely on the scrambled-sentence task—it's just that those scrambled-sentence studies have proven flashy and attention grabbing. Perhaps my favorite study yoking the Big Gods ideas to a better experimental methodology comes from the lab of Mark Aveyard.[44] He wanted to use a more ecologically valid experimental protocol, something that more directly evokes religious concepts in participants. In his paper, he first used the same scrambled-sentence procedure as Shariff and Norenzayan, and got precisely zilch (as we'd expect, given revelations that the priming task itself does zilch). Next, however, he primed religious concepts in a clever way. His participants were Arabic-speaking Muslim students at the University of Sharjah, in the United Arab Emirates. He had them listen to a two-minute audio clip prior to completing a task that measures honesty (which is in the same conceptual ballpark as prosociality and cooperation). Half of the participants got a clip that merely had city sounds, full of traffic and whatnot. Half of the participants got a clip that was identical except that partway through the clip, the *adhan*, or Muslim call to prayer, blared. Here was a more blatant, more ecologically valid, way to get some participants thinking religious thoughts. And in this study those participants who'd heard the call to prayer were more honest in their subsequent responses. An overt religious prime increased honesty, precisely as predicted. As a great parallel study, Erik Duhaime obtained a similar result in an even more naturalistic field study in Marrakesh.[45] Duhaime found that marketgoers were more prosocial immediately after the *adhan* had been made—when religion was at its most salient to marketgoers. The take home message of these studies is that scientists can get results much like the original Shariff ones—they just have to first abandon the Shariff methodology using the scrambled sentences. Testing the same conceptual hypothesis with a better tool, researchers like Duhaime and Aveyard provide some vindication for the religious prosociality thesis. They put away the dowsing rod and dug until they found water.

I strongly suspect that if we scientists rolled up our sleeves and redid all of the studies that used the scrambled-sentence task to prime God concepts, only using priming methods that actually work, we'd find that a lot of the conceptual hypotheses actually hold up—even if the original results using the scrambled-sentence task aren't worth much. It's probably safe to assume, however, that lots of the results would vanish, even using stronger methods. There are dozens of published papers claiming a causal relationship between religious cognition and one outcome or another (it's a real grab bag), all based on results using the scrambled-sentences primes. Despite the considerable effort that went into each and every one of these papers, I unfortunately don't think they can teach us much. At best, they're marker flags for where we should dig with something better than the dowsing rod that the scrambled-sentence God primes ended up being.

This tour of the sausage-making factory behind the scenes of published papers isn't meant to cast doubt on the broad Big Gods hypothesis—thankfully there's far more support than the original Shariff priming paper and its 128 total participants could even in principle offer. We're seeing a growing number of new and improved laboratory and field studies using religious primes that actually work, like the Aveyard and Duhaime results above.

In sum, the most cited paper linking religious reminders to a cooperative outcome doesn't hold its water. Thankfully, stronger studies have shown promising results linking the momentary salience of religion to cooperative outcomes.

TAKING STOCK

In this chapter, we learned about cultural group selection—merely the notion that cultural groups thrive or struggle in part because of the consequences that norms have on group functioning. Cultural group selection is far from the naive group selection ideas that were prevalent decades ago, notions that critters might sacrifice themselves "for the good of the species." We saw how outright dismissal of group selection—by many theoretical biologists in the 1960s and 1970s, and extending to biology-adjacent popularizers today—may have been premature. Group selection is a unique lens through which to view evolution. It's a language, if you will, for modeling evolutionary change. It's a language that's less frequently spoken than counterparts like gene's-eye-view inclusive fitness modeling, but it's no less mathematically and theoretically rigorous for its relative lack of popularity. Indeed, group selectionist thinking is experiencing a bit of a resurgence, particularly in the domain of culture. Cultural transmission provides mechanisms for maintaining group boundaries that genetic transmission lacks, making cultural group selection an easier theoretical sell than genetic group selection.

Cultural group selection may have played a key role in shaping the world's current religious landscape. Today, most people believe in one or a few Big Gods—deities that are powerful, knowledgeable, and morally concerned. Big Gods may have captured the world's religious marketplace because they've proven to be good "tricks" for cultural groups. Religions act as norm accelerators, ramping up commitment. Threats of eternal punishment (or promises of eternal reward) can increase adherence to group norms. Where those norms pay reproductive or cooperative or missionistic dividends, groups thrive and bring their Big Gods with them as they spread.

WHICH RELIGIONS "WIN" AND WHY IT MATTERS

The past dozen or so millennia have seen drastic cultural shifts, with parallel changes in both the global cooperative landscape and the global religious landscape. I see two main upshots of these changes.

First, as a handful of religions gained followers and success and became truly global, we've seen more and more people come to believe in a very specific type of god—a peculiarly powerful, knowledgeable, and morally concerned god. Most humans today believe in a type of god that most world religions have lacked. Cultural groups prosper or perish largely because of the norms and beliefs they hold, and the effects of those norms and beliefs on group behavior. Religious beliefs are inextricably linked to cultural groups—religions act as norm accelerators that ramp up commitment to a group's norms. Successful religions, including especially those focused on Big Gods, have spread throughout the globe, outcompeting the myriad small and local sects that define most global historical religious beliefs. Cultural group selection has seen a winnowing of religious diversity, with a few Big Gods supplanting myriad small and local gods in the minds of believers worldwide—plausibly because Big God religions are nifty cultural evolutionary tricks that ease cooperation within groups that adhere to them.

This shift toward a few Big God religions dominating the global religious marketplace has brought a secondary shift in how people conceive of morality.[46] As big, successful religions spread, they brought with them their once unfamiliar notions of gods with deep and universalistic moral concerns, gods who deeply care what people do and believe. Big Gods act as surveyors and guarantors of group norms—in short, Big Gods come to be seen as fundamental to morality itself. Over time, this means that there has been a gradual blurring of lines between religion and morality, to the point where, to many people today, religion and morality are practically synonymous. In large-scale global surveys, most people (who in all likelihood believe in one Big God or another) see religion as a necessary bedrock of morality. People in these polls overwhelmingly report that a religious upbringing is a key component of kids developing moral identities. Morality became essentially religious.

This leaves us today in a world where just a few Big Gods have "won"—they've effectively become global religious monopolies. Because Big Gods tend to have intimate moral concerns, as Big Gods religions spread, so too has spread the notion that morality is inextricably linked to religious belief. We'll see in the next chapter that this blurring of religious and moral lines has important and sometimes shocking implications for those of us who don't believe in any gods.

Here ends our section on the Puzzle of Faith. Along the past few chapters, we've seen how cognitive scientists of religion attempted to Darwinize religion, focusing on the ways that our innate dispositions and cognitive biases make some religious concepts attractive and memorable. Next, we learned that content biases—like those that are the primary focus of the cognitive science of religion—are just the tip of a cultural evolutionary iceberg. People don't believe in their gods simply because those gods have the right conceptual content. They come to believe in their gods (and not other supernatural agents like Mickey Mouse or Santa Claus, or nowadays Zeus) because their gods are supported by relevant context biases in cultural learning. Conformist learning, prestige-biased learning, and especially credibility-enhancing displays go a long way toward explaining why and how people come to believe in (just) their gods. Zooming out, this chapter showed how some religions have come to dominate the globe, through a process of cultural group selection where religious norms around cooperation and reproduction and outreach give some faiths a boost over others. This has been my best effort to sketch out a plausible scientific answer for the Puzzle of Faith.

Moving forward, we turn from the Puzzle of Faith to the Puzzle of Atheism. We'll ask how people become atheists, and how large-scale atheism can arise and be sustained. Before we jump into answering questions about who atheists are and how they come to disbelieve in gods, in chapter 8 we'll first explore perceptions of atheists, and ask: Why are atheists so disliked, distrusted, and reviled globally?

INTERLUDE

The Puzzle of Atheism

As we grapple with the Puzzle of Atheism, we need to answer a few key questions:

- Why are atheists disliked and distrusted?
- Are atheists morally trustworthy?
- Are agnostics distinct from atheists?
- How many atheists are there? Are there "closeted" atheists?
- What are the origins of atheism, at the level of individuals? Are there multiple pathways to atheism?
- What explains pockets of stable secularism in the world today?
- Is atheism improbable, or cognitively unnatural?

CHAPTER EIGHT

DO YOU BELIEVE IN ATHEISTS?

Morality, Trust, and Anti-Atheist Prejudice

> *Promises, covenants, and oaths, which are the bonds of human society, can have no hold upon an atheist. The taking away of God, though but even in thought, dissolves all.*
>
> —JOHN LOCKE, *A LETTER CONCERNING TOLERATION*

In 2016, a man in Saudi Arabia was sentenced to ten years in prison and two thousand lashes for voicing his atheism on social media.[1] The next year, another man was sentenced to death on charges of atheism and blasphemy after he'd uploaded videos renouncing Islam and the Prophet Mohammed. The man appealed and attempted to escape punishment through an insanity plea—after all, he'd been intoxicated when he made the videos. Nonetheless, the Saudi Supreme Court upheld the charges.[2] These cases are far from isolated. After all, King Abdullah in 2014 passed several royal decrees which formally labeled atheism as terrorism.

In 2013, the government of Bangladesh arrested a number of dissident bloggers and publicly labeled them as atheists. Even after their formal charges had been settled, the public accusation of atheism lingered. Post-release, they faced regular death threats—people even posted bounties for their deaths on social media.[3] In one instance, five people confessed to the murder of a blogger, stating that it had been their religious obligation to slay him.[4]

In Egypt, a family court ruled that a mother should lose custody of her two children because she was an atheist.[5] In New Mexico, a family court ordered an atheist mother to take faith-based classes or risk losing her children;[6] when she stopped attending the religious course, she lost custody of her children. UCLA law professor Eugene Volokh has documented dozens of similar cases in the United States,[7] where courts discriminated against irreligious (or merely less religious) parents on the theory that religion is in the child's best interests.

Beyond execution, torture, imprisonment, or loss of children, atheists face legal hurdles in countries around the world. Just in the United States, seven states still have laws on the books forbidding atheists from holding office. For example, the Mississippi state constitution says that "No person who denies the existence of a Supreme Being shall hold any office in this state." Legal prohibitions against atheists holding office are no longer enforceable in the United States, thanks to a 1961 Supreme Court ruling, but occasional challenges still arise. Given the current court makeup in the United States, how secure are these precedents?

These tragic cases highlight the many legal challenges that atheists face worldwide. But legal challenges aren't the end for atheists. Outside the courtroom, atheists face stigma, prejudice, and outright discrimination. This book tries to understand the origins of atheism in our religious species. Before we try to figure out where atheism comes from and how it is sustained, let's step back and view atheism through the lens of public perception. Are atheists popular or reviled? What might explain why people view atheists as they do?

ATHEIST AS "OTHER"

In 2006, Penny Edgell and colleagues at the University of Minnesota published a fascinating sociological study of the perceptions of atheists and other groups in the United States.[8] They were especially interested in cultural inclusion and exclusion—the degree to which everyday American citizens viewed atheists and others as fundamentally like themselves and worthy of inclusion.

In the paper, Edgell and colleagues report on a large and representative survey of people from all over the United States. To measure the broad concept of cultural inclusion, the team asked specific questions about which groups of people were preferred or tolerated in various roles, both public and private. This gave them a nice barometer of where people tended to draw symbolic boundaries, and which groups were systematically placed outside of them. The authors note that their paper examines stigmatization of atheists against a backdrop of general trends toward greater religious tolerance in the United States: they open their paper stating that "Despite the declining salience of divisions among religious groups, the boundary between believers and nonbelievers in America remains strong." Savvy readers will no doubt mark some salient counterexamples to the general pattern toward religious tolerance in the early 2000s—vilification and persecution of Muslims in the wake of September 11 comes readily to mind. But nonetheless, the United States had seen general trends toward fewer and less obvious religious divisions over the preceding decades. Against this backdrop of piecemeal tolerance, atheists remained locked out.

Consider political inclusion: which groups of people would respondents like to see as leaders? Polling services like Gallup have been looking into this question for decades, which gives us a nice picture of how attitudes evolve. The general setup is to ask people if they'd vote for a *well-qualified member of their own preferred political party* who happened to belong to one group or another. And there's a general (though far from perfect) trend toward tolerance. For instance, in a 1958 poll, fewer than 40 percent of Americans said they'd vote for a qualified Black candidate of their preferred party; this number climbed to over 95 percent by 1999. We see similar trends toward tolerance for Catholic, Jewish, and gay candidates.

Edgell and colleagues used the 1999 Gallup data as a starting point in their paper about atheists. Shockingly, the 1999 data show that atheists are among the only groups who can't garner a majority of votes—only about 48 percent of respondents claimed they'd vote for a qualified atheist. Tolerance for Catholic, Jewish, Black, and gay candidates had steeply increased over the decades. In contrast, tolerance toward atheists had increased much less rapidly.

A lot has happened since 1999. The United States has had a Black president. An openly racist businessman and reality show host defeated a woman who'd been both a senator and a secretary of state in a presidential election. Then a Black woman became vice president. Border walls, Proud Boys, Muslim travel bans, but also the Obergefell decision legalizing same-sex marriage—it was a busy time. How had attitudes changed between 1999 and 2020?

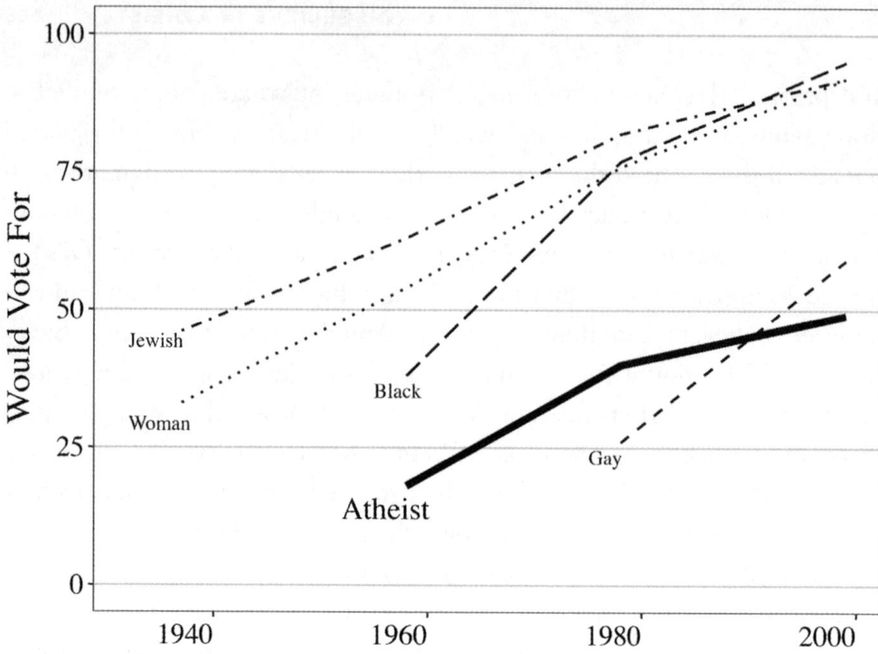

Figure 8.1. Increasing tolerance for many groups of people, 1937–1999. *Source:* P. Edgell, J. Gerteis, and D. Hartmann, "Atheists as 'Other': Moral Boundaries and Cultural Membership in American Society," *American Sociological Review* 71, no. 2 (2006): 211–34.

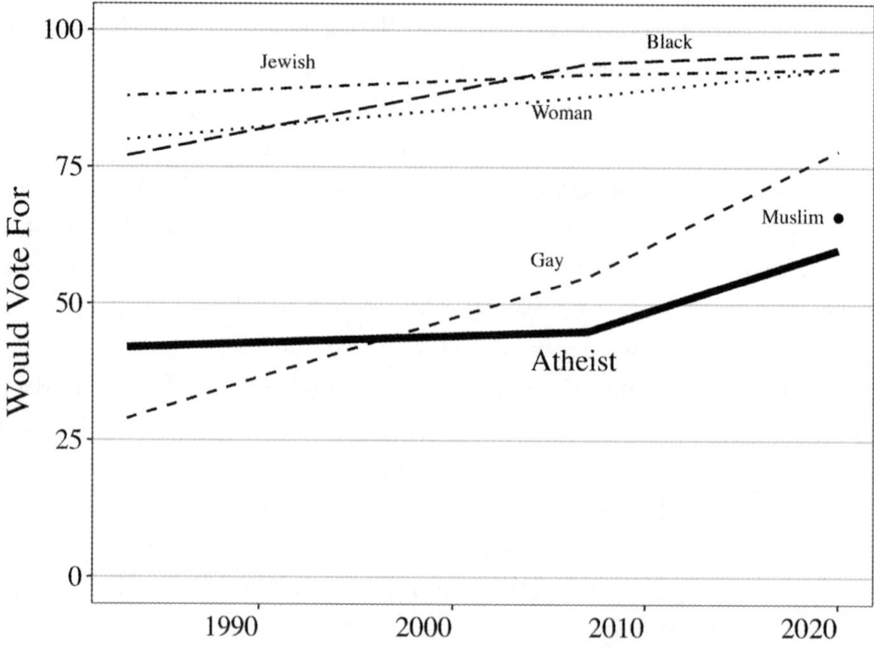

Figure 8.2. Rising political tolerance for many, 1983–2020. *Source:* Gallup data.

There is still a steady trend toward tolerance. Three decades saw people consistently express more willingness to vote for pretty much everyone. But the progress wasn't consistent across all groups. Tolerance for gay candidates jumped from about 30 percent in the 1980s to about 80 percent in 2020. Atheists experienced some, but not all, of this trend. Voting intention polls like these showed lots of progress for atheists, but as of 2020 they remained stubbornly among the least popular groups of people.

It's especially striking to compare attitudes toward atheists to attitudes toward Muslims in these polls. Both are minority religious groups in the United States. But Muslims had been targets of intense post-911 stigma. The War on Terror was often painted as a clash between Christendom and Islam. Hate crimes against Muslims spiked and remain high. In 2016–2020, Trump's Muslim travel ban and consistent vilification of Islam were in play, yet in 2020, tolerance for atheists still lagged behind Muslims in voting polls.

Returning to Edgell and colleagues, they recognized that voting intentions are just one sliver of the pie when it comes to cultural inclusion. Further, these polls are asking about who people want as president—a rather high bar. I certainly have friends and colleagues for whom I bear no ill will, but wouldn't let anywhere near the Oval Office or any other seat of power. Saying you wouldn't want an atheist (or a Muslim, or a woman) as president tells us something about attitudes, but that "something" is quite limited and quite strong.

Another way to get at cultural inclusion and exclusion is just to bluntly ask people about it. Edgell and colleagues directly asked people about who shares their vision of America: "Now I want to read you a list of different groups of people who live in this country. For each one, please tell me how much you think people in this group agree with YOUR vision of American society."

The research team coded how many people reported that each of a list of groups did *not at all* agree with their vision of America. Very few people, for example, said that white people (2.2 percent), Black people (4.6 percent), Asian Americans (7.0 percent), or Jews (7.4 percent) didn't at all share their vision of America. Things got a bit worse for some other groups: recent immigrants (12.5 percent), gay men and lesbians (22.5 percent), and Muslims (26.3 percent) were excluded by a broad plurality of respondents.

And atheists? Nearly two in five Americans (39.6 percent) reported that atheists do not at all share their vision of America. It seems that Americans have a circle of people who they think shares their vision of America, and people from most ethnic groups are situated within the circle. The circle's border is a bit fuzzy, and people aren't quite sure whether immigrants, gay men and lesbians, or Muslims fit inside. But atheists reside well outside the circle for something like 125 million Americans.

Americans don't want atheists as president, and they don't think atheists share their vision of America. Here, the exclusion is rather impersonal—it's asking about public power and symbolic identity. What about more personal attitudes? Edgell and colleagues used another survey item to see who Americans wouldn't want to join their family. Specifically, it asked about marriage preferences for their children: "People can feel differently about their children marrying people from various backgrounds. Suppose your son or daughter wanted to marry [a person in given category]. Would you approve of this choice, disapprove of it, or wouldn't it make any difference at all one way or the other?"

Mirroring the previous poll results, Americans again excluded atheists. Few people would object to their child marrying a white person (2.3 percent), a Conservative Christian (6.9 percent), or a Jew (11.8 percent). Things got a little precarious for ethnic minorities, with lots of Americans rejecting Hispanics (18.5 percent), Asian Americans (18.5 percent), or Black Americans (27.2 percent) as partners for their children. And about one in three Americans would reject an eligible Muslim partner for their kiddo (33.5 percent to be precise).

Atheists? Almost half (47.6 percent) of Americans reported that they'd disapprove of their son or daughter marrying an atheist. Based on these results, Edgell and colleagues concluded that atheists were broadly viewed as "other" in America. Per the authors, "Atheists are less likely to be accepted, publicly and privately, than any others from a long list of ethnic, religious, and other minority groups."

As a budding social scientist just beginning my graduate career, these data both horrified and fascinated me when I read this paper back in the day. Atheists are people with little collective or individual power, who may not even constitute a group in any meaningful sense. To illustrate the point here: can you name distinctively "atheist" music, cuisine, attire, or powerful leaders, the way you can with the other groups mentioned above? Atheists don't really do anything to stand out as a group. Yet they're among the most excluded groups in America. What gives? There's a genuine scientific puzzle here.

THE SOCIAL PSYCHOLOGY OF STIGMA (AND WHAT IT DOESN'T TELL US ABOUT ATHEISTS)

When I first read the landmark Edgell paper, I remember being both blown away by the paper's results and inspired by its very existence. I had just begun getting really curious about what science said about atheists and was growing frustrated by the overall lack of research out there. Seeing a huge paper like this published in a flagship sociology journal gave me some hope that there was room for the sort of work I wanted to do. Sure, sociology wasn't my home discipline (my interests were in evolutionary and cultural psychology, and my PhD program was in social psychology). But it still showed that it was possible to carve out some space to study atheists and publish that work in mainstream outlets. I just had to figure out a way to make it work in my discipline too.

Beyond enjoying the proof-of-concept that it was possible to make mainstream contributions by studying atheists, I was also amazed by the data themselves. Poll respondents were reporting quite extreme attitudes about atheists, excluding them in both public and private. Atheists seemed an odd group to stigmatize like this. So I turned to work in my home discipline of social psychology to figure out what might be going on. And I hit a dead end.

Within social psychology, there are a few main ways to explain prejudice and stereotyping. A hall of fame social psychology idea is *social identity theory*.[9] The basic idea is that people really love to categorize themselves and others in terms of their social identities. Consider all the social categories into which you might fit. Personally, I belong to several different social categories. I'm a husband and a father. I'm a dog owner. I'm a psychology professor. I study cultural evolution. I'm a fan of the Colorado Avalanche hockey team. I'm a football player (although back in the United States I was a soccer player). I'm a native Coloradan. I'm a resident of London, England. My belonging in these various categories helps define me, and helps me find others who are like me if I'm so inclined.

Over time, people tend to do more than just categorize themselves—eventually we start to really identify with some of the categories. We develop group allegiances. We develop social identities around the categories that we belong to and find especially important. A likely (though not inevitable) result is that as we come to identify strongly with groups that we belong to, we also define outgroups—people who belong to different or opposing groups. My social identity as a Colorado Avalanche fan might make me dislike fans of our longtime rival team the Detroit Red Wings, for example. The rivalry has cooled over the years, but too much blood has been shed by both sides to let that one go. Fierce sports rivalries often breed violent conflict between fans. Just try a Google search for the string "crossbow death celtic v rangers old firm" and you'll see multiple hits for news stories about matchday crossbow-related violence between supporters of the historically Protestant- and Catholic-supported Glasgow football clubs Rangers and Celtic (respectively), collectively dubbed The Old Firm. The seeds of mere categorization grow into trees of group identity and allegiance. These trees can then bear fruits like prejudice, discrimination, and even violence against other groups.

The stakes get raised even further when there's some sort of realistic conflict between the groups.[10] Where there's competition over resources or status, that makes conflict more likely, and can spill over to produce stigmatization of, and prejudice against, people on the other team. Even highly symbolic or arbitrary group boundaries can become battle lines drawn in the sand, once the forces of social identity and realistic conflict take over.

Supposedly high-minded academics who know all about social identity theory can even fall prey to the very intergroup dynamics it predicts. If you spend enough time following academics on social media, you'll see upwellings of conflict across group lines. Evolutionary psychologists frequently spar with cultural evolutionists. "Blank slatist!" cry the evolutionary psychologists. "Just so stories!" holler back the cultural evolutionists. Bayesian statisticians will face off against those who prefer frequentist statistics. There's been about a decade-long rift between people urging rapid methodological reforms in psychology and those who are more committed to defending the status quo. Even among us reformers, there's a schism between those who advocate for relatively quick bureaucratic fixes (changing policies in how people report and conduct studies) and a smaller group who urge a more moderate, nuanced, and theory-driven approach that recognizes fewer silver bullets to slay our monsters of iffy science. This is all quite esoteric to outsiders, but tempers run hot. Harsh invective gets thrown around. I've seen people called "shameless little bullies" and "methodological terrorists." I've seen a prominent researcher paternalistically liken his disappointment in the authors of a critical paper on research methods to how a father would feel learning his children voted for Trump.* I've seen someone claim that psychologists failing to publish negative results is the biggest ethical lapse of our profession—quite a claim considering that our profession had only recently classified most of the letters in LGBTQ as mental illnesses and also sanctioned the US government's torture programs. Calls to dial back the hostile rhetoric a few notches got dismissed as "a load of honking bullshit." These people—adults! professionals! professors!—are ostensibly discussing the minutiae of how scientists should conduct and report their studies, and yet they throw around insults like kids on the playground.† This ain't productive scientific discourse—it's moralized social identity in action.

Social identity theory and realistic group conflict can explain a lot about prejudice in general. They're among the most prominent theories in all social psychology. So surely they'll explain stigmatization and exclusion of atheists, right? Surprisingly, these theories don't seem to have much to offer when it comes to explaining anti-atheist prejudice. Dislike of atheists is a peculiar form of prejudice, in part because atheists are a peculiar "group" of people. I put group in scare quotes because many features of atheism make it a very poor candidate for the types of intergroup dynamics that social identity theory helps explain.

To begin with, atheists aren't a group of people in any meaningful sense. Sure, there are atheists who join groups with other atheists. There are atheist meetups, and national and international atheist organizations. There are atheist podcasts and reddit communities. But these highly identified atheists are a tiny minority among atheists. Indeed, in my surveys I consistently find that most atheists out there don't even identify as atheists. Atheism just means that someone doesn't believe in a God (or gods). It's the absence of belief. There are tons of people who don't believe in any gods but who

* To his credit, the author of this piece walked it back, under a measure of public pressure.

† Full disclosure: I've been as guilty of this silliness as anyone else, Tweeting burns on behalf of and then against several of these teams at different points in my career.

identify themselves as nonreligious or agnostic (more on this in a subsequent chapter), or who simply skip poll questions about religious identity. Religious belief isn't for them, so why does that absence need a name?

To illustrate the fact that most definitional atheists don't identify as atheists, consider a couple of results. In 2017, talented then-graduate student (and now doctor) Maxine Najle and I ran some studies to see how many atheists there are in the United States.[11] As a starting point for our exploration, we looked up some poll numbers. Big survey companies like Gallup and Pew ask about religion in different ways, and an estimate of atheist prevalence varies greatly depending on what specific question is asked. A 2015 Gallup poll asked people whether or not they believed in God and gave them a binary yes/no response option. Here, 11 percent of people indicated that they didn't believe in God; so that's 11 percent of Americans saying that they are definitional atheists. Around the same time, Pew asked people to indicate their preferred religious identity, and gave them a long menu of response possibilities (e.g., Evangelical Christian, Sikh, Muslim, atheist, none, etc.). Here, only about 3 percent of people ticked the "atheist" box. Putting these polls side by side, you might see the problem: 11 percent of Americans are by definition atheists, but only 3 percent actually identify as atheists, per our gold-standard pollsters. Assuming there are some three hundred million people in the United States, the two atheist prevalence estimates differ by *twenty-four million.* Moving from the large-scale polls to our own work, Maxine and I fielded two big nationally representative surveys with two thousand people apiece. In these surveys, about 17 percent of people said they didn't believe in God. But only about 7 percent of people identified as atheists. Most people who are by definition atheists don't actually identify as atheists. This is one challenge to any theory that makes social identity a necessary ingredient for explaining stigmatization of atheists—there's not much social identity to be found.

Social identity accounts seem to be missing some key ingredients when it comes to atheism (namely, social identity). Realistic conflict accounts also come up short. Atheists on the whole don't constitute an easily identifiable or socially identified group of people—they're just a bunch of individuals who happen to not believe in God. Atheism is simply something that a bunch of folks don't believe. There's not much there to bring about group categorization, let alone group cohesion and intergroup conflict.

While there certainly are some atheist groups who come into conflict with religious groups, this is a clear exception to the general trend of disaffiliation and low identity. Most definitional atheists don't identify as atheists. Even then, most self-identified atheists aren't especially active in the few atheist communities that have cropped up. Social identity theory and realistic conflict theory describe some key ingredients that drive prejudice, but these key ingredients are missing in the case of atheism. These prominent social psychological theories don't clearly predict prejudice against atheists. Instead, they would seem to predict a general apathy toward and ignorance of atheists. Atheists shouldn't be shunned and scorned—per these theories at least—they should just be overlooked. And yet the Edgell results clearly show an intense stigmatization of atheism. Clearly another explanation is needed.

Warmth, Competence, and Stereotype Content

Social identity theory is a one-size-fits-all approach to prejudice. It describes a pretty general process whereby people lump themselves into groups, come to like people in their groups, and come to dislike people in different or opposing groups. This approach has led to a lot of really important insights over the years and gives a nice lens through which to look at intergroup conflicts. It can teach us important things about racism, about football hooligans, and about many religious conflicts. It's a very general framework for understanding prejudice.

But its generality is also at times a weakness. While it can say a lot about prejudice, writ large, it is often not specific enough when we want to understand a specific form of prejudice as it manifests against a specific group. There are quirks and peculiarities that differentiate racism, Islamophobia, transphobia, or sexism, for example. Humanity is complex and diverse. Against a backdrop of great cultural, ethnic, and religious diversity—not to mention huge individual differences within these groups—is it really all that realistic to assume that prejudice always follows the same template? Over the past few decades, social psychologists have tried to expand their repertoire to better capture the nuanced reactions people have to each other.

A prominent attempt to break up stigma into more manageable chunks is known as the stereotype content model, a theory of stigma developed by

Susan Fiske and her colleagues Amy Cuddy, Peter Glick, and Jun Xu.[12] The general idea is pretty straightforward.

Social identity theory views prejudice as existing along one simple dimension. We *like* people who are similar to us, and we *dislike* people who adopt different social identities. That's it: everything flattened down to like versus dislike along a gradient of perceived similarity.

In contrast, the stereotype content model adds some nuance by representing our attitudes toward others as existing along two intersecting dimensions. Instead of flattening everything down to a single like vs. dislike dimension, the stereotype content model says that we view others along one dimension of *competence* and a second dimension of *warmth*. Both are pretty self-explanatory. Competence describes how confident, intelligent, capable, and—well—competent people are. Warmth describes how friendly, approachable, good-natured, or sincere people are. These two dimensions vary independently of each other: people can be high or low in either attribute.

A nice insight of the stereotype content model is that our reactions to others depend on the specific combination of warmth and competence we perceive. If somebody is high in both warmth and competence, we'll probably view them with admiration; these folks are high-status insiders, and we want to curry their favor. If somebody is low in both warmth and competence, we'll probably view them with contempt; these folks are the lowest of the low, and we want to avoid them across the board. Things get interesting, however, for the mixed or ambiguous combinations. If somebody is high in competence but low in warmth (think: stereotypical lawyer), we might not like them. But we're far more likely to react to them with a bit of envy or jealousy than with other emotions. These people have status but seem to wield it only for themselves. In contrast, if someone is high in warmth but low in competence, we view them with pity or sympathy. We like them, but without expecting much.

In their seminal paper on the topic, Fiske and colleagues present some stereotypical people who might fit in each quadrant of a grid that crosses warmth and competence. People viewed as both warm and competent might include close allies and prestigious in-group members. People seen as low in both warmth and competence might include homeless people or welfare recipients (remember: we're just talking about commonly held stereotypes here). High warmth–low competence people might include the elderly, or people with disabilities. High competence–low warmth people might include really rich people. Anti-Semitic tropes about cabals of rich Jews secretly running the world strongly evoke both high competence and low warmth, for example.

Might the stereotype content model help explain anti-atheist prejudice? The Edgell poll results don't really paint a clear picture of how warm or competent people might think atheists are. Not wanting someone as president might speak to competence. But then again not wanting someone to marry your kid could speak to warmth. And thinking that atheists fundamentally disagree with one's vision of America doesn't neatly map onto either dimension.

Curious about this, I ran a quick study trying to pin down where exactly atheists fall on both dimensions. The results? Atheists fell in a sort of undifferentiated middle ground. They were seen as a little higher on competence than on warmth, but not especially high or low on either. Atheists were more-or-less comparable to groups like feminists, Jews, and to a lesser extent gay people. But recall that atheists fall well behind Jews and gay people on the various Edgell poll results. Whatever is leading to atheists being so excluded in Edgell's work, it doesn't look like the stereotype content model can explain it. Back to the drawing board.

From Prejudice to Prejudices

A key thrust of social psychology work on prejudice has been to try to explain it as a relatively unitary phenomenon. Social psychologists have historically loved theories that capture complex phenomena in broad strokes. This is useful in lots of cases, and both social identity theory and the stereotype content model have produced impressive scientific insights. But both can be quite underpowered if one wants to explain a particular type of prejudice against specific people. Broad theories are great tools for the job of understanding lots of manifestations of prejudice in general; they're often poor tools for understanding any particular manifestation.

Here, evolutionary psychology might be able to offer a rich theory for drilling deeper into the particulars. Evolutionary psychologists look to our evolutionary history to form hypotheses about our modern psychology. And one key challenge is outlining the myriad specific adaptive challenges our ancestors faced. Our ancestors needed to avoid predators, seek shelter, find nutritious foods, avoid toxic substances, join coalitions, fight off rivals, attract and retain mates, raise offspring, and do countless other very specific things. Evolutionary psychologists tend to view our psychology as a set of specific mental adaptations that helped our ancestors navigate specific challenges.[13] A common metaphor is the Swiss Army knife, which is really just a collection of gadgets, each one useful for one specific thing.

In this view, it's not realistic to view "prejudice" as a single phenomenon. Instead, we might have really specific and nuanced reactions to people, commensurate with the threats they may pose. What we call "prejudice" is actually a lot of specific "prejudices" shaped by different specific evolved reactions we have to threats, according to Steven Neuberg at Arizona State University,[14] who's been a leader on this sort of work. If somebody is a hulking brute who looks prone to violence, they're a threat to our physical safety and we might view them with fear. On the other hand, if someone is hacking and coughing up phlegm, they're a pathogen risk and we might view them with disgust. If someone has been taking food from our clan's common pool without doing their share of the gathering labor, they're a resource threat, and we might view them with anger.

This evolutionary approach to prejudices—rather than to prejudice, singular—gives scientists a powerful tool for figuring out what specific reactions to expect. People like Neuberg and his colleague Mark Schaller at the University of British Columbia are at the forefront of this work,[15] and their research provides a bit of a model for how to productively study a given form of prejudice. First, consider the evolutionary threats that a potential prejudice target might be seen to pose. Then, figure out what reactions might be appropriate when it comes to avoiding or mitigating the threat. As a young graduate student, this seemed a powerful recipe. So, what's the threat atheists might pose? And what's an appropriate reaction?

I first came across this evolutionary psychology work on prejudices right around the same time I'd begun really thinking about the idea of religious prosociality discussed in the previous chapter. Religions, it seems, have been really good at getting large groups of people to cooperate with each other. Beliefs in—and frequent reminders of—Big Gods can help people curb their selfish impulses and behave more prosocially. Not only does religious prosociality imply that people will alter their own behavior because of their beliefs in moralizing gods, it suggests that the religious beliefs of others might be used as a cue to how cooperative they are likely to be. But by not believing in gods, atheists are sending the wrong signals. Without beliefs in moralizing gods, atheists might be viewed as threats to cooperation.

If someone is seen as a cooperative threat because their lack of belief in gods makes them more likely to lie, cheat, and steal with impunity (or so the perception goes), then what kind of a reaction might we expect? Since the threat is cooperative and moral in nature, I hypothesized that stigmatization of atheists might be especially driven by a sort of *moral distrust*. Here's the power of the evolutionary approach to prejudices: I was able to move from a stubborn puzzle about why atheists were viewed with such scorn to a quite specific prediction about *how exactly* atheists were stigmatized. Instead of a general dislike (per social identity theory) or some combination of warmth and competence (per the stereotype content model), I could predict instead that negative attitudes toward atheists would be specifically about moral distrust.

In Gods We Trust

Compelled and confounded by large-scale polls showing intense stigmatization of atheists, I'd set out to figure out why this was the case. Classic approaches from social psychology, including social identity theory and the stereotype content model, hadn't really helped me crack the code. But by combining an evolutionary view of prejudices with a cultural evolutionary view of religious prosociality, I'd arrived at the prediction that antipathy toward atheists might be specifically driven by moral distrust.

Time to test the hypothesis. As we saw in previous chapters, there are lots of ideas that sound great in principle but ultimately fail when tested (or in the case of my experiments on analytic thinking and atheism, fail when tested rigorously). Data are often where the scientific rubber meets the road. So I began testing moral distrust of atheists in a bunch of different ways, in work that would eventually produce my master's thesis, my doctoral dissertation, and a handful of scholarly publications with some of my collaborators. My graduate school mentor Ara Norenzayan was my most frequent sounding board for ideas, and a key contributor to this early work.

To begin with, we went with a fairly obvious approach: we just designed some questionnaires to ask people how they felt about atheists and some other groups of people. For various reasons, we thought that attitudes toward gay men might be an interesting comparison. Both atheists and gay men have historically scored near the bottom on cultural inclusion polls. Both groups are frequently targeted by the religious right. Both are also to some extent stigmas based on concealable identities—people might be able to pass as being straight or devout to avoid backlash. But according to our evolutionary approach to prejudices, we'd expect different reactions. Steve Neuberg's work on evolved prejudices pinpointed a specific disgust reaction toward gay men, born of a suspicion that they represent a pathogen and disease threat (once again, we're talking about people's stereotypes here). Disgust and distrust are really quite different, so in effect we were predicting a different profile of prejudice against both atheists and gay men. So we asked a few hundred participants to rate both atheists and gay men according to a few key things: how much they generally like or dislike each, how disgusting they find each, and how much they distrust each. The results showed that atheists and gay men weren't hugely different in terms of overall like and dislike (the currency of theories like social identity theory). But they were entirely different when it came to the more specific reactions. People showed a distinct disgust reaction for the gay men, but specific distrust toward atheists. There we had it—anti-atheist prejudice was reflected in specific distrust, at least when it came to the crude self-reports we used in this study.

To drill deeper, we then developed other ways to test whether anti-atheist prejudice really boiled down to distrust. In one study, we had people rate how likely they'd be to hire atheists for various jobs that varied in how trustworthy an ideal candidate needed to be. For high-trust jobs like babysitters, atheists were seen as unacceptable. But for low-trust jobs like a waitress, atheists were just fine. This showed that discrimination against atheists was context sensitive, especially likely only when trust mattered a lot. In a separate study we used a quirky reaction-time task called the Implicit Association Test (IAT) to see if people showed a gut-level association between atheists and the concept of untrustworthiness. Without boring you with the methodological details or inferential quirks of the IAT, we again found evidence that distrust was a main driver.‡

‡ Inasmuch as that's something the IAT could measure—and exactly what the IAT measures is a somewhat open case, despite its widespread use and the degree of popular attention it's received.

So across three different experimental paradigms (self-report, job candidate preferences, and IAT performance), we'd found some evidence that distrust drove anti-atheist prejudice. But more convincing evidence would have to come from additional types of experiments, pitting atheists against lots of other different potential prejudice targets. And by a strange bit of serendipity, I stumbled across an experimental setup that seemed perfect for the job, but—to my knowledge at least—hadn't been deployed to measure stereotypes or prejudice before. I've used this task now quite a lot over the years, and will feature some of the results obtained with it throughout this chapter. So let's begin by walking through it in some detail.

Stereotyping, Fast and Slow

I'd been brushing up on some classic work in psychology for some of my coursework. This included foundational work on judgment and decision-making, and the intuitions and biases that lead to some predictable departures from rationality. Lots of this work is outlined in books like *Thinking Fast and Slow* by Nobel Laureate Daniel Kahneman. Specifically, I'd read about the *representativeness heuristic*, a classic finding in this domain. Read the vignette below and quickly answer the question.

> Linda is thirty-one years old, single, outspoken, and very bright. She majored in philosophy. As a student, she was deeply concerned with issues of discrimination and social justice and also participated in anti-nuclear demonstrations.
>
> Which is more probable?
>
> A. Linda is a bank teller.
> B. Linda is a bank teller and is active in the feminist movement.

Did you pick A or B? Stumped and picked neither? Just take a stab and go with your gut.

Most people, it turns out, pick Option B (60–80 percent, depending on details), but Option B is logically incorrect. You see, Option B is just a small subset that is already contained by Option A. If Linda is a bank teller who happens to be an active feminist, she also belongs to the category of bank tellers. A contains B, plus all of the bank tellers who aren't active in the feminist movement. Option B is known as a *conjunction error*; picking it is sometimes called the *conjunction fallacy* because people are mistakenly saying that the conjunction of two things (bank teller *and* feminism) is more probable than one of the things on its own (bank teller). So why do most people pick B? Are humans just stupid? Not at all.§

In this problem, we have a description of Linda, and then some question options with one option implying membership in some group. In the Linda example, the description doesn't necessarily sound like the category "bank teller" but it does sound like the category "feminist." If people intuitively think that the description is representative of the implied group membership, then they tend to pick Option B. The logical error in people's responses isn't driven by stupidity—it's the result of our brains trying to see what information fits with what. Because the description provided of liberal activist Linda sounds representative of someone who could be active in the feminist movement, people pick that option.

One day I was thinking about the representative heuristic as I was walking in the woods near my flat.¶ And I had a sudden realization: the representativeness heuristic task is all about stereotyping. The intuitive fit between a description and an implied group membership really came down to the compatibility of stereotypes. Our stereotype of someone active in the feminist movement just fits easily with the stereotypes that are evoked by the description of Linda. That would make the representativeness heuristic task a natural fit for examining specific stereotype reactions people might have for different groups—exactly what I was hoping to investigate with atheists! By tinkering with the descriptions given and the implied group memberships, I could see which concepts people stereotypically associate with different people. This representativeness heuristic task would prove an

§ And yet . . .

¶ As an aside, I don't think I've ever had a good scientific idea sitting in my office. Walking and pondering, going for a bike ride, kayaking, or just aimlessly strolling about all do more for me. I can really see why Charles Darwin built regular walks into his daily routine. That said, the people in his life who took care of his household and life aside from work no doubt would've appreciated the leisure time for daily contemplative strolls, and I wonder what scientific insights we've missed over the years by only giving the thinnest and most entitled slice of humanity the privilege of such intellectual leisure time.

invaluable tool for pinning down specific intuitive associations that people have about atheists.

To confirm that the representative heuristic task boiled down to stereotype compatibility, I tried to make the effect disappear. In experimental psychology, this is a common tactic: if you want to show that you understand how an effect "works," you find a straightforward way to kill the effect. It turns out that it's really easy to break the representativeness heuristic effect: if you provide a different description, or a different implied group, then this disrupts the intuitive flow. For example, if I gave you the same description of Linda but a different Option B, how would you respond?

> Linda is thirty-one years old, single, outspoken, and very bright. She majored in philosophy. As a student, she was deeply concerned with issues of discrimination and social justice and also participated in anti-nuclear demonstrations.
>
> Which is more probable?
>
> A. Linda is a bank teller.
> B. Linda is a bank teller and is an avid big-game hunter.

In this case, there's nothing about the description that screams "big-game hunter." Without a tight fit between the description and the implied group membership, the spell is broken and there's no intuitive pull to pick Option B. And indeed, when I ran a study with this exact setup, exactly nobody picked Option B. The classic Linda problem performance dropped from 60–80 percent conjunction errors at baseline to 0 percent in the big-game hunter version. Effect killed.

The conjunction error turns out to just be a gauge of stereotype compatibility: people pick Option B when it portrays someone who participants could see fitting the description provided. This was exciting, because it showed that we could use the probability with which people pick Option B in this task to gauge the intuitive fit between a given description and an implied group membership. If lots of people commit the conjunction error, this indicates a tight intuitive fit between description and group. If few people commit the conjunction fallacy, this indicates weak or no intuitive fit between the description and the group. In short, the conjunction fallacy makes for a nice, straightforward measure of people's intuitive endorsement of specific stereotypes for specific people.

Armed with these insights about the representativeness heuristic, the conjunction fallacy, and their use for measuring intuitive stereotypes, let's return to atheists.

Intuitive Moral Distrust

Through happenstance, I'd hit upon a neat experimental method for testing whether people held specific intuitive stereotypes about specific people. Now I wanted to tweak this tool to measure the very specific sort of moral distrust that we'd postulated was at the root of anti-atheist prejudice. Religious prosociality speculates that beliefs in big moralizing gods might be especially useful in preventing people from selfish freeriding—a tendency to take what you can if you think you can get away with it. So I designed a representativeness heuristic task describing an archetypal untrustworthy free rider who lies and steals when the taking's easy. It starts with a story and question about a man named Richard:

> Richard is thirty-one years old. On his way to work one day, he accidentally backed his car into a parked van. Because pedestrians were watching, he got out of his car. He pretended to write down his insurance information. He then tucked the blank note into the van's window before getting back into his car and driving away. Later the same day, Richard found a wallet on the sidewalk. Nobody was looking, so he took all of the money out of the wallet. He then threw the wallet in a trash can.

Armed with this vignette about Richard, I could give different research participants different follow-up questions to see which groups of people my participants intuitively associated with this description of a sketchy and untrustworthy guy. So, for example, some participants would get the following question:

> Which is more probable?
>
> A. Richard is a teacher.
> B. Richard is a teacher and a Christian.

Other participants would get this version:

> Which is more probable?
>
> A. Richard is a teacher.
> B. Richard is a teacher and a Muslim.

Few people picked Option B in either of these experimental conditions. Nor did they tend to pick Option B if it implied that the person in question was gay, or a feminist. Conjunction error (Option B) responses were rare, and basically just chance errors. This happened about 5–20 percent of the time.

To calibrate our measure, we also included one implied target group that would be unambiguously distrusted. Namely, rapists:

> Which is more probable?
>
> A. Richard is a teacher.
> B. Richard is a teacher and a rapist.

Lots of people picked Option B if it indicated that our sketchy thief and fraudster also was a rapist (a hair under 50 percent of people picked this option). In contrast to low conjunction-error rates matching the untrustworthy description with Christian, Muslim, Jewish, gay, or feminist targets, the conjunction error popped right out for rapist targets. This is a sanity check for the method: we found evidence for intuitive moral distrust of unambiguously distrusted rapists. The key question then is whether the pattern of results for atheist targets would look more like rapists, or more like everyone else. Here was the atheist question prompt we used, giving both the name "atheist" and also a definition:

> Which is more probable?
>
> A. Richard is a teacher.
> B. Richard is a teacher and an atheist (someone who does not believe in God).

In our first version of this experiment, about 50 percent of participants picked Option B for atheists, showing a degree of intuitive distrust for atheists that was statistically comparable to their intuitive distrust for rapists. That's right: according to this one measure at least, intuitive distrust of atheists was similar in strength to intuitive distrust of rapists.

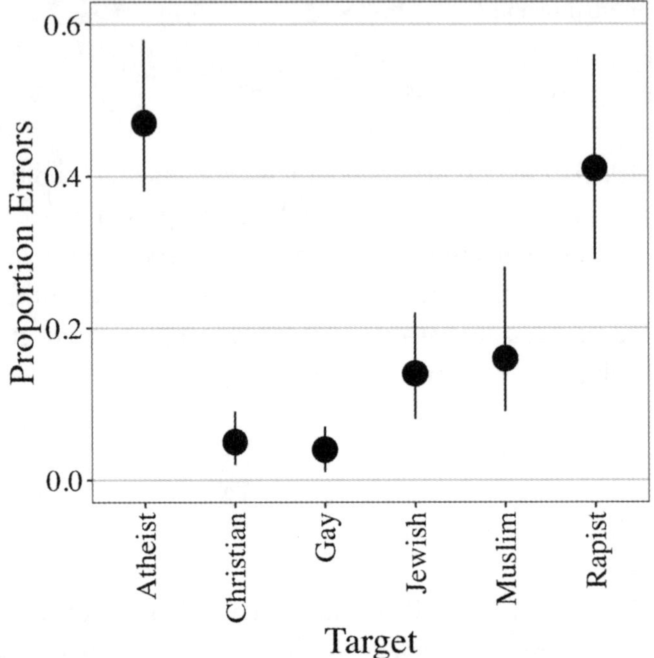

Figure 8.3. Intuitive moral distrust of atheists, relative to other groups. *Source:* W. M. Gervais, A. F. Shariff, and A. Norenzayan, "Do You Believe in Atheists? Distrust Is Central to Anti-Atheist Prejudice," *Journal of Personality and Social Psychology* 101, no. 6 (2011): 1189.

We did some follow-up study to confirm that we were measuring a specific distrust reaction rather than a more knee-jerk general revulsion. For example, we gave people a description that was quite unpleasant, but in a way that doesn't at all evoke trust or distrust:

> Richard is thirty-one years old. He has a rare inherited medical condition. This leads him to have dry, flaky skin and produce excess mucus. His skin often flakes off at embarrassing times, and he almost always has a dripping nose and phlegm in his throat. On his way to work one day, Richard was scratching his itchy shoulder. Some of the dry skin that flaked off caused him to sneeze, and some snot ended up on his tie. He failed to notice that the phlegm got on his tie. He wore this dirty tie through an entire workday.

The conjunction error rate that had spiked when atheists were paired with a distrust vignette now disappeared entirely. It wasn't any old unpleasant description that triggered the conjunction error for atheists—it was specific to distrust.

I can still vividly remember analyzing the data from these initial studies. The experimental paradigm felt almost too simple to work, but the Linda problem had been well-trodden research territory since Kahneman and Tversky developed it in the 1970s. I'd just tweaked it a little to add different descriptions and new target groups. And the results suggested that intuitive distrust of atheists was incredibly strong. This was one of a very few statistical results in my research career that stopped me in my tracks. I checked and rechecked the data, and the result held. We replicated it, and replicated it again. Every time, the conjunction errors spiked when a description of an untrustworthy person was paired with an atheist target (or, it turns out, a rapist target). It's no exaggeration to say that this is both the most surprising and most robust empirical result of my career as a scientist. As for the puzzle that this chapter considers—why is it that atheists provoke such disdain?—it was another compelling piece of evidence that it boiled down to moral distrust.

My coauthors and I published our first paper on atheist distrust in 2011. The publication journey had been a bumpy one. We initially wrote up just a couple of the studies mentioned above and quickly sent it out for publication starting in about 2008, fearing that we were about to be scooped by the numerous other teams that were surely working on the same puzzle (how wrong we were). And our submission got rejected from journal after journal. Some commented that prejudice against atheists was a fringe topic, too niche for a mainstream psychology journal like them to touch. Others pointed out that the studies in our paper weren't especially strong—compellingly, I can admit in retrospect. At this point, the paper consisted of the reaction time study and the job candidate study, which are admittedly both quite weak little studies. But after the frustration of multiple rejections, I got serious and ran a bigger study to pin down the details. And sometime in this period I hit on the ideas with the conjunction fallacy studies that really tied the package together. The paper was finally published in the *Journal of Personality and Social Psychology*,[16] a flagship journal in social psychology. I'm generally quite averse to rankings of journal prestige, but having our work published in that journal definitely felt a bit like I'd felt reading the original Edgell paper. There was room for this work in mainstream outlets, it just took a lot of work to get there. The rejections along the way stung, but were great learning experiences. And landing a *JPSP* (as insiders call the journal) on this niche little topic was quite vindicating.

The Varieties of Moral Distrust

The initial *JPSP* results pointed to distrust as a contributor to anti-atheist prejudice. But I suspected we'd just barely scratched the surface. Some of the evidence we'd gathered so far came from experiments that treated the concept of distrust very broadly (say, looking at reaction times to words synonymous with *trustworthy*). This was nice, but didn't give a lot of nuance. Other studies, like the conjunction fallacy work, were if anything too specific. It showed that people intuitively associate atheism with theft and insurance fraud—very specific types of moral distrust. I really wanted to explore this conceptual space a bit more, to see what other types of actions people would associate with atheism.

I'd just completed graduate school (my doctoral dissertation was cheekily and grandiosely titled "The Peculiar Psychological Properties of Anti-Atheist Prejudice") and had embarked on my first full academic post as an assistant professor of social psychology at the University of Kentucky. My lab space was under construction for much of my first year there, and I didn't yet have collaborators in the area. So I decided to run a bunch of low-cost online studies to get my independent professorial career rolling. Kiley Hamlin—a brilliant developmental psychologist back at UBC—had been on my dissertation committee and had posed a really interesting question. She asked if my conjunction fallacy results on distrust were really about morality in general, not just the type of cooperative trust we'd tested. To the extent that people intuitively assume that morality is more-or-less synonymous with religion—thanks to millennia of religious supremacy borne by religious prosociality and cultural evolution—mightn't they intuitively associate atheism with lots of other types of moral violations?

To test this possibility, I decided to run a bunch more conjunction fallacy studies. By tweaking the descriptions given, one can assess moral intuitions with a bit more precision than is possible with a lot of other standard social psychology experimental tasks. And for a first-year professor with a toddler at home who had just moved to a new city and didn't yet know anyone or really even know how to do my job yet, these experiments had another huge advantage: they were quick and easy to run. I could put together some conjunction fallacy vignettes, put them online, and have ready results overnight. I really can't recommend these experiments enough for any researchers out there looking for a quick and interesting methodology.

To assess a wide range of moral violations, I turned to moral foundations theory,** a social psychological approach to morality developed by Jonathan Haidt, Jesse Graham, and their collaborative team. Moral foundations theory has been popularly summarized in Haidt's book *The Righteous Mind*, and it goes something like this: Human morality is not a unitary phenomenon. Instead, we have a number of moral intuitions about specific types of actions. These specific intuitions are the moral foundations, and there's variability in how much people rely on them. I think of the moral foundations as knobs that can be dialed up or down for different people. One of the knobs is *harm* and another is *fairness*. Basically everyone agrees that harm and fairness are morally relevant: thou shalt not kill, thou shalt not steal, and the like. These knobs are dialed up for most people, most of the time.

Other moral knobs are only dialed up for some people. For example, political conservatives in the United States also consider *respect for authority* and *loyalty to one's ingroup* as highly morally relevant; liberals, not so much. This can somewhat explain huge partisan gaps in views on issues like flag burning (disloyal desecration), or public protest (anti-authority rabble rousing).

Finally, there's one moral knob that really seems to drive a lot of culture war issues. Haidt and company dubbed this the *purity* or *sanctity* foundation. Basically, people who endorse purity-based morality think that there's a natural order to the world that we oughtn't screw around with—and this moral dial cares deeply about screwing! The purity-defining natural order proscribes a lot of things having to do with what we use our bodies for and what we put in them. Sometimes even where we put things in our bodies, and in which things we put parts of our bodies. Drugs (my body is a temple!), sex (Adam and Eve, not Adam and Steve!), food (no mixing milk and meat!), and holding some things sacred are the purview of purity-based morality. Like the authority and loyalty foundations, political conservatives tend to have their purity dial turned up higher than do liberals.

** As an aside, I think moral foundations theory is a misnomer. Moral foundations are a descriptive typology that loosely clusters people's moral judgments into five (or now more) chunks. It lacks the explanatory depth or predictive specificity that most philosophers of science would recognize as a proper theory. It's a hunch and a clustering of themes—interesting but probably falling short of a theory. Per a famous saying, in the land of the blind, a man with one eye is king. And in a field as light in strong theory as social psychology is, I suppose moral foundations "theory" will have to do.

Returning to atheists, moral foundations theory proved a nice entry point for testing Kiley Hamlin's hypothesis about people just generally associating atheists with immorality. Would people intuitively associate atheism with violations of all the moral foundations?

I constructed a series of conjunction fallacy vignettes, targeting each specific moral foundation violation. Table 8.1 is a sampling of the nasty business my characters got up to.[††]

My online participants would each be given one of these vignettes to read, and a standard conjunction fallacy question, such as (using the last example):

> Which is more probable?
>
> A. Jack is a doctor.
> B. Jack is a doctor and [insert group membership]

Crucially, many of my participants got this as their Option B: "Jack is a doctor and does not believe in God." In this way, I could see if people intuitively associated the vignette with atheism, but we didn't actually use the word *atheist* in case it had its own unsavory associations in the minds of my participants. To check whether any results were specific to atheism, I also included a lot of other contrast groups, including lots of ethnic and religious group comparisons.

Any given participant would receive just one vignette-target group combination in isolation (say, a harm vignette with a potential atheist target, or one purity vignette with a potential Hispanic target). This part's crucial: nobody is being asked, for example, whether they think the people doing incest are more likely to be atheists or to be Muslims or Hispanics or Jews or anything else. Each participant makes one judgment, and we infer overall rates of how much each target is associated with the moral violations by looking at the aggregate data across all combinations.

The results? People didn't reliably associate any of the moral violations with any of the contrast groups. People weren't imagining cannibalistic

---

[††] Fun fact: I named these characters after friends and family. I tried to tailor the moral violation to each personality in an ironic way—my fictional characters tend to be doing things that most directly contradict their real-life counterpart's personality. So, if my brother Jack invites you for a barbecue and serves chicken, it is probably still virginal poultry. As far as I know.

Table 8.1. Moral Violation Vignettes

Foundation	Vignette
Harm	Russell was on the bus on his way home from a long day at work. An overweight woman got on the bus. Rather than give up his seat for the woman, Russell made a number of cruel remarks to her about her appearance. After getting off the bus, Russell was walking to his apartment. A stray dog walked up to him to beg for food and Russell kicked it in the head, hard.
Fairness	Brad just moved into a new apartment. A coworker, Jan, helped Brad move his belongings. One day, Jan emailed Brad to see if Brad would help Jan move into a new apartment. Brad ignored the email and did not help Jan. Brad also enjoyed playing poker at a local bar. When he was playing with people he did not know well, Brad would usually cheat in order to win money.
Loyalty	Lesley grew up in the United States. After university she spent a summer backpacking around Europe. In Europe, she would often pretend that she was Canadian and say derogatory things about the United States. She also rooted against the US team during the Olympics that year. This caused some conflicts with her family, so she cut off all ties with them for one year.
Authority	Drew did not like her boss. One day, her boss was scolding Drew for missing a deadline. Drew got frustrated and flipped her boss off as soon as the boss turned around. Later that day, Drew was walking home. The police had a barricade set up on one block for a parade the next day. When a police officer asked Drew to find another route home, Drew said, "Why won't you f#$%@! pigs just leave me alone?" and walked through the barricade anyways.
Purity	Catherine works in a medical school pathology lab as a research assistant. The lab prepares human cadavers that are used to teach medical students about anatomy. The cadavers come from people who had donated their body to science for research. One night Catherine is leaving the lab when she sees a body that is going to be discarded the next day. Catherine was a vegetarian, for moral reasons. She thought it was wrong to kill animals for food. But then, when she saw a body about to be cremated, she thought it was irrational to waste perfectly edible meat. So she cut off a piece of flesh, and took it home and cooked it. The person had died recently of a heart attack, and she cooked the meat thoroughly, so there was no risk of disease.
Purity	Graeme and his sister were traveling together in France. One night they were staying alone in a cabin near the beach. They decided that it would be interesting and fun if they tried making love. At the very least it would be a new experience for each of them. Graeme's sister was already taking birth control pills, but Graeme used a condom too, just to be safe. They both enjoyed it, but they decided not to do it again. They keep that night as a special secret between them, which makes them feel even closer to each other.
Purity	On the way home from work, Jack decided to stop at the butcher shop to pick up something for dinner. He decided to roast a whole chicken. He got home, unwrapped the chicken carcass, and decided to make love to it. He used a condom, and fully sterilized the carcass when he was finished. He then roasted the chicken and ate it for dinner alongside a nice glass of chardonnay.

Source: W. M. Gervais, "Everything Is Permitted? People Intuitively Judge Immorality as Representative of Atheists," *PLoS ONE* 9, no. 4 (2014): e92302.

Buddhists or boss-hating Native Americans. But across the board, people intuitively felt that atheists might be puppy-kicking, Canadian-feigning, poker-cheating, cop-insulting, incestuous, chicken-fucking cannibals.[17] Below is an aggregate graph showing the overall conjunction error rate for each of my target groups, collapsing across all of the moral violations I tested across each moral foundation. Atheists were intuitively associated with every single moral violation; no other group was strongly associated with any moral violation.

You may now be asking yourself a question that I get a lot when I give talks about these results. Namely, who the hell are the people in my studies who think atheists are into incest and the like? All of the participants in this group of studies were adults in the United States who agreed to do surveys online for a bit of money, via Amazon Mechanical Turk. Relative to the general American populace, MTurkers tend to skew slightly liberal,

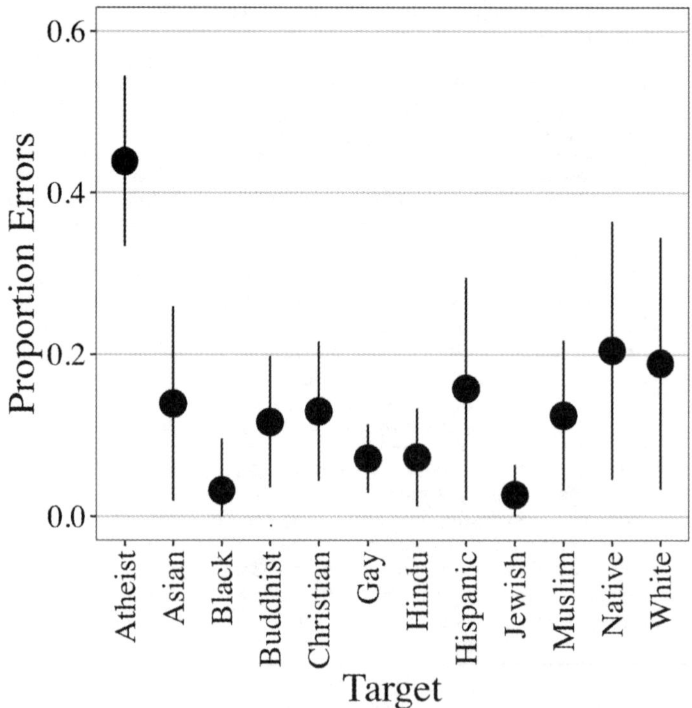

Figure 8.4. People intuitively associate atheists, but not many other groups, with gross moral violations including cannibalism, abuse, incest, and necrobestiality. *Source:* W. M. Gervais, "Everything Is Permitted? People Intuitively Judge Immorality as Representative of Atheists," *PLoS ONE* 9, no. 4 (2014): e92302.

and slightly less religious. This isn't a sample of conservatives in the Bible Belt who think atheists are up to no good; if anything, the opposite. I was also able to run an aggregate analysis just looking at atheist participants—people who rated their belief in God at exactly zero on a 0–100 scale, and who self-identified with the term *atheist*. Amazingly, even my atheist participants intuitively associated immorality with atheism! Moral suspicion of atheists runs deep.

All of these participants were from the United States, which is by global standards a peculiarly religious country considering its overall prosperity and education levels. So next I wanted to explore things in a global context. Over about four years, I assembled an all-star team of global scholars to test intuitive moral distrust of atheists in thirteen countries around the globe. We included both strongly religious countries (the United States, United Arab Emirates, India) and some of the most secular places on earth (China, Czechia, Netherlands, Finland). To pinpoint intuitions about really extreme moral violations, we used the following vignette:

> When a man was young, he began inflicting harm on animals. It started with just pulling the wings off flies but eventually progressed to torturing stray cats and other animals in his neighborhood. As an adult, the man found that he did not get much thrill from harming animals, so he began hurting people instead. He has killed five homeless people that he abducted from poor neighborhoods in his home city. Their dismembered bodies are currently buried in his basement.
>
> Which is more probable?
>
> A. The man is a teacher.
>
> B. The man is a teacher and . . .

For the end of Option B, half of our participants saw "does not believe in any gods" and half saw "is a religious believer." This allowed us to see, in each of thirteen countries, the degree to which people intuitively associate torture and serial murder of homeless people with either atheism or religious belief. The results—published in the journal *Nature Human Behaviour* in 2017[18]—both astounded and horrified us.

In every country except Finland (and to a lesser extent New Zealand), people reliably associated serial murder with atheism. Additional analyses showed the results varied way less among people with different religious beliefs within each country than they varied between countries overall. In other words, our models and data suggested that even atheists in highly secular places like the Netherlands nonetheless hold an intuitive moral suspicion of atheists. Yes, this pattern was strongest among the most religious people in the most religious countries. But it was not wholly eliminated anywhere except for among our Finnish participants.

Across lots of studies and lots of locations, our conjunction fallacy studies showed a deep intuitive association between atheism and immorality and distrust. This intuitive moral suspicion wasn't just seen among strongly religious participants, and in two sets of aggregate studies it even showed up among atheist participants. Dostoevsky's *The Brothers Karamazov* includes a rather (in)famous line, in which a character suggests that belief in God might be a necessary set of brakes to inhibit immorality: "Without

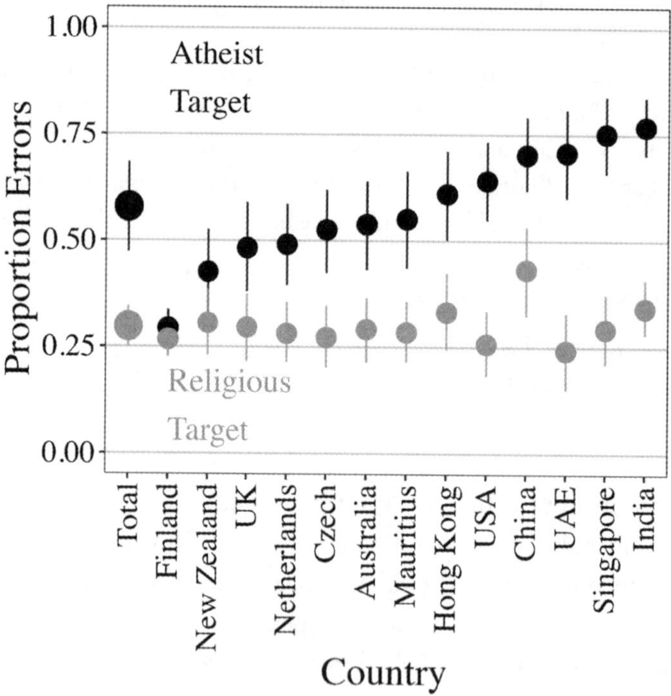

Figure 8.5. Across thirteen countries, serial murder is intuitively associated with atheists. *Source:* W. M. Gervais, D. Xygalatas, R. T. McKay, R. M. Van Elk, E. E. Buchtel, M. Aveyard, . . . and J. Bulbulia, "Global Evidence of Extreme Intuitive Moral Prejudice against Atheists," *Nature Human Behaviour* 1, no. 8 (2017): 1–6.

God and the future life? It means everything is permitted now, one can do anything?" Our participants seemed to intuitively agree. Without belief in God, truly anything might be permitted: torture, murder, cannibalism, incest, and necro-bestiality included.

Religious Haloes and Atheist Horns

The various conjunction fallacy studies show an intuitive link between immorality and atheism. But the studies only speak to an intuition running in one direction: from immorality to atheism. Given a vignette depicting immorality, people seem to intuitively assume the perpetrator is an atheist. The intuition infers atheism from immorality. But this doesn't necessarily tell us much about what people naturally infer using atheism as a starting point. Put differently, people assume that immoral people are atheists, but what do they spontaneously assume if they're just thinking about atheists? Is the pattern reversible—will people spontaneously infer immorality and untrustworthiness from mere atheism?

Jazmin Brown-Iannuzzi joined us as an assistant professor at the University of Kentucky in 2015, and was easily and by far our best social psychologist until she left for the greener grass of the University of Virginia where she has since well-earned tenure. She's made landmark contributions in social cognition, the social psychology of inequality, and stereotyping and prejudice research. Her studies exemplify creativity and rigor, and she came up with a very clever way to see how people spontaneously pictured atheists.

There's a nifty experimental task called the reverse correlations procedure that lets researchers see how people picture others—it gives us a snapshot of people's mental representations. Here's how it works. Imagine you're a participant in a study, and you're seated at a computer. You're told that you will see a pair of pictures, and you're just supposed to pick which one looks more like a given category. But the catch is that the images are all sort of degraded and they don't look a hell of a lot like anything. But you do this task lots and lots of times, and eventually researchers can take all the pictures you chose and merge them together into a composite. The composite image blends together whatever incidental features you chose along the way and shows your spontaneously generated mental representation of the category you were given.

Along with Stephanie McKee, we ran a reverse correlation study to see how people spontaneously represented both atheists and believers. If you're a participant, you'd be given two pictures, as in figure 8.6, and asked which one you think doesn't believe in God.

Not much to work with, is it? But if hundreds of people make hundreds of these choices, the final blended results can be quite striking. For comparison, we had some people do a round where they'd select the face that looks like it doesn't believe in God and other people did a round selecting the face that does believe in God. In this way we could generate two composite faces, as in figure 8.7: one depicts a spontaneous mental representation of atheists, one a spontaneous mental representation of believers. Guess which is which.

The atheist face (on the left if you couldn't guess) looks entirely sketchier than does the theist face (on the right). He—and the atheist face does look decidedly masculine—looks like he has both seen and done some shit in his time. And the theist face? She looks positively angelic in comparison.

The next phase in a reverse correlations study is showing the composite images to a new batch of participants without telling them anything about the faces or how they were made, and having this new bunch of people rate

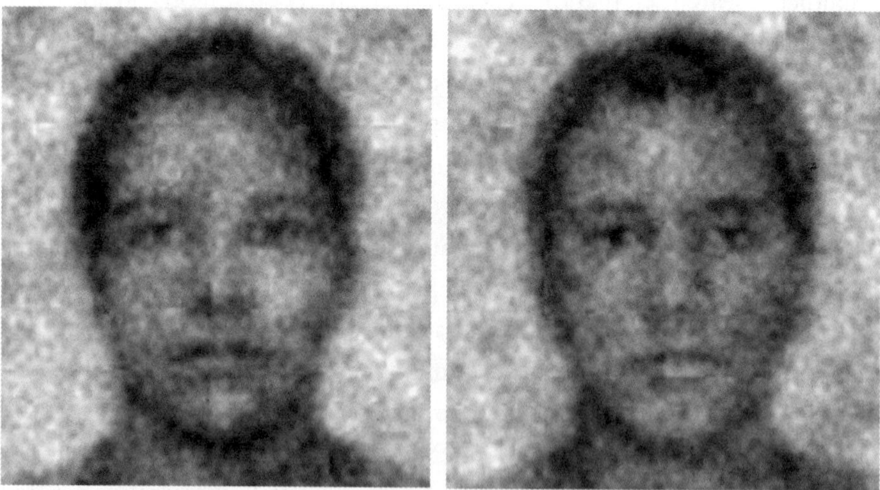

Figure 8.6. Sample reverse correlations stimuli. *Source:* J. L. Brown-Iannuzzi, S. McKee, and W. M. Gervais, "Atheist Horns and Religious Halos: Mental Representations of Atheists and Theists," *Journal of Experimental Psychology: General* 147, no. 2 (2018): 292.

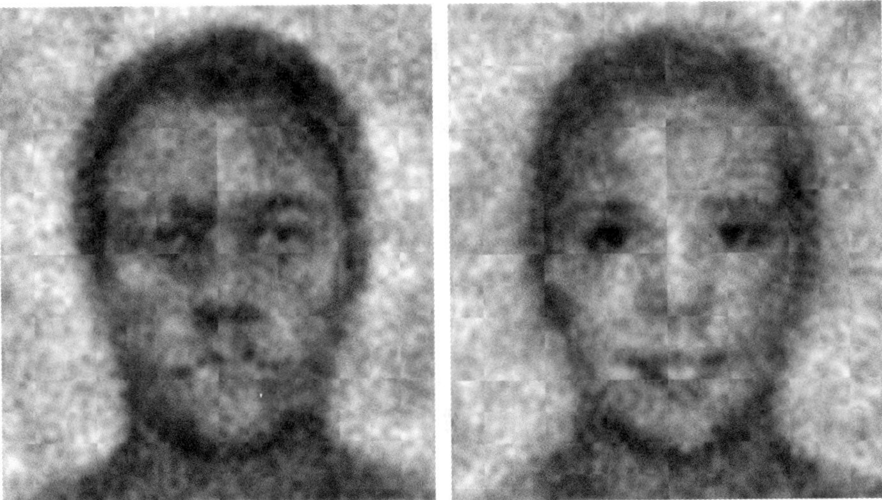

Figure 8.7. Composite mental image of atheists (left) and composite mental image of religious believers (right). *Source:* J. L. Brown-Iannuzzi, S. McKee, and W. M. Gervais, "Atheist Horns and Religious Halos: Mental Representations of Atheists and Theists," *Journal of Experimental Psychology: General* 147, no. 2 (2018): 292.

the faces on various attributes. We were interested in a lot of specific traits here. First off, we wanted to see how religious people would think each face was—this is sort of a validation check. If you generate a face based on people's representations of atheists, will new people guess that the face isn't very religious? Beyond this sanity check, we were especially curious to see if the spontaneously generated mental representation of atheists would somehow connote immorality and untrustworthiness as well. So we included those traits. Finally, we included a whole bunch of other associations people might have about the faces. As you can see in figure 8.8, our second wave of participants did, indeed, think that the atheist face was less religious than the theist face. But interestingly, they felt even more strongly that the atheist face depicted lower morality and trustworthiness. From an atheism prompt, people readily infer moral untrustworthiness! Beyond these crucial attributes, you can see that people just generally didn't like the atheist face: it was seen as less competent, less warm, less gentle, and even a bit less fundamentally human.

The conjunction fallacy studies suggest that people readily assume that people who behave immorally are likely to be atheists. These reverse correlation studies show the opposite association: that merely thinking about

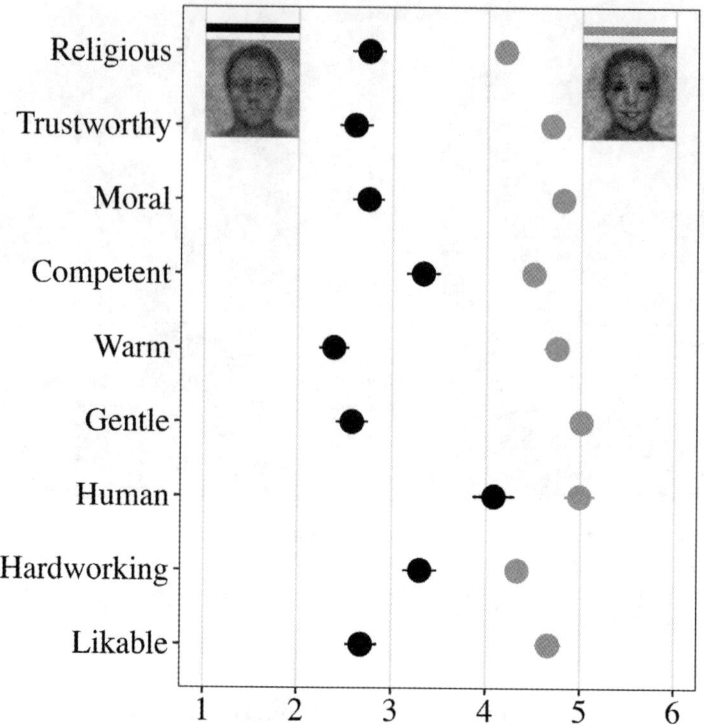

Figure 8.8. Trait attributions to composite mental images of atheists and believers. *Source:* J. L. Brown-Iannuzzi, S. McKee, and W. M. Gervais, "Atheist Horns and Religious Halos: Mental Representations of Atheists and Theists," *Journal of Experimental Psychology: General* 147, no. 2 (2018): 292.

atheism leads people to spontaneously picture immorality. People's robust intuitions about immorality and irreligion are even stamped in the faces that people imagine atheists to have. As we wrote in the conclusion of our paper,[19] "Although data suggest that the relationship between religion and morality is complex, the present research presents a clear picture: People tend to imagine devilish atheists and angelic theists."

JUST MORAL DISTRUST?

Throughout this chapter, I've focused on just one account of where anti-atheist prejudice comes from: moral distrust. It's the account I've done the most work on over the years, and I think it does a reasonable job at explaining the phenomenon in question. But it's not the only account out there. Lots of other fantastic scientists have done great work in this domain, and there's a lot more work on this topic than there used to be back when we started in about 2007. I'd like to highlight a few of these approaches, and make the case that they're largely complementary (rather than contradictory) to my own work.

Jordan Moon, a rapidly rising star in the world of evolutionary psychology and research on atheism and religion, who has also joined us at the Centre for Culture and Evolution, has done some really great work looking at the overlaps between religiosity and mating—mating psychology being a core domain of research in evolutionary psychology. Along with Adam Cohen and Jaimie Krems, Moon found evidence that people's attitudes about short-term mating can also predict anti-atheist prejudice.[20] People seem to infer that atheists (relative to believers) are more sexually uninhibited and into quick hook-ups; opposition to these short-term mating opportunities can thus fuel distrust of atheists. Moon also points out that there are domains where atheists are positively stereotyped: they're viewed as fun, and scientifically curious.[21]

Do these patterns undercut the general moral distrust story? I don't think so. Regarding short-term mating opportunities and stereotypes that atheists are fun, I think this is consistent with a view that atheists are seen as just sort of uninhibited. Remember: without God, *everything* is permitted. This cuts both ways. Religion is a huge source of moral inhibition and social control in the world. If atheists don't have this inhibition (or so goes the stereotype), they're moral wildcards; but they're also sexually adventurous, scientifically curious, and a good time at parties! Combining this possibility with all the work on moral violations, we get an odd image: atheists as freewheeling amoralists who like science and sex and parties, but have few moral hang-ups about anything. They can be a good time (especially for a one-night stand), but they're also capable of some twisted shit and great evil. Like a kinky Dr. Strangelove.

In graduate school, I was surprised and confused to see atheists emerge in polls as among the least accepted groups of people in America. They just didn't seem to do enough to merit that kind of scorn—there are few recognizable atheists out there, and collectively they're neither organized nor powerful.

Over the last fifteen or so years, I've done a lot of research trying to figure out what's going on here, and it looks like people's intuitions about religion and morality are a key ingredient. Thanks to the forces of cultural evolution and religious prosociality (see chapter 7), religion has increasingly been central to cooperation and moral regulation over the past few millennia. This influence persists today, even in some strongly secular countries. We've now found that atheists are intuitively associated with all sorts of immoral actions: lying, cheating, chicken buggery, and even murder. And the images people spontaneously call to mind when they think about atheists are of creepy and untrustworthy dudes. People infer atheism from immorality, and imagine immorality stamped on the faces of atheists. Moral distrust looks central to anti-atheist prejudice. In chapter 9, we'll turn to the thorny issue of whether or not there's a kernel of truth to stereotypes that atheists can't be trusted.

CHAPTER NINE

TAKE ME TO YOUR SECULAR WORLD

Can Atheists Be Trusted?

The fool hath said in his heart, there is no God. They are corrupt, they have done abominable works, there is none that doeth good.

—PSALM 14:1

You must teach me the ways of the secular flesh.

—ANN VEAL TO GEORGE MICHAEL BLUTH, *ARRESTED DEVELOPMENT*

The sitcom *Arrested Development* may seem an odd jumping-off point for a chapter weighing the moral trustworthiness of atheists, but bear with me. In the show, Jason Bateman plays Michael Bluth, the lone semi-competent member of a family chock full of fools, narcissists, crooks, and foolish narcissist crooks. His son, George Michael, has a steady girlfriend named Ann Veal.* Ann is a caricature of a young Evangelical Christian from a highly religious and conservative family: prude, closed-minded, judgmental, fond of burning sinful CDs. Eventually, it's time for the families to meet, and Michael joins George Michael to meet Ann's parents. Pastor Veal and Mrs. Veal are apparently thrilled with Ann and George Michael's plan to get pre-engaged as a sign of their chaste commitment to each other. When Michael mentions that the pre-engagement might play

* Although even while dating Ann, George Michael's real love interest is his maybe-cousin, Maeby Fünke. It's a busy show.

differently in the secular world, chaos gradually ensues. Eventually Mrs. Veal corners Michael on a balcony and begins sensually grinding all over him, seductively sighing, "Take me to your secular world."

Throughout, religion is consistently portrayed as rigid, controlling, and bland, while "the secular world" is an enticing den of sensual disinhibition. This stereotype hearkens back to Jordan Moon's work, discussed in the previous chapter, finding that atheists are seen as sexually uninhibited and adventurous—a stereotype on which Mrs. Veal hopes to romantically cash in!

Recall, however, that stereotypes of atheist disinhibition run much darker than just amorous friskiness. Atheists aren't just seen as willing to engage in illicit romance, they're seen as capable of gross misdeeds. Incest, cannibalism, and even serial murder are parts of "the secular world" according to deep-seated intuitions that seem to transcend geographical and cultural boundaries. To people who equate morality with religion—potentially most people on the planet, by the by—atheists are moral wildcards who cannot be trusted. In this chapter, we'll ask a straightforward question: *Can atheists be trusted?*

I'll wager that many readers think that the answer to this question is incredibly obvious. I'll also wager that the incredibly obvious answer differs starkly across readers with different religious backgrounds—some think that *of course* atheists can't be trusted while others think that *of course* they can. First, I'll present the logic for why a degree of relative distrust for atheists might seem rational. Next, we'll look at the evidence for atheist morality and trustworthiness across a few levels of analysis.

THE LOGIC OF ATHEIST MISTRUST

I wrote both my master's thesis and my doctoral dissertation on the topic of atheist distrust, with both documents summarizing my work on the topic over the years. During my dissertation defense, I presented my work in a brief presentation[†] and then steeled myself to face questions from my committee members. One member, from outside my department, asked the

[†] On the topic of how long the presentation should run, one committee member jokingly replied, "If it runs longer than thirty minutes, I will slit your throat." Between that and the snake fight portion (https://www.mcsweeneys.net/articles/faq-the-snake-fight-portion-of-your-thesis-defense), one best remain on guard at all times when defending one's dissertation.

main question we're considering in this chapter: in some sense, isn't distrust of atheists perfectly rational?

He unpacked the logic, roughly as follows: A key challenge in the world is figuring out who we can trust to not hurt us or rip us off. We can't directly perceive trustworthiness in this regard and have to make some educated guesses about how people will behave. People have various reasons to refrain from lying, cheating, and stealing. Maybe they're afraid they'll be caught and punished by the police or some other authority. Likewise, people might be on their best behavior due to their own personal standards and internalized norms. They might be concerned about what others close to them would think—don't steal that candy bar, what would your dear old grandmother think? We could make quite a lengthy list of reasons like this.

Believers and atheists share all of these reasons, more or less. But someone who believes in a morally concerned god will always have one more reason to inhibit their basest urges than will an atheist.

Stripping religion out of the calculus entirely, we could think of people's various reasons for choosing good behavior and list them. Doesn't it make a certain amount of cold rational sense to trust the person with reasons A, B, C, and D to choose good over the person who only subscribes to reasons A, B, and C? All else equal, isn't it perfectly rational to preferentially trust people with one additional salient reason to choose good over bad, whether or not we place any stock in that particular reason?

There's the logic, if you will, for why it might be rational to trust believers over atheists. In my dissertation defense, this struck me as a legitimately interesting question, and one that isn't all that easy to solve.

There is some intriguing evidence out there that people do seem to use religious beliefs (some of them, at least) as a cue to trustworthiness in this way. Anecdotally, for example, adherents of some religions make appealing candidates for specific jobs. Economist Robert Frank notes that New Yorkers view Latter-Day Saints as especially trustworthy nannies—the LDS combination of alcohol abstention and pro-family norms, paired with belief in a moralizing God, is quite enticing in childcare.[1]

Moving from anecdata to actual data, Tan and Vogel ran a nifty study looking at financial trust for religious believers.[2] They used an experimental economic game called the Trust Game. In this game, players are paired off (while remaining anonymous) and take on different roles—let's call them the Sender and the Receiver. The Sender gets a stake of money, say $10 for example. They decide how much of the stake to transfer to the Receiver, and any amount transferred gets tripled en route. So if the Sender transfers $5, the Receiver gets $15; a $10 transfer becomes $30 for the Receiver. Upon receiving the multiplied stake, the Receiver then gets to transfer any amount back to the Sender. None of this re-transfer is multiplied. This is called the Trust Game because both players can prosper, to the extent that the Sender can trust the Receiver.

For example, our Sender could ship the full $10 to the Receiver, who ends up with $30. A trustworthy Receiver could send half back, and both players walk away $15 richer—all it took was a little trust! Recall that the Receiver doesn't have to transfer a cent back to the Sender, however. A trusting Sender might send $10 the Receiver's way, who could just walk away with the full $30 leaving the Sender empty-handed for their trust. If the Receiver can't be trusted to reciprocate in good faith, the Sender may want to hedge and keep the stake. In this game, researchers can use the Sender's offer as an index of how much they trust the Receiver.

In Tan and Vogel's study, they gave the players a bit of information about their partner, specifically divulging their degree of religiosity. The result? Senders shipped more money to Receivers who they learned were more religious. That is, they trusted religious Receivers more. This effect was more pronounced for Senders who were themselves more religious. In other words, in an incentivized and anonymous economic game, people used religiosity as a cue to trustworthiness, and this cue was especially strong among more religious Senders. Among all the reasons one might act trustworthy in a game like this, people assume that religiosity is at least one more reason added to the pile.

Given all the evidence for moralized distrust of atheists from the last chapter, this result shouldn't be all that surprising. If people think atheists might cut up homeless people for fun, it's not a shocker that believers don't want to trust atheists with a few bucks either. Both in the last chapter and in these examples, we're only looking at evidence that atheists aren't *perceived to be* trustworthy. This doesn't quite answer this chapter's central question, however. In the remainder of the chapter, I want to consider available evidence at different levels of analysis on just how moral and trustworthy atheists *actually are*. Will our best experimental evidence accord with lay suspicions about atheists? Or is the Veal family's dreaded-but-desired secular world not so scary after all?

ARE ATHEISTS TRUSTWORTHY?

There are lots of ways one could try to find evidence about how trustworthy atheists actually are. None of them are perfect, but together they might be useful. We'll consider five different sources of evidence: cross-cultural comparisons, economic games, moral judgments, everyday morality, and the effects of religious upbringing on children. But before digging into the evidence, some clarifications and caveats are in order, to clearly spell out the types of claims I shan't be making.

The Scientific Futility of Body Stacking

Arguments about religion and morality can often end up focusing on questions of which group has, over history, killed the most people or done the most damage. I call this the body-stacking approach. We look at world atrocities and sort them into a "religious" pile and an "atheist" pile, then we weigh each stack of bodies to see who's the worst. We can put body stacks from the Crusades on the religion tab, Maoist purges on the atheist tab, and argue back-and-forth over who needs to take Hitler's stack. This approach shows up in online discussions, and in popular books like *The End of Faith*[3] or *The God Delusion*.[‡] These body-stacking efforts flat-out get the science wrong on the topic of religion and conflict. Beyond the severe scientific limitations of specific body-stacking efforts, there is a fundamental futility of body stacking as a way of thinking about the relationship between religious belief and morality, as we're hoping to do in this chapter.

No series of atrocities can be wholly (or even mostly) chalked up to religion, or to atheism. It is impossible to fully disentangle a religious or atheistic motivation from the myriad other factors that foment small-scale intolerance and prejudice; things get vastly more complex when trying to attribute causes to large-scale genocide and warfare. Serious social scientists

‡ Sometimes, books like this will even try to sneak explicitly nonreligious movements (like, say, Stalinist purges) onto the "religious" pile, saying that the coalitional fervor was religion-like in its intensity. These efforts rather tip the hand about the intellectual unseriousness of their body-stacking enterprise.

have recognized this, going back to at least the turn of the twentieth century. William James, a founding father of empirical psychology in America, had this to say about the apparent connection between religion and nasty outcomes like violence and intolerance: "The baseness so commonly charged to religion's account are thus, almost all of them, not chargeable to religion proper, but rather to religion's wicked practical partner, the spirit of corporate dominion. And the bigotries are most of them in their turn chargeable to religion's wicked intellectual partner, the spirit of dogmatic dominion."[4]

To James, and to generations of scholars after him, it was important to acknowledge real-world correlations between religions and things like violence and bigotry—the correlations are real, after all, and apparent enough to anyone who looks for them. But it was also important to dig a bit deeper and ask whether it is anything about religion, per se, that causes violence, or whether it's instead the case that religion—a cultural universal, after all—might be incidentally bound up with other factors that are more directly responsible. James clearly viewed religion as a bystander to crimes that were committed (often in its name, it must be acknowledged) by "wicked partners" like dogmatism and pernicious group allegiances. Given religion's ubiquity, and its ubiquitous links to groupishness and coalitional alliance, it is only natural that it is also bound up in conflicts; indeed, it would be quite surprising if a human universal like religion wasn't involved in intergroup conflicts.

As a digression, to illustrate how the complexity of real-world conflict undermines the credibility of body-stacking efforts, let's take a detour through some research on terrorism. Even a form of violence that seems transparently religious in origins, such as the terrorist attacks of September 11, the reaction to which went on to shape the global geopolitical landscape for the worse for decades, cannot be so simply attributed to religion as the body stackers would have us believe. Dawkins waited just four days after September 11, 2001, to publish an infamous piece titled "Religion's Misguided Missiles" that pinned the blame for the attacks squarely on religious faith.[5] In that piece, Dawkins writes that "testosterone-sodden young men too unattractive to get a woman in this world might be desperate enough to go for 72 private virgins in the next," before expanding the claim: "Religion is also, of course, the underlying source of the divisiveness in the Middle East which motivated the use of this deadly weapon in the first place. . . . To fill a world with religion, or religions of the Abrahamic kind, is like littering the streets with loaded guns." According to Christopher Hitchens,[6] religion is inherently "violent, irrational, intolerant, allied to racism, tribalism, and bigotry." To Sam Harris, "a glance at history . . . reveals that ideas which divide one group of human beings from another, only to unite them in slaughter, generally have their roots in religion." Alas, the confident religion-blaming of the New Atheists fails to find support from researchers who actually study this stuff.

Here, I highly recommend Scott Atran's book *Talking to the Enemy*,[7] written by a global expert in both religious cognition and terrorism. Atran sought to discover what motivates suicide terrorists by combining both quantitative and qualitative research, as well as his own experiences conducting this research. Some of the work Atran summarizes comes from interviews with close family and friends of successful suicide bombers, as well as failed bombers themselves.[8] Failed bombers are an important group to study; these are people who were fully prepared to blow themselves up in order to kill others. In a lot of cases, they were dressed and ready to do the deed, only to have a mechanical miscue—their bombs didn't go off. In almost every case, they mention that they wanted to kill their group's enemies, and were willing to sacrifice themselves to do so—here recall James's "wicked partners" of corporate dominion. Almost wholly absent from their accounts were appeals to divine reward. In contrast to frequent New Atheist claims, beliefs about gods don't appear to drive suicide terrorism. Body stackers would no doubt heap Manhattan's dead from September 11 on the religious stack, another mark against religion. According to people with the most expertise on the topic, they'd likely be wrong to do so—far more than religious belief drove those men.

Beyond interviews with would-be bombers, others have done in-depth survey and experimental work trying to understand the dynamics that drive extremism and violence often attributed to religion. Ara Norenzayan, Ian Hansen, and Jeremy Ginges were interested in testing some of the Jamesian ideas about whether religion's links to conflict are more inescapable or incidental—whether "religion proper" or "her wicked partners" were more to blame. In a series of studies, they found that the best predictor of support for suicide terrorism wasn't religious faith, it was other markers of coalitional commitment to one's group of people.[9] This directly contradicts charges by New Atheists and other body stackers that suicide bombers, for example, were motivated by heavenly rewards and promises of celestial virgins. Instead, the primary predictor was a feeling of close allegiance with their religious community, echoing Atran's interviews. Direct measures of allegiance to a God (for instance, prayer frequency) predicted more tolerance and less support for suicide attacks. On the other hand, measures of group allegiance (attendance at religious services) predicted greater support for attacks.

A second line of evidence contradicting the New Atheist's simplistic narrative that religious belief causes violence and warfare comes again from the work of Jeremy Ginges.[10] Ginges and colleagues like Mikey Pasek have spent years doing field research in the Middle East, in sites where conflict along religious divides is an everyday occurrence. Much of their work comes from Israel and Palestine in hotbed areas of intergroup strife. In an elegant series of studies, Ginges and colleagues have tested the degree to which the conflict derives from people's perception that mistreating outsiders is condoned by God (or Yahweh, or Allah). To test this, the team has several surveys in which they ask people their opinions on an issue—whether they dehumanize folks from the opposing group, whether they are prejudiced against the other group, whether the lives of outgroup members are worth less. Predictably bleak patterns emerge. "We" are human, "they" less so; "we" are worthy of praise, "they" contempt; "our" lives matter, "theirs" are valueless.

But Ginges also asks people to complete the questionnaire and adopt the position of their god—does their god think outgroup members are worth less, for example? Basically, Ginges is indirectly asking people to rate both the degree to which they think violence and intolerance against a religious other is condoned by their god.[11] And across every set of studies from this team, people consistently think that their god is more tolerant, less violent, and less prejudiced than they themselves are.[12] The New Atheists claim that violence and intolerance happen because people are trying to please their God. According to this research, they couldn't be more wrong. Ginges has been demonstrating for years that violence and intolerance happen *in spite of* what people believe about their gods. If anything, people tend to think that their gods are more tolerant than they themselves are—a peculiar state of affairs if belief in gods was driving intolerance.

Body-stacking comparisons of atheists and believers ignore all this nuance and—well—reality, in order to force a crude dichotomous comparison. I find the exercise futile and distasteful. It's also scientifically hollow. The sections to come don't at all try to body stack, or even to rank believers and atheists on any sort of moral superiority index. Instead, we'll try to stick to quantitative and psychological analyses of moral judgments and actions, and try to see how different atheists and believers, on average, look. A modest goal, admittedly. But unlike grand body-stacking comparisons, it's a goal that might be productive. We can look at five different questions regarding atheist morality: (1) do societies with more atheists function well? (2) are atheists less prosocial in the lab? (3) do atheists and believers have comparable moral intuitions? (4) do atheists and believers take comparable moral actions? And (5) are kids without religion morally different than kids raised religious?

SOCIETIES, SACRED AND SECULAR

Our first way to see if atheists are trustworthy is to zoom all the way out and look at cross-cultural comparisons. Presumably, if atheists really were the puppy-kicking, Canadian-feigning, poker-cheating, cop-insulting, incestuous, chicken-fucking cannibals met in the last chapter, this would leave some broad societal trace in places where there are lots of atheists. More secular societies, populated with a higher concentration of atheists, would presumably show higher rates of immoral stuff. Crime ought to be higher, violence rampant, chickens wary.

In *Society without God*,[13] sociologist and scholar of secularism Phil Zuckerman makes the case that the least religious countries on earth might in fact be the safest and most secure—quite the opposite of what one might expect, based solely on atheist stereotypes. He takes a close look at Scandinavia, and Denmark and Sweden in particular. In these secular havens, most people are nonreligious. Believers aren't wholly absent, but public life discourages overt religiosity for the most part. Rates of church attendance are low, and self-reports of atheism sky-high. Atheists are everywhere, and life is good.

Crime rates tend to be low, and violence is a rare aberration. Beyond that, however, there seems to be a lot of interpersonal and societal trust.

Institutions perform well, and good social safety nets guarantee a measure of security for all. All Scandinavian countries have (by American standards) high taxation rates and socialist redistribution programs. But far from stifling economic productivity and growth, as libertarians might object, these countries tend to punch above their weight class (well, population base) on economic indices. On most measures of health, prosperity, peace, and stability, the atheist hotbeds in Scandinavia are among the world's leaders.

This is not to say that life is perfect in Scandinavia. Among other things, there's recurrent strife over immigration and refugees, with frequent clashes between the white nonreligious-but-essentially-Christian-in-origin historical majority and various ethnic and religious minority groups. There is a distinct air of privilege for insiders, and a treatment of others as essentially foreign, to be excluded. Ethnic homogeneity is a strong historical norm, and changing demographics invite backlash, as seen in resurgent far-right nationalist movements.

On a recent conference trip to Aarhus, Denmark, my colleagues and I experienced this duality of secular stability overlaying ethnic tension and confusion firsthand. The city was lovely and safe. It was quiet, calm, and clean. The citizenry biked everywhere, from the downtown corridor (replete with Viking figures as crosswalk signals) to the university up the hillside and along the seafront. Everyone seemed to quite peacefully get along—but nearly everyone was very white. We saw little ethnic diversity in the people and had a couple of jarring reminders of how the country was but gradually coming to terms with global diversity. By chance, I was allocated a luxury suite in our hotel, with a bedroom and washroom separate from a large and ornately decorated sitting room. As my friends and I took in the furnishings of my ludicrously plush conference accommodations, we were struck by a shockingly racist table, with its legs being crudely caricatured slaves grinning up as they held the glass tabletop. It truly wouldn't have been out of place in a plantation sitting room in the antebellum South. We were puzzled about the table—different countries shouldn't necessarily be expected to have identical norms around décor, and maybe there was something to the table that we were missing. Nonetheless, smiling caricatures of enslaved humans as table stands in a modern twenty-first-century hotel? Our deeper suspicions were confirmed later in the trip, when two members of our Brunel contingent—women from India and Mauritius, respectively—returned to the hotel after dinner and were mistaken by the concierge for cleaning staff arriving for the night shift. Evidently brown-skinned young women are more frequently "the help" than guests at this hotel.

Festering ethnocentrism aside, let's return to the broad issue of atheists and trustworthiness.[§] On a first pass, it looks like the parts of the world with the highest concentration of atheists, far from being sinful dens of iniquity, crime, and strife, are actually among the most peaceful and stable societies in the history of our planet. Now, this correlation is not evidence that atheism is causing peace and stability—as we'll see in a later chapter, the arrow of causation probably runs the other direction—but it is at least one piece of evidence showing that atheists aren't as morally untrustworthy as stereotypes portray. If they were, their societies would quickly crumble, and that's hardly happened.

Large-scale cross-cultural comparisons are fraught. There's so much that differs between countries and regions, beyond the atheistic makeup of their respective populaces. The rest of our comparisons drill down from the country level of analysis to consider whether individual-level differences in religious belief are associated with various morally loaded outcomes.

LAB PROSOCIALITY

A couple chapters ago, we considered the concept of religious prosociality—the idea that beliefs in moralizing Big Gods might've helped ease cooperative tensions, giving people a good reason to eschew selfishness without needing other people to constantly surveil each other. I argued that certain types of religions might've helped make cultures more cooperative, and that this helps explain the global religious landscape today, typified by just a few Big Gods religions having near-total global religious market capture. Does religious prosociality imply that atheists—who after all don't believe in any gods, let alone Big ones—aren't cooperative?

[§] Any atheists of North American background tut-tutting the Danes about their ethnocentrism should take a long, hard look at the prevailing ethnic demographics of atheist groups in the United States.

Not at all. Our religious prosociality explanation was about how some cultural groups might've stabilized cooperative norms in some societies in the past, not about the necessity of individual-level belief in Big Gods today. It's entirely consistent to think that religions might've helped upscale human cooperation, without it necessarily following that people without religion can't be cooperative. Over the millennia, norms of cooperation have stabilized in many societies, along with institutions to maintain them. Religions may have helped instill and sustain those norms and institutions, but religious belief isn't necessary for people in societies defined by those norms to uphold them today.

We can look for direct evidence to compare cooperation and prosociality across religious believers and nonbelievers today. Recall the lab-based priming studies we discussed in chapter 7. I argued that the experimental methodology used in the most famous priming study was useless, and the priming results themselves likely spurious. However, we can still meaningfully compare religious and nonreligious participants in these studies to ask whether religious participants give more prosocial Dictator Game allocations than do atheists, priming manipulation aside. To do so, we can compare all the participants assigned to the control conditions,[¶] those who received no priming to remind them of religion. In effect, we can compare the baseline settings of cooperation between atheists and believers. In the priming studies I highlighted, and in lots of follow-up studies in Western samples, there seems to be no reliable difference between atheists and believers in the control condition Dictator Game offers. In student samples in studies like this, the norm is selfishness across religious divides; in nonstudent adult samples, people tend to split the stakes more equally—again across religious divides. Students keep most of the money, atheist or believer. Nonstudent adults share half-ish, atheist or believer.

At baseline, when tricksy researchers haven't subtly nudged anyone to think about their religious beliefs, atheists and believers tend to give more-or-less the same offers in games like the Dictator Game. There are some

[¶] For the scrambled-sentence studies, I suppose you could also compare the "primed" participants, since the prime itself doesn't seem to do anything. But for purity of comparison, it's simplest to just compare control condition rates.

interesting differences in overall giving rates across cultures, but within cultures people seem to converge on pretty stable norms, whether they're believers or not. On this one specific type of task popular among researchers who study cooperation and prosociality, it seems to not matter a ton whether individual participants believe in God or are atheists.[14]

MORAL INTUITIONS

Moving from trustworthiness and prosociality in economic games to broader considerations of morality, researchers have done a lot of interesting studies looking at people's moral intuitions. The idea here is that when confronted with moral judgments, people seem to rely first on a set of quick-and-dirty moral intuitions that largely shape our judgments. We can then reflectively elaborate on these judgments—giving long-winded justifications for why we think that this-or-that act should be permitted or forbidden. But most of the key moral action is happening at a gut-level of intuition. Moral psychologist Jonathan Haidt likens the situation to a rider steering an elephant. The rider in this case is our effortful conscious deliberation, and the elephant is our intuitions. The rider (read: deliberation) might be able to nudge the elephant a bit, but at the end of the day the elephant (read: intuition) has the locomotive juice.

Do core moral intuitions differ between atheists and believers? Here, the answer is complicated, and ends up depending on what you count as a valid moral intuition.

Moral psychologists and experimental philosophers love checking people's moral intuitions by giving them little vignette thought experiments. One classic example is the trolley problem. Imagine you're standing by a trolley track, where a runaway trolley is careening toward five clueless people who will be killed by the trolley impact (why are they on the track? not our problem). You can flip a switch to redirect the trolley onto an alternate track, where but a single fool is walking. Should you flip the switch, five lives will be saved at the cost of this one solitary fool's life. Would you flip the switch?

Now consider a common alternative trolley problem. Picture the same runaway trolley running toward five pedestrians. This time, you don't have the option to flip a switch to redirect the trolley down another track. But you are standing on a footbridge over the tracks, alongside a man burdened by a large backpack. If you push this man off the bridge, he will land on the tracks where he will be fatally crushed by the trolley. The man and his backpack, however, have sufficient mass that they would stop the trolley and save the five pedestrians. Should you push the dude, five lives will be saved at the cost of this one man's life. Would you push the dude?**

Most folks ("folks" here referring to the overwhelmingly Western samples of university students who end up in these studies) report that they'd definitely flip the switch in the first example, but would not push the man in the second example. Even though the calculus of lives is identical in both (killing one to save five), people have consistent intuitions and gut feelings to the effect that redirecting the trolley into a man is permissible, but redirecting a man into the trolley is not.

When it comes to this type of moral judgment, people seem to have a relatively universal set of intuitions. John Mikhail dubs this set of intuitions a "universal moral grammar" that underpins our judgments.[15] When comparing atheists to believers, similarities in these sorts of moral intuitions are far more evident than are any differences. Summarizing a large internet survey of moral intuitions, Konika Banerjee and colleagues state, "We conclude that gender, education, politics and religion are likely to be relatively insignificant for moral judgments" of the sorts studied by experimental philosophers and moral psychologists.[16] In short: the universal moral grammar isn't much different depending on whether one believes in God.

Our core moral grammar can be elaborated through culture, but moral intuitions are pretty robust across populations. Some core moral intuitions, according to primatologists like Frans de Waal (check out his excellent book *The Bonobo and the Atheist*)[17] are probably shared with our closest primate ancestors. And according to developmental psychologists like Kiley

---

** I posed these two trolley problem examples to my daughter. For the track-switching example, she calmly considered and then unemotionally replied that of course she would flip the switch to save five lives. When I then gave her the bridge example, there was no calm or measured contemplation: her eyes lit up and she excitedly announced her intention to push the man. This is, uh, not the typical pattern. That said, she is not the only psychologist's child to give an atypical trolley answer: https://youtu.be/-N_RZJUAQY4.

Hamlin, Karen Wynn, and Paul Bloom,[18] core moral intuitions reliably develop even in pre-verbal infants.[19] If the building blocks of morality are evident in our nonreligious primate relatives, and in pre-religious infants, then how could morality really boil down to religion? However, morality isn't one-size-fits-all, and there might be different domains in which religion might be important.

Our moral judgments come in different flavors. Consider the trolley problem examples we just played with. Each of them pits two different sorts of moral thinking against each other. On the one hand, each asks us to consider the overall consequences: kill one, save five. This is a consequentialist or utilitarian calculus, weighing goods and bads across affected agents. On the other hand, we also have some firm and largely nonnegotiable moral principles, rules such as "thou shalt not kill." Simple dictates like this form a deontological system of morality, an ethic built on rules and principles. Across the two trolley problems—our switch flipping example and our man pushing example—the utilitarian calculus remains identical (5 > 1), but the strength of deontological commitments is less stable. Pushing a man off a bridge directly violates a deontological "don't kill people" rule, whereas flipping a switch to redirect a train obscures things a little. Yes, flipping the switch causes one man to die, but the death is easy to cast as a side effect of the train's redirection rather than a directly intended consequence. In contrast, pushing a man off a bridge rather directly causes his death, the harm is direct and obvious. One example moves a train and indirectly kills a man; the other example directly uses a man's death to stop the trolley. We all rely on both utilitarianism and deontology in various judgments, albeit to differing degrees. Where researchers find differences between atheists and believers on trolley problem-like moral judgments, the pattern is that believers slightly favor deontology (following strict moral commandments, often handed down from their god) whereas atheists rely more heavily on utilitarian judgments. Atheists and believers have both utilitarian and deontological systems, it's just that the believers lean on deontology a little more.[20]

Beyond utilitarianism and deontology, other moral psychologists have proposed more than just two systems underlying different moral judgments. In the last chapter, we met the moral foundations approach popularized by

Haidt's team over the years. This moral foundations framework[††] argues that people make distinct moral judgments in the categories of harm, fairness, respect for authority, loyalty to one's group, and purity/sanctity. They've since added a "liberty" framework, seemingly motivated to better capture moral divides in US politics. The moral foundations framework has proven immensely successful in popular culture, but this popularity has outstripped its scientific acceptance. For example, critics have pointed out that the statistics underlying the moral foundations framework don't hold up well—one has to crunch the numbers in a specific way to yield five or six distinct moral foundations, and equally, if not more, sensible statistical approaches reduce the foundations down into just two categories. It turns out that, empirically speaking, harm and fairness concerns cluster together, as do all the others, yielding just two foundations. These two meta-foundations are sometimes called the "binding" foundations (loyalty, deference, purity, sometimes liberty) and the "individualizing" foundations (harm and fairness).

Quibbles about the theoretical status and underlying stats of moral foundations aside, where does religion fit in? A classic moral foundations finding is that pretty much everyone endorses the "individualizing" foundations of harm and fairness, but only political conservatives endorse the full suite of foundations. Given the recurrent links between religious beliefs and political ideology, it's unsurprising that differences in moral foundations concerns across believers and atheists largely mirror the political divides. Atheists tend

[††] As a reminder: they call it moral foundations theory, but it's not really a theory in the sense that philosophers of science would recognize. Theories build on lots of observations and give concrete mechanistic explanations for them, pointing the way toward lots of novel predictions. Moral foundations aren't much like this. Observing a set of five or six different categories isn't a proper theory—there's just not enough explanatory depth or reach. Instead, moral foundations theory offers a classification scheme or a descriptive categorization. There's no shame in being a classification scheme instead of a theory. The five-factor model of personality tells us that personalities vary in about five core ways. The Linnean classification scheme organizes all life into a series of hierarchically branching mappings (Kingdom, Order, and so on). The moral foundations framework is far more like these other observational classification schemes than like a full-fledged scientific theory such as, say, evolution via natural selection. Why did the popularizers of moral foundations call it a theory then? That's just what social psychologists love to do as soon as they've gathered a few interesting observations. In 2008, Walter Mischel, in *APS Observer*, dubbed this the *toothbrush problem:* "Psychologists treat other peoples' theories like toothbrushes—no self-respecting person wants to use anyone else's." Thus every set of surprising findings seems to generate its own catchily named "theory."

to strongly endorse harm and fairness concerns, while largely ignoring the other foundations. Believers still recognize harm and fairness concerns, but tend to place a higher weight on things like respect for authority, loyalty to one's group, and (perhaps especially) purity concerns about a sacred natural order to things that we oughtn't disrupt. Atheists almost exclusively consider the "individualizing" foundations, believers are more likely to consider the whole spectrum and include the "binding" foundations as well.

Trolley problems and moral foundations alike suggest that atheists and believers don't so much differ in overall levels of morality, but rather in more nuanced conceptions of how morality works and in what's perceived to be morally relevant. Atheists tend toward utilitarianism and concerns of harm or fairness. Believers are more likely to follow deontological commandments and view a wider suite of things as morally relevant, including loyalty to groups, respect for authority, and spiritual purity. These are differences in subtle views of morality, rather than overall amounts of it.

EVERYDAY MORALITY

Turning from moral judgments to moral actions, we can next ask whether there's evidence that atheists actually behave less morally in the world. Moral intuition research often occurs in psychology laboratories and online surveys, with clever experimental philosophers crafting clever vignettes to cleave our moral intuitions at their joints. This is a fascinating exercise, but when the rubber hits the road, we're interested in people's moral actions. Moving from laboratory experiments and economic games to the real world, do atheists seem to behave any less morally than believers?

My favorite study in this genre comes from Wilhelm Hofmann, Daniel Wisneski, Mark Brandt, and Linda Skitka. Their *Science* paper, titled "Morality in Everyday Life," used a nifty tool called ecological momentary assessment to get snapshots of people's everyday moral lives.[21] About twelve hundred participants took part in the study. Each participant downloaded an app to their phone that would ping them at a handful of random intervals throughout the day to ask a few questions. This included some routine mood questions ("How happy do you feel at the moment?"), for example. Crucially, the app asked everyone about their moral experiences: had they committed, were the target of, witnessed, or learned about a moral or immoral act within the past hour? If so, participants could provide additional context in a text box.

The overall results are fascinating, religion aside. Most momentary responses didn't include a lot of moral content. In fact, only about 29 percent of the snapshots were morally relevant. Of the morally relevant snapshots, people were relatively unlikely to report being the target of or witness to morally charged actions, be they moral or immoral. However, people were a bit more likely to report that they'd performed moral actions, and that they'd heard about immoral actions. Morally relevant experiences tended to be about people reporting their own good deeds, and hearing gossip about the misdeeds of others. There was some evidence of moral licensing—the idea that when people do a good deed, they feel entitled to take a bit of a moral breather for a while. Folks who'd reported doing a good deed early in the day were more likely to report later immoral actions, and less likely to report moral actions later in the day. A good deed a day seems to be enough, and even buys people some license to sin later on.

For each participant, the research team also had some basic demographic data, including religiosity. This allowed them to see who was reporting what sorts of moral or immoral actions. They split people into a nonreligious group (folks who indicated the lowest level of religiosity) and a religious group (everyone else) for a straightforward binary comparison. People who indicate that they're not at all religious might not identify as atheists, per se (an issue we'll address in a later chapter), but they're as close as this study gets to letting us ask whether atheists actually behave less morally than believers in everyday life.

Atheist stereotypes of craven sinners would have us predict that the nonreligious participants would be engaging in immoral acts more frequently, and moral acts less frequently, than would religious participants. On the religious split, Hofmann and colleagues' results turned up—drum roll—basically nothing. There was hardly any difference in the everyday moral experiences of nonreligious and religious participants. Recall that for both moral and immoral acts, the researchers had been interested in four different types of behaviors: whether people had (1) committed, (2) been the target/recipient of, (3) witnessed, or (4) learned about a moral act. Collapsing all four targets together, there was precisely zero difference between religious and nonreligious people on moral actions. Nonreligious folks hadn't committed fewer moral acts, nor had they witnessed, experienced, and learned of them. Nothing, zip, zero, zilch. The results are among the most comprehensively null you're likely to find in a journal like *Science*. Turning to immoral actions, we can see that there was a small overall difference, with religious folks overall reporting fewer immoral experiences. Does this mean the nonreligious are out committing more immoral actions? Not at all. It turns out that the overall immorality difference was entirely driven by gossip and what people attended to. Relative to the nonreligious, religious folks were less likely to learn about immoral actions from others, but there was no difference in actual commission or even direct witnessing of bad deeds.

There were some interesting wrinkles to the data, mostly in terms of reactions to moral and immoral actions. Religious folks, it turns out, were more positively affected by moral deeds and more negatively affected by immoral actions. But when it comes to the question of whether nonreligious people are less moral in their everyday lives than are religious folks, these data suggest a resounding lack of a difference between the groups. Nonreligious people were no more likely to commit immoral actions, and no less likely to commit moral actions, than their religious peers.

To recap this: researchers taking snapshots of people's everyday moral lives found zero difference in the rates at which religious and nonreligious people commit either good or bad deeds. In terms of moment-to-moment actions, religiosity predicted exactly nothing. The everyday morality of believers and atheists[‡‡] doesn't look to be very different at all.

NONRELIGIOUS KIDS ARE MORE GENEROUS? (OR NOT)

In 2015, a study related to religion and morality generated quite a media frenzy. The paper, published in the journal *Current Biology*, reported on an investigation of generosity in children around the world.[22] The take-home headline-grabbing finding was that worldwide, children raised in nonreligious homes were more generous than were children from religious homes, using a standard task for measuring generosity in kids. Ancillary analyses also showed religiously raised kids to be more judgmental and punitive.

---

‡‡ Again, with the caveat that people indicating no religion aren't necessarily atheists: the data in the study almost but *don't quite* get us all the way there. Defining and identifying atheists is a tricky issue, to which we'll devote an entire chapter coming up.

Perhaps unsurprisingly, atheist and nonreligious advocacy organizations jumped on the results. The Freedom from Religion Foundation's summary stated, "In what amounts to good news for secular parents and nonbelievers, children who grow up in nonreligious environments appear to be more generous than those who are raised with religion, according to a new study." In separate stories, the Richard Dawkins Foundation for Reason and Science headlined the results with: "Far from Bolstering Generosity, A Religious Upbringing Diminishes It,"[23] and "Religious Upbringing Linked to Less Altruism, Study of Children Suggests."[24]

It wasn't just the secularist press on this beat, either. Here are some representative headlines and claims:

- "Religion Makes Children More Judgmental, Less Generous" (CBS)
- "Children with a Religious Upbringing Show Less Altruism" (*Scientific American*)
- "Religious Children Are Meaner Than Their Secular Counterparts, Study Finds" (*The Guardian*)
- "Religion Makes Children More Selfish, Say Scientists" (*Forbes*)

According to these results, not only is religion unnecessary for instilling morality in our children, but secular upbringings might also actually lead to even more moral kids. In a media report on the study, the lead author is quoted thusly: "Our findings support the notion that the secularization of moral discourse does not reduce human kindness. In fact it does just the opposite."

These results seem to flip the dynamics considered in this chapter. Not only are atheists (well, kids of nonreligious parents) moral, but they might actually be *more moral* than kids raised in religious homes. It's not hard to see why groups like FFRF and the Dawkins Foundation celebrated these results.

Unfortunately, the results didn't hold up under scrutiny. I'll unpack why, and offer my best summary of the study's actual results.

An independent team of researchers read the article closely, and something didn't quite add up. The study itself tested more than a thousand children, across six countries (United States, Canada, Jordan, Turkey, South Africa, and China). The paper claimed to have controlled for country of origin when analyzing the religious/nonreligious split, but the statistical output didn't quite match what one would expect for results nested within countries like this. Eventually, the original authors shared their raw data with the new team, and the new team discovered a mundane error in the dataset's coding.

For the column in the dataset indexing country of origin, each country had been given a numerical code (for example: United States = 1, Canada = 2, and so forth). But the analysis code didn't specify that countries should be treated as discrete clusters that were merely indexed using numbers for convenience. As a result, the analyses effectively treated those country numbers as quantities. Doing so means that instead of countries being treated as discrete (United States, Canada, China, Turkey), the analyses effectively modeled some quantity we might term "countriness" and assigned values of this quantity (1, 2, 3, 4) to each country. Canada would have twice as much "countriness" as the United States, and Turkey twice as much as that. This coding error—practically a typo, as far as these things go—had profound consequences for the pragmatic conclusions of the paper. You see, generosity rates varied a lot across countries, religion aside. And since that variation tended to also go along with country-level differences in overall religiosity, what was actually a country difference in generosity (communist China shares more than capitalist United States, for example) was erroneously viewed by the statistics software as a religion difference in generosity.

The new team communicated their concerns to the journal and were largely met with radio silence. Eventually they wrote up and submitted a commentary piece on the original research—commentaries of this sort are entirely commonplace, nothing unusual, published all the time as a matter of routine. This one, however, took a while in editorial and peer review. The months trickled by. Although four of five reviewers of the commentary (an unusual although perhaps necessary number of reviewers for a mere commentary) recommended it be published, the journal originally rejected the commentary for publication. Eventually, after some back-and-forth, the journal agreed to publish a softer version of the commentary.[25] The original article still stood in the scientific record, albeit alongside a short commentary noting that all of the headline-grabbing results vanished as soon as analyses treated countries properly—as discrete countries, rather than quantities of countriness.

The new team had advocated to the journal that a commentary was insufficient. After all, the journal had published a paper whose results rested entirely on a coding error; the published record was substantially incorrect, and a firm correction or retraction of the original was in order. Again, the months dragged on. The original article continued to accrue attention and citations. As is often the case, the commentary was easily overlooked. To date, the original paper has been cited in 134 other scientific papers and the commentary cited just 26 times. Eventually, concrete action was taken. In 2019, roughly four years after the initial publication and three after the critical commentary, the original paper's authors retracted their paper from the scientific record. Unlike the original article, the commentary and eventual retraction merited barely a blip from the media. The claim that nonreligious kids are more generous was expunged from the scientific record, but not the public one. The Dawkins Foundation, which explicitly claims to be about science and skepticism, never corrected their own record, do not seem to have covered the correction or retraction, and their initial summaries claiming moral superiority for nonreligious kids remain online as of early 2023. The sole notable media coverage I can find of the back-and-forth is an admirable and interesting *Vox* article on the affair.[26]

I'm recounting this paper and ensuing saga not to impugn the characters or scientific chops of anyone involved. Coding errors are routine, they happen all the time. Sometimes scientific papers don't hold up well—something I know all too well. Retraction isn't easy, and the authors do deserve some credit for taking eventual action to clear up the record. Instead, I'm hoping to shed some light on how the sausage is made, when it comes to the scientific record. You've probably heard that science is self-correcting, and that self-correction is what makes and keeps science useful. Well, science is self-correcting—in principle. In practice? Corrections are arduous, slow, and relatively rare, and people doing the hard work of correcting the record swim against a powerful current of incentives pushing scientific careers in the opposite direction.

So, if proper analyses invalidated the claim that nonreligious kids were more moral than religious kids, what do the results in fact show? After all, the data in this study were solid and it was only the analyses that were invalid. In this case, I think that the actual results are at least as fascinating as those originally claimed. There are, as always, different ways to statistically model things. Looking at all the data, and treating countries as properly discrete, the overall comparison between religious and nonreligious kids reveals a pleasing nothing. There's no difference overall.

Aside from the overall non-difference, it's possible to look within each country and weigh the evidence for and against a religious difference in generosity. And in each and every country, the evidence rather strongly supports the conclusion that religious upbringing—or not—doesn't much matter, at least for the tasks and questions in this paper. Kids raised with and without religion are just about as generous as each other within each country, and any differences between individual kids seem to be soaked up by prevailing country-level differences in overall cooperative norms. Religion or no, kids in each country converged to national norms of cooperation. (Remember our discussion of how cultural learning can stabilize norms across groups? Here you go!) Nonreligious kids aren't better than religious kids, but nor are they worse. They're all just kids!

THE BIRD'S-EYE VIEW

The last few sections took the micro-view of various strands of evidence looking at the morality and trustworthiness of athcists. Let's assemble each of these pieces and take a holistic bird's-eye view (or perhaps a god's-eye view if such is your persuasion) of the evidence.

Zooming all the way out, there's no evidence that more atheistic countries fare more poorly than religious countries on morally laden outcomes. If anything, the opposite pattern emerges: atheistic societies trend toward peace, safety, and stability. Cross-cultural comparisons of this nature are incredibly fraught, and the causal arrow between atheism to stability might actually run in the reverse direction, as we'll see in a later chapter.

Turning from countries to individuals, we next looked at anonymous generosity in economic games like the Dictator Game. A few chapters ago we met (and then largely rejected) some studies on religious priming. Ignoring the experimental manipulations in these studies allows us to check whether atheists are any less anonymously prosocial than their more faithful peers. It turns out, they aren't.

Beyond economic games, we next considered moral judgments—this gets us more direct comparisons on whether atheists are any less moral than believers when it comes to under-the-hood psychology. Here, it's not the case that believers are more moral than atheists. Instead, it looks like atheists and believers just use slightly different moral frameworks for their judgments, with believers relying more on deontological rules and binding foundations, and atheists sticking to utilitarian calculations about harm and fairness. In a sense, this means that atheists might hold a somewhat narrower view of morality than do believers. There's little atheistic moral regard for sacred teachings and unbendable rules, little moral concern for things like deference to authority or pledging allegiance to a group, or to respecting the sanctity of some metaphysical natural order we're meant to uphold. But bringing different (or even narrower) sets of moral considerations to bear doesn't make atheists any less moral overall than believers, unless the more religious moral frameworks are held up as an initial benchmark.

Some folks—and especially religious believers—might prefer to deal with people who share their brand of deontologically derived full-spectrum morality, but that's as much a case of preferring self-similarity as anything else. Everyone finds it easier to deal with folks who share their moral concerns, no surprises there. But endorsing slightly different moral principles and foundations doesn't imply that someone is less moral, only that they view the moral universe through a slightly different lens. When it comes to moral intuitions and judgments, atheists look just as moral as believers—unless one chooses to adopt a religiously deontological view of morality.

Moving from moral judgment to moral behavior, work by Hofmann and colleagues found a striking non-difference between nonreligious and religious people on everyday morality. On a day-to-day and moment-to-moment basis, nonreligious folks are no more likely to be engaging in immoral behavior, and no less likely to be engaging in moral behavior, than are religious believers.

Finally, we considered the moral effects of a religious upbringing—a domain in which the moral benefits of religion are often discussed. Despite initial results suggesting that in fact nonreligious kids were morally superior—results that were met with media acclaim—proper statistical analysis revealed, once again, no difference between religious and nonreligious kids.

Putting all of this together, there's converging evidence that atheists are no less morally trustworthy than believers. There's some intuitive logic behind mistrust of atheists—why not preferentially trust people with more reasons to do good instead of bad, after all. Believers and atheists have differing moral concerns (per moral foundations), and might rely on slightly different sorts of judgments and frameworks (pitting utilitarianism against deontology). But when it comes to concrete evidence, we found that religious belief doesn't predict consistent differences in moral actions.

The secular world? It's probably just fine, morally speaking. Atheists don't look any less (or more) moral or trustworthy than anyone else.

CHAPTER TEN

HOW MANY ATHEISTS ARE THERE?

There are dozens of us! Dozens!
—TOBIAS FÜNKE, *ARRESTED DEVELOPMENT*

Agnosticism is of the essence of science, whether ancient or modern. It simply means that a man shall not say he knows or believes that which he has no scientific grounds for professing to know or believe.
—THOMAS HENRY HUXLEY, *AGNOSTICISM: A SYMPOSIUM*[1]

The 2022 United States congressional elections ushered in the most diverse legislature in the nation's history.* In 1945, Congress was 99+ percent white; in 2022, 28 percent of the House of Representatives identified as Black, Hispanic, Asian American, American Indian, Alaska Native, or multiracial. The 2022 seated Congress had the highest share of women (28 percent) and younger generations (50 percent of Congress were Gen X or Millennial). And thirteen members identify as gay, lesbian, or bisexual, another new high.

That broad demographic diversity—at least by the standards of an institution that's always been solidly white, straight, rich, male, and Christian—had one large exception: atheists. Various backgrounds were better represented than before, but the lawmakers still overwhelmingly professed belief in a god, and mostly in the specific God of Christianity. Only one member, Congressman Jared Huffman from California, stands out as a tiny ripple against the otherwise God-fearing current.[2] He identifies as a secular humanist, and in one interview stated that he doesn't actively believe in God (although he leaves the door open to various spiritual possibilities).

* A low hurdle to clear, to be fair.

Atheists are far from a majority in the United States, but they're not vanishingly rare. Congressman Huffman existing as the sole nonbeliever among all 535 members of the federal legislature is wildly improbable—effectively a statistical impossibility. To figure out the sheer improbability of Congressman Huffman's sole religious disbelief, let's crunch some numbers.

Congressman Huffman stops short of calling himself an atheist, and no other members of Congress do either. Yet the United States average is that about 3 percent of Americans call themselves atheists. *How improbable is a complete lack of self-identified atheists in Congress?* Some back-of-the-envelope calculations show that the odds that 0 of 535 people are atheists (against a background base rate of 3 percent) are approximately 1 in 12 million.

Although he doesn't identify as an atheist, per se, Congressman Huffman makes it clear that he does not believe in God. That makes 1 in 535 congresspeople who don't believe in God (regardless of whether they call themselves atheists). *How likely is it that there is truly only one member of Congress who doesn't believe in God?* Here, our estimate is complicated because there are multiple different estimates of the background prevalence of atheists. But if we take a recent Pew survey at face value, about 17 percent of Americans don't believe in God. The odds that no more than one of the 535 congresspeople disbelieve in God (against a background base rate of 17 percent): approximately 1 in 100 duodecillion. If, like me, you aren't familiar with the term "duodecillion," the odds of Huffman being the sole disbeliever are 1 in 100 thousand billion billion billion billion.[†]

Now, all these estimates assume that we're drawing congresspeople at random from the US populace, which we know isn't the case. Federal lawmakers, relative to the US average, are overwhelmingly wealthy, educated, male, and white. Far from undermining our probability estimates, this actually implies that the estimates might've been too conservative. After all, wealth, education, maleness, and paleness all demographically ride with atheism.[3] All else equal, we'd expect that groups of wealthy, educated, white men are probably less religious than the population average.

How can we explain the demographic peculiarity of Congress concerning atheism? I can think of at least two possibilities. First, maybe voters

---

[†] 1.17×10^{41}, to be pseudo-precise. That's the precise probability estimate, based on assumptions too messy to give much confidence or precision.

effectively barricade atheists from the halls of Congress. A couple chapters back, we saw that atheists are incredibly unpopular in places like the United States. Polls even ask people if they'd be likely to elect an atheist, and people say they wouldn't. Atheists trail lots of other groups when it comes to people saying that they'd vote for a candidate who happened to be one.[4] Here, lack of nonreligious representation in Congress might simply reflect the clearly stated preferences of the voting populace, paired with a keen ability to sniff out atheism in candidates. Informed democracy in action.

A second possibility is that—bear with me here—our politicians aren't perfectly honest with us.[5] It's possible that there are lots of privately atheistic lawmakers who are savvy enough to realize that open atheism would be electoral suicide. So, they keep their doubts to themselves, put those hands on Bibles, and go through the motions of sincere belief to win and keep votes.

So, two possible explanations. One is that the United States voting populace is incredibly savvy at choosing politicians who well-represent their interests and preferences, and also able to spot atheists. The other possibility is that some lawmakers are less than forthcoming and honest about aspects of their lives and beliefs. I'll let the reader decide which possibility they find more plausible: savvy electorates or dishonest politicians.

The remainder of this chapter will try to make the case that lots of people conceal their atheism—and not just in the halls of Congress. This is a possibility that we should take seriously because it has important implications for our understanding of both faith and atheism. After all, theories of religion and atheism need to grapple with basic facts about these phenomena, including the overall numbers we're talking about. Basic figures about atheist prevalence let us test theories of religion.

In this chapter, we'll try to figure out how many atheists there might be in the world. We'll do so by asking a series of nested questions:

- According to large scale surveys, how many atheists are there?
- Who counts as an atheist—and what about agnostics?
- Are people generally accurate and honest about religion?
- Why might people hide atheism?
- How many atheists might there actually be once we account for all of the above?

So, how many atheists are there? The answer to this question depends heavily on how you ask it, and the true value could be much higher than large-scale polls to date have suggested.

SURVEY SAYS . . .

Any decent scientific theory of religion needs to explain atheism as well. This means that basic facts about atheism should have great import for our theories of religion. A theory of religion that predicts low rates of atheism ought to be abandoned if atheists turn out to be common; in contrast, theories of religion that predict higher or more variable rates of atheism are better fits if the true prevalence of atheism is higher or more variable across cultures. So, how many atheists are there?

Turns out, this is an incredibly challenging question to answer, because there aren't many good data sources that can track atheism across countries in a principled apples-to-apples way. Countries don't uniformly track atheism in census reports. Even large-scale polling companies have patchy coverage of countries across some world regions—data are plentiful in Europe, for example, but sparse across the Global South, for reasons of entrenched scientific norms and insidious global resource allocation inequities stemming from centuries of exploitation of the Global South by the Global North.

Even if large-scale polling operations were equally active in all countries, there's an issue of inconsistency in how questions about religion get asked. Different polls use different questions about religion, and atheism rates aren't often possible to directly infer from the data, thanks to inconsistencies in polling questions. Some surveys ask people straightforwardly whether they believe in God (or a god); here, atheists are the people who answer in the negative. Other surveys give people a menu of religious identity categories with which they might feel aligned: are you Catholic? Protestant? Sunni? Atheist? Agnostic? None of the above? Nothing in particular? On these surveys, we can estimate atheist prevalence by simply checking how many people tick the "atheist" box. You might assume that atheist rates would look similar across these two questions, but you'd be quite mistaken.

To illustrate the research challenge introduced by these differences in question wording, consider a pair of polls run by Gallup[6] and Pew[7] around the same time, a handful of years ago. Both polls were conducted in the United States, meaning that discrepancies aren't down to international coverage issues. Both are reputable survey firms, well versed in the intricacies of representative sampling. These polls should be about as close to an apples-to-apples comparison as we'll find in the literature, with equivalent sampling plans for both surveys, and just a minor difference in questions. One survey used the religious identity menu approach outlined above (Catholic? Protestant? Atheist?), and found that only about 2–3 percent of people are atheists—in this case meaning that's how many people ticked the "atheist" box. The other survey instead asked people about belief in God, using a binary choice measure. Basically, it asked people whether they believed in God, with "yes" and "no" as the primary choice options. If we treat people who answer "no" when asked whether they believe in God as atheists—disbelief in gods being the definition of atheism, after all—then this 2017 poll suggests that 12 percent of Americans were atheists at the time. Atheism clocks in at either 3 percent or 12 percent, a fourfold difference in atheism prevalence resulting from asking the question in a different way, within the same country, using the same sorts of rigorous representative sampling methods. Neither atheism estimate is inherently "truer" or more "correct," they're just giving us slightly different pieces of information because they've asked different questions. This is apparent when you have both sorts of polls within the same country, but it can make atheist prevalence estimates challenging when some countries only have polling data on one question or the other. It's not possible to translate between the currencies of "identify as atheist" and "don't believe in God" in an especially principled way, leaving us in a bit of a data quagmire.

The bottom line: Intersecting issues of patchy and inequitable international survey coverage and inconsistent question wording means that it's not possible to estimate atheist prevalence worldwide from survey data alone with any degree of confidence or precision, but nonetheless a good-faith effort can be made. Sociologist Phil Zuckerman tried to squeeze some inferential lemonade from the global survey lemons, amalgamating across data sources. His estimate was that there are five hundred to seven hundred million atheists in the world (this was in 2007, so a bit dated by now). Crucially, this estimate red flags some countries, like China, where top-down government mandates could artificially inflate atheist numbers.[8]

When the government requires atheism, self-reported atheism becomes an empirically hollow measure.

For now, let's treat this seven hundred million number as a firm lower-bound estimate of atheist prevalence. It's the best that Zuckerman could do with the data at hand, but it relies on a lot of assumptions that mightn't hold (for instance, whatever the non-government-induced atheism rate of China's billion plus people happens to be, it's probably much higher than Zuckerman inferred). In addition, that number was based on data available in 2007. Both the global population and the share of nonreligious people in lots of places have risen since 2007. Even if we wiggle our estimate upward to adjust for those parallel trends and come up with an estimate of, say, eight hundred to nine hundred million atheists, I suspect we're still falling well short. The rest of this chapter will argue that even an estimate adjusted in this way is probably vastly lower than the actual number of atheists in the world, for reasons that go conceptually deeper than just question wording and patchy survey coverage. In short: the fundamental social consequences of talking about religious belief and disbelief might fundamentally skew all self-report estimates of atheist prevalence worldwide, by a potentially substantial amount.

Before diving into the minutiae of what polls get right and wrong, and what the actual number of atheists might be, let's think a bit about estimates derived from the "religious menu" approach above. Yes, people who self-identify with the label "atheist" are safe to count as atheists, but what about people who indicate other nonreligious identities? If they don't believe in God, but didn't tick the "atheist" box for one reason or another, how should they be counted? And most puzzling of all, what should we do with the self-described agnostics?

WHAT ABOUT AGNOSTICS?

When I give talks about my research, there is one follow-up question that I get more than any other. I get the question from academic and public audiences alike, across talks of different topics.

What about agnostics?

If I'm talking about work on moral distrust of atheists (stuff from a couple chapters back), people inevitably want to know if agnostics are also distrusted. When I talk about work in this chapter—trying to figure out how many atheists there are—people want to know how many agnostics there are, and how they get counted. Especially audience members who themselves identify as "I'm not an atheist, I'm agnostic" are keen to know which bin they get sorted into when it comes to research like mine. This section is my attempt to answer that question, in a way that respects both the philosophical aspects of atheism and agnosticism, and the types of scientific measurements that underpin a lot of my research.

So, what about agnostics? For me, the answer has three facets to it:

1. "I'm not an atheist, I'm agnostic" isn't an especially meaningful descriptor of belief—it conflates different branches of philosophy to force a false dichotomy between two wholly compatible religious stances.
2. Substantively and empirically speaking, most people who identify as agnostic are also atheists.
3. It's much more productive to think of atheism and agnosticism as endpoints of separate continua that are largely independent of each other, philosophically and psychologically speaking.

To unpack these points a bit, we'll have to detour through some psychological work on identity, some popular but misconceived notions from Dawkins's *God Delusion*, and some intro-level philosophy. To really nail home the point that atheism and agnosticism are separate continuous dimensions, we'll close by seeing where a few prominent historical thinkers might land on both dimensions.

Identity Labels

People love labels for their social identities. There's a vital importance to the words we choose to use to describe who we are. The words we choose for ourselves can help us communicate important aspects of our personhood to others.

Those labels often aren't meaningful and philosophically consistent descriptors of our beliefs.

In lots of surveys, people can give identity labels for their religious and nonreligious beliefs, and many of these surveys give separate tick boxes for "atheist" and "agnostic"—there's thus a forced dichotomy between the two categories. This is unfortunate, because as we'll soon see one can easily be both an atheist and an agnostic. Or just one, or neither. Atheism and agnosticism reflect independent types of beliefs, different stances on philosophical questions, not just mutually incompatible identity categories.

That's not to say that lots of people don't have a firm social identity as either an atheist or an agnostic. Telling someone you're an atheist, or an agnostic, can convey different things. To lots of recipients hearing about these identities in others, "atheist" might convey anti-theism, science-mindedness, and perhaps a touch of judgmental close-mindedness. It gets associated with the loudest public New Atheists that hit their peak cultural cachet a decade or two ago. Lots of people hear "atheist" and think of a know-it-all out to debunk religion, confident in their own rational disbelief—a Dawkinsian sort of smugness. In contrast, "agnostic" conveys an inherent open-mindedness. These folks in a principled way don't know if there's a god. Gone is the certainty that atheism is seen as connoting, replaced with a high-minded above-the-fray recognition that nobody can be certain when it comes to God (or Zeus, or myriad other little-g gods).

People choosing to call themselves either an "atheist" or an "agnostic" are in part making a choice about what image others will hold of them, based solely on the tag's connotations. People identifying as agnostic aren't just sending a signal (intentional or not) about how open-minded they are, they might also be signaling something about their background. One of my favorite findings in this area is that self-identified agnostics tend to be more highly educated than people from most religious groups—but also than self-identified atheists. Does this mean that education makes people more open-minded and agnostic about religion? Or that agnostics are naturally curious people who seek out more knowledge via education? There's a simpler, largely noncausal, possibility: maybe it just takes a bit more education to be able to describe one's core religious worldview with a fancy Greek word (from Greek *agnōstos*, "unknowable"), which entered popular discourse through fancypants public intellectuals like Thomas Henry Huxley and Bertrand Russell. Like calling oneself an oenophile or a gastronome, "agnostic" is precisely the type of identity tag that we'd expect to correlate with education, *no matter what specific beliefs or attitudes it entails.*

The point here isn't to malign people who identify themselves as an agnostic. For big chunks of life, that was me. The point is to show that the words people use to signify and communicate their social identities might not precisely reflect their underlying beliefs. There's so much social and cultural baggage attached to the words we use to describe our identities, especially words like "atheist." In my research, I tend to focus on what people do and do not believe, not on what they call themselves. Questions of belief aren't in any way scientifically superior to questions about identity labels; it's just that if I want to study (and now write a book about) religious beliefs, social identity labels are a bit of a distraction from the core issues of what people do or don't believe, and why.

If identity labels aren't informative about belief, how else might we represent agnosticism and atheism?

The So-Called Dawkins Scale

Sometimes, people don't portray atheism and agnosticism as discrete and mutually exclusive categories. Instead, they are portrayed as separate points on a single continuum of religious faith running from staunch atheism at one pole to devout theism at the other, with agnosticism perched at the precise midpoint.

In *The God Delusion*, Richard Dawkins took this idea and fitted it to that mainstay of social science research, the seven-point Likert-type scale.[‡] He provided descriptors for each of the seven ordered levels, each roughly assigned a probability that people viewed God's existence as likely. It's usually summarized with points at least roughly analogous to those listed below, with each rung getting a verbal descriptor and a numerical estimate of the probability of God's existence:

1. *Strong theist*: 100 percent probability of God. In the words of Carl Jung: "I do not believe, I know."
2. *De facto theist*: Very high probability but short of 100 percent. "I don't know for certain, but I strongly believe in God and live my life on the assumption that He is there."
3. *Weak theist*: Higher than 50 percent but not very high. "I am very uncertain, but I am inclined to believe in God."

[‡] Named after originator Rensis Likert, these are questions that ask for your agreement on a seven-point scale (e.g., 7. strongly agree; 6. agree; 5. mildly agree; 4. neither agree nor disagree; 3. mildly disagree; 2. disagree; 1. strongly disagree).

4. *Pure agnostic*: Exactly 50 percent. "God's existence and nonexistence are exactly equiprobable."
5. *Weak atheist*: Lower than 50 percent but not very low. "I do not know whether God exists, but I'm inclined to be skeptical."
6. *De facto atheist*: Very low probability, but short of zero. "I don't know for certain, but I think God is very improbable, and I live my life on the assumption that he is not there."
7. *Strong atheist*: 0 percent probability of God. "I know there is no God, with the same conviction as Jung knows there is one."

This representation does have a few strengths that we should acknowledge up front. First off, people have a pretty easy time representing degrees of confidence in rating scales like this, and mapping degrees of belief about gods to a Likert scale is a decent way to get numerical representations for variability in belief. Second, it's punchy and memorable. Once the scale became popular, it was easy for people to say they're like a 6.5 atheist, for example—pretty damn sure we live in a Godless world, but not dogmatically certain. And finally, I appreciate that instead of forcing people into categorical labels, degree of belief is represented as a continuum. This is probably a closer match to psychological reality than a view of discrete belief identities. Those positives aside, I don't find the Dawkins scale useful, for several reasons.

First off, it's worth acknowledging measurement of religious beliefs had been underway for decades in the psychology of religion and other fields before Dawkins popularized a single-item sort of belief scale. There are dozens of much more rigorously validated measurement tools out there that do a better job of capturing subtle variations in people's degrees and kinds of religious belief. In comparison to the measurement toolkit that was already available at publication date, *The God Delusion*'s scale is crude. That said, lay audiences don't need a psychometrically validated instrument, they need a handy tool to communicate with others, and for this sort of chatroom-and-social-media dialogue the Dawkins scale works well enough.

When it comes to conceptual limitations, however, the Dawkins scale offers plenty. First off, there's the issue of mapping degrees of belief to probabilistic judgments. There's nothing wrong with this in principle—indeed, Bayesian approaches to probability fundamentally map probability to subjective uncertainty like this. But when I look at the Dawkins scale, I really don't know what to make of statements like "100 percent probability of God" or "Lower than 50 percent but not very low." Is this my subjective appraisal of God (the Judeo-Christian capitalizer)? All gods? If someone is certain that Yahweh exists, and places the probability of Zeus existing at zero, what's their overall score? The Dawkins scale (and, if we're being blunt, most of *The God Delusion*) fixates narrowly on the Abrahamic deity. Zooming out to consider all world gods—which both atheists and agnostics do—the scale is tough to apply. Notice also that the probabilities don't map closely to the rungs on the seven-point scale. Moving from 1 to 2 takes us only from "100 percent certain" to "very high but short of 100 percent," so maybe 1 to 2 represents movement from 100 percent to 85–90 percent? But then a single interval gap, from 2 to 3, moves us from not quite 100 percent all the way to just above 50 percent. Then moving from 3 to 4, probability shifts only from above 50 percent to exactly 50 percent. The gaps across intervals are imprecisely and inconsistently mapped to subjective probabilities; interval width and scaling is wildly inconsistent.

A far more serious issue than inconsistent probability mapping is the treatment of agnosticism. This issue is fundamental, and it shows a deep conceptual confusion in the Dawkins scale and what it seeks to measure. The scale considers agnosticism as the exact midpoint between fully devout theism and certain atheism. Using the subjective probability values, it describes atheism as exactly a 50 percent probability of God's existence. Fundamentally, it places agnosticism as an intermediate or indeterminate position on the probability of God's existence, a stance on how likely it is that there's a God. But this gets the basic philosophy (and, I suspect, psychology) of agnosticism all wrong. Let's head back to Philosophy 101.

Atheism and Agnosticism: Answers to Different Questions, from Different Branches of Philosophy

A man may be an agnostic, in the sense of admitting he has no positive knowledge, and yet consider that he has more or less probable ground for accepting any given hypothesis about the spiritual world. . . . [He] may think one or other of the current views on the subject, to some extent, probable.

—THOMAS HENRY HUXLEY,
AGNOSTICISM AND CHRISTIANITY

There are a lot of assumptions bundled into the Dawkins scale, some better than others. But for the purposes of this section, I just want to focus on the placement of agnostics as a "4" on a scale running from atheism to theism—agnosticism as a halfway stop between devout belief and certain disbelief. On the Dawkins scale, an agnostic is someone who thinks God's existence and nonexistence are perfectly equiprobable. I think that this placement does grave injustice to agnosticism, as discussed by publicly identifying agnostic thinkers like T. H. Huxley (who initially popularized the term "agnostic" in the religious sense) or Bertrand Russell. And it does so because the Dawkins scale's version of agnosticism tramples all over centuries-old philosophical distinctions.

Atheists and theists disagree about *whether a god exists*. Ultimately, this is a question of *metaphysics*, the branch of philosophy concerned with the ultimate nature of reality.

On the other hand, agnosticism is a stance that *we can't ultimately know* for sure whether a god exists. Agnosticism isn't a statement about the probability that a god exists (let alone that the probability is precisely 50 percent), it's a statement about what we can know. Agnosticism is a position on *epistemology*, the branch of philosophy concerned with the ultimate nature of knowledge.

"I'm an atheist" is a statement about someone's beliefs about whether God exists, an answer to a question of metaphysics. "I'm agnostic" is a statement about someone's beliefs on the fundamental knowability of God's existence, an answer to a question of epistemology.

With this scale, Dawkins (and a great many others) conflates entire branches of philosophy and mistakes a principled stance on epistemology for a waffling stance on metaphysics. As a result, there's now a whole lot of confusion out there surrounding the term "agnostic," and this confusion makes life difficult for researchers like me who study this stuff. In my research, people who call themselves agnostics tend to be one of several things:

- People who don't believe in a god but don't want to call themselves atheists
- People who care deeply about religious claims but are uncertain about whether there's a god

- People who really don't care if there's a god
- People who stake a strong epistemological claim that we can't know if there's a god

All of these people might adopt the social identity label "agnostic." But they are likely to have quite different ideas both about the existence (or not) of gods, and about their conceptions of the limitations of human knowledge thereof. Given this variety, why insist that these folks all occupy a metaphysical position exactly intermediate between dogmatic theism and dogmatic atheism? It's a philosophical and conceptual mess.

I think a much more productive approach is to split people's beliefs into separate metaphysical and epistemological dimensions. On the metaphysical front, people can range from being strong theists to strong atheists. On the epistemological front, people can range from being extremely agnostic (thinking we can't know if a god exists) to extremely gnostic (thinking we definitely can). And along a two-dimensional space, people can figure out where they fit. To illustrate what such a grid would look like, see figure 10.1.

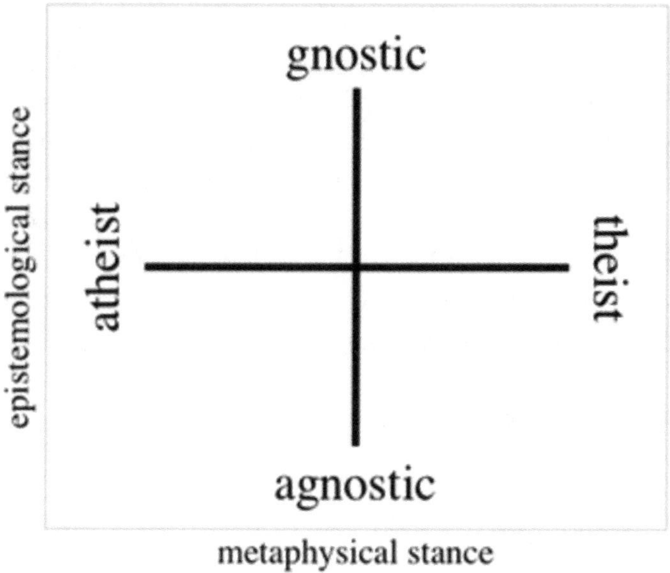

Figure 10.1. Atheism and agnosticism as endpoints of two independent continua.

By splitting the metaphysical and epistemological aspects of religious belief and disbelief from each other, there's much more room for people to express their nuanced viewpoints. One doesn't have to choose between categorical labels of "agnostic" or "atheist." Likewise, one doesn't have to let their views on the metaphysics of gods impinge on their views about epistemology—separating what we believe about whether or not a god exists from our beliefs about our own states of knowledge. People can be atheists and agnostics, or just one, or neither.

Let's illustrate the utility of partitioning atheism and agnosticism in this manner using prominent historical examples.

Gnostic Theist: William Paley

Every indication of contrivance, every manifestation of design, which existed in the watch, exists in the works of nature; with the difference, on the side of nature, of being greater or more, and that in a degree which exceeds all computation.

—WILLIAM PALEY, *NATURAL THEOLOGY*[9]

British clergyman and Christian apologist William Paley's an especially good example for our gnostic theism quadrant, as he argued that the apparent design in nature necessarily implied the existence of God, much as the intricate design of a watch implied the existence of a watchmaker. He thought that the intricate design evident in nature was positive proof of God's existence, giving us rational proof of God. God is real, and we can logically infer this with certainty from what the world looks like—it's plain and provable for all to see. Observation and reason in this case get you all the way to theism. Paley's a believer, and he knew it (and knew that he could know it). Theistic metaphysics, gnostic epistemology.

Agnostic Theist: Søren Kierkegaard

to see what a tremendous paradox faith is . . . which no thought can master, because faith begins precisely where thinking leaves off.

—SØREN KIERKEGAARD, *FEAR AND TREMBLING*[10]

In *Fear and Trembling* Kierkegaard argues that reason, logic, and facts can only get you so far in a journey to knowing God. But you ain't about to prove God's existence rationally or with evidence. Instead, you must take a leap of faith. In the quote above, he isn't saying that faith begins where thinking leaves off because he thinks faith is stupid or irrational—it's because he thinks that faith can only exist once rationality has been pushed to its limits and is still found lacking. "Infinite resignation is the last stage before faith, so anyone who has not made this movement does not have faith, for only in infinite resignation does an individual become conscious of his eternal validity, and only then can one speak of grasping existence by virtue of faith." The tingling agnosticism left when reason was fully exhausted is precisely where Kierkegaard found faith necessary, and beautiful. Our friend Søren was a devout believer who believed in God despite not rationally knowing He existed (and he knew he couldn't know it). Theistic in his metaphysics, agnostic in his epistemology.

Agnostic Atheist: Bertrand Russell

The Christian god may exist; so may the gods of Olympus, or of ancient Egypt, or of Babylon. But no one of these hypotheses is more probable than any other . . . and therefore there is no reason to consider any of them.

—BERTRAND RUSSELL, *WHY I AM NOT A CHRISTIAN*[11]

Bertrand Russell (author of *Why I Am Not a Christian* and, with Alfred North Whitehead, *Principia Mathematica*) maintained that his agnosticism was merely a philosophical stance and not a statement about his religious beliefs or lack thereof. He didn't think we could positively and rationally disprove the existence of a god, hence a degree of agnosticism. Yet he also made it clear that he didn't believe in any gods. He was, simply, both atheist and agnostic. Russell said that one can't disprove the existence of the Christian God or the Greek pantheon on strict rational or evidentiary grounds—gods have too much metaphysical wiggle room to be ruled out entirely. Yet he never espoused belief in any gods either and opined that the gods who he'd heard described all sounded quite implausible. "Therefore, in regard to the Olympic gods, speaking to a purely philosophical audience, I would say that I am an Agnostic. But speaking popularly, I think that all of us would say in regard to those gods that we were Atheists. In regard to the

Christian God, I should, I think, take exactly the same line."[§] So Russell by all appearances was a definitional atheist who took the further epistemological stance that ultimate disproofs of God's existence aren't forthcoming. He was a disbeliever who disbelieved in spite of not being able to logically prove the nonexistence of gods; Russell was an atheist and an agnostic. Atheistic in his metaphysics, agnostic in his epistemology.

Figure 10.2 shows where this cast of famous thinkers would probably fall, both in our two-dimensional grid and in the Dawkins scale. Which visualization do you prefer? Which preserves the philosophical nuances reflected in their writings?

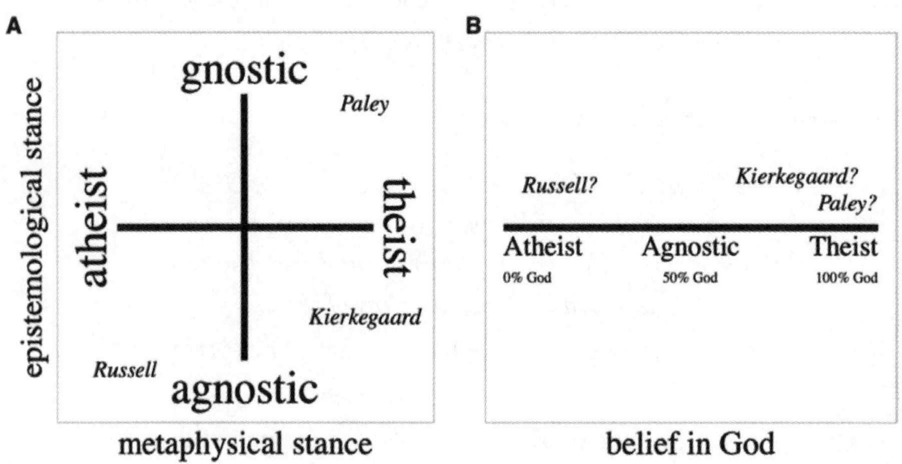

Figure 10.2. Kierkegaard, Paley, and Russell's beliefs, depicted across two- and one-dimensional scales.

From Principle to Practice

This all sounds nice in principle and accords well with the philosophical and etymological roots of atheism and agnosticism. But is this how people represent their beliefs about gods? It's all fine and well to argue that atheism and agnosticism are endpoints of separate continua, but it's vital to check whether this distinction maps onto people's own experiences. Can people easily split their views about gods into different atheism/theism and agnosticism/

§ From his essay "Am I an Atheist or an Agnostic?" in which he concludes "both."

gnosticism stances? One possibility is that people represent beliefs essentially as the Dawkins scale depicts, with agnosticism no more than the midpoint between atheism and theism. If this is the case, then all my linguistic prescriptivism about what these words mean doesn't count for much—if my definitions don't match ground truths in how people structure their beliefs, then so much the worse for my definitions. Alternatively, people might be able to think about atheism and agnosticism as separate dimensions of disbelief, suggesting that there's some merit to my proposal about how we should think about atheism and agnosticism. An empirical test is in order.

Over the past few years, my lab has been working on teasing apart atheism and agnosticism in this way. Sometimes, we explain the metaphysics/epistemology grid and ask people to simply place a mark where they feel they belong on it, as in figure 10.1. Other times, we explain the two dimensions to them and ask them to indicate where they'd place themselves on each individually (see figure 10.3). Here's what those questions look like:

> When it comes to belief in a god or gods, there are two different components to consider. One is your belief about whether or not a god (or gods) exists. This continuum ranges from not believing in a god or gods (atheist) to believing in a god or gods (theist). The other is the degree to which you think it is in principle possible to know the ultimate truth about whether or not a god exists. This continuum ranges from believing that humans cannot ultimately know that a god or gods exist (agnostic) to believing that humans can know that a god or gods exist (gnostic).

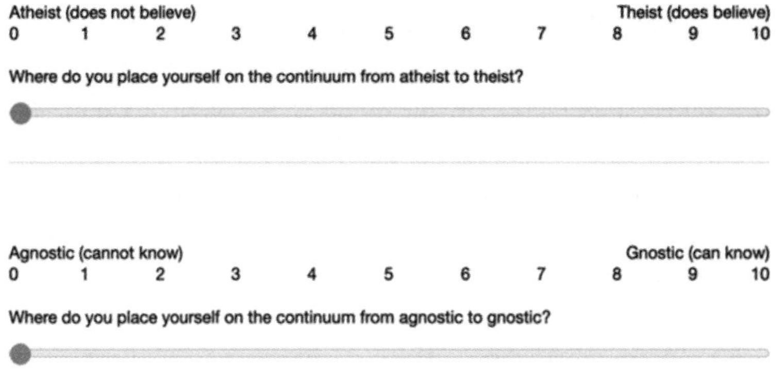

Figure 10.3. Sample slider bars to independently measure atheism and agnosticism.

If people represent agnosticism like the Dawkins scale depicts—as a midpoint between faith and atheism—then people scoring high on the agnosticism continuum ought to cluster in the middle of the theism-atheism continuum. The scale, after all, assumes that agnostics necessarily fall in the middle. In contrast, if people can separate atheism and agnosticism into separate underlying continuous dimensions, then we'd expect more spread across both axes. Some people might indicate that they're firm theists, but high in agnosticism. Others might be agnostic atheists. Yet others might be atheists with more gnostic leanings, certain of their disbelief. Figure 10.4 is a typical graph of what we find, at least in samples from the United States.[¶]

This graph is precisely what we'd expect if atheism/theism and agnosticism/gnosticism are independent dimensions, and people can separate them with ease, given the right instructions. Notice that folks on the gnostic end of the epistemological dimension are incredibly polarized—they're either strong theists or strong atheists, no middle ground. Strong agnostics, far from clustering at the midpoint of the atheist/theist continuum (as the Dawkins scale forces), trend toward atheism, although they are present across the entire spectrum from devout theism to staunch atheism. Overall, theists tend to be more gnostic in their views, but plenty of agnostic theists are apparent. Atheists tend to be agnostic, although there's also a smattering of atheists with more gnostic leanings. The general pattern was that atheists tend to be agnostic, and theists more gnostic in their belief. But there's a lot of variability around this general trend. Insights like these are impossible if everything is forced into a unidimensional scale where agnosticism lies halfway between theism and atheism.

The next stage in our research is seeing what this distinction buys us, empirically and inferentially speaking. Do the two dimensions correlate with different demographic or individual differences variables? Do they predict different behaviors? Time will tell, but so far results are promising.

In the meantime, I think there's a lot to recommend abandoning the Dawkins scale entirely. It conflates entire schools of philosophical thought and erases important distinctions in how folks might view gods. Importantly, it also means that no nonreligious person would have to choose whether

---

¶ This particular graph came from a study where we oversampled people who don't believe in God/a god. That explains the abundance of folks who indicate high levels of atheism, hardly a typical US pattern.

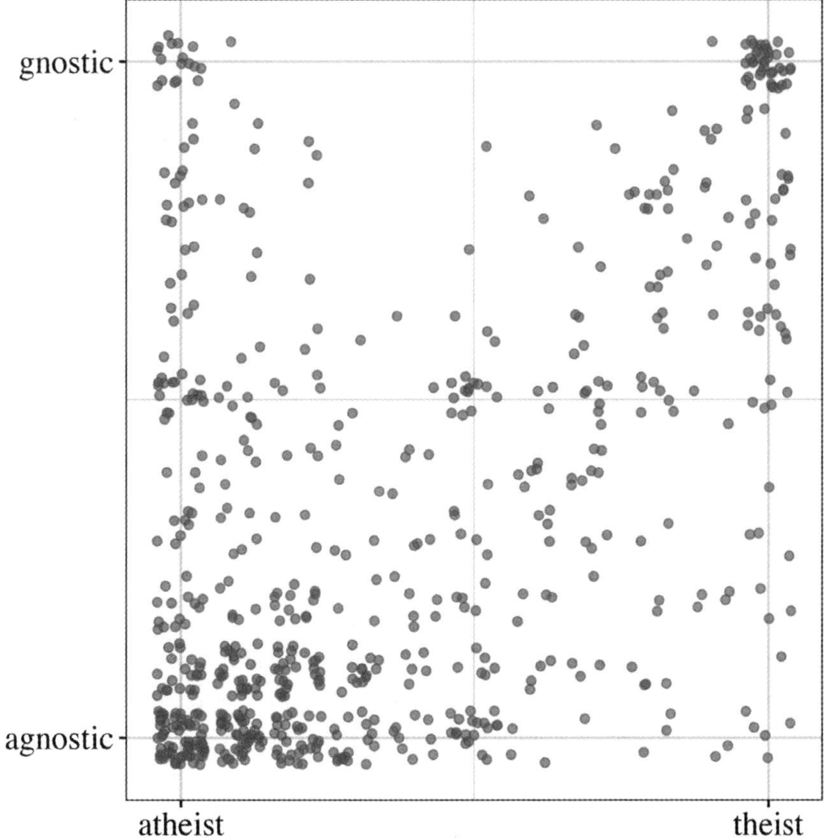

Figure 10.4. People can easily separate their beliefs along two dimensions, one indexing metaphysics (atheism-theism) and one indexing epistemology (agnosticism-gnosticism).

they're agnostic or atheist—listen to Bertrand Russell, and choose both if so inclined. Our preliminary data show that people are pretty good at placing themselves along both dimensions. Importantly, people high in agnosticism don't have to force themselves to the midpoint of the scale: check out that graph and you'll see that highly agnostic folks populate the entire theism/atheism spectrum, not just the midpoint. On top of that, it looks like most agnostics are fairly atheistic, and most atheists quite agnostic. The tick box survey approach presenting "atheist" and "agnostic" as mutually exclusive forces a binary choice where no strict binary exists. The Dawkins scale similarly imposes a choice between atheism and agnosticism. As you can see, a large chunk of atheists simultaneously view themselves as agnostic and vice versa. Updating our descriptive and measurement tools to embrace this nuance is in order.

Me, personally? Gun to my head,** I'd describe my own religious beliefs or identity as an agnostic atheist. I'm an agnostic. And I'm an atheist. These are entirely compatible philosophical stances. I think that, as an idiosyncratically evolved hominid on an insignificant Milky Way planet, there are fundamental limits on what we can know about ultimate reality, and maybe some sort of a god exists; I'm agnostic, in a scientific and epistemological sense. But given all the descriptions of gods I've seen, none of them accord especially well with other evidence I tend to rely on, so I'm a pretty convinced atheist about the gods I've heard about so far. There you have it: I'm an atheist agnostic or agnostic atheist, and I suspect a lot of this book's readership is as well. You're not a 4 on the Dawkins scale—you just score highly on both atheism and agnosticism.

Regarding my agnosticism, I suspect I share this stance with a great many of my devoutly religious friends and readers as well. Indeed, abandoning the Dawkins scale gives theists the option to signal whether they're more of a Kierkegaard "leap of faith" agnostic theist or more of a Paley "we can prove God's existence" gnostic theist. These two thinkers had really different conceptions of what things like "faith" even are, and the Dawkins scale squeezes all the juice out of important distinctions, then discards it. I suspect our research will reveal interesting differences between theists of agnostic and gnostic bent, as it will reveal interesting differences between gnostic and agnostic atheists.

There you have it, atheism and agnosticism aren't separate categories that are mutually exclusive, and agnosticism isn't some intermediate point between faith and atheism. Instead, they are answers to different sorts of philosophical questions. Atheism (or theism) is a stance on what we believe about whether a god exists; agnosticism (or gnosticism) is a stance on what we think we can know. There's plenty of space within each dimension for

---

** I genuinely doubt anyone will put a gun to my head and ask me to clarify whether I'm an atheist or an agnostic. But my grad school stats instructor Ralph Hakstian would open questions to the class with a preface about how you'd answer if a gun were put to your head. "Gun to your head, how do you think you'd calculate variance here?" and so forth. Knowledge of variance formulae has yet to rescue me from a firearm-related incident, but like most UBC psychology doctorates for a time, I'm well prepared.

graded differences, and I encourage you to play around with the grid above and see where you might land.

Terminological side quest complete, let's return to the question of how many atheists there are, with the recognition that "what about agnostics" might be a red herring of a question.

PIETY, PUBLIC AND PRIVATE

Beware of practicing your piety before others in order to be seen by them
—MATTHEW 6:1

Large-scale surveys, of the sort we've used to gauge atheist prevalence, tend to be straightforward self-reports. Either via an online survey or a phone call, pollsters ask respondents a bunch of questions about their beliefs. In return, the respondents provide answers—whatever answers they like. There's no way to guarantee truth from respondents, but pollsters hope that conditions of anonymity give respondents the freedom to speak their minds.

Commitment to anonymity, commendable as it is, will not perfectly guarantee honest or truthful responses. Some participants might consciously fib to the pollster—they could cast themselves in a favorable light to project a more positive image. Less cynically, but equally pernicious from a researcher's perspective, respondents could subtly shift their responses and project a positive image without any overt fibbing, without nefarious intent. They might leave out or gloss over some unsavory details and play up the nicer bits. This could even occur in a wholly unintentional or unconscious manner. Maybe people are more likely to forget mistakes and remember successes. Survey questions asking people to recall events or behaviors will thus be biased by this recall advantage for positive information.

This all amounts to a *social desirability bias*,[12] a tendency for people to use their responses in questionnaires to project a positive image—they don't just tell the pollster who they are, they also tell them who they'd like to be seen as. People tend to overreport good stuff and underreport bad stuff ("good" or "bad" in their prevailing cultural milieu, an important note). You can easily imagine how this would play out for really sensitive topics. Surveys on touchy topics like drug use, illegal activity, problem drinking, prejudicial attitudes, and such will end up with unrealistically low levels of sin and vice. Surveys on things like charitable giving, norm compliance, or other positives will find unreasonably high rates of saintliness and virtue. Inasmuch as a survey's topic is socially sensitive, researchers need to always be mindful of the fact that aggregate results will reflect both the truth of whatever's being asked about, plus or minus some wiggle room introduced by social desirability biases.

When it comes to religion, this can be tricky indeed. As we saw a couple chapters ago, people tend to intuitively assume a tight link between religion and morality. This means that when a pollster asks questions about religious beliefs or practices, respondents might hear or infer a question about their perceived moral worth. As a result, they might—again, consciously or not—find ways to inflate their claims of religiosity. The tendency to do so won't be equal across all contexts. In the United States Bible Belt, for example, we'd expect to see people fudging their claims of piety in a positive direction. In an atheist stronghold like Scandinavia, the social desirability bias favoring religiosity might disappear, or even reverse.

Given that the world is largely religious (with just a few strongly secular holdouts like Scandinavia), we'd expect that global surveys might tend to subtly skew toward religion, in accordance with prevailing norms and social desirability biases. This is precisely what we find, at least according to a couple lines of scientific evidence. As with much social science work, it relies heavily on data from the United States. The United States doesn't provide better data than other countries in any particularly meaningful way—in many ways, it's worse—but it's plentiful and thus occupies a position of undue influence in social scientific conversations.

Surveys routinely ask people how frequently they attend church or other religious services. Based on questions like this, we get headlines like "Losing Their Religion: Why US Churches Are on the Decline"[13] or "Churchgoing and Belief in God Stand at Historic Lows, Despite a Megachurch Surge."[14] Stories like this rely on a pattern whereby people are reporting lower levels of church attendance. I've no doubt that a genuine dip in attendance in the United States is happening—this would fit well with lots of other data. But in addition to an actual dip, there might also be an increase in honest reporting going on. For years, you see, surveys on religious attendance in the United States have presented unrealistically high estimates.[15]

Phillip Brenner and others have conducted studies[16] to see just how trustworthy people's self-reported religiosity is, looking at church attendance as a nice behavioral proxy. It's hard to measure an abstract concept like "religious commitment" but attending church or not is a nice concrete behavior that folks can report on, and researchers can track in other ways. In Brenner's work, something like 40–50 percent of people report church attendance on a weekly or greater basis, when they're directly asked how often they go to church. This is a lot of regular church attendance. But when Brenner uses a different methodology, the number drops.[17] Specifically, Brenner looked at time-use diary research,[18] where people are asked to record what they do each day or week. He found that people weren't listing churchgoing nearly as frequently as self-reports of churchgoing might lead one to expect. If you ask people how often they think they go to church, almost half of people say they're in the pews on a weekly basis. But if you ask people what they do each day, and then count how often church is listed, the weekly attendance number drops to 20–30 percent. In other words, if you ask Americans how often they go to church, they'll tell you they go all the time. But if you reconstruct how often they actually go to church, from regular reports of how they're using their time, people are far less churchgoing than they'll let on. In short, it's easier to say you go to church weekly than it is to actually, you know, attend church weekly.[19]

Brenner's results suggest that social desirability concerns lead Americans to pad their church attendance stats by about 80 percent, relative to better measures of people's behavior. There is padding in other countries he's examined, although the degree of padding varies across context. As we might expect, there's less padding in less religious countries. Comparing the United States to its less religious progenitor Great Britain, and that whopping 20-point pad the Americans tack on (45 percent–25 percent) drops to only 4 points of padding in Great Britain. The Netherlands, which is normatively even less religious than Great Britain, sees only 2 points of padding.

This same pattern—people overreporting their church attendance—shows up in work by other researchers in the United States and seems to generalize to other cultures that place a social premium on religiosity. John Shaver and colleagues, for example, found that self-reports of church attendance in a Fijian village setting were much higher than peer reports.[20]

Seemingly more people report that "I was there" than have other people confirm "yes, they were there."

Inflated piety in self-reports isn't confined to just church attendance. Broader measures of religiosity are also routinely overinflated when people give self-reports. Interestingly, this pattern is more pronounced in situations where the social stakes are higher. When people respond to religion surveys over the telephone—an objectively anonymous and confidential context, but one that doesn't feel especially anonymous, due to the human conversation required—they describe themselves as more religious than when they take the same exact surveys in online questionnaires. Evidently verbalizing answers to a human makes people report being more religious than just mashing buttons on a keyboard. Increasing the interpersonal and social stakes leads to a corresponding increase in self-reported religiosity.

Exaggerated religiosity can be decreased if people are given a nudge toward truth-telling. Keenly attendant to social desirability concerns, researchers have devised various experimental techniques to encourage truthful responding. One experimental setup is the "bogus pipeline," a technique in which participants are hooked up to a machine that they are told is a lie detector (in reality, it's often some vaguely scientific-looking junk scrounged from the lab surplus). Participants thus hooked up to this sort of "lie detector" tend to report lower levels of religiosity than do folks who aren't.[21] Thinking that one might get caught in a lie makes people report being a bit less religious than they otherwise might.

The general pattern is that people like to project a positive image of themselves, even to pollsters who they'll never meet in real life. The social desirability biases to present positively can skew our estimates of religiosity, given how socially loaded religion is in most of the world. People (in highly religious contexts) tend to inflate their self-reported religiosity in polls, saying for example that they attend church more than they actually do. When people are given a reason to respond more truthfully—even if it's just via a bogus lie detector—self-reports of religiosity decline. In sum, self-report polls of religiosity probably give us padded estimates of just how faithful most folks are, at least in areas where religion is normatively favored.

HIDDEN HEATHENISM

So, how many atheists are there? Zuckerman guessed five hundred to seven hundred million, largely based on self-report surveys. Within the United States, polls from 2017 and 2018 suggest that 2–3 percent of Americans identify as atheists, and 10–12 percent of Americans don't believe in God. Both numbers have crept up over the past half decade—for example, Pew's disbelief-in-God numbers held steady at 10–12 percent from 2013–2017 and then jumped to 17 percent in 2022. Does this mean that we can be confident that less than 20 percent of Americans don't believe in God?

I don't think so.

We have converging evidence that people overreport church attendance and overall religiosity, presumably because these are socially desirable things to report. If we return to the research covered a couple of chapters ago, atheism is hugely socially undesirable to a lot of people. Research participants in the United States, remember, spontaneously conjured a mental image of a creepy and immoral man when thinking about atheism, and they intuitively assume that atheists are capable of gross immorality ranging from puppy kicking and poker cheating to cannibalism, incest, and serial murder. Other lines of research show that atheists are well aware of stigma against religious disbelief and stereotypes of atheists (with predictably poor consequences for their well-being).

So, when a pollster calls and asks people, "Do you believe in God?" this is an incredibly loaded question. Yes, polling data are *objectively* anonymous and confidential. The respondent has no rational fear that they'll one day meet the pollster and be recognized as a heathen, but the situation isn't *subjectively* anonymous at all. After all, a telephone survey is basically a conversation with a stranger. Guarantees of data confidentiality don't make things feel anonymous. And to the extent that atheism is seen as socially undesirable—and this certainly seems to be the case in the United States—it's precisely the type of topic that we'd expect to generate skewed survey numbers, thanks to social desirability biases.

Back in about 2015, this chain of thinking led Maxine Najle and me to seek out indirect ways to measure atheist prevalence, ways for us to see how many atheists there are without relying on the sorts of polls that might be especially sensitive to social desirability biases. Maxine was one of the first doctoral students I was privileged to work with over the years, and she is now a successful polling researcher in the private sector, after completing her doctoral work at the University of Kentucky back in 2018.

We stumbled across a measurement tool for indirectly getting prevalence estimates of things people are loath to admit. This tool is called the "unmatched count technique" or "list technique," and it allows researchers to get indirect prevalence estimates by giving respondents a way to indicate that something is true of them, without them having to overtly admit it.[22] Here's how it works.

Imagine you're trying to estimate the prevalence of problem drinking or shoplifting or illicit drug use or something of that nature—something that your respondents will be motivated to conceal. You could directly ask them if they drink and drive, or shoplift, or do meth. Some folks will honestly fess up and confess their misdeeds, but presumably many people will refrain from telling the truth. And again, this needn't be conscious deception. "Aww, that was one time." "I wasn't that tipsy." It's really easy to avoid answering these sorts of questions in a forthright manner. What if you could pull an aggregate estimate from lots of people, without any single respondent having to openly confess?

In a list technique study, you gather a large sample of respondents—the larger the better, really—and randomly split them into two groups. Everybody then completes a list or count task. People are given a list of statements, and asked to count how many are true of them, but they are never asked *which specific statements are true*. The key trick is that our two groups of respondents get slightly different lists of statements, and the difference between lists lets researchers indirectly infer the prevalence of something socially undesirable.

One group of respondents, those we might think of as being in the baseline condition, gets a list of unremarkable statements, like this:

- I can drive a car.
- I exercise regularly.
- I have set foot on the moon.
- I was born on a weekday.
- My favorite color is red.
- I am a vegetarian.

Remember that each respondent is just asked how many of these statements are true of them. Item plausibility ranges from some that will be true for basically nobody (have set foot on the moon) to others that will be true for many more people (driving, weekday birth). Each person just counts the statements that fit them and replies with that number. For example, one respondent might answer "three," but the researcher doesn't know which three are true. Our "three" could be a weekday-born driver of red cars; it could be a vegetarian who works out in a red outfit; it could be a vegetarian who drives to the gym. The researcher knows nothing of each respondent, beyond their number.

Now's when things get interesting. Remember that we had two groups of respondents, randomly split. Our baseline group got a boring list, full of items we don't really care about. Our second group, which we might call the sensitive group, does the exact same task, but their list is slightly different. It contains all the same items that the baseline group got, plus our socially sensitive item, the thing we're hoping to measure. For example, if we wanted to estimate the prevalence of shoplifting, we might provide this list:

- I can drive a car.
- I exercise regularly.
- I have set foot on the moon.
- I have taken items from stores without paying.
- I was born on a weekday.
- My favorite color is red.
- I am a vegetarian.

If we wanted to estimate the prevalence of drunk driving, we might provide this list:

- I can drive a car.
- I exercise regularly.
- I have set foot on the moon.
- I have driven a car after drinking too much alcohol.
- I was born on a weekday.
- My favorite color is red.
- I am a vegetarian.

Respondents in these conditions never have to directly tell the pollster that they've shoplifted, or that they've driven drunk. Each respondent, remember, only gives a number. A "four" reply could mean an exercise junky who drives a red car to the mall to shoplift, an exercise junky who drunk drives their red car, or an exercise junky who drives red cars to vegetarian restaurants. On an individual respondent-by-respondent basis, researchers don't know who has done the socially undesirable things. But by comparing overall scores between the baseline and sensitive conditions, researchers can figure out *roughly how many people* do them. Because people were randomly allocated to the two conditions, and the only difference between conditions was the addition of our socially sensitive item, the difference in averages between the two conditions can be attributed to the proportion of people in the overall sample for whom the socially sensitive item applies.

Imagine that we conducted a list technique survey using the baseline condition and the shoplifting version of the sensitive condition. A few thousand respondents are given one list or the other; each respondent gives no more than a number in response. If the average in the baseline condition is 2.15 and the average in the sensitive condition is 2.60, the researcher can infer that 45 percent of people have shoplifted (the math: 2.60 – 2.15 = 0.45, or 45 percent).

Now imagine that we conducted a list technique survey using the baseline condition and the second, drunk driving, sensitive condition. If the average in the baseline condition is 2.50 and the average in the sensitive condition is 2.65, the researcher can infer that 15 percent of the overall sample has driven drunk (the math: 2.65 – 2.50 = 0.15, or 15 percent).

Not a single respondent had to directly fess up about their drunk driving or shoplifting. But we can nonetheless make an informed indirect inference about how common these behaviors are across the entire sample.

Thus armed, Maxine Najle and I set out to estimate how many atheists there are in the United States, using the list technique to sidestep the social desirability concerns that might lead Americans to not out themselves as atheists in polls.[23] Maxine and I fielded two large surveys using the polling company YouGov to recruit nationally representative samples of 2000 people apiece. Each of our surveys had slight variants on question wording and such to rule out idiosyncrasies of any question that might skew things. This work began in about 2015 and was published in 2018, so let's recall the atheist prevalence estimates coming from polls at that time. Using the "menu of religious/nonreligious identities" approach, some polls had atheists at about 2–3 percent of the US population. Using a binary-type "Do you believe in God" question, other polls clocked atheists at more like 11–12 percent.

First, we included a self-report item gauging belief in God, not unlike the binary choice version in polls (that at the time was yielding an 11–12 percent estimate). While our sample was broadly representative of the population, our survey itself was delivered online—there was no need for people to verbalize their atheism to a stranger, buying us a little bit of ground on overcoming social pressures to conceal atheism. Our self-report estimate was 17 percent atheists. It's possible that the online response option led people to give us more honest answers, yielding a higher estimate of self-reported God disbelief than telephone polls at the time tended to deliver.

Most importantly, each of our surveys had a version of the list technique to measure the prevalence of disbelief in God in a way that didn't actually require a single person to directly tell us they didn't believe in God. We collected the data and crunched the numbers using some statistical tools that let us represent just how credible different atheist prevalence estimates were. Our best guess—the single most credible atheist prevalence value collapsing across both of the surveys we fielded—was 26 percent atheists. Not 3 percent, not 12 percent, not even the 17 percent we found from an online survey, but 26 percent. Our statistical tool allowed us to state with greater than 99 percent confidence that existing poll estimates at 11–12 percent were too low. We were about 80 percent confident that atheist prevalence surpassed 20 percent. Our data and model suggested that an 11 percent prevalence was no more credible than a 40 percent estimate—a value that few scientists would take seriously. Given our data, a true US atheist prevalence of 11–12 percent in 2017 looks really quite improbable.

Gallup ran polls in 2013, 2014, 2016, and 2017, and in each year the atheism prevalence estimate wavered between 10 percent and 12 percent. In 2018 we published our report claiming with 99 percent certainty that this was too low. Their 2022 estimate was 17 percent, right in line with our computer survey self-report estimate from a few years prior, but still lower than our list technique estimate topping 25 percent.

If that 26 percent figure holds, it has profound implications. It would mean that there are far more atheists than our polls have been estimating. Comparing a 26 percent figure to the 11 percent that polls at the same time estimated, it would imply that most atheists remain hidden from our polls, and that all large-scale polls could have downwardly biased estimates of atheist prevalence. That would be a big deal, upending some foundational assumptions in the social scientific study of religion and atheism.

Now, let's not rush to overconfidence here. The list technique is nifty, but it leaves us with an admittedly imperfect and imprecise estimate, based provisionally on one type of measurement tool. That estimate is, like all decent science, open to revision as additional evidence rolls in. Some of our validation work on the measurement tool raised pink-to-red flags, as we got nonsense answers if we included nonsense items in variants of the task—such as a list-technique-derived inference that something like 30 percent of Americans believe that 2 + 2 = 13. But over the years, we've refined this measure again and again, and we keep finding that list technique estimates of atheist prevalence in the United States are markedly higher than self-reports imply. Future work can help us narrow the range a bit, but based on the evidence I'm betting that there are a lot more atheists out there than are showing up in our polls.

HOW MANY ATHEISTS ARE THERE ACTUALLY?

So what's the actual prevalence of atheists in the United States? Is it the 3 percent who call themselves atheists in polls? The 11–12 percent who said they don't believe in God in polls in 2017? The 17 percent estimate pollsters get from doing the same in 2022? Our 26 percent estimate? Even higher to account for both the higher indirect estimates we found in 2018 and the uptick in self-reported atheism in the ensuing years? My money's on the last option, but time will tell.

Zooming out from the peculiar and peculiarly overstudied United States to the rest of the globe, how many atheists might there be? We can't take the estimates that Maxine Najle and I derived in the United States and assume that atheism rates are uniformly double what polls suggest worldwide. The list technique diverges from self-reports due to social pressures favoring religion, but these very social pressures vary hugely worldwide. In Scandinavia atheism is normative; in Saudi Arabia it's forbidden and severely punishable. Presumably in countries like Saudi Arabia, overall rates of atheism are much lower than in somewhere like Sweden, but however many atheists there are, atheists are vastly more likely to hide it. Genuine Saudi Arabian atheism rates are probably low, but given social and legal risks the few atheists out there are vastly more motivated to keep it secret.

Since that 2018 paper, I've been working with a team[††] to expand the list technique measurement of atheism to more sites globally. After years of vetting and validation work on the list technique itself, we submitted a plan to generate atheist prevalence estimates to the journal *Nature Human Behaviour* as what's called a Registered Report. This exciting innovation in scientific publication is basically a twist on the standard publication model. In standard publications, I'd do some studies, write up the results, and then submit the manuscript to a journal who would decide to accept or reject the paper (acceptances usually come after several rounds of peer-suggested revisions). In the Registered Report format, I'd submit a study plan to the journal, before collecting a single bit of data. I'd specify what the study idea and design were, how I was planning to analyze the data, and what different results would imply for the theories I was working with. At this juncture, the journal sends my plan out for peer review, to see if the plan itself is solid and the proposed interpretations sensible. Once they decide the plan's solid, the paper is provisionally accepted for publication. And then I get to do the actual study, confident in the knowledge that the resulting paper will be published no matter what the results show. This means that the journal can't pick and choose which results to publish, based on their impact or statistical significance or headline-grabbingness. Based only on the study rationale and methods, they commit to publishing the results, outcome-be-damned.

We submitted a Registered Report plan to the journal, aiming to use the list technique (leaner and meaner, thanks to years of our validation work) to generate atheist prevalence estimates in several countries: United States, France, Argentina, China, Saudi Arabia, and Indonesia. This group of countries represents strongly religious and strongly secular countries, countries with different dominant languages and religious demographics, and vastly different economic and political systems. This will be our first check on the assumption that atheism isn't uniformly underreported—it's

[††] The paper's lead author is our oft-mentioned Nava Caluori, along with myself, Brett Mercier, and Azim Shariff.

mainly underreported in places (like the United States, Argentina, Saudi Arabia, and Indonesia) where religion is normative and socially sanctioned. In signing off on our Registered Report, the journal has effectively said, "We trust your plan, it looks scientifically solid. We will publish whatever atheist prevalence estimates you obtain in these countries."

The results, as they currently stand:

In the United States, we saw similar patterns as in our original surveys from five years ago. Self-reported disbelief in God/gods was up slightly, to 24 percent; our indirect estimate was even higher than before, up to 32 percent. This is nice confirmation of our first attempt to indirectly estimate atheist prevalence in the United States, while also giving us a bit of a barometer on how things are changing. In the United States, nearly one in three may disbelieve in God, even though a smaller number would openly admit as much. Argentina looked similar to the United States, although if anything slightly less religious. Atheism prevalence was 34 percent on self-reported God belief, and 43 percent on our indirect measurement.

In our more explicitly nonreligious countries, atheism rates were high—both self-reported and indirectly measured. China saw an 82 percent self-reported rate of disbelief, and 88 percent on indirect measurement. In France, respective figures were 73 percent and 78 percent. The differences between self-report and indirect measurements are small, but their very existence is nonetheless noteworthy. Even in countries where atheism is relatively normative, it looks like there are some disbelievers who are closeted from pollsters.

In many ways, the data from Indonesia and Saudi Arabia are of the most potential interest. These are two countries with strong social (and even legal!) pressure favoring religious belief, or the presentation thereof. Alas, some surveying challenges mean that the estimates aren't ready yet—at least at time of writing—but initial pilot data hint at a similar pattern as in the United States and Argentina, where many-to-most atheists remain concealed in self-report polls. As far as precise atheism prevalence estimates go in Indonesia and Saudi Arabia, time will tell, and hopefully our journal article on this work arrives around the same time as this book hits the shelves. Stay tuned.

Our survey also included some questions about how much people feel like there is pressure favoring religion in their community. Eyeballing the general trends, things were about as you might expect. Where do people hide their atheism? In the same countries where people tell us there's more social pressure favoring religion.

Now, there are some necessary clarifications and cautions here. We contracted a survey company to give us approximately representative samples in each country. Our samples were representative on some demographic features, but nonetheless probably skewed toward affluent, educated, and urban citizens of each country. We suspect that the overall atheism rates in some of our samples are unrepresentatively high, relative to the overall populaces of their respective countries. But again—even if our samples skewed urban, affluent, educated, and secular, we still found striking evidence that lots of people were hiding their atheism, even in anonymous surveys.

To close, let's return to Zuckerman's opening estimate of five hundred to seven hundred million atheists and see if we can update it. Caveats abound in such an exercise. The global data spread isn't great—data coverage is patchy, in highly inequitable ways. We only have six data points to work with for indirect estimates. Even those estimates come from just one methodology. But if we revise upward from Zuckerman's account, assume that regardless of government pressures there are probably still lots of atheists in countries like China, and then figure that our largest polls have probably been systematically undercounting atheists everywhere that there's social pressure favoring religion—most of the world, that is—and the atheist prevalence estimate steadily rises.

We've now found evidence that polls understate the prevalence of atheism, in countries strongly religious and strongly secular. Closeted atheism appears to be fairly robust and general, albeit hugely varying in magnitude in accordance with local norms around religious self-presentation. Put differently, we've found some countries where there's a large divergence between self-reports and indirect estimates, and some countries where the gap narrows. But—with the acknowledgment that we've only looked in a handful of countries so far—we've yet to find a country where self-report polls alone wouldn't produce an underestimate of just how common atheists actually are.

Given all of these patterns, and a healthy dose of extrapolation, I'd guess that the number of atheists in the world is probably closer to two billion than to the seven hundred million maximum that Zuckerman estimated.

And this number is only likely to rise, as both the global population and its atheist share are potentially on the rise. That's a huge number of atheists, one that should rattle the foundations of some prominent theories of religion—a rattling we'll more explicitly amplify in a couple of chapters.

Counting atheists is tricky. Like United States congresspeople, most folks in many countries have an incentive to hide their atheism from others. Religion is normative throughout the world, and popularly equated with moral living. Atheism, on the other hand, evokes immorality and vice. So if a pollster calls and asks someone if they believe in God, lots of folks will answer in the affirmative, even if they privately doubt.

Systematic undercounting of atheism is likely. And, as we'll see in subsequent chapters, it's hugely important for testing theories of how religion and atheism work.

In the next chapter, we'll turn from counting atheists to understanding how people become atheists in the first place. Different theoretical approaches—including the cognitive by-product and dual inheritance approaches we met back in chapters 4 and 6–7, respectively—make very different predictions about what factors ought to predict atheism. In the next chapter we'll see that the evidence is only recently letting us put these theories to the test and sort out the cognitive origins of religious disbelief. In the process, we'll see that there might be different pathways to atheism, owing to the different cognitive and cultural pressures that lead people to disbelief.

CHAPTER ELEVEN

PATHWAYS TO ATHEISM

The road goes upward towards the light;
but the laden traveler may never reach the end of it.
—URSULA K. LE GUIN, *THE TOMBS OF ATUAN*

I hope two ideas resonate from the previous chapter. First, that atheism and agnosticism aren't mutually incompatible identities; agnosticism isn't some midpoint position between faith and atheism. Instead, agnosticism is a philosophical stance that someone doesn't think we can ultimately know or prove the (non)existence of gods, regardless of whether one believes a god exists or not. Agnosticism can commingle with either belief or atheism. Second, and more importantly for the big-picture theoretical story of this book, the last chapter argued that there are probably a lot more atheists in the world than we realize—and perhaps substantially more than even rigorous representative polls suggest. Survey methods that mitigate social desirability concerns and let people indirectly tell researchers they disbelieve in gods return atheist prevalence estimates that are vastly higher than simple self-reports tend to.

Now, we turn from defining and counting atheism to trying to understand where it comes from, at a cognitive, evolutionary, and cultural level. The subtitle of this book is "the origins of atheism in a religious species." We'll uncover those origins at different levels of analysis in the next two chapters. Somewhat mirroring the structure of chapters 6 and 7, we'll first look at the origins of atheism at the level of individuals, and then zoom out to larger cultural and historical levels of analysis. This chapter covers the various factors that can predict which folks become atheists; the next chapter asks why atheism arises and persists where it does, and when.

"TYPES" OF ATHEISTS???

Before we consider the different ways that people might become atheists, a note of caution is needed about the temptation to classify atheists as belonging to discrete categories of atheists.

Like religions, atheism is complex and multifaceted. When people ask me where atheism comes from, the shortest and most honest answer is "it depends." Our research over the years tends to converge on the idea that there are multiple different pathways to atheism—different cognitive or cultural factors that tend to predict people being less religious. One possible extension of this is to think of these pathways to atheism as characterizing different types or flavors of atheism (e.g., these atheists are Rational Atheists, those are New Atheism–tinged Antitheists, and the ones over in that pile are the Culturally Disaffected Apatheists, etc.). Every now and then I see a book[1] or article[2] claiming that there are five (or six, or seven) different "types" of atheists out there, based on some quantitative or qualitative pile-sorting exercise. I'm always intrigued by these typologies, but ultimately not terribly scientifically persuaded, for a couple of different reasons. Let's begin with a general reservation and then proceed to a more specific one.

My first reason for skepticism about typologies of atheism comes from the psychological study of individual differences, more broadly. Scientists who rigorously study individual differences in personality, for example, have reached the conclusion that there aren't discrete "types" or categories of personalities—personality just doesn't work that way. Instead, serious scientists engaged in the study of how personality varies from person to person recognize a few basic traits that vary continuously across individuals. Some people are more extroverted while others remain socially reserved; some folks are curious and high in openness to experience, others more traditional and prefer their routines; some are highly agreeable, others grumpy; some of us are organized and conscientious, others more slovenly and chaotic. People can be high or low in any of five or so dimensions of personality.[3] It very much does not follow from this that people can be bundled or clustered into groupings based on personality "types." The variation we observe is best viewed as continuous along a few fixed dimensions, not as categorical differences among different personality "types."

The firm scientific consensus that personality types are bunk hasn't stopped some personality typing schemes from achieving mainstream success—in spite, not because, of their scientific legitimacy. Those personality profile projects that claim to be able to discover your personality type and give you tailored advice (looking at you here, Myers-Briggs and your ENFJ/INTJ flimflam) are scams, with little to no scientific backing.[4] The clue to the scam is that it's free to take some online quiz to find out what your personality type is, but then you have to pay for custom-tailored life advice for people fitting your category. Scam-bashing aside, I hope readers take away from this section some newfound skepticism for personality typologies that give you the first hit (or online personality test) for free. When they start charging money you know the game's afoot.

I suspect that atheism is a bit like personality, something defined by continuous variation in a few important traits, rather than something defined by discrete "types." In this chapter we'll meet four candidate factors, but keep in mind that each individual factor is just a dimension along which people tend to vary, that also tends to predict being less religious. They're definitely not meant to be viewed as discrete categories of atheism: by my read, that's not really how individual differences in core aspects of our personhood work, generally speaking.

Turning from psychological variation in general to atheism specifically, complex phenomena like religious disbelief will have multiple overlapping and intersecting causes. Some cognitive or cultural factors predispose people to be a bit less religious, and lots of these intersecting factors can lead to atheism. But this doesn't necessarily imply categorical clustering among the diversity of disbelief.

Atheists are a diverse group, and we might even expect more diversity among atheists than within other religious groupings, because atheism itself is a negatively defined category. Catholics all have shared norms with each other, as do Jews or Muslims, whereas the only thing atheists necessarily share is an absence of belief in gods. It would be odd and surprising if the world operated in such a way that there would be essentially distinct categories of some negatively defined thing, just waiting for clever scientists to discover. Think about this with other negatively defined categories you can come up with. Are there distinct types of people who don't watch ice hockey? Different categories of non-joggers, non-jugglers, or people who don't eat phở? In all of these cases, you can probably identify a few different factors nudging people into their negative-space categories, but that in no way implies a discrete typology of phở-non-eaters or hockey-non-watchers.

If likening atheists to hockey-non-watchers seems odd, keep in mind work on atheist prevalence from a prior chapter. Yes, there are some positively identified atheists, people who make their atheism a core part of their identity. Numerically, these are atypical atheists. Once you get past the loudest and most visible atheists, you discover that most folks who disbelieve in gods probably don't even identify as atheists, and they mightn't even tell an anonymous pollster about their atheism. Most atheists are merely god-non-believers. Like hockey-non-watchers, it's odd to assume that there will be a meaningful typology of categorical differences within the weird negatively defined category of god-non-believers.

If there turned out to be more or less distinct categories of atheists (rather than continuous variability in underlying traits that predict atheism), it would genuinely surprise me. Neither individual differences in psychology generally nor religious doubt specifically seem to work like that. Maybe one day solid evidence of atheist categorical clusters will emerge. I'll no doubt find that work interesting. But given our current evidence base, I find all current claims of categorical clustering of atheists scientifically premature. For what it's worth, I suspect that any categorical clustering we eventually find among atheists will stem not from the factors that nudged them toward their atheism, but from differences in their life experiences with religion prior to their arrival at atheism. Lifelong atheists, who grew up without much religious influence, plausibly differ in lots of interesting ways from people who grew up religious and abandoned religion for one reason or another later in life. But we'll have to just wait for better evidence to see if this prediction is empirically borne out.

This section is no more than a cautionary reminder that discussing different pathways to atheism—along with some handy shorthand labels I'll give them—doesn't give us license to think about people as being different "types" of atheists as a result. Discussing the pathways to atheism gives us no reason to reify the labels below and treat them as discrete categories of atheist. There may be many different roads to a destination like atheism, but that wouldn't necessarily imply that travelers of each road end up categorically or essentially different once they arrive at the destination.

WHAT IT TAKES TO BELIEVE

About a decade ago now, Ara Norenzayan and I wrote a brief little article summarizing what we knew about the sources of atheism in light of recent work on the cognitive and evolutionary science of religion.[5] This piece, which we titled "The Origins of Religious Disbelief," opened by considering the origins of religious belief instead. How do people believe? And what does this suggest about disbelief?

We reasoned that in order for a given person to believe in a given god, at a given time, at least four things must be true. To wit:

First, that person must have the general cognitive capacity to imagine and mentally represent supernatural agents. If you're not great at imagining supernatural agents, belief in some of them is going to be tricky business.

Second, that person must have some motivation to entertain the possibility that at least some of the imaginable gods are real. Religious belief isn't cold and abstract, it's generally about perceived relationships with gods—for this, motivation is key.

Third, of all the gods a person might imagine and be motivated to mentally entertain, people still only tend to believe in those for which the surrounding culture models belief. As we saw back in chapter 7, it takes context-biased cultural learning and especially credibility-enhancing displays to engender belief in a given god.

Those first three steps are crucial for producing initial belief in a god, but that belief must be maintained over time. People might find gods in general intuitively compelling, and have both motivation and cultural support for a given god. But presumably, people reconsider their beliefs from time to time. So, fourth, for belief in a given god to persist, these occasional mental check-ins have to yield consistently positive results, and the temptation to override a religious belief must be avoided.

If people can imagine lots of supernatural agents, are motivated to treat some of them as real, and see cultural support for just one or a handful of them, they're likely to believe in that one god (or handful of gods). Unless they somehow override this belief, they're going to remain a believer. All four steps complete, this is a recipe for believers: imagine, motivate, learn, and maintain. Inverted, they also point to the steps that might lead to atheism instead.

PATHWAYS TO ATHEISM

Ara and I reasoned that if these are the four necessary ingredients for sustained belief in a god, then atheism might result from disruptions to any of them. If, for one reason or another, somebody has a tougher time imagining supernatural agents, they're unlikely to proceed to subsequent steps. Similarly, without motivation to pursue gods, or cultural support for a specific god, belief is unlikely to develop. Finally, if people initially come to believe in a god (that they can imagine, are motivated to treat as real, and have seen cultural support for), only eventually to reflectively override that belief, we'll have a once-believer-turned-atheist, a religious de-convert.

Herein we saw four potential pathways to atheism. We considered the types of psychological factors that might be especially important for each pathway—after all, things that make gods tougher to imagine are quite different than things that might lead people to override their beliefs—and in an early-grad-student departmental talk pitching the idea, I gave each of the pathways a catchy little name, which we'll reproduce here. But again, recall the previous cautionary note: these different pathways don't entail different "types" of atheists. Such a typology might or might not be useful, but it goes beyond our current evidence base. Each pathway names a different sort of atheism, but keep in mind that this is just shorthand for describing the underlying cultural and psychological dimensions at play. Because it seemed like there were four necessary steps for belief that could be disrupted to yield atheism instead, I suggested four pathways. In the talk and subsequent paper, we termed the pathways *mindblind atheism*, *apatheism*, *inCREDulous atheism*, and *analytic atheism*. Let's delve into each, and the evidence supporting it.

Mindblind Atheism

To believe in a supernatural agent, you first have to be able to imagine them, to be able to intuitively entertain their existence. We can imagine gods, yes, but we can also imagine supernatural agents of folklore and fiction. Alongside Shiva, we imagine smurfs and Snuffleupagus. As far as we can tell, other animals don't populate their mental lives with imagined agents in this way.

What does it take to imagine gods and other supernatural agents?

Recall the insights from the cognitive science of religion, back in chapter 4. A core tenet of the cognitive science of religion is that religions come naturally to us, in large part because we have lots of cognitive gadgets that are well-adapted to help us solve recurring challenges. Specifically, cognitive science of religion has converged on the idea that our suite of mentalizing abilities—those cognitive gadgets that make it easy for us to reason about, to "read," the minds of others—underpin our capacity to imagine gods.[6] The mental representation of gods and other supernatural agents rests on a cognitive foundation of our intuitive mind-reading abilities.[7]

It just so happens that there are notable individual differences in these mentalizing skills. Most people are quite adept at mentalizing. It is, after all, one of the defining traits of our hyper-social species. But within our general species-wide excellence at intuitive mindreading, there exist gradations in just how adept individuals are.[8] Some folks truly excel at decoding mental states in others. But some people, as with pretty much any ability, find the task a bit more challenging.

Our first pathway to atheism is inspired by the cognitive science of religion approach, and focuses on individual differences in advanced mentalizing abilities as fundamental constraints on religious beliefs about personal gods. If people have a bit of a tougher time with advanced mentalizing, this will make it just a little harder to entertain thoughts of disembodied minds, of the sorts that gods seem to have and be. If decoding the wants and whims of other humans is a semi-demanding cognitive task, doing the same for an incorporeal agent is just a notch or two more difficult. If we think about the mental representation of supernatural agents as a sort of extreme exercise in mentalizing, then individual differences in advanced mentalizing abilities might be important in constraining people's abilities to mentally entertain the existence of supernatural agents.

If this logic holds, then we'd predict that individual differences in advanced mentalizing abilities might predict religious disbelief. People a bit less adept at intuitive mindreading might find disembodied supernatural minds a touch less fathomable. Mentalizing constraints become religious belief constraints. Religious cognition is after all, in some ways, mentalizing writ large. Thinking about (and mentally interacting with) gods is an advanced extension of our ordinary mentalizing abilities, supernatural thinking built atop ordinary everyday social cognition. As a result, we'd expect that individual differences in mundane mentalizing ought to be associated with differing levels of religious belief and disbelief. People who have a harder time decoding human minds might be just a bit less likely to entertain thoughts of, and seek to form personal relationships with, supernatural minds.

Ara and I dubbed this *mindblind atheism* in that initial paper, and I somewhat regret the title, although it seems to have stuck. Our use of the term *mindblind* followed some of the developmental and autism literature lingo, but seems quite dated now.[9] People who find advanced mindreading tasks a little challenging aren't blind to other minds at all; they merely find them a bit tougher to decode than do other people, who can do so with unconscious ease. The gap is wide between being able to carry on social interactions with other humans, lubricated by the ability to "read" their minds from the behavior and communications, and being able to intuit the presence of supernatural minds with whom we can interact. People who have a harder time imagining personal relationships with invisible and incorporeal gods aren't "blind" to anything; it's just a subtle difference in high-end mentalizing inclination and ability. So, poor terminology apologetically acknowledged, there remains the theoretical prediction that individual differences in high-end mentalizing might constrain beliefs in supernatural agents, like a personal God.

So goes the logic. Now, how about evidence?

Ara and I, along with Kali Trzesniewski, tested the mentalizing-disbelief hypothesis back in 2009 or so, eventually publishing our results in 2012.[10] Our results: across various measures, people scoring on the lower end on tasks measuring advanced mentalizing abilities also were a bit less religious and more likely to disbelieve in gods. We found that this mentalizing–religious belief correlation might help explain a puzzling demographic pattern. In many societies, including the United States, women tend to be a bit more religious than men are. There are lots of social or cultural reasons for this religiosity gap—in many places, for example, churches offer forms of social and childcare support that might otherwise be unavailable, making religions appealing for reasons well beyond eschatology and religious metaphysics. But mentalizing might offer an additional cognitive explanation for the gap. You see, women tend to on average score a bit better than men on tests measuring advanced mentalizing abilities.[11] We found that mentalizing scores substantially explained gender differences in religiosity in our samples.*

Does this mean that mentalizing challenges strongly constrain religious beliefs, or that mindblind atheism is likely to be an especially potent pathway? While the cognitive science of religion approach clearly predicts the patterns we found, I think the dual inheritance model we've been developing does a better job of contextualizing the prediction. Indeed, follow-up work by David Maij and colleagues makes it clear that mentalizing is at best a bit player in predicting atheism, when considered alongside other factors like childhood religious CREDs—a point we'll return to at the chapter's close.[12]

The fact that mentalizing has proven to be a relatively minor predictor of atheism is another positive tally for our dual inheritance approach. Yes, people with less-adept high-end mentalizing might have a harder time believing in a personal god, but this is likely to be a quite tiny effect overall. The vast majority of people on earth have mentalizing abilities more than good enough for imagining gods and other supernatural agents. Subtle mentalizing variation around the edges might predict a bit more atheism than otherwise, but this is not likely to be a key player in explaining atheism worldwide. And that's precisely what we found: all of our observed correlations were quite tiny, explaining only a small amount of variability in faith and atheism.

We'd found evidence for mindblind atheism, at least inasmuch as it looks like one potential way people might become atheists, one small factor nudging people in that direction. But over the years I've come to view this

* For the sake of completeness, our paper also included a small study looking at religious beliefs in a sample of autistic individuals, reasoning that among other things the autism spectrum is correlated with differences in mentalizing. We thought that the mentalizing differences experienced by people with autism might predispose them to being less religious. Although our data fit this story, I'm not especially convinced by our less-than-nuanced treatment of autism, or our measurement of some key constructs. I recently saw a conference talk by the brilliant Ingela Visuri on the religious and spiritual lives of people with autism and it was vastly more interesting and nuanced than our little study; there's so much more to the story than we presented. So I wouldn't put too much stock in this little finding. The broader point of our paper wasn't the autism results, but the broader patterns linking mentalizing challenges to religious disbelief. For further reading: Visuri, I. (2018). Rethinking autism, theism, and atheism: Bodiless agents and imaginary realities. *Archive for the Psychology of Religion*, *40*(1), 1-31.

work as a nice example of the difference between statistical significance and practical significance. The negative correlations we found between mentalizing and religiosity were statistically significant, but that doesn't mean they're practically important. The statistical apparatus called null hypothesis significance testing invites us to imagine how implausible a given result would be, under a lot of typically quite unrealistic assumptions, including the assumption that there's no actual effect to be found. When observed data are sufficiently surprising, under our garbage assumptions (including the assumption that there's no actual effect) we declare the result "statistically significant," which people who've only learned a little about statistics equate with the result being "real" or "important" or perhaps "replicable." It just means it was surprising, under assumptions we probably don't believe in the first place. Better statistical tools are available, but much like the QWERTY keyboard, null hypothesis testing persists because once upon a time it solved a problem that we can better solve in other ways today.[†] A pattern being "statistically significant" doesn't mean the relationship is strong, or of practical importance.[13]

In the case of our mentalizing work, we're talking about rather weak correlations, that don't reliably turn up across different cultural contexts, that are usually dwarfed by other more robust predictors of atheism. So our data were consistent with the broad theory that mentalizing is important for religious belief—if we're just talking about a binary decision on whether or not the results were statistically surprising enough to meet an arbitrary significance threshold. But work over the years also points strongly toward other factors being more important. Theories (like the cognitive by-product approach) that focus strongly on mentalizing are likely to miss lots of the most important action when it comes to atheism. Mentalizing matters, but not very much if we're trying to predict broad patterns about global atheism.

Apatheism

Mindblind atheism focuses on one key cognitive constraint that might lead to atheism. Turning from cognitive to motivational approaches, Ara

---

[†] If this piques your interest, I once blogged about some statistics books that embiggened my thinking on the topic: http://willgervais.com/blog/2016/6/17/books-for-kids-who-cant-statistics-good-and-want-to-learn-how-to-do-other-stuff-good-too.

suggested we dub atheism resulting from a general lack of religious motivation *apatheism*. The general idea is that lots of (usually harsh or unpredictable) everyday circumstances of life drive religious motivation, they lead people to seek out gods and religious communities. Where these conditions prevail, religion flourishes; where these conditions abate and become absent, so too eventually goes faith.

I've not personally worked on the motivational aspects of religion much, but there are thriving research trajectories in both sociology and social psychology that have helped outline the general conditions that motivate faith, and that undermine it over time. Specifically, when life is harsh or unpredictable—when life is "solitary, poor, nasty, brutish, and short" to Hobbes, or when people confront Tennyson's "nature, red in tooth and claw"—people are drawn to religion. Under conditions of greater safety and security, religion tends to fade gradually away. People attend religious services less, and over generations belief follows behind. People secularized in this way aren't fighting against religion, they just sort of disaffectedly move apart from it. It's atheism, but apathetically—apatheism. Sociologists and social psychologists working on this reach similar conclusions, while positing different underlying dynamics.

Sociologists of religion have long been interested in trends of secularization, focusing especially on how large swathes of Western Europe rather rapidly moved away from religion in the decades following the World Wars. Secularization theory, as it's called in various forms, is closely associated with the work of sociologists like Norris and Inglehart. In their classic book *Sacred and Secular* they outline converging patterns of evidence from large-scale surveys showing that countries experiencing security and abundance tend to show subsequent dips in religious attendance, fervor, and belief.[14] Countries experiencing less security and stability—due to causes natural, political, or complex mixtures of both—tend to see high rates of religiosity. Inglehart and Norris term this broad sense of security, safety, and stability "existential security" and in wave after wave of surveys it shows up as a primary predictor of secularization across societies. Indices of existential security—normally encompassing combinations of health, wealth, education, and the like—tend to predict lower levels of religious attendance and belief.

There are a handful of countries that stand as outliers against the general pattern linking prosperity to lower religiosity. If you plot a graph with per-capita GDP against some measure of religiosity, you'll find a nice tight trendline, with one incredibly obvious outlier—the United States. It's by far the most religious nation among the planet's wealthiest countries, uniquely religious for its economic standing. Does American oddity mean that the secularity thesis fails? Hardly. It turns out that the United States is a secularization outlier for reasons well-explained by secularization theory itself. It has immense wealth, but distributed incredibly inequitably. Given wealth inequality and immobility, per-capita GDP tells us little about the conditions that most folks live in. On top of inequality, the full-throated embrace of capitalism and "pull yourself up by the bootstraps" mythology has left it a country bereft of safety nets and social support that most developed nations consider basic necessities. Without much in terms of public education promises, health care, or even public transit, the United States has condensed its wealth among just a few, rather than invested in the collective good. On top of this, there is the US love affair with firearms (which incidentally is related to its religious expression[15]) making life less safe for basically everyone—and especially for gun owners, per the best statistics. Make a plot of religion against GDP, and the United States is an outlier. Do the same for GDP and gun fatalities, and the extremity of outlying is even more obvious. The conditions described by secularization theory as inimical to religion—relative health, safety, security, and prosperity enjoyed by most—are not present in the United States, where life for typical citizens and residents tends to be far more precarious than the country's immense overall wealth would suggest. When it comes to how wealth translates to well-being of its citizenry, the United States is effectively a "third world" nation with a handful of incredibly rich people living with wealth beyond that which bygone magnates and feudal warlords could've imagined.[16] Judged on this standard, the country is no longer an outlier when it comes to religion; it is about as religious as you'd expect, given the day-to-day precarity among the majority of folks that its inequitably condensed wealth masks.[17]

Turning from sociology of religion to social psychology, let's consider another way that favorable conditions might lead to the sort of disaffected atheism we dubbed apatheism. Researchers like Kristin Laurin and Aaron Kay have written about the links between religiosity and political conditions, under the theoretical banner of compensatory control.[18] The general idea here is that people are motivated to seek a sense of control in the world. We don't like chaos and disorder, feelings of being less than the pilot of our own lives. We're thus motivated to seek out sources of control to keep the chaos at bay. Religions are great sources of control—they furnish both divine sources of control, and also communities with norms to which they can adhere. But religions aren't the only sources of control. Governments, done well, can also furnish people with a sense of control and order. Within the compensatory control model, people just need a source of control, and they're willing to trade off between different available market options when it comes to sources of control.[‡] Where governments are fickle, weak, or unpredictable, they can't offer much in terms of sating a deep psychological desire for control. In conditions like this, people turn to religion instead. In contrast, where governments are strong, transparent, and effective, religion fades away. In a hydraulic way, as one source of control becomes more salient, competitors in the control domain fade to the background. As governments get better, gods are less motivationally appealing.[19]

As you can see, secularization theory and compensatory control make the same sorts of predictions. Both predict that as secular institutions—police, judges, courts, social safety nets—become strong and stable, religions will fade away. The atheism that eventually results isn't hostile to religion, it just views religion as something from a bygone, chaotic, era. Apatheism is what happens when secular conditions render religion motivationally impotent.

InCREDulous Atheism

Lots of people might be able to imagine lots of supernatural agents, and even live in conditions where they're motivated by gods and religion. Nonetheless, these people might not come to believe in any specific gods simply because they don't culturally learn that this god is real, to be worshipped, whereas those gods are fictions and myths.

[‡] In the interest of transparency, the compensatory control work summarized herein includes both archival and comparative work looking at large-scale patterns in government and religious trust—which I find reasonably compelling—and also lots of flashy experimental social psychology tasks not unlike studies we've already discussed and found to be lacking empirical robustness—which I do not find especially compelling. I think the general idea that people might psychologically make tradeoffs between trust of God and government is more compelling than most of the small experiments mustered in its support.

Back in chapters 5 and 6 we saw that context biases in cultural learning—figuring out from whom we should learn what—are immensely important for our cultural species. The Zeus Problem (chapter 6) asked how people only come to believe in one god (or a select few gods), and the solution was cultural learning, with a particular emphasis on credibility-enhancing displays.[20] Converging learning biases help determine what we end up believing. Adopting norms and beliefs of "our group" via conformist transmission, or following those idols worshipped by elites (prestige bias), helps naive cultural learners figure out which of the myriad gods they can imagine are to be treated as real. Credibility-enhancing displays of faith in these specific gods helps show learners that their cultural models are serious and sincere in their professions of faith.[21] Where cultural cues converge on a single deity or pantheon, belief naturally results. Where cues are absent or jumbled, learners are left uncertain in whom to believe, and are likely to simply not develop beliefs in any gods as a result. In an unwieldy bit of wordplay, I called this *inCREDulous atheism*,[§] and despite how much of a pain in the ass it is to type, it stuck.

In the by-product framework popularized by early cognitive scientists of religion, belief in a god is so natural it's almost inevitable, and culture just furnishes some details. In contrast, the dual inheritance framework posits that belief in any god takes cultural work. Cultural learners need converging and consistent cues, backed by credible displays of faith, to come to believe that any given god is real. Lots of little cues all need to point in the same direction. If our species had a strong default content bias favoring belief in gods, then learners might arbitrarily adopt belief in whichever gods they've heard about, or pick one god to believe in more or less at random. That's not what we see at all. When people believe in gods, they tend to believe in only the gods of their surrounding culture. The exceptions here prove the rule as well. When you see pockets of folks believing in a god foreign to their surrounding community, there's a really good chance that explicit missionary work was at play: it takes a lot of cultural work to get a pocket of people to believe in a god other than the locally normative one.

[§] It's easy enough to say, but try slipping "inCREDulous" past spellchecks and autocorrects, through an entire book—nay, *career*. The terminology is catchy and pithy enough, but in terms of regular usage I've made a huge mistake.

In places where cultural signals are either weaker (say, if baseline rates of religious attendance or display wane) or jumbled (say, in a globalized and pluralistic society with lots of religious "signals") then far from believing in an arbitrary or randomly chosen god, atheism becomes a viable and likely option. By now we have several lines of evidence pointing toward this conclusion.

Anthropologist Jon Lanman's doctoral dissertation looked at predictors of atheism in European samples. He included some measures relevant to the cognitive science of religion approaches prevalent at the time (including one measure of exposure to HADD-triggering stuff, that ended up predicting basically nothing), as well as measures of how much people witnessed credibility-enhancing displays of faith in a specific god when they were growing up. The best predictor of atheism? Low religious CREDs.[22]

Lanman (joined by Michael Buhrmester) developed and validated a questionnaire to measure childhood religious CREDs, and in sample after sample, people who score lower on this measure—folks who witnessed less church attendance, tithing, or costly religious actions—are far more likely to grow up atheists.[23] I've used this measure in loads of surveys (some which we'll discuss later this chapter), and it's pretty much always the best predictor of atheism. People who see few religious CREDs growing up tend to end up as nonreligious adults—as inCREDulous atheists. Having low levels of relevant cultural cues leads to atheism.

Atheism can also be a natural result when it's not so much that CREDs are low as that they're mixed. In an archival analysis project led by Nava Caluori, we (Nava, Jazmin Brown-Iannuzzi, and I) find that measures of globalization predict secularization. Where cultures are mixed—and religious CREDs correspondingly jumbled—there's less of a distinctive signal for people to believe in any specific god, and religious belief wanes.[24]

A microcosm of this same trend for mixed signals to yield atheism comes from the example of children coming from mixed-faith families. Imagine a family where one parent is Hindu and the other parent Christian. Both parents engage in CREDs proving faith to their gods. What signal will their children receive? None that's consistent. Without that consistent signal to believe in a given god, no god seems especially compelling. In another project with Nava and Aiyana Willard, we find that children of mixed-faith parents are less religious, and more likely to be atheists, than their religiously homogamous peers. This holds even for mixed faith families where the doctrinal difference is seemingly slight. We isolated a subsample of people for whom both parents are nominally Christian but belong to different denominations—like, say, a Catholic who's married a Baptist—and the children again tend to be less religious, more likely to become atheists.[25]

As in chapter 6, this work shows that belief in any given god takes cultural work. The cognitive science of religion makes atheism sound difficult, unnatural. The dual inheritance approach recasts it as a natural and likely result in environments lacking consistent cultural cues to believe in any specific god (a theme developed in greater depth in chapter 14, stay tuned). Learners need to see converging and credible signals that they ought to believe in a given god. Where these signals are comparatively absent, and even when they're mixed (via globalization or mixed faith parentage, for example), inCREDulous atheism can result.

Analytic (or Rational) Atheism¶

Religious beliefs enjoy a lot of intuitive support (think: dualism, teleology, minimal counterintuitive-driven memory boosts, maybe even intuitive creationism). But we don't always blindly follow our intuitions. Alongside our gut-level hunches, we have the capacity for rational, reflective overrides of our intuitions. One pathway to atheism—much discussed popularly, by the New Atheists and others—is through rational, analytic thought. Dual process accounts of cognition describe parallel intuitive and analytic systems that process information in different ways. One quick, effortless, and intuitive; the other slower, effortful, and reflective or analytic. Given the links between intuition and religion, might rational thinking be a viable path to atheism, at least for some?

Now, you might be thinking that we met this idea in chapter 3, and I dismissed it as a myth. Why is it showing back up in a chapter discussing pathways to atheism?

¶ As a terminological aside, "rational" and "analytic" are used somewhat interchangeably in the literature here. Chapter 2 framed the Rational Atheism Thesis. In the paper with Ara, we called it Analytic Atheism, for alliterative purposes. Both work just fine, so both get named here. I've kept the focus on the Rational Atheism terminology here, for continuity with chapter 2, but this footnote provides continuity to our previous paper, which called it Analytic Atheism.

I think the notion that atheism *primarily or necessarily* results from rational or reflective analytic thinking to be bunk. The science just hasn't panned out, despite lots of scientists (including a younger me) trying really hard to find that evidence. Early "wins" for the rational atheism thesis crumbled under scrutiny from subsequent researchers (including a slightly less-young me).[26] But that doesn't mean there's no relationship between analytic thinking and atheism, just that the link isn't all that strong or consistent.

This section is my attempt to get the story straight, given that I've been on both sides of this discussion at different points in my career. At the end of the day, I do think that in some limited contexts there's a viable connection between effortful cognitive reflection—analytic or rational thinking, in other words—and atheism. It's just not a link that is especially strong, consistent, necessary, or sufficient for atheism. The connection between a rational cognitive style and atheism is a messy one, fickle across samples and measures, inconsistent across cultures. And this is precisely what we'd expect, under the dual inheritance theory of faith and atheism that I've been developing in this book. Rational thinking can be one path among many—not the strongest or most important one, but still a viable one—toward atheism, in at least some contexts. Let's check the evidence.

Recall that early investigations of the rational atheism hypothesis turned up some positive results. Independent teams found correlational links between a more rational cognitive style and religious disbelief. A couple of teams claimed experimental successes as well, but these efforts proved unreliable—false positives and likely no more. Further digging into the correlations turned up a lot of variability from culture to culture.[27] What looked to be a mild-but-stable correlation between analytic thinking and atheism in North America proved to be even weaker or nonexistent in other societies. There's a genuine pattern here: in lots of samples, analytic cognitive style predicts atheism. But the pattern is weak and obscured by more obvious and apparent cultural trends.

To me, this pattern fits quite well with a dual inheritance account that centrally features culture and cultural learning. Despite connections between religion and intuition, we wouldn't expect cognitive style to be a strong predictor of global atheism, simply because cultural learning is more potent and immediate an influence on people's beliefs. We're a cultural species, and religion is a cultural phenomenon; it would be exceedingly strange if culture weren't a primary cause of people's beliefs or lack thereof. Of course, other factors are still important, and an analytic cognitive style is just one of those bit-player factors than can predict a bit about atheism around the edges.

There you have it. Rational or analytic atheism is one viable pathway to atheism. But we shouldn't expect it to be the main one or even an especially important one overall. This consideration of the relatively minor role for analytic atheism leads us to the very important question addressed next.

WHICH PATHWAYS TO ATHEISM ARE MOST IMPORTANT?

So, which pathways to atheism are the most widely trod? Are any of our four pathways the most important?

By now there are a couple of good large-scale investigations that have tried to pit the pathways against each other to see which carries the most empirical weight. This sort of "which factor predicts the most" exercise can be really useful in this context because different theories of religion make quite different predictions about which pathway ought to be the most important. Let's consider three different theories that have risen to some degree of prominence, and which pathways they'd predict to be especially important.

First comes secularization theory, which we met when discussing apatheism. It describes a pattern whereby better living conditions lead people to be less motivated to seek out religion. This can be viewed through either a sociological or social psychological (under the name "compensatory control") lens. This is a prominent and successful approach to studying religion and secularism, backed by tons of large-scale survey evidence, well-presented in books like Norris and Inglehart's *Sacred and Secular*. The theory is largely silent on cognitive and cultural factors, and clearly predicts that apatheism should be the strongest pathway—it's basically the only pathway within the theory's purview.

Next comes the cognitive science of religion's approach to atheism, based on the notion that religious belief reliably develops as a cognitive by-product. Cognitive science of religion describes religious belief as largely tied to intuition and heavily driven by our mentalizing faculties. Cognitive by-product theorists would likely find mindblind atheism theoretically compelling (the prediction directly fell to us from reading cognitive by-product summaries) and analytic atheism (ditto) as well. Indeed, in their writings, by-product theorists generally describe atheism as powerfully—and perhaps necessarily—rooted in effortful cognitive reflection. As Pascal Boyer puts it in a think piece in *Nature*, "Disbelief is generally the result of deliberate, effortful work against our natural cognitive dispositions—hardly the easiest ideology to propagate."[28] Cognitive by-product approaches highlight analytic atheism as the most important pathway, but leaves room for mindblind atheism as well. Indeed, my having been steeped in the cognitive science of religion framework for my early graduate school years inspired me to do initial studies on both mindblind atheism and analytic atheism in the first place.

Finally, our dual inheritance framework unites the cognitive science of religion with modern approaches to cultural evolution. Being intimately connected to cultural learning and cultural evolution, our dual inheritance approach predicts that inCREDulous atheism should be the most important pathway. But in incorporating insights from the cognitive science of religion, the dual inheritance approach also predicts roles for both mindblind atheism and apatheism, albeit smaller ones. In the case of apatheism, the dual inheritance approach would suggest that it's at best an indirect pathway, influencing atheism via CREDs, rather than separately from them. This theme will be developed in the next chapter.

Along with Nava Caluori and Maxine Najle—names that should be familiar by now—figure 11.1 shows how we summarized these predictions in a recent project in which we sought to test which pathways were most important.[29]

Theory	Discipline	Mindblind	Apatheist	inCREDulous	Rational/ Analytic
Secularization	Sociology; social psychology		++++		
Cognitive Byproduct	Evolutionary psychology; cognitive science of religion	++	+		++++
Dual Inheritance	Gene-culture coevolution	+	indirect	++++	+

Figure 11.1. Different theories of religion make different predictions about pathways to atheism. *Source:* W. M. Gervais, M. B. Najle, and N. Caluori, "The Origins of Religious Disbelief: A Dual Inheritance Approach," *Social Psychological and Personality Science* 12, no. 7 (2021): 1369–79.

Maxine, Nava, and I collected a large, nationally representative sample from the United States. We included standard (though inevitably imperfect) measures of each pathway, and essentially sought to see which could predict atheism the best. Our mentalizing measure (to gauge mindblind atheism) was a short self-report measure, specifically the Perspective Taking subscale of the Interpersonal Reactivity Index. It measures the extent to which people say they're able to think through and reason about other people's perspectives—basically a self-report measure of how good people are at the cognitive mindreading that lets us decode other people's mental states. We measured the conditions associated with apatheism by asking people about perceptions of their everyday safety and stability, using a questionnaire we borrowed from others in the field. We measured exposure to religious CREDs using the aforementioned questionnaire developed by Lanman and colleagues. Finally, we measured reflective cognitive style using an extended version of the cognitive reflection task, discussed back in chapter 3.

With data from almost fifteen hundred people, broadly representative of the US population, we compared all four pathways simultaneously. The results were quite clear: fewer religious CREDs was by far the best predictor of religious disbelief, followed distantly by a rational cognitive style and weaker advanced mentalizing. Self-reports of instability and insecurity were uncorrelated with religion, once other factors were accounted for. This pattern of results is precisely what the dual inheritance approach predicted: a heavy dose of inCREDulous atheism, with a smattering of mindblind and rational atheism on the side.

Even more compelling results come from a larger international study by Aiyana Willard and Lubomír Cingl, who tested all four pathways in parallel in both the Czech Republic and Slovakia.[30] These two countries, once coercively joined, provide a fascinating natural experiment for understanding the dynamics of secularism. Although in Soviet times they were joined as Czechoslovakia, the two independent countries have had vastly different religious fates since the dusk of the Cold War. Czechia is now counted among the most secular and least religious nations on earth, while Slovakia is fairly religious, at least by European standards. What predicts atheism in these countries, and can that help explain overall differences in secularity between them? Willard and Cingl found that the best predictor of atheism within countries was exposure to fewer CREDs, and that CRED exposure also largely explained the national-level differences in secularity. Analytic thinking, mentalizing, and social conditions were again rather minor predictors of religious disbelief. Once again, inCREDulous atheism appears more potent a pathway than mindblind atheism, apatheism, or analytic atheism.

About a decade ago Ara Norenzayan and I pitched the possibility that there are (at least) four distinct pathways to atheism, based on evidence at the time. Each pathway to atheism comes from disruption to a process that has to happen for a given person to believe in a given god over time. Mindblind atheism results from people not finding the (mentalizing-derived) notion of gods intuitively compelling. Apatheism results when people just don't find gods motivationally compelling. InCREDulous atheism results from people who don't find signals favoring any given god culturally compelling. And analytic atheism results from people not finding culturally endorsed gods rationally compelling.

Mindblind atheism happens when people *don't get* gods. Apatheism results when people *don't give a shit* about gods. InCREDulous atheism occurs when folks *don't learn* to believe in specific gods. Rational or analytic atheism can happen when people *don't think* their group's gods make much rational sense. At the outset, I tried to be clear that these are separate pathways to atheism, not a typology of different classes of atheists. At this juncture, we don't have especially compelling evidence regarding how these different pathways might engender different "types" of atheists. They're just different paths to the same endpoint.

While there's independent evidence of each pathway in isolation, the crucial theoretical test is of how important they each are in conjunction with each other. We saw data from representative samples in three countries (United States, Czechia, and Slovakia) converging on the conclusion that a relative dearth of exposure to religious CREDs is the best predictor of atheism. Other factors, like mentalizing or cognitive style, do play a role. It's just a less pronounced role. These patterns are exactly what a dual inheritance approach to religion and atheism predict, but are largely inconsistent with the predictions of secularization theory or the cognitive by-product account coming out of the cognitive science of religion.

Chapter 6 asked how individual people come to believe in individual gods, and found that religious CREDs are key. After that, chapter 7 zoomed out and considered the global religious landscape across longer spans of time, asking why entire religions rise and fall, and why some religions "win" the cultural evolutionary arms race.

This chapter and the next are to atheism what chapters 6 and 7 were to religious belief. Mirroring chapter 6, this chapter asked how individual people become atheists, and highlighted four distinct pathways. But once again, cultural learning and religious CREDs proved vital. Where CREDs are plentiful and consistent, belief naturally emerges. Where they are absent or muddled, atheism is the natural result. Mirroring chapter 8, our next chapter asks why—at the level of societies—atheism and secularism can emerge, take root, and stabilize over broader cultural and historical scales.

CHAPTER TWELVE

STABLE SECULAR SOCIETIES

When, Where, and How

I don't want to go to heaven. None of my friends are there.
—OSCAR WILDE

It isn't where you came from, it's where you're going that counts.
—ELLA FITZGERALD

In the world today, atheism and secularism are geographically clustered. In most countries of the Americas, Africa, the Middle East, and much of Asia, the world continues to be about as religious as ever (which is to say: very religious).* In contrast, the countries of Scandinavia and the rest of Western Europe are the seats of global atheism, with overt religiosity and belief in God being a minority metaphysical opinion. Belief in gods and religious attendance are persistently low, and often getting lower.[1] Religion is not a major factor in public life.[2]

* From time to time, I see a news piece or even scientific paper talking about the "global withdrawal of religion" or similar. Whenever I see this, I think that the authors must have either a very selective reading of the relevant literature, or a very narrow view of which "global" regions matter. Across most of the globe, including many of the world's most populous nations and regions, religion is doing just fine, thank you very much for apparently not noticing! That said, our recent data indirectly measuring atheist prevalence suggest that even overtly religious places likely harbor some level of covert atheism. It's far more complicated than a "global collapse of religion" narrative, is what I'm saying.

To illustrate just how secular Europe has gotten (relative to the United States) over the past several decades, consider some polling data from Pew.[3] They rate Romania as the most religious European country. Yet there are a whopping twenty-four states in the United States whose rates of fervent God belief are at least as high as Romania's—Romania would be a middle-of-the-pack US state, religiously speaking. Massachusetts boasts the lowest rate of God belief among the states, yet twenty-four of Europe's thirty-four countries are even less God-fearing than Massachusetts. When it comes to prayer frequency, Moldova is Europe's highest-ranking country with 48 percent indicating daily prayer. This would make Moldova the tenth-least-prayerful state in the United States. Only six European countries report prayer frequency rates higher than the least prayerful US state, Vermont. The most secular US states are on a par with the most religious countries in Europe.

Famous thinkers for centuries have been projecting that the rest of the globe would follow the Western European example—see, for example, writings of Hume, Marx, Durkheim, Weber, and Freud, who all predicted the imminent demise of religion. Like predictions of Jesus's imminent return, projections that global religion would fade within decades have been as easily disproven as they've been numerous. Yet, in pockets, the world today is perhaps as atheistic as it's ever been. Why has atheism flourished, but just in a few select locales?

The last chapter detailed the cognitive, motivational, and cultural pathways that lead individuals to atheism. This chapter extends the argument from individuals to societies, asking how individual-level pathways to atheism might combine to yield larger-scale aggregate trends in global disbelief. Given what we've learned about atheism's origins in cognition, motivation, and culture, why is secularism prevalent today, and why is it prevalent in certain places but not others? And what lessons does this teach us about the stability of emerging atheist movements? The goal of this chapter is to scaffold up from the processes we learned about in the last few chapters, to see how they'd play out at a more macro scale.

Thus far, the dual process account—incorporating both insights from the cognitive science of religion and cultural evolution—has been useful for explaining who believes in which gods (chapter 6), how some religions have spread and persisted (chapter 7), and why individual folks might end up as atheists rather than believers in one god or another (chapter 11). Let's see if it can also explain why and how secular societies stabilize and even spread.

The historical example of Scandinavia, paired with a theoretical understanding of cultural evolution, hints at a possible three-step process to stable, long-term secularism. By my reading, this multi-stage theory of secularism was initially proposed by Queen's University, Belfast anthropologist Jon Lanman,[†] and I hope to both do the initial proposal justice and give it a thorough and accessible treatment here, updated by recent findings.

In simple form, this three-stage account proposes that atheism can take root in a society over successive (cultural) generations, following three general steps. Following secularization theory, increased existential security drives religious complacency, characterized by a mixture of private belief and apatheism. Complacency yields fewer religious CREDs, which in turn leads subsequent generations of learners to inCREDulous atheism. Widespread atheism doesn't imply that religion's influence is quickly or completely absent. More gradually than belief in gods, bundles of pro-religious norms and intuitions fade from societal consciousness. Religious influence outlasts religious practice and belief if one looks beyond surface-level measures of religious thinking.

Different secular (and secularizing) countries around the world seem to be at different stages in this process. In the rest of the chapter, I want to develop the ideas behind each stage, and to consider candidate countries that seem to typify each. This latter exercise is necessarily tentative, as the underlying dynamics can shift quite quickly, and some of the processes involved are challenging to measure and quantify in a principled way, at least given our current base of evidence.

STEP 1: SECURITY DRIVES RELIGIOUS COMPLACENCY

Phil Zuckerman's book *Society without God* takes a sociological approach to understanding life in normatively nonreligious Scandinavian countries

---

[†] I recall a sketch of some of these ideas at one of the first conferences I attended, back in about 2010. Jon highlighted the first two stages we cover here—how security breeds complacency, leading to lower CREDs, and then disbelief. The story has been fleshed out further by lots of us over the years, and the third-stage proposal about intuitions is very much a work in progress, but the initial shout-out to Jon is important. Cheers, buddy!

like Denmark and Sweden. In these countries, much of the populace is nominally religious, in that they've been baptized or married in a church, but explicit belief in God is remarkably low. They're as close to organically atheistic societies as we can find on earth, now or ever in our history. Do these societies, Zuckerman asks, collapse without religion?[‡]

Quite the contrary. Zuckerman finds life in these Scandinavian secular sanctuaries to be calm, peaceful, and stable. Indeed, following other sociological work by Norris and Inglehart in *Sacred and Secular*, it is possible that the very stability of life in these countries helps explain their secularism. In an argument that should be familiar from our discussion of apatheism in the previous chapter, Norris and Inglehart, across a series of large-scale international surveys, find that a consistent predictor of societal secularism is conditions of what they call existential security: basically, how well-off, safe, and stable your typical citizen's life is. In countries with effective social safety nets, good public health care, comparatively little wealth inequality, and good education systems, it increasingly looks like people simply fall out of religion due to a lack of motivation or necessity.

Apatheism is one potential outcome here—folks are no longer motivated by religion and cease believing, somewhat apathetically. This outcome is largely consistent with Norris and Inglehart's findings that places with higher levels of existential security also have lower levels of things like prayer and belief in God/gods. That said, the survey data that are the backbone of their work don't quite have measures specific enough to pin down whether the irreligion first associated with existential security looks apatheistic in a meaningful way. Questions about belief in or prayer to gods can reveal when they are low, but not whether atheists in these places would be characterized by apathy and disregard of religion rather than, say, opposition to religion. Large-scale data are consistent with the argument I'm making here, but are often not granular enough to be conclusive.

But apatheism is not the only possible outcome in an increasingly existentially secure society. Instead, many people may continue to privately believe in God but just downgrade their public religious participation. As living conditions and stabilizing secular institutions become the norm in societies, people seem to be less excited about religion, and especially about

‡ Flip back to chapter 9—of course they don't.

public religion. Church attendance wanes. Politicians spend less time bloviating about how faithful and churchgoing they are. Athletes thank their coaches instead of their saviors for sporting achievements. Belief persists, but a bit more subtly and privately. Again, this is consistent with what Norris and Inglehart find regarding things like church attendance—where life gets stable and easy, pews empty.

One crucial piece of the argument in this chapter is that the first wave of secularism links existential security first to religious complacency, and only later to widespread disbelief. If that's the case, then we'd expect to see declines in church attendance preceding large-scale dips in belief. Konrad Talmont-Kaminsky, David Voas, and colleagues have been working on some very exciting projects to explore the timing of secular shifts in Europe over recent decades.[4] Their work shows that, as a general pattern, existential security immediately precedes dips in public religiosity (things like church attendance) but does not immediately drive down private belief. In terms of this chapter's theory, that's exactly what we'd expect. Core beliefs, like whether or not someone thinks there's a God out there, are stable, and tend not to change on a whim. Shifts in economic or social fortunes within a society are unlikely to have people changing their core metaphysical beliefs about the cosmos. But economic and social changes can easily drive lots of small shifts in everyday behavior, like going to church less, skipping a tithe, or being less vocal about religion than one might've otherwise been. Religious behavior changes more easily than core beliefs, as this chapter's theory predicts and the European data suggest.

So one initial step to explaining the current (localized) upswell in secularism in Western Europe seems to lie in the accumulated wealth and advantage, translated into effective secular institutions that have lifted everyday existential security above some threshold point at which people stop being especially interested in religion. There arises a populace that may or may not privately believe in God, but most folks simply don't pay it much public attention. Religious attendance and pageantry dwindle, and a nation becomes less publicly religious—with important implications for the subsequent cultural transmission of faith, as we'll see.

The crucial first step toward societal secularization is the link between existential security and public, outward religiosity—remember, after existential security rises, we tend to see drops in religious attendance and identification, but not belief at first. Where can we see this pattern happening in the world today? Outside Scandinavia (which has progressed well beyond this stage) it's entirely possible that many Western democracies outside Europe, including places like Canada and Australia, are in more or less the first stage of secular development (religious complacency), with some edging into the next phase quite rapidly. In Canada, for example, some researchers have noted a recent "decoupling" between religious beliefs and identifications.[5] Belief in gods is dipping a bit, but remains fairly stable. Meanwhile, the numbers of people who identify with specific religious traditions are dipping rapidly. People are believers still, but are no longer publicly identifying Catholics or Protestants, for example. Religious attendance also dips in concert with identification. Canada is quickly becoming *less religious* (in terms of people identifying with religions, and publicly practicing them) without necessarily becoming *atheistic*. Canada makes a decent reference point for our first stage of secularism: security driving religious complacency.

STEP 2: APATHEISTS AND PRIVATE BELIEVERS RAISE INCREDULOUS ATHEISTS

If rising existential security leads to religiously disaffected people who are no longer publicly religious (whether they privately believe or not), this quickly leads to a second cultural generation of more explicit atheism, via the cultural evolutionary pathways sketched in previous chapters. Apatheism and private belief breed a secondary wave of inCREDulous atheism.

Imagine growing up as a cultural learner in a newly existentially secure society that's experiencing its first wave of secularity. You might hear your elders discussing religious matters on occasion, or speaking their private opinions about God. But you don't see much in terms of credibility-enhancing displays of faith. Regular religious attendance in your local surroundings has fallen from a weekly rite to a practice reserved for weddings, funerals, and other momentous occasions. Politicians move from pontificating about their spiritual life to largely withholding words about religion, which is seen as a private matter. Public holy rituals are less and less evident. Tithing isn't visible or regular. Holidays might remain nominally religious-themed, but Christmas becomes more about Santa than about Jesus; Easter becomes less reanimation and more candy bunny. People might still get married in the local church, but they'll merely do so because it's the nicest building in town, not because there's any real religious significance to the act. There are few consistent cues in your environment supporting belief in any given god.

Religious complacency deals a serious blow to the cultural transmission of religious faith across generations of learners, and lends support to emerging secularism. As we've seen in previous chapters, a lack of consistent behavioral cues favoring belief in a specific god is the death-knell for belief and a harbinger for inCREDulous atheism. Rising existential security can produce a mixed generation of sincere-but-private believers and apatheists. The next generation of cultural learners, however, is quite likely to be composed largely of inCREDulous atheists. Within just two generations—a relatively quick span of cultural evolutionary time—a strongly religious society can become a fairly atheistic one.

This logic sounds fine, but, as always, evidence is crucial. In this case, we have converging lines of evidence supporting the theory.

Agent-Based Models: A Theoretical Proof-of-Concept

First, a simulation-based proof-of concept. Back in chapter 7, we discussed how evolutionary models can make nice, simplified playgrounds for testing ideas—ways to find out if proposed dynamics even pan out as expected under idealized and controlled conditions. One of my current projects is building agent-based models of religion, incorporating different sorts of cultural evolution–inspired learning biases. Basically, I can build a miniature model world in my computer, and populate it with computer agents whose learning apparatus I fully control. Then I can tweak parameters in my agents' learning biases, and see what happens to the beliefs of my little simulated computer minions.[6]

To make this concrete, imagine a world with agents who either do or don't believe in a given god. Here belief is a discrete trait, that my little agents either do or do not have—my minions are either atheists or believers, no middle ground. Each agent also has a few different in-built biases in how they come to learn and believe. As the (on a good day, after coffee) intelligent designer of this model universe, I have full control over the strength and operation of these learning biases.

First, my agents have a *content bias* favoring belief in their god. I can dial the strength of this content bias up or down—basically I can make it so that pretty much everyone believes, regardless of other input, or I can make it so people just get slightly nudged toward belief, all else equal. Recall that the cognitive by-product approach posits a strong-to-nearly-inevitable content bias favoring religious belief, whereas the dual inheritance approach makes no such assumption (although is compatible with content biases of varying strengths).

Second, my agents exhibit *conformist transmission*. They preferentially adopt beliefs modeled by the majority of their peers. As with the content bias, I can tinker with the strength of the conformist learning bias. I can make my agents totally ignore others, or I can make it so that they're virtually certain to adopt any majority-held belief.

Finally, my agents have *religious CREDs*, again of varying strength. Agents will display their beliefs, with varying degrees of zeal. I can again tinker with the strength of this CREDulous zeal. Basically, this setting controls how behaviorally visible religious belief is. I can make it so that every believer is out-and-proud about it, I can make it so that every believer keeps their faith secret, or I can simulate some intermediate level of CREDs.

By independently tinkering with the settings of these three parameters—strength of content bias, strength of conformist learning, probability that believers show CREDs—we can explore the emerging dynamics in our world. Do some combinations of parameters tend to produce belief? Under which parameters does disbelief reign instead?

I'm particularly interested in finding combinations of learning bias parameters that can mimic two observed real-world trends. First, universally high religious belief seems to be a norm for much of our species' history, but presumably (given the dearth of religion elsewhere in the animal kingdom) this wasn't always the case. At some early point in our evolutionary history, our ancestors had no religious beliefs; but eventually, our forebears became religious. Something changed. It would be nice to find parameter values that can saturate belief in a simulated world, from a starting point where belief is initially absent (as it once was during our evolution). Second, at least in places like Western Europe we've seen a rapid decline in religious belief, from historically high levels (as we see in much of the rest of the world still) to their current low (but nonzero) levels. At some point in history, our lineage moved from no religion to essentially universal religion; in some regions, things rapidly shifted from near-universal religion to majority disbelief. Can we simulate a world that can reproduce both trends, with only slight changes to our inputs?

The first trend—getting near-universal belief from universal disbelief—is straightforward. Trivially, I could create agents with a strong content bias to believe, and it wouldn't matter even a little bit whether they engage in social learning or CREDs. Belief would come easily and naturally, just as cognitive by-product theorists might expect (recall chapter 4's focus on content bias and omission of other forms of cultural learning). But this simulation setting makes our second desired outcome—the ability to culturally evolve high atheism rates from a starting point of near-universal belief—effectively impossible. If we have a strong content bias, we won't get stable disbelief in the population.

Strike one, time to try something else. Given the importance of cultural learning to our species, it makes sense to play with simulations that lean more heavily on context-biased learning than on content biases alone. And here's where things get interesting.

Pairing even a weak content bias (say, a bias where 10 percent of people become believers regardless of other learning) with realistic rates of conformist learning quickly saturates our simulated world with believers. A handful of people, thanks to content biases, come to believe no matter what. But as soon as enough people believe in this way, conformist transmission takes off, and the population quickly converges on belief. Crucially, this only happens when CREDs are high. Conformist transmission only works when belief is visible, and the rate of visible belief (e.g., CREDs) is way more important than our agents' invisible underlying beliefs. Learners see others' CREDs, not their mental states. Here's a recipe to culturally evolve near-universal belief from a starting point of pure disbelief: Weak content bias, plus moderate conformist learning, plus high CREDs among believers.

To simulate our second desired dynamic—the crash from near-universal belief to low belief, as observed in recent decades in Western Europe—is the next crucial test. Ideally, we want our simulations to reproduce this dynamic, given only minimal tweaks to our inputs. Think of it this way: if I can get my simulation to produce disbelief after fiddling extensively with the amount of content bias and conformist learning, this isn't very impressive or informative. I would effectively be positing a seismic shift in the underlying psychology of my agents, from ones who slightly tend to believe in gods and who like to copy each other, to ones who do neither. If it takes that magnitude of change in parameters to produce our desired results, that would imply that belief is quite resilient, and we'd have to make outlandish assumptions about rapid psychological shifts to produce disbelief—assumptions that go well beyond our current evidence back in the real world.[7] On the other hand, if we can leave our agents' psychologies largely intact and simulate a rapid drop in belief with only minimal tweaking, that implies a lot more malleability, and would give me confidence that we're on the right track with this project.

As is often the case when trying to understand religious belief and disbelief (see chapters 6, 7, and 11), CREDs are crucial. Our simulated society is full of believers when CREDs are common, given weak content biases and plausibly moderate rates of conformist learning. But if the likelihood that believers display CREDs of their faith dips even slightly, population-level belief quickly crashes from near-universal to relatively uncommon (though not ever wholly absent). The plots in figure 12.1 show the rates of belief that evolve in a simulated world with identically mild content bias and moderate conformist learning, but the percentage of believers who engage in CREDs drops from 95 percent to 85 percent. As you can see, this tiny shift in CREDs—while leaving the rest of our agents' psychology entirely untouched—makes a profound difference. Disbelief becomes normative, even with a content bias favoring belief and a sizeable majority of people walking the religious walk with CREDs.

In this simulated world, agents learn to believe in a god in one of two ways. Via a content bias, some small number of agents (10 percent) come to believe no matter what. The rest adopt their beliefs by observing and preferentially copying others. Because our agents can't "see" underlying beliefs, only the behaviors that believers display, CREDs are hugely important. If believers display CREDs at a very high level (95 percent), our population quickly evolves to believe. But if CRED rates dip only slightly, from 95 to 85 percent, belief rapidly collapses.

As is always the case with simulations and models, this is an idealized toy example, a way to look for proof-of-concept and no more. But in this limited role, it's performed admirably. We've seen how, in a simulated and

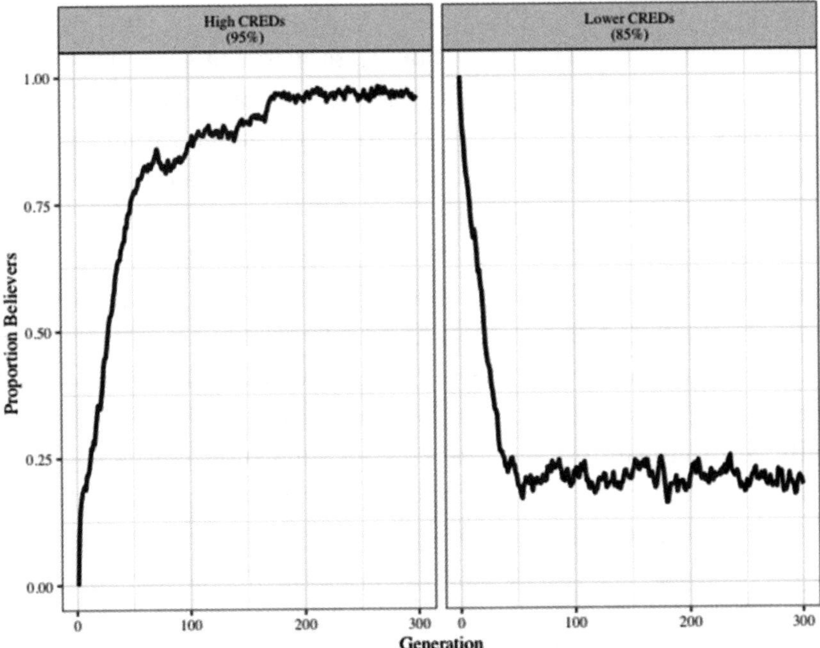

Figure 12.1. Varying levels of CREDs can determine the cultural evolution of populations toward widespread faith or atheism. Results from an agent-based model of cultural learning.

simplistic world, the same underlying psychology (a weak content bias favoring belief, and a tendency toward conformist learning) can produce both belief from disbelief and widespread atheism from a starting point of universal faith. The only thing that needs to change between these outcomes is the degree to which believers credibly display their faith. As public religious behavior becomes decoupled from private religious beliefs, a once-devout society can quickly culturally evolve to be largely nonreligious. This pattern has been observed in many countries, and this simulation shows—in at least a minimal and idealized way—one possible way it can happen.

First Practice, Then Belief: Real-World Data and Rule-Proving Exceptions

Turning from simulated worlds to our own world, the aforementioned work by Voas, Talmont-Kaminsky, and colleagues again looms large. This work looks at secular shifts in numerous countries, and found a consistent pattern across them. In general, turns toward secularism tend to happen across successive cohorts of people, not within them.[8] In other words, it's not the case that as people grow older in secularizing countries, everyone gets less religious in lockstep with each other. It's not like Baby Boomers, Millennials, and GenZeds[§] are all showing comparable within-generation shifts in religiosity; the action is instead that each generation looks a bit less religious than the one preceding it, and beliefs remain stable over time within each generational cohort. Successive generations become less religious, one after another, with individual within-cohort belief levels crystalizing by the time folks are about twenty-five years old. The cohort-level shifts come in a predictable order. First, attendance and identification decline. Then, in subsequent cohorts, belief follows.

This fits well with our proof-of-concept simulations. Declines in belief predictably follow from declines in the more public aspects of religion. Existential security moves an initial cohort from the pews to private faith; the next cohort comes up as inCREDulous atheists. This general pattern holds across most of the countries where we have decent data, but there are exceptions. As is often the case, the exceptions themselves prove highly illuminating.

One of the countries that stood out as exceptionally religious (by European standards) for a long time is Ireland. Proudly and fervently Catholic for centuries, even as Ireland saw its economic fortunes turn upward in the latter half of the twentieth century and early twenty-first, it remained steadfast in its faith. Existential security rose well above the levels that precipitated religious declines in the rest of Europe, but the faith held strong. Only very recently has Ireland started to see mass religious disaffiliation, and is quickly falling in line with its European counterparts in terms of secularization indices.

What's going on with Ireland? Why did its Catholic faith persist past the point where existential security tends to initiate secular shifts? And why the incredibly rapid correction back to the trend line in recent years? Hugh Turpin, an Irish expert on secularism in the Republic, is leading a project with Konrad and me to find out.

Our working model is that in Ireland, national and religious identity have historically been tightly fused: to be Irish is to be Catholic. The centrality of Catholicism to Irishness has helped to keep public religious fervor strong, even as existential security increased over the decades. Many countries

[§] GenZees in some of the former colonies?

saw public religiosity dip as economic fortunes rose, but in Ireland public Catholicism persisted, in large part due to the fusion of religious and national identities. In short, Catholicism's prominent role in the Irish national identity helped buffer the Republic against the religious complacency that often sets in as economic and social prosperity emerge. Economic fortunes improved, but public religiosity remained buoyed by Catholicism's prominent role in the national identity.

In recent years, Ireland has been becoming more secular at an astonishing rate. Looking at indices of religiosity that Konrad and crew have collected throughout Europe (things like church attendance, religious identification, and reported belief) Ireland remained highly religious longer than expected, by the standards of the rest of Europe. But then it shot back to the trend line—and potentially beyond it. Ireland is currently in the midst of what may be the most rapid secularization trend that Europe has seen. In talks, Hugh vividly illustrates this rapid shift with images of crowd size at papal visits to Ireland over the years—which look not unlike the infamous side-by-side Obama and Trump inauguration images. When Pope John Paul II visited in 1979, nearly a third of the country was in attendance (almost a million out of three and a half million total citizens).¶ When Pope Francis visited a handful of years ago, only about one hundred fifty thousand folks turned up (roughly 3 percent of the since-grown population).

What precipitated Ireland's rapid secularization? In his book *Unholy Catholic Ireland: Religious Hypocrisy, Secular Morality, and Irish Irreligion*,[9] Hugh Turpin details how the Irish people grew rapidly disenchanted with Catholic orthodoxy in the midst of revelations of ongoing child rape scandals, and subsequent coverups by Church leaders. As if one credibility-eroding scandal wasn't sufficient, other revelations ensued around the same time: Magdalene Laundries (i.e., where "fallen women" were imprisoned and more or less enslaved), Industrial Schools (places where poor children were brutalized and tortured), and Mother and Baby Homes (think: taking unmarried women's babies and de facto selling them).** As Catholic leaders

¶ And they did more than just watch—there was a corresponding baby and marriage boom some nine months later.

**These are Hugh's pithy summaries of several overlapping and complex scandals that could serve as Credibility Undermining Displays (CRUDs) that undermine the cultural transmission of faith.

were revealed to be hypocrites, rapists, and hypocritical enablers of rapists, many Irish people felt markedly less compelled to identify with the Church.[10] The fusion between Irish and Catholic identities was broken. People didn't lose all faith and turn to atheism, but Hugh tells me that an unprecedented number of Irish people would identify as agnostic, or perhaps as merely privately religious. Either way, Catholic CREDs plummet. Without the religious-nationalist fusion buffering Ireland against the familiar patterns of secularization seen across Europe, religious complacency and disbelief quickly set in. As with Voas's data, Ireland is getting less religious, one cohort of people at a time. Younger generations, in particular, have turned away from Catholicism en masse, and agnosticism and atheism are become more mainstream among young people.

If we combine the Ireland insights with the simulation work above, it's easy to see how various factors (national identity, for example) might artificially inflate the rate of CREDs above what economic and social conditions might predict, keeping belief at a perhaps unsustainably high level. But other conditions (say, a widespread Church conspiracy to conceal decades of child rape) can rather rapidly drive down CREDs, leading to widespread disaffiliation and eventual disbelief. Here Ireland, what was once a secularization outlier in Europe, becomes an interesting case study in how specific historical dynamics can interact with more general cultural evolutionary dynamics, leading either to persistently high levels of belief or rapid shifts toward disbelief.

This chapter's three-stage model of secularizing societies is now two-thirds complete. Rising existential security breeds religious complacency—a mix of private belief and apatheism. These conditions, via by now well-trodden processes like context-biased cultural learning and CREDs, lead subsequent generations of learners to widespread disbelief, a rapid spread of inCREDulous atheism. This sounds like the endpoint of secularization, but it turns out that religious influence can linger intuitively, even in explicitly secular societies.

STEP 3: MORE GRADUALLY, PRO-RELIGIOUS NORMS AND INTUITIONS FADE

Our first two steps describe a society in which security has driven down public religiosity, which then leads subsequent generations of learners to inCREDulous atheism. Without public displays of faith, learners naturally trend toward atheism. It might seem that such a society has now fully secularized. Religious attendance and identification are down, as is belief in gods. Indeed, a lot of social scientific work on secularization treats these indices—low church attendance, low prayer, low belief—as an endpoint.

But loss of belief in gods might not be the endpoint of secularism at all. Our work over the last decade or so is starting to show that even when overt religiosity wanes, religious influence can persist in society, albeit at a more implicit or intuitive level. Most societies have been defined by religious supremacy for centuries, millennia, and longer. Yes, individual faiths come and go, but for at least 10,000 years, Big Gods and their religions have been reshaping our social ecosystem in profound ways. Tens of millennia of religious influence isn't erased from public psyches in mere decades.

Cultural Ripples

After a generation of private believers and apatheists is followed by a generation of largely inCREDulous atheists, religion is far from absent in a society. After all, religious norms can have profound long-term effects on cultural evolution. To take just one example, Joe Henrich's recent book *The WEIRDest People in the World* provides a startling theory of cultural evolution and psychology, tracing the original roots of our peculiar Western psychological proclivities all the way back to the Catholic Church's prohibitions on near-cousin marriage in medieval times.[11] Religious proclamations begat a cascade of shifts to norms and practices that continues to be felt today, centuries later. Cultural learning is a secret to our species' success, and the quirks of how we learn and maintain norms mean that cultural causes can continue to have rippling effects far downstream of where they're initially identified. Small and initially localized shifts in norms about family life cast ripples outward in space and forward in time, yielding waves of psychological shifts that we can map today. If Henrich's theory is true—or at least has a grain of truth to it—then it shows how much of the psychological variability we see worldwide today can be traced back to one major religion tinkering with some norms a mere handful of centuries ago.

Interestingly, those initial norm shifts, implemented by the medieval Church, might help us explain where atheism has taken root today.[12] Among the psychological shifts that tweaks to family norms might've triggered: shifts toward broader and more impersonal cooperation; toward institutions that galvanize cooperation; institutional changes that led from monastic societies to guilds and even large-scale educational efforts; psychological shifts toward a more analytic (and less holistic) cognitive style. Henrich's book details these shifts, and evidence for them, in far greater detail than we can here. But what's incredibly interesting to me is that each of these shifts fits in well with the pathways to atheism that we outlined in the previous chapter. Institutions underlying cooperation and civil society pave the way for institutions that improve existential security, which eventually drives down attendance and the cultural transmission of faith as a result (our first two steps in this chapter). Shifts toward an analytic cognitive style, paired with changes in educational norms, institutions, and practices, also pave the way for pockets of analytic atheism.

In an ongoing project, Nava Caluori, Joe Henrich, and I are investigating whether there's anything to these hints that Church-catalyzed norm shifts in medieval times might predict atheism today.[13] Using the sorts of variables that Henrich marshaled in his book and associated papers (things like regional exposure to the Western Church over previous centuries, exposure to the Church's family norm packages), we can predict things like atheism rates and church nonattendance today. Early exposure to the Western Church's emerging norms on family life led regions to develop cultural, institutional, and psychological patterns that are all fertile ground for atheism in modern times. The Church's own teachings centuries ago might've helped plant the seeds for empty pews in Western Europe today.

I find these Church exposure–atheism links provocative and interesting in their own right. At the end of the day, they may prove solid, or they may prove to be a false alarm—it's notoriously difficult to pin down historical dynamics underlying contemporary psychological patterns, and sometimes a good theoretical[††] story is the best we can do.

The broader point of this section isn't that I think we have proof-positive that the medieval Church accidentally planted a time bomb that

[††] I don't mean this in the colloquial and deeply mistaken sense of "oh that's just a *theory*" which is meant to dismiss an idea as a mere hunch. I do mean "theory" as a coherent idea that binds together a vast number of observations, structures our inferences, and generates more ideas to be fruitfully tested. It's just that when linking history to present, our options for empirical substantiation are necessarily more limited.

would sabotage its membership some centuries later—although it would be incredibly fascinating if that proved to be the case. The broader point is that *cultural patterns can exert long-lasting and unpredictable influences.* If Church-driven shifts to family life could reshape the psychological globe centuries later, imagine how millennia of religious influence around the globe—those Big Gods helping various societies scale up and stabilize—might persist in cultures.

Big Gods Changed (Intuitions about) Morality

Even after overt markers of religion fade, Big Gods and their influence might linger. As we saw back in chapter 7, Big Gods religions somewhat changed the landscape of moral intuitions. Ben Purzycki's work shows us that pretty much all gods moralize, but they differ considerably in their scope to monitor and enforce morality. The gods of smaller-scale societies tend to moralize locally, and with limited capacity for punishing wrongs. Big Gods, on the other hand, have the skill sets to enforce morality on a broader scale—even universally for some gods.

Within Big Gods religions, people tend to assume that morality is ultimately rooted in religion. Over time, norms and practices linking religion and morality become psychologically and culturally embedded. The circles of religion and morality overlap more and more, to the point that many people see them as effectively synonymous.[14]

This manifests in people's explicit responses. For example, Pew asks people in countries around the world whether they agree with the sentiment that morality requires belief in a god, or the sentiment that religious belief is a necessary component in a child's moral upbringing. In most of the world, most people agree with these ideas (as you might guess, Western Europe is again the persistent exception).[15]

Religious influence can be felt in more subtle ways as well. Consider linguistic tells. In lots of places, saying that something is "the Christian thing to do" signals moral good. Calling someone "a good Christian" is tantamount to saying they're a good person, an upstanding moral citizen. Merriam-Webster dictionary provides three definitions for "Christian," when used as an adjective. The first two define Christian in ways relating to Christianity (e.g., "based on or conforming with Christianity"). The third definition? "Treating other people in a kind or generous way."

Patterns like these are the consequences of religions holding moral sway in societies over cultural evolutionary time. Norms and institutions are shaped by religions, so what happens as religions fade away? Because cultural shifts can cast ripples forward, as Henrich's examples show, it's possible that even explicitly secular societies still retain some latent religious influence. In particular, I think that attitudes toward both atheism and religious belief can help us test whether intuitions favoring religion might persist, even in secular societies where explicit religious influence has largely disappeared, along with religious belief.

Next, we'll consider two lines of evidence that point toward an intuitive persistence of preferences for religion. Both of them come from our work on anti-atheist sentiments over the years.

Psycho Killer, Qu'est-ce que c'est?

Back in chapter 8, we explored some research on people's moral intuitions about atheists. Our research participants intuitively assumed that people doing immoral things (things like kicking dogs, lustily romancing dead chickens, or snacking on people meat) probably didn't believe in a god.[16] This reflects a deep-seated intuitive moral distrust of atheists. Without belief in God, immorality is possible—or so goes the intuition.

Our strongest demonstration of this phenomenon involved a vignette in which we described a guy who, after tormenting animals as a kid, ends up mutilating and murdering homeless people for fun as an adult. Our participants intuitively assumed that this psycho killer must not believe in a god, at least when it came to the gut-level intuitions we were measuring. This overall finding was intriguing, but I think the most important and fascinating finding came with our more fine-grained analyses.

We conducted this study in thirteen different countries that spanned the global religious spectrum, from highly devout places like the United States, the United Arab Emirates, and India, to more secular locales like Czechia, Finland, Australia, and the UK.[17] Overall our participants intuited that serial killers are probably atheists, but there was variability in the strength of this effect across research sites. One of our most secular countries—Finland, firmly Nordic—showed no hint of anti-atheist intuitions on our experimental task. New Zealand, a second highly secular country, showed just a whisper of an effect—probably there, but not strong. In every other country, however, people were more likely to attribute serial murder to atheists than to believers.

Our sample included many countries that look quite secular if one focuses on measures like religious attendance or rates of belief in gods. In Czechia, for example, a recent poll finds that two in three adults don't believe in a god.[18] In Great Britain, the Netherlands, and Australia, belief in gods is relatively low, and an increasingly large percentage of the populace identify as nonreligious. Yet, in all these countries, our participants intuitively blamed serial murder on atheists. Digging deeper still, we ran a set of analyses looking at participants' own beliefs about god. We found that even atheist participants across these countries still tended to intuitively assume that the serial killer didn't believe in a god.

Neither personal atheism nor societal-level secularity was a bulwark against intuitive moral suspicion of atheists. Naturally, the patterns we observed were stronger among more devout participants and were stronger in the more strongly religious societies. But anti-atheist moral intuitions weren't solely evident in more religious countries. Even explicitly nonreligious societies—like Czechia, where most adults don't believe in a god—still show evidence of deep-seated intuitions linking extreme immorality to atheism.

If intuitive moral distrust of atheists was evident in most of our sampled countries, why was it not evident in Finland? Frankly, I've no clue—or at least I've no direct evidence supporting my hunches. One possibility is that it was just a quirk of the data: maybe our sample in this country was skewed in one way or another. Another possibility—one that merits focused investigation—is that Finland is more fully and intuitively secular than lots of the other countries we sampled. Maybe their secular shifts began earlier, for example, or took root more quickly for unknown reasons. In the parlance of the three steps of secularism in this chapter, maybe Finland is more fully in the third stage of secularization than are the other countries we've studied. It's certainly possible that lots of our countries are teetering between Stage 2 and Stage 3, where overt religiosity and explicit belief has toppled, but latent religious influence lingers in people's intuitions. This latter possibility is consistent with other work we're just now publishing, work that delved deeper into the strongly secular countries of the world to tease apart their intuitions about religion and atheism.

Belief in Belief

In this section I've hypothesized that, due to millennia of religious influence, overt and explicit secularism might overlay more subtly ingrained pro-religious intuitions. Simply, people might not attend religious services or believe in God, but nonetheless somehow still have the intuition that religion is a fundamentally good thing, preferred over atheism. In his book *Breaking the Spell*, Daniel Dennett dubbed this sort of gut-level feeling that faith is intrinsically good (even if one doesn't have it) "belief in belief." If we could measure and document a sort of intuitive belief in belief in even secular countries, that would help substantiate the hypothesis that religion's influence lingers on, even in nominally nonreligious societies.

How might we measure such an abstract intuition? Consider this vignette:

> The CEO of a company is sitting in his office when his vice president of R&D comes in and says, "We are thinking of starting a new program. It will help us increase profits, but it will also harm the environment." The CEO responds that he doesn't care about harming the environment and just wants to make as much profit as possible. The program is carried out, profits are made, and the environment is harmed.

Now comes the crucial question: Did the CEO intentionally harm the environment?

Given this vignette, most people answer "yes." The CEO shows blatant disregard for the environment and prioritizes profits. His policy—with his foreknowledge—harmed the environment. He made money, and did so by (according to our intuitions) intentionally harming the environment. Now let's flip the vignette and see if the intuition holds. Consider this version:

> The CEO of a company is sitting in his office when his vice president of R&D comes in and says, "We are thinking of starting a new program. It will help us increase profits, but it will also help the environment." The CEO responds that he doesn't care about helping the environment and just wants to make as much profit as possible. The program is carried out, profits are made, and the environment is helped.

Did the CEO intentionally *help* the environment in this example? Most people don't think so. His clearly stated goal was profit, and environmental benefit seems like an incidental side effect of profit motives, not an intentionally chosen goal.

Across these two vignettes, only a single word differs: *harm* is thrice changed to *help*. And this produces a stark difference in results. Joshua Knobe's initial results on this pattern—since dubbed the "Knobe effect"—showed that 82 percent of respondents felt that environmental harm was intentional, but only 23 percent of respondents felt environmental help was intentional.[19]

What gives? The vignettes are identical save a single word, but people's intuitions sharply diverge. One explanation that's held up reasonably well focuses on an asymmetry in how people view positive and negative outcomes and how they think about intended outcomes versus side effects. Lots of actions have multiple outcomes, causes rarely have singular effects. Parsing intent isn't always straightforward—after all we can't directly observe intentions and other mental states, we have to rely on our mentalizing system to infer them. For one reason or another (and many potential ones have been offered), negative outcomes are seen as intended outcomes, whereas positive outcomes are viewed as unintended side effects. Another name for the Knobe effect is the side-effect effect.

What does all of this have to do with latent religious influence lingering under overt secularism? It turns out that the Knobe effect makes a lovely tool for investigating people's subtle intuitions, the sorts of intuitions posited by my hypothesis about sneaky intuitive belief in belief persisting in ostensibly secular societies. Specifically, it might help us test whether people in highly secular countries nonetheless intuitively view religious belief as a good thing and atheism as a bad thing. After all, in the Knobe effect good things (like helping the environment) are seen as unintended side effects, whereas bad things (like harming the environment) are seen as intended outcomes.

An all-star team of researchers—Jazmin Brown-Iannuzzi, Ryan McKay, Gordon Pennycock, Jon Jong, Jonathan Lanman, Robert Ross—and I set out to test the possible existence of an atheism Knobe effect in highly secular countries. The whole research group was already fielding a survey about atheism in eight largely secular countries: Canada, China, Czechia, Japan, the Netherlands, Sweden, the United Kingdom, and Vietnam. This is a nice test, because by focusing primarily on secular countries we are in effect being more stringent and conservative in testing the hypothesis. If even people in highly secular countries intuitively disfavor atheism, that would be reasonably compelling evidence for the notion that explicit secularism might overlay a deeper intuitive preference for religion.

Our survey included a Knobe effect vignette that had been tailored to gauge intuitions about the intuitive positivity or negativity of both religious belief and atheism.

Half of our participants got this version:

> A journalist went to her editor and said, "I have written a news story about religion. I'm sure that it will help us sell newspapers and make money, and I think it will also make some people believe that God exists." The editor answered, "I don't care at all if people believe that God exists. I just want to make as much money as I can. Let's publish this news story." The newspaper published the news story. After reading the news story some people who didn't believe in God changed their mind and started to believe that God exists.
>
> Did the editor intend to make people believe that God exists?

Half got this version instead:

> A journalist went to her editor and said, "I have written a news story about religion. I'm sure that it will help us sell newspapers and make money, and I think it will also make some people believe that God doesn't exist." The editor answered, "I don't care at all if people believe that God doesn't exist. I just want to make as much money as I can. Let's publish this news story." The newspaper published the news story. After reading the news story some people who did believe in God changed their mind and started to believe that God doesn't exist.
>
> Did the editor intend to make people believe that God doesn't exist?

The key test is whether people are more likely to say that the editor's publication decision is more intentional when she was creating more atheists in the world. This would be consistent with the possibility that our participants intuitively favor religious belief over atheism—they see more atheists as an intentionally caused negative, and more believers as an unintended positive. In other words, are our participants viewing a world with more atheists as a negative, akin to a world where the environment is harmed (as in the original Knobe effect)?

For our final analysis, we had about 3,800 respondents to our survey—just shy of 500 from each of our secular countries. Each saw one version of the above vignette, and indicated whether they felt the resulting religious change (journalism that either created atheists or believers) was intentional.

The results? Overall, we saw that the odds of judging the religious change as intentional were about 40 percent higher when the journalism created atheists than when it created more believers. This, again, is consistent with the possibility that our respondents intuitively viewed a world with more atheists in it as more negative than a world with more believers. The magnitude of this intention rating gap varied a bit country-by-country. It was largest in the United Kingdom, for example, and practically nonexistent in Vietnam. With only eight countries to work with, we can't form very solid inferences about what's going on here, why some countries show larger intuitive anti-atheist sentiments than others. That's a question that requires more research.

In addition to the focal vignette intentionality question, we also asked people about their own religious beliefs in various ways. We included one multiple-choice item asking people their views about gods, with one response item starkly indicating atheism: "I don't believe in God (or gods)." This item specifically allowed us to check to see whether any pro-religion intuitions in secular societies were present even among atheist respondents. Across different statistical analyses, we consistently found that personal atheism didn't matter much—the intentionality gap between experimental conditions wasn't different across atheist and believer respondents. One statistical model even let us produce a predicted pattern of response across all countries for just atheists. And this model provided evidence that across countries overall, and within each individual country, even atheists saw the creation of atheists as more intentional (thus, presumably, negative) than the creation of believers.

In short, we found an atheism Knobe effect, even among atheists in highly secular countries. One interpretation of this pattern of results is that, at an intuitive level, even atheists in largely secular countries nonetheless harbor some intuitive preference for religious belief. In other words, this could be evidence of what Dennett might call belief in belief persisting at the level of intuition among atheists in secular societies.

Caveats and Caution

As with pretty much all science, there are caveats and possible alternative explanations for these results. The data are consistent with the interpretation I've outlined, but they're consistent with other possibilities as well.

To start with: the Knobe effect vignette task is an odd one. We experimenters have full control over the contents of the vignette, but don't have much of a say in what our respondents imagine as they're reading it. They read about a piece of journalism with the power to shift people's core religious beliefs, producing either atheism or belief. What on earth might the contents of such a story be? Let's imagine a couple of scenarios for the atheist condition. All participants know is that there's a revelatory piece of journalism that leads people to abandon their religious faith and become atheists. Some participants might conceivably be imagining some breakthrough scientific discovery that proves our gods to be mere myths.[‡‡] Others might imagine that it's a story of religious hypocrisy of some sort—maybe it's an expose of the Catholic Church's complicity in covering up decades of sexual abuses, or about residential schools' role in genocide against indigenous people worldwide. As experimenters, we don't know which of these routes, or others as-yet unimagined by us, our respondents have in mind. The outcome measure is a judgment of intentionality, which (by assumption) seems to track a negative valence judgment; negative outcomes are seen as more intentional. It's possible that people imagine that a story capable of generating atheism is a negative story, and it's negativity from the imagined journalism topic (rather than inherent negativity of atheism) that drives the intentionality judgment. Or so a critic might suggest, in good faith. A defender of the belief in belief hypothesis I've outlined might push back and ask whether people imagining that an atheism-causing event must be negative sort of fits the broad story that there's a latent anti-atheism that still pervades nominally secular societies. Who's right, the critic or defender? Based on our evidence right now, we don't know—it's supposition either way. Hopefully follow-up studies will more conclusively point one way or another.

The conjunction fallacy results, pointing to an intuitive moral distrust of atheists, face a similar need for caution. As with the Knobe effect, that result rests on a kind of quirky experimental task. Kahneman and Tversky's original

[‡‡] For a fun twist on this, I'd recommend Ted Chiang's short story "Omphalos."

work on the representativeness heuristic dates back to the 1970s, and the intervening decades have seen waves of critique, defense, and rethinking. As with the Knobe effect, the primary experimental result rests on inferences we researchers make about how participants are responding to a rather contrived question, deliberately designed in some ways to subvert how people normally communicate. If I ask whether it's more probable that someone is (A) a bank teller or (B) a bank teller who's active in the feminist movement, the pragmatics of conversation bring the implication that Option A describes a bank teller who isn't a feminist, rather than that they're a bank teller who may or may not be a feminist. This pragmatic quirk is shared across experimental conditions, so the fact that people are more likely to answer B when a description of a serial killer is paired with an atheist more than when the description is paired with a believer tells us that the results aren't pure dreck and noise. But still, the results warrant some inferential caution.

Across both sets of results, people are giving nonsensical replies to a contrived and unusual question, but they're doing so in predictable ways. Both sorts of studies—quirky as they are individually—give results that point in a similar direction. This gives me a bit more confidence in their reliability, and the fit with this chapter's theory. But at the end of the day, I'll need lots more studies using lots more tasks. Hopefully accruing enough individually odd experimental paradigms will continue to lead to a convergence of results. Time will tell.

How do some societies shift toward secularism? What drives shifts in religious demographics, producing the pockets of atheism that we see around the globe today? In this chapter, I sketched out a preliminary three-stage theory of secularism that stitches together various empirical threads, united by the general dual inheritance approach we've developed across this book.

Following secularization theory in the sociology of religion, it looks like a shift in underlying social and economic fortunes serves as a societal catalyst for secularism. Rising existential security triggers religious complacency. Public religiosity wanes, leading to a mixture of sincere—but increasingly private—belief, and apatheism. Countries like Canada seem to be teetering at this stage right now.

Eroding public religiosity is a serious threat to the cultural transmission of religious faith across generations, via cultural evolutionary mechanisms we've explored in previous chapters. Cultural learners in a religiously complacent society don't witness strong and consistent religious CREDs favoring a particular god. Without CREDs, belief in any given god is much less likely. A generation of private believers and apatheists gives way to a generation of inCREDulous atheists. Much of Western Europe is about here right now.

Dips in public proclamations of faith and even private belief don't herald full secularism, complete at deeper cultural and psychological levels. Chapter 7 argued that for millennia, Big God religions were central in the gradual upscaling of human cooperation. Many features of our large-scale cooperative societies may owe a debt to millennia of originally religious norms. And there's no reason to expect that these sorts of pro-religious norms would evaporate from a society overnight, simply because a couple generations of people stopped participating in, and then believing in, religion. In the domain of religion and atheism, it looks like various pro-religious norms continue to have their influence felt, even after overt religion has largely faded from a society, and even among individuals who aren't explicitly religious. For example, we found that even atheists in secular places like the Netherlands still tend to be morally suspicious of atheists, at least at the level of gut-feeling. We also found an atheism Knobe effect—results consistent with the possibility that even atheists in secular countries intuitively feel negatively about the prospect of more atheists in the world. On the surface, these findings seem absurd: why would atheists in majority-atheist countries distrust other atheists, or intuitively prefer a world with fewer atheists? But when viewed through the lens of cultural evolution, it makes a lot of sense. Cultural evolution enables causes to trigger consequences that cascade across decades and centuries, and religion might still exert an intuitive influence on atheists in nominally nonreligious societies. That said, our evidence for this possibility is, at this stage, preliminary and suggestive rather than conclusive. It will be fascinating to perform additional studies in increasingly secular societies to evaluate the degree to which the speculation of this chapter—that pro-religious norms and intuitions might outlive religious belief in secularizing societies—continues to fit the data.

CHAPTER THIRTEEN

ATHEISM IS NATURAL

Changing Visions of Faith and Atheism

Nothing is so painful to the human mind as a great and sudden change.
—MARY SHELLEY, *FRANKENSTEIN*

It is an interesting and demonstrable fact, that all children are atheists and were religion not inculcated into their minds, they would remain so.
—ERNESTINE L. ROSE

Here is as good a point as any to pause and take stock of what we've learned about atheism, in light of different theories we've considered. Back in chapter 4, we met the cognitive by-product approach to religion—one potential answer for the Puzzle of Faith, that also makes predictions of varying degrees of specificity about atheism. Over the next handful of chapters, we then developed a dual inheritance theory of religious belief and disbelief, as applied to both the Puzzle of Faith (chapters 5–7) and then the Puzzle of Atheism (chapters 8–12). In this chapter, I want to explicitly juxtapose these theories, to first ask what they predict about atheism, then to evaluate the evidence we've encountered thus far. Finally, I'd like to step back and consider what both theoretical approaches suggest about atheism, at a more basic and fundamental level.

Each of the preceding chapters zoomed in to describe a small but important part of the scientific landscape. Now, let's soar higher above the landscape thus described, and see what broad features our world contains. Instead of focusing on waves, let's think about currents; mountain ranges instead of slopes; watersheds instead of streams.

Viewed with sufficient distance, we can see that the theories of religion encountered in this book don't just describe slightly different psychological mechanisms for how religion and atheism work. These theoretical visions diverge on core questions of *just how natural* religion is, and *just how unnatural or improbable atheism is.*

FROM BY-PRODUCTS TO CREDS: THEORETICAL EVOLUTION*

Fifteen or twenty years ago, many cognitive and evolutionary scientists were tackling the Puzzle of Faith, but fewer were tackling the Puzzle of Atheism. The central questions emerging from the literature included ones like: "Why is pretty much everyone religious?" and "Why are religions similar in some fundamental ways once you abstract away superficial differences?" Religious belief in our species was taken almost as a given, and scientific explanations skewed heavily toward assuming and then explaining its universality. Out of this scientific milieu, the cognitive by-product account from the cognitive science of religion emerged.

I think the cognitive by-product approach gave us some profoundly important insights and helped build a strong foundation for subsequent generations of theories. First, it grounded the spiritual in the cognitive. Instead of using odd high-level psychological and philosophical abstractions—like an existential dread of death, or some need to explain the cosmos, for example—the by-product account started building an understanding of religion from a foundation of things we already knew or suspected about how basic cognition works.[1] Scientifically, it's a good move to ground religion in simpler and more basic cognitive processes, rather than in complex abstractions that themselves require psychological explanation.

Second, at its best, the cognitive science of religion's by-product approach specified empirically testable hypotheses about how cognition connected to religion. The approach was fundamentally mechanistic, which lent itself to

---

* Theoretical evolution can be seen in both prevailing ideas among successive cohorts of researchers and in shifts within individual researchers' own thinking. Many people whose quotes I've used to illustrate by-productist thinking would be copacetic, if not supportive, of what I'm calling the dual inheritance theory. Ideas change, as do idea-havers, and in this chapter I hope no false dichotomy of social identities among theorists is inferred, for none is intended.

productive study. In principle, if by-product theorists posited a cognitive linkage that researchers couldn't empirically connect the dots on, that hypothesis could be abandoned in favor of more scientifically generative alternatives. As we saw, this ideal wasn't always fully realized—scientists being inevitably and frustratingly human, after all—and some ideas like HADD have persisted long past the date when they should've either yielded more impressive empirical results or been conclusively dropped. But other prominent by-productist ideas were furnished with more consistent empirical support over the years, in part because they started with known cognitive gadgets and built upward to religion. For example, mind-body dualism[2] and promiscuous teleological thinking[3] both seem to be stable enough cognitive proclivities to underpin aspects of religious thinking.

Third, I think that the by-product account laid important groundwork for connecting the study of religion to the study of culture more broadly. Pretty early on, cognitive scientists of religion hit on the idea that minimally counterintuitive concepts—practically universal among religions—might be successful in part because they're good fits for our minds. If there are some concepts out there that people tend to find more memorable, those concepts will naturally fare well in cultural transmission over the years. Stories with these concepts will become and remain popular; religious stories with them will be passed from generation to generation of cultural learners. The evidence that minimal counterintuition is fundamental to religion looks shakier today than it did a decade ago, but I think the effort—linking core cognitive biases to broader cultural patterns—is an important one. This is grounding the cultural success of some concepts in a basic feature of our psychology, which is kind of a profound idea if you play with it for a while. Lots of features of our cultural world stick around over the years simply because our minds evolved in such a way that some concepts are stickier than others (to minds like ours, at least. A capuchin or caterpillar or cuttlefish mind would find entirely different concepts sticky). We didn't at all *have to evolve* in such a way that supernatural concepts would be memorable; the contingent fact that we did is fascinating.

Finally, I think an enduring take-home message from the cognitive science of religion is that religion is not only natural, but psychologically *ordinary* as well. We don't have some fixed God center in our brains, there aren't specific God genes. Our everyday and mundane psychological apparatus generates religion, much as it generates lots of other cultural phenomena. Religion isn't some cognitively special category of concepts. Religious belief probably isn't genetically hardwired into us because it's a naturally selected adaptation that helps us solve some environmental challenge or other. Instead, religion's a universal feature of our evolved psychology, but as a sort of side effect. Our brains work in a way that makes religion possible and probable, but they didn't evolve *to have religion*. Our evolved minds—the bundle of abilities, biases, proclivities, and cognitive gadgets we collectively call "human nature"—helped our ancestors solve lots of recurrent adaptive challenges, and the capacity to imagine gods is just along for the ride.

Despite these strengths, the cognitive by-product approach has gradually given way to its own evolutionary descendant and successor, the dual inheritance approach. Around the time of the Zeus Problem paper I wrote with Joe Henrich, researchers had started taking belief a bit more seriously.[4] After all, the cultural popularity of a minimally counterintuitive concept tells us little about whether people actually believe in it. Just ask Mickey Mouse, or ask adults about Santa Claus. And even the most successful god concepts aren't so cognitively sticky that people believe in them on contents alone. Missionaries don't just pull up in a new spot, tell people about Jesus's features and skill set, and watch belief spread. Anthropologists don't learn details of Zeus today, and start believing in him tomorrow. For the most part, people don't add new gods to the pantheons they believe in just by hearing about them. Belief seems to take more than just content biases, in the parlance of cultural evolution.

In addition to focusing on belief, researchers also began connecting the dots between the memory biases cognitive scientists of religion wrote about, and the broader cultural evolution literature. *What religions are about* (supernatural agents with strategic information) is plausibly explained by content biases that emerge in our evolved minds. But *patterns of who believes* in which supernatural agents are largely explained by context biases in cultural evolution. Conformist learning, imitation of elites, and especially attending to credible displays of faith—religious CREDs—give us a lot of theoretical traction for understanding patterns of belief and disbelief in various gods.[5] Yes, our evolved cognition constrains which supernatural agent concepts are likely to catch on, as cognitive by-productists quite rightly pointed out, but content biases alone make questionable explanations for patterns of belief. This was the genesis of the dual inheritance approach: content biases explaining the cross-cultural recurrence of some sorts of supernatural agent concepts, context biases and CREDs explaining patterns of belief and disbelief in them.

By being more fully integrated with the full toolkit of modern cultural evolution, the dual inheritance approach has proven quite successful at not only solving challenges like the Zeus and Mickey Mouse problems, but also challenges that the by-product account never seriously grappled with. Why have just a few religions (with similar sorts of gods) conquered the globe? Why links between religious beliefs and cooperative outcomes? Why do negative views of atheists center on moral perceptions? Content biases are mum on those scientific questions. The dual inheritance approach, in contrast, tackles those questions with aplomb, building on notions of cultural group selection and religious prosociality.[6] Different religions have different gods with different skill sets. Pretty much every religion that sticks around for a while has a set of gods that fit the by-product account's content template—minimally counterintuitive agents, etcetera—but only a few have features conducive to broader competitive success at the cultural level. Big Gods, and the religions built around them, might've helped our species upgrade its cooperative skill set over the millennia, profoundly reshaping this world and our place in it, as well as our intuitions about morality.[7]

Above all, I think that the by-product account and the dual inheritance account differ when it comes to atheism. And, although I may be heavily biased here because I happen to be a dual inheritance theorist who studies atheism a lot, I think that studying atheism helped progress and refine the dual inheritance approach, and convincingly show how it is an upgrade over its theoretical ancestor. The dual inheritance approach includes more plausible mechanisms for belief. It is more capable of explaining broad patterns in religion and secularism. Studying these mechanisms necessarily entails studying differences in belief—the conditions under which people do or don't believe in gods. Which, naturally, means studying atheists.

As we studied atheism more, from a dual cognitive and evolutionary lens, the dual inheritance approach garnered more support. The theoretical refinement of the dual inheritance approach and the empirical refinement of our understanding of atheism happened in parallel over about the last ten or fifteen years. This temporal correlation is no coincidence: empirical results on atheism are simply better fits for the predictions derived from dual inheritance than from the by-product approach. This didn't have to be the case. Both frameworks make predictions of varying specificity about atheism, and the fun thing about science is that ultimately you get to check your pet theory against the stubborn world to see how it performs. When it comes to atheism, the dual inheritance account's predictions have simply worked better. Taking atheism more seriously spurred improvement in basic theory on religion.

TESTING THEORIES AGAINST OUR WORLD

Let's briefly consider just three sets of predictions that each approach can make about atheism.

Recall that the by-product view holds that religions persist because they are such phenomenally great fits for our evolved minds—that we are all, in a sense, born ready to adopt religious beliefs with little or no cultural prodding. The idea isn't that we're born Christian or Sunni or Zoroastrian, but that we are born with a sort of natural religious inclination, with doctrinal details ready to be filled in by culture. That we are *born believers*, as one prominent book on the cognitive by-product approach is entitled.[8]

Alas, the notion that kids are born believers runs afoul of empirical work we met in previous chapters. For example, in chapter 2 we discussed how kids think and learn about religious concepts. Far from automatically encoding religious claims as facts, as one might expect born believers to do, kids actually view religious claims as somewhat intermediate between fact and opinion—that is, unless those kids have been explicitly raised to be religious. Likewise, we looked at work on how kids learn from testimony—how they come to believe their elders that there are things like gods or germs, that are important but unseen.[9] If you recall, kids showed an intuitive skepticism of supernatural unseens, and they required a bit more testimony on their behalf.[10] Once again, not the pattern one would expect from born believers, who would only need culture to fill in the blanks of religion, like some cognitive paint-by-numbers.

If we concede that the hardline "born believers" thesis is too strong to be supportable by current evidence, can we perhaps salvage a more nuanced version of the by-product thesis? Recall that a central premise of the by-product view is just that religion comes naturally, a by-product generated by our evolved minds. This view, with varying levels of explicitness across prominent writings, predicts that although religion is natural, atheism is cognitively unnatural. Not impossible, but something that takes either cultural or cognitive work. "Natural" and "unnatural," recall, take on a technical meaning that might translate more into "ease of picking up" rather than having the semi-judgmental connotations that might otherwise occur if something is called "unnatural."

The by-product account, in claiming that religion comes easily and atheism only with work, predicts that atheism is probably fairly uncommon and improbable. Boyer's 2012 *Nature* summary article opens with the byline "Atheism will always be a harder sell than religion" and closes by saying that atheism is "hardly the easiest ideology to propagate."[11] Barrett's seminal 2004 cognitive science of religion book calls atheism "unsurprisingly, a very uncommon worldview,"[12] and his follow-up book's atheism chapter includes the major subheading "Atheism is rarer than you might think."[13] With these descriptions of atheism, flip back to chapter 10: is atheism improbable and uncommon? Hardly. If anything, atheism is *more common and prevalent* than we'd previously assumed.

Finally, we can look at whether atheism is difficult to initiate or maintain. If theism comes as naturally as the by-product view suggests, then we might predict that atheism would take work—either cultural or cognitive effort would need to be mustered on atheism's behalf. Here are some representative quotations, coming from summaries of the cognitive by-product approach:

- Atheism "is generally the result of deliberate, effortful work against our natural cognitive dispositions."[14]
- Atheism "just requires some special conditions to help it struggle against theism."[15]
- "Compared with the near inevitability of theism, atheism appears to lack the natural, intuitive support to become a widespread type of worldview. . . . Religious belief is the natural backdrop to the oddity that is atheism."[16]

The general gist of the by-product account is that religious belief largely just happens, whereas something extra needs to be added to get atheism.

It could be unusual cultural circumstances, maybe even overt cultural scaffolding to support atheism—public institutions that actively foist atheism upon citizenry, somehow or other. Or it could be some cognitive special sauce that helps people overcome their natural, presumably religion-supporting, intuitions. How have these predictions fared, in light of evidence? Again, not well.

On the cultural front, we have indeed found that some cultures are more conducive to atheism than others, but these haven't necessarily been cultures where atheism is actively supported or deliberately promoted. It doesn't take consistent cultural scaffolding to support atheism; instead, atheism emerges where consistent cultural support for specific religions is lacking.[17] Culture needn't push people toward atheism. Rather, atheism is the destination to which people will naturally gravitate, unless culturally pushed toward a specific religion.

On the cognitive front, the empirical record is perhaps even more bleak, from the perspective of a by-product prediction. Does atheism require cognitive effort, rational rebuttal to our religious intuitions? Recall our third chapter, on the more-or-less myth of rational atheism. Although there are some theoretical hints that lend plausibility to the rational atheism thesis—religions are supported by intuitions, but intuitions aren't the only way we think—work that directly tests whether rational and reflective cognitive effort underpin atheism has proven disappointing. Experimental work flared,[18] then fizzled.[19] Correlations between rational thinking and atheism are weak and fickle across cultures.[20] Among people with strongly religious upbringings, the correlation between rational thinking and religious disbelief disappears entirely.[21] In large representative surveys looking at which factors predict atheism in different countries, rational thinking didn't pull much weight.[22] Far from rational thinking and cognitive effort being central to atheism, instead they look like rather minor contributors.

On each of these fronts—born believers, the prevalence of atheism, and the effort needed to sustain it—evidence has stubbornly refused to support the clearest predictions made by the by-product account. But in each case, the evidence is firmly in line with predictions made from the dual inheritance theory developed throughout this book.

By my reading, this theoretical dispute is settled, with the evidence clearly showing the dual inheritance theory to be a better solution to the

Puzzles of Faith and Atheism than its theoretical predecessor, the by-product account. And in a sense, this is as we should expect. The dual inheritance theory takes a more expansive view of cultural evolution and was from its inception deeply concerned with issues of belief and disbelief. Over the years, my own views shifted from the by-product view to the dual inheritance view, largely because I was actively studying atheism, and the dual inheritance theory simply does a better job describing and explaining it.

Now, I'd like us to step back from the theoretical melee, and ask not *which theory is better* but instead to ask *what are these theories' visions of atheism itself*. At a broader level, what does it mean for our view of atheism if we describe it as cognitively unnatural, in need of effortful propping-up? What does atheism look like if we view it instead through a dual inheritance lens?

CONTRASTING VISIONS

Cognitive By-Products: The Naturalness of Religion and the Improbability of Atheism

The cognitive by-product approach grounds religious belief in everyday, natural cognition. Our species evolved to solve a bunch of recurrent adaptive challenges in our ancestral environments. Some of the mental adaptations that helped us solve these challenges just so happen to, purely as a by-product, make it really easy for us to think religious thoughts. To summarize: Our ordinary social cognition and mentalizing—which presumably evolved to help us navigate our social ecosystems—give us the capacity to imagine gods and spirits. We have minds capable of imagining gods, and also minds with specific evolved features that make it so that we can more easily remember some candidate gods than others. Some gods are good fits for the conceptual nooks and crannies of our evolved minds and will be cognitively "sticky": easy to remember, recall, and tell others about. The idiosyncrasies of our mental evolution make it more likely for some gods than others to catch on and persist in cultures.

As a species, we seem to get really hung up on purpose and meaning. We care deeply about questions of *how* and *why*, and successful gods can help people make teleological sense of their world. According to some interpretations of some research, we might even intuitively favor creationist accounts as answers to these *why* and *how* questions.

If you put all these elements together, the cognitive by-product account presents a vision of our religious world as one in which belief is a nearly inevitable outcome. A constellation of intersecting cognitive biases produces a human psychology that is irresistibly drawn to religious concepts. Popular and influential summaries of the cognitive science of religion reference a "belief instinct" and call people "born believers" and "intuitive theists."

Under the strongest versions of this approach, religious belief is natural and practically inescapable. Atheism, in contrast, is seen as comparatively challenging and improbable. The by-product approach to atheism states that whereas religion is natural, *atheism is unnatural*. At minimum, atheism is described as an unlikely outcome that takes special cultural or cognitive work to get off the ground; at its strongest, the by-product account describes atheism as a psychologically superficial blip that obscures deeper patterns in cognition, including a latent intuitive theism underlying self-reports of atheism. By-product theorists stress the assumption that atheism is less cognitively natural than is faith.[23] The overwhelming implication from by-product accounts is that atheism must be hard to sustain, is perhaps psychologically superficial,[24] and is expected to be a rare exception to our species' overwhelming faith.

In sum, the by-product account presents a vision of religion as practically inevitable, and a vision of atheism as a rare aberration that's difficult to sustain without cultural and cognitive work. This view of atheism as a rare and effortfully maintained stance against our species' default intuitive religious faith has garnered support from beyond the academic study of religion, finding seemingly unlikely support with some of the world's foremost atheism advocates and apologists.

New Atheism and By-Products: Oddly Comfortable Bedfellows

As someone who discovered his latent atheism in the discussion board of a university philosophy class, briefly flirted with New Atheism as it emerged, and then chose to study religion scientifically instead, I've long been fascinated by the fact that the cognitive by-product account has reached a measure of popular success in New Atheist circles. Sketching pet hypotheses of religion in *The God Delusion*, Dawkins gives the by-product account a rather positive evaluation, describing it as the kind of evolutionary theory of religion that we need: "I am one of an increasing number of biologists who see religion as a *by-product* of something else" (his emphasis). Dawkins echoes the positive by-product sentiment a decade and a half later in *Outgrowing God*. Dennett and Shermer both give the by-product account positive reviews in their respective books on religion and atheism.[25]

In a lot of ways, the by-product theory seems an odd fit for this crowd. Why, after all, would the world's most strident atheists embrace a theory that explicitly describes atheism as *unnatural*? It took me a while to sort out the appeal of the cognitive by-product approach to New Atheists, but here's my current guesses as to the odd-couple fit between New Atheists and by-product theory. Three or four things tie these ideas and ideologies together.

First is coincidental timing, mere happenstance of history. The New Atheists rose to popularity around the turn of the millennium. This is precisely the same period of time when the cognitive science of religion was making its most headway. If popularizers like Dawkins or Shermer did a quick skim of the scientific literature on religion, they probably would've stumbled across some cognitive science of religion work, including books by Boyer and Barrett outlining the then-current state of the cognitive science of religion, with heavy emphasis placed on the by-product account.

Second, I think that New Atheists likely found the by-product account appealing because it describes religion as fundamentally an evolutionary accident—a mere Darwinian "oopsie." Other theories at the time posited that religion might've emerged as a directly selected adaptation for helping our species navigate cooperative dilemmas, for example. Against the backdrop of adaptationist theories of religion, which spoke of religion as fulfilling some core adaptive function in our species' evolution, the by-product account was an evolutionary theory of religion that posited no specific Darwinian utility for religious faith. The by-product account, unlike other competitors at the time, *wasn't saying that religion was good for anything in particular* or that it had any direct evolutionary value—an obvious selling point for those ideologically opposed to religion. The by-product account was a fully evolutionary theory of religion that managed to not say anything all that complimentary about religious belief.

Third, I think that the vision of atheism implied by the by-product account was probably attractive to New Atheists as well. Indeed, in many ways it was *positively flattering* to them. Prominent by-product accounts describe religious belief as nearly inevitable, because it's simply such a good fit for our evolved minds. The key to atheism? Rational thinking. Cognitive effort. Cultural artifices like fancy education. Atheists could only be atheists if they were quite clever. If one reads between the lines a bit, it seems that any old rube will probably be religious in the by-product account. But atheists? They're the select few able to use their effortful analytic System 2 processing to think their way out of religion—to *intellectually outgrow God*. Making education and cleverness central to its view of atheism, the by-product account directly appealed to the vanity of atheists who valorize rationality and learning.

A few other historical quirks likely played a part. In proposing and then defending memetics as an approach to culture, Dawkins (intentionally or not) seems to have distanced his approach from the mainstream study of cultural evolution that was gaining steam through the late 1970s to 1990s. Memetics was first a rival to cultural evolution approaches (although memetics always had more popular than scholarly adherents), but over time it kind of just gradually got either abandoned or absorbed into mainstream cultural evolution.[26] Memetics pinned itself to some hard assumptions (particulate inheritance of cultural information; neutrality to host fitness) that didn't really empirically hold.[27] Memetics ultimately faded because it didn't bear scientific fruit. Given Dawkins's outsized influence in the New Atheist world, this might have led other New Atheist–aligned thinkers to overlook good cultural evolution work in favor of memetics, a scientific bet that paid increasingly poor dividends over the years.

Admittedly, this is all supposition on my part, but it does sort of fit. We have a theoretical approach to religion that became popular just as the New Atheists were gaining momentum. This theoretical approach has a vision of religion as nonfunctional and nonadaptive, an accident of evolution. The vision of atheism for this theory is one of effortful cognitive work, with some select few folks able to rationally outgrow their childish religious impulses. The New Atheist appeal seems pretty straightforward: in the by-product account, religion isn't special, but atheists sure are!

Viewing religion as nonadaptive, atheism as a product of superior thinking, and culture as fundamentally memetic, New Atheists were perhaps culturally predisposed to favor the by-product view to one like the dual inheritance approach developed in this book. After all, the dual inheritance theory views many religious features as at least culturally adaptive (Big Gods, CREDs, and the like), and atheism largely resulting from mundane forces other than superior thinking.

Although the by-product account's vision of religion and atheism might be well-suited to the sensibilities of New Atheists a couple decades ago, I think the visions of faith and atheism presented by the dual inheritance approach is one that modern atheists can identify with and embrace. At least for me, moving from the New Atheism's stark view of atheism's rational supremacy over religious irrationality to one that asks better scientific questions about religion and atheism—and then, crucially, listens to the empirical answers the world provides—has only deepened my appreciation for both atheism and religion. Let's consider that view next.

Dual Inheritance: The Cultural Naturalness of Atheism and the Contingent Fragility of Religions

The by-product account describes religious belief as a sort of default for our species and atheism as a rare aberration that takes superior thinking and cultural work. The dual inheritance account inverts this vision.

Under the dual inheritance theory, religious belief doesn't just emerge on its own, as a content bias in the parlance of cultural evolution. Instead, any specific religious beliefs—belief in Yahweh rather than Zeus, or Mithras instead of no gods at all—only emerge and persist over time to the extent that they are backed by the right cultural context. Conformist learning, prestige-biased learning, and credibility-enhancing displays attesting to the sincerity of faith held by cultural models all combine to produce specific religious beliefs in learners. Without this consistent cultural support for any one god (or pantheon, for the polytheistic among us), belief in any one god is unlikely. Religious beliefs don't just emerge on their own, because they're such good fits for our evolved minds; instead, belief in any specific god takes consistent cultural nurturing.

What does this mean for atheism? If specific religious beliefs take specific cultural support, does this imply that atheism takes special cultural work too? I don't think so. Atheism is the natural result, in the absence of the specific conditions required for faith. Atheism is not something that requires special cultural scaffolding, or special cognitive resources; it's just what happens when there isn't consistent cultural support for any specific religious belief.[†] Atheism is the basin to which we fall, unless consistent CREDs push us upward to a specific faith.

Under the cognitive by-product account, atheism happens rarely, under narrowly circumscribed circumstances. Under the dual inheritance framework, the pathways to atheism are far wider and more passable. If we want to push things even further, we might say that whereas under the by-product framework belief is a cognitive default, in the dual inheritance framework atheism is the baseline stance until the conditions for a specific religious belief arise. Each and every specific religious faith—Catholicism, or Mithraism, or worship of Zeus, Odin, Papa Gede, Lord Xenu, or any other gods—is a fragile thing, requiring cultural cultivation and nourishment. In contrast, atheism naturally results whenever the cultural conditions aren't especially conducive to any particular faith.

Atheism can additionally arise through other cognitive pathways—through individual differences in mentalizing or reflective cognitive style, for example—but analytic atheism and mindblind atheism are smaller tributaries in the watershed of global atheism, whereas inCREDulous atheism (often triggered by a previous generation's apatheism and the private belief of a religiously complacent society) is the surging Amazon or Nile. InCREDulous atheism isn't a pathway defined by any special cognitive or cultural resource; it doesn't require effort, or indoctrination. It's merely an absence—an absence of the specific cultural practices that sustain specific religious faiths.

So is faith the default, or atheism? Before offering a hesitant answer, a necessary caveat: I'm a bit wary to speak of default or baseline states when it comes to religious belief. Some cognitive scientists of religion have written of belief as a "cognitive default" and that verbiage has always struck me as inappropriately strong, given what we know of minds, cultures, and their interactions. There are psychological proclivities that have been assumed to be core aspects of human nature (assumed by Western psychologists studying Western participants, that is) that turn out to be ephemeral psychological patterns that don't generalize widely across cultures.[28] Things that might

[†] Could atheistic CREDs culturally push people toward atheism? Absolutely. Indeed, merely being an open atheist is itself a CRED in large parts of the world where religion is normatively enforced. But atheism *doesn't require* specific atheist CREDs.

appear as "cognitive defaults" when studying one population might look like rare aberrations or even maladaptations in other contexts. The empirical track record of cross-cultural cognitive defaults is mixed at best. Where we find human universals, they tend to be in basic mechanisms, rather than in complex psychological and cultural artifacts like religion.

Throat clearing aside, is faith or atheism the default? Neither, or both. It really comes down to context. Throughout most of human history, being surrounded by kin and clan-mates practicing a consistent religious faith was pretty much something one could expect. Most members of our species could count on seeing consistent religious CREDs favoring one god or another. In a context like this, belief in the local deity would be the natural outcome, and atheism quite odd. Does this mean that belief is the "default" because being surrounded by co-believers is a "default" human environment? Perhaps. Or would we choose to define the "default" as what would happen if someone were raised apart from others? If that's the bar, then I think atheism would be the likely outcome.

Our best developmental psychology work shows kids to not be "born believers," but rather sort of innately suspicious and skeptical about things; they're savvy information consumers. They want to know which adults are good sources of information about what. As we saw in an early chapter, kids aren't widely gullible and credulous. When it comes to religion specifically, they aren't quite sure whether religious beliefs are more like facts or like opinions. Recall our discussion of work on intuitive creationism,[‡] where the youngest kids give nonsystematic responses, even though their surrounding culture is absent of evolutionary instruction and chock full of religion. If there's a religious default belief here, we certainly haven't found it.

Specific religious beliefs take some cultural work. It needn't be the type of heavy-handed indoctrination that Barrett (rightly) dismisses as the indoctrination thesis, or that New Atheists condemn as abusive. But, indoctrination aside, specific religious faiths are learned, and are learned against the apparent grain of childhood skepticism and curiosity. Developmental psychologists Konika Banerjee and Paul Bloom penned an interesting short piece called "Would Tarzan Believe in God? Conditions for the Emergence of Religious Belief" and imagined whether religious beliefs would likely emerge in a child raised apart from other people.[29] Their conclusion?

[‡] Chapter 4.

"Drawing on evidence from developmental psychology, we argue here that the answer is no: children lack spontaneous theistic views and the emergence of religion is crucially dependent on culture."The default position—if indeed it makes sense to talk about defaults at all—seems far more likely to be atheism rather than belief.

ATHEISM COMES EASILY, AND NATURALLY

When I first started studying atheism, I was convinced that I'd be able to find some special cognitive proclivity or ability that set us atheists apart from the overwhelmingly faithful masses. The view that there was a key ingredient, some magic bullet, that made atheists special didn't just fit my early New Atheist leanings, it also fit with what the cognitive by-product theory prevalent at the time had explicitly predicted. Whereas religion is natural and all but inevitable, atheism is comparatively unnatural and must therefore arise only in unique circumstances, or with the help of special cognitive effort among special individuals.

Over about a decade, I saw my own research efforts to find evidence of atheism's special cognitive origins frustrated. Rational cognitive style looked to be a bit player, rather than a starring cast member, in the global production of atheism. In contrast, study after study after study consistently pointed toward fewer religious CREDs as the most likely source of atheism worldwide—an almost boringly consistent result.

Following the evidence, my views shifted. My early infatuation with the by-product account cooled, as my research inspired by it failed to really take off. My interest in cultural evolution led to lots of the speculation we met back in the Zeus Problem chapter. Larger-scale projects to test the theory-derived predictors of atheism consistently pointed in the direction of cultural context being crucial. In short, as the evidence rolled in, something like the dual inheritance approach looked more and more necessary. I, and other like-minded researchers, have been fine-tuning the dual inheritance theory for about a decade now, and it's proven quite productive. As the previous dozen or so chapters show, it's a theory that can explain important things about both religion (why people believe in some gods rather than others, why some religions persist) and atheism (the pathways to and prevalence of atheism, how secular societies stabilize).

Although I started out thinking that atheists like me were somehow special, I've now come around to viewing atheism as rather mundane. It arises naturally and easily, in cultural contexts comparatively devoid of consistent religious CREDs. This accords well with my own introspection about my atheism. I had an epiphany that I was an atheist in a university philosophy class discussion board, but it wasn't like learning about logic and philosophy led me to atheism. They just revealed my long-present, but hitherto unacknowledged, atheism, which was largely the result of me having grown up in a cultural context where religion—while apparent and present—just wasn't a big deal. I was aware of Christianity (my area's overwhelming majority faith), but aside from a few unsuccessful attempts at Sunday School, I didn't really see it or practice it. My upbringing was the religious complacency we met last chapter, writ small. As a predictable result, my own atheism came easily and naturally. Reason and debate didn't produce my atheism, they merely revealed and crystalized it, and made me realize that I'd probably been an atheist for quite some time.

WHEN ATHEISM ISN'T EASY

I suspect this "atheism comes easily" insight comes as little surprise to many or most atheist readers, but is one that some readers will vehemently disagree with. When I talk to atheist groups, it is apparent that lots of atheists out there attribute their own atheism to a rational struggle against their religious indoctrination. What of the atheists who came to doubt later in life, not because of their upbringing but despite it? Has my argument in this chapter just missed the mark?

I think a few points are worth keeping in mind. First, the dual inheritance account developed in part to explain large-scale aggregate patterns in atheism. Aggregate explanations are often unsatisfying for lots of individuals. I can confidently state that most atheism worldwide results not from feats of cognitive effort and rationality, but from the far more banal lack of religious CREDs. In explaining the potentially billions of atheists around the world, the dual inheritance model works well. But it mightn't feel compelling to lots of people who became atheists despite a strong religious upbringing. If you're one of those atheists, my apologies that the aggregate theory we've developed over the years doesn't seem to explain your own idiosyncratic path to atheism. That's, unfortunately, how aggregate explanations often work.

Here, it may be worth remembering the pattern we discussed back in chapter 3, where we looked at the interaction between religious CREDs and rational cognitive reflection. Among people raised in strongly religious contexts, there was precisely no relation between rational cognitive style and disbelief. None. Lots of atheists from religious backgrounds probably feel like their superior analytic prowess was key to their atheism. But I'll bet that a lot of highly analytic *theists* who had strongly religious upbringings attribute their *religious faith* to rationality as well. Highly analytic people probably feel like lots of their beliefs are the product of rationality—this is precisely the sort of attribution that highly analytic people are likely to make, for a wide range of beliefs.

Just as there are undoubtedly lots of highly rational and analytic theists out there, we also know with some certainty that there are lots of atheists out there who aren't highly rational and analytic. Even in studies where we do find a small advantage on rational thinking tasks for atheists, the results aren't especially impressive. In the cognitive reflection test results, for example, atheists do score a bit higher on these questions, which require grade school mathematics to solve. But far from acing the test, the atheists' average performance is right around 50 percent. That's sobering, isn't it? Even our clever atheists are pretty bad at questions that just require a little bit of reflection and childhood-caliber mathematics.

Most atheists aren't hyper-rational. People raised with strong religious upbringings who are also highly rational show no systemic trend toward atheism. Rationality is compatible with the entire spectrum of religious belief and disbelief—as is irrationality. But for atheists who've left religion, rationality makes a compelling narrative, even though its underlying evidence isn't strong.

Is this a satisfying answer for the atheists out there who attribute their atheism to their rationality? I doubt it, to be perfectly honest. But it's the best I can come up with as a scientist, at least for now, by following the empirical evidence.

In the coming years, I'm hoping to devote a lot more research time trying to directly understand the processes that lead some people (but not most) in highly religious contexts to atheism. This isn't the most common path people take to atheism, as revealed by our work over the years, but it is hugely important to study.

To close this side discussion, I hope that atheist readers who don't feel they came from lower-CRED environments can at least step back, zoom out, and see how the broad sweep of the religious landscape looks different today, under the dual inheritance theory, than it did fifteen years ago, under the by-product theory. Atheism is no longer an improbable aberration that needed some special explanation. Instead, atheism is every bit as natural and easy to come by as any specific religious faith, under the right conditions—and under conditions that are increasingly common in the world today. Atheism looks easier and more natural than it used to, a sentiment that I hope most atheists (and believers) can appreciate on some level. Personally, I've quite enjoyed shifting my perspective from viewing atheism as "special" to viewing it as rather ordinary and commonplace.

We've now come to the end of our section on the Puzzle of Faith, appropriately enough concluding that atheism is perfectly natural, and even likely in many contexts. It is my hope that considering the by-product and dual inheritance theories alongside each other helped consolidate a lot of the ideas we've been working with, to better appreciate how the study of atheism has spurred theory development in this space, and how shifting theories have fundamentally changed our vision of atheism.

Next, let's have some fun and try to predict the future of faith and atheism.

INTERLUDE

A Gods'-Eye View

Now that we have a theory that answers both the Puzzle of Faith and the Puzzle of Atheism, we can zoom out and ask some really big questions:

- What is the future of faith and atheism? Will religions disappear? Or will they continue to flourish?
- What does our solution to the Puzzles of Faith and Atheism tell us about human nature?

CHAPTER FOURTEEN

THE FUTURE OF FAITH AND ATHEISM

[Religion] is crumbling by itself, and its fall can only be made more rapid.
—FREDERICK THE GREAT, LETTER TO VOLTAIRE, 1767

There is not a young man now living in the United States
who will not die a Unitarian.
—THOMAS JEFFERSON, 1822

[By] the 21st century, religious believers are likely to be found
in small sects, huddled together to resist a worldwide secular culture.
—PETER BERGER, 1968

Marx, Weber, Durkheim, Freud, Jefferson, Voltaire. For centuries, a steady stream of heavyweight intellectuals predicted the imminent demise of religion.[1]

Keen cultural observers may note that, in the third decade of the twenty-first century, religion persists.

What gave these learned men such confidence that religion was on its last legs? And can we—armed as we are with a shiny new theory of religious belief and disbelief—offer a more plausible prediction about faith and atheism? This is among the shortest chapters in the book. It is short because instead of recounting facts and findings, theories and models, I'll be making guesses. Guesses based on facts I don't definitively know, domains of inquiry where I have little formal expertise. Predicting the future is tricky business, so at least I'll keep my prognostication brief.

RELIGION'S NEVER-ACTUALIZED IMMINENT DEMISE

Like Jesus's imminent return, forecast numerous times over the centuries, religion's imminent demise hasn't happened yet.

Thinkers predicting that religion would soon collapse tended to share the view that modernity, prosperity, education, and the onward march of science would prove incompatible with widespread religious faith. They'd seen, within their respective decades and centuries, great advances in the material conditions in which people in their social circles lived. These thinkers were animated by new technologies, intermingling cultures, advances in science, and a general optimism that further progress was just around the bend.

These thinkers had witnessed such progress, and had also witnessed a reduction in signs of overt religiosity, at least in their well-heeled circles. They'd simply connected the dots between these trends. Correlation, meet causation. Material and technological progress was viewed as undermining support for religion. As science advances, mustn't religion decline? Wouldn't superstition be replaced by a solid mechanistic understanding of our cosmos?

Over the decades, and then over the centuries, modernization marched on. First the industrial revolution, and then the capture of new fuels to power its steadily improving machines, brought tremendous prosperity to some pockets of the globe. In these same pockets, religion lost much of its influence. Our scientific understanding of the world improved, step by steady incremental step.

As technology, wealth, and progress marched on, the world did see some dips in religiosity, but unevenly so. Many countries, as we saw two chapters ago, became quite nonreligious. But the predicted global collapse of religion simply never materialized. Why not?

The primary issue with all the failed predictions of religious collapse is that they started with faulty assumptions about how religion actually works.

Thinkers who viewed science's progress as a needed incursion into the domains traditionally held by religion presupposed a deeper incompatibility between science and rationality on one hand, and faith on the other, than is warranted. This same perceived incompatibility underlies some prominent New Atheist rhetoric even today. Consider the popular books of Dawkins, which view religion as a primitive way of thinking that can be culturally outgrown through engagement with rationality and science.[2] Recall our third chapter though: the rational atheism thesis has repeatedly failed to deliver the scientific goods. Regarding some fundamental incompatibility between scientific and religious thinking, this too is an artifact of selective attention rather than a general psychological pattern.[3] Recent research by Jonathan McPhetres, Jonathan Jong, and Miron Zuckerman finds that although religious participants from the United States show resistance to science, this pattern doesn't generalize to most other countries.[4] Far from being deeply incompatible, religion/science conflicts in the United States are usually driven by particular political battles that have stoked strategic debate, to capture ideologically aligned voters. As these authors summarize their results, "Our findings are inconsistent with the idea that science and religion are necessarily at odds, undermining common theories of scientific advancement undermining religion." When politicians lament conflicts between secular science and religion, they do so because it is politically expedient, not because there is any general psychological incompatibility between the two. Most folks have little trouble endorsing both science and religion simultaneously.[5]

Starting with the wrong theory of religion, unsurprisingly, produces poor predictions about religion's future. Rationality, science, and modernity haven't undermined faith, simply because that's not how faith has ever worked. Can a better theory make better predictions?

Armed with a (hopefully) solid theory of religion, one that answers both the Puzzle of Faith and the Puzzle of Atheism, I'd like to try something that history suggests is foolish. I'd like to stake my own prediction about the future of faith and atheism.

We can build a prediction by extrapolating from what we learned two chapters back about how societies secularize. To recap: First, material changes bring increased existential security to citizens, which in turn breeds religious complacency.[6] Second, religious complacency deprives learners of the religious CREDs that produce belief.[7] Within a couple brief cultural generations, near-universal religious belief can collapse to quite low levels. Computer simulations show how just small tweaks in CREDs act as a dial that tunes belief up or down within a society. Observational data across Europe matches this general pattern quite well.[8] Security breeds complacency, disbelief soon follows. Waves of secularity occur, with public religiosity falling before private belief. This pattern occurs again and again across Western Europe, the most heavily secularized countries on earth.

But religion remains strong in much of the rest of the world. In order to forecast religion's future, we need to consider in more detail why secularism has taken root where it has, and the material conditions separating secularizing countries from those that remain steadfast in their faith.

SECULARISM: WHERE AND WHY?

Secularism throughout the twentieth century followed a fairly predictable pattern. It occurred in most of the wealthiest countries on the planet. Western Europe, populated as it is with former colonial powers that had amassed incredible wealth over the centuries, was well poised for the material shifts that are the first domino to fall in the cascade of secularism outlined in chapter 12.

Where did these societies obtain the wealth that fueled their secular shifts? To a first approximation, the wealth of the West (and the Global North, by extension today) was extracted from the rest of the globe to Western benefit and everyone else's loss. First were direct colonial spoils, land and resources and human beings forcibly taken from well-populated lands through either violence or threat of violence, with lingering effects today. Consider Haiti, currently among the most impoverished countries on earth, and the poorest in the Western hemisphere. For more than a century, Haiti's colonizer, France, demanded direct payment, as reimbursement for the human "property" it lost when enslaved Haitians revolted and gained independence. A century of Haitian wealth, diverted to help maintain France's high standards of living, the precisely invoiced price of freedom. Although former colonial powers have largely packed up their outposts in the face of independence movements, they kept their accumulated colonial riches, and often left behind mechanisms to maintain flows of wealth and advantage. France is not exceptional in this regard, especially if one considers less overtly formalized patterns of upward wealth transfer and exploitation in the world today.

Widespread adoption of fossil fuels throughout the nineteenth and twentieth centuries only exacerbated these global inequities. In transferring carbon from the ground to the atmosphere, and wealth from Global South to Global North, people created pockets of immense wealth, which not coincidentally became pockets of secular stability.[9] But these pockets did not lead to truly global improvements in everyday living conditions.

The countries that took the wealth had the wherewithal to build institutions conducive to secularization, and thus secularized. The countries whose wealth had been stolen? Not so much. A map of religion and secularism today is largely a map of colonial and neocolonial wealth transfer, of exploitation.

Coming to terms with that fact helps us to understand one key reason that predictions of a global religious collapse never bore fruit. There has never been a sustained effort to globally and equitably increase the existential security of humanity—wealth extraction and inequity ruled instead.

In pinning secularism to a hypothesized direct link between scientific progress and religious decline, religious collapse prognosticators got the details wrong. As rapidly secularizing countries redoubled their wealth extraction efforts and subsequent hoarding, they undermined any chance of a global religious collapse, as wealth extraction came at the expense of equitable global human development.

If we want to make solid predictions about the future of religion and atheism over the next couple of centuries, we first need to recognize that secularism doesn't stem from the scientific and technological advances developed by people with opportunities afforded to few; secularism stems from the living conditions of the many.

By the by, here lies a tremendous irony in the New Atheist project of the early 2000s. They sought to undermine religion by arguing against it, by advocating on behalf of science. Wrong diagnosis of religion, leading to an ineffectual "cure" for it. Using science as a wedge against religion probably did more to pry believers away from science than to undermine religion. Had they put their influence behind efforts to ameliorate global poverty, to produce equitable human development worldwide, they may have put a more measurable dent in global religious faith than that produced by all their books, debates, podcasts, and social media proclamations. And if their efforts didn't directly undermine religion, at least they would've helped people along the way.

I digress. What, then, can we expect from religion and atheism in the coming decades and centuries?

DUAL INHERITANCE (DIS)BELIEF AND THE FUTURE OF FAITH AND ATHEISM

Understanding current patterns in global secularism requires an appreciation of two broad factors: flows of wealth, and everyday living conditions. The two are intimately intertwined. If we want to predict where atheism will flourish in a century's time, we need to understand where public religiosity will remain strong some decades prior to that. And if we want to predict where public faith will remain resilient in eight or nine decades, we need to project wealth and global conditions—two projections that I need to note I'm not especially well-qualified to make. Nonetheless, I can see two likely outcomes.

Outcome 1: Global Chaos and Instability, Widespread Faith, Enclaves of Affluent Atheism

My first prediction. Caution: it gets dark.

Over the past century, wealth has been tremendously condensed, to the point that much of global wealth is held by a small number of people, corporations, and countries. One key to unlocking this wealth has been an unprecedented shift of carbon from the earth to the atmosphere. Fossil fuels, keys to global prosperity for a time, have brought us to the brink of climate collapse.

As the warnings our climate sends us become increasingly dire, these warnings go largely unnoticed by those with the power to respond to them. A few headlines, from recent years in which we're stumbling over climate tipping point after climate tipping point: "Texas Paid Bitcoin Miner More Than $31 Million to Cut Energy Usage during Heat Wave," describing how cryptocurrency schemers were so depleting local power grids during Texas heatwaves that the state paid individuals vast sums of money to merely temporarily stop pumping carbon into the atmosphere to fund their enterprises, so that people could have refrigeration and air conditioning to survive the heat. "Thirsty Data Centers Are Making Hot Summers Even Scarier," describing how the vast computer banks needed to run tech billionaires' AI startups are depleting water supplies in already drought-ridden communities in which they operate. These are the headlines of a society deeply and fundamentally unprepared to reap what it's sown.

Although the wealth made possible by fossil fuels tends to be concentrated in the wealthiest countries of the Global North, the dire consequences of climate change will be disproportionately felt in the Global South.[10] In the words of Olúfẹ́mi O. Táíwò, "As climate impacts accelerate, we can expect them to perversely distribute the costs and burdens of climate change, disproportionately impacting those who have been rendered most vulnerable given the accumulated weight of history. . . . The people who will be most protected tend to be whites in the Global North, and those least protected tend to be Black and Indigenous peoples in the Global South."[11] The true pain that overconsumption of fossil fuels causes will be least felt by those who benefitted most from it, while the juice was freely flowing. This is among the sickest ironies imaginable, the *coup de merde* on several centuries of injustice.

As global climate conditions worsen, large chunks of the planet will teeter toward—and then beyond—inhabitability. Fires, floods, ever-worsening tropical storms. Food scarcity, crop failures, drought, desertification, ocean acidification, rising ocean levels. Cities that have been home to humans for millennia will become unlivable. We are approaching a century of unprecedented human misery and displacement, what author Gaia Vince terms the Nomad Century in a book of the same name.[12] Picture here Bangladesh's population of over 100 million, scrambling to find purchase as nearly 20 percent of the country's land is submerged over the next couple decades, and you'll start to realize the scale of destabilization and forced migration that's already underway.[13]

Shit's going to get very bad, very rapidly, for most humans on the planet. But I expect it will continue to be fine for stable and wealthy enclaves, at least for a while. Pockets of the Global North will remain prosperous, for as long as possible. As the rise of far-right ethnonationalist movements throughout Europe and North America attest, there will be populist political opposition to immigration—to letting in those people displaced by centuries of exploitation. Wealthy countries will double down, focusing on keeping what's (currently) theirs. In these countries, ideological capture of major institutions, on behalf of wealth and capital, will render effective mitigation of climate disaster impossible.[14] For those of us lucky enough to be housed in areas of close proximity to global wealth, we can expect a degree of stability and security. And in these bubbles, I predict that we'll see a continuation of decades-old trends toward secularism. In enclaves of security, protected by inequitably hoarded societal wealth, atheism will do just fine.

Outside these enclaves? In an increasingly unstable and unlivable world? Religion will positively thrive. Let down by secular institutions and forced into an increasingly precarious existence, most people on earth will find much appeal in their religions. Most people on earth will remain as religious as ever. If there is any change, it may be toward increasing religious fervor, commensurate with the increasing instability of everyday living.

So, one path forward is basically the world we see now, only more so. Pockets of stable secularism, continuing its decades-long trajectory in wealthy and secure countries that gained an early leg up through colonialism and exploitation. The rest of the globe? Increasingly unstable and precarious; correspondingly, increasingly turning toward religion for salvation where secular governance has globally failed to prevent catastrophe.

As humans, we've utterly failed to look out for one another, to produce the kinds of stable and equitable living conditions that breed stability, that phase religion out of society over time. We've praised technology and progress, projecting that they'd undermine religion while they've instead continually produced the very conditions in which faith thrives.

Outcome 2: By Luck, Climate Reprieve—and a Future Still Unwritten

That first prediction is glum, but relatively specific. This one will be vague, but much more hopeful.

It is hard not to despair about the future of our planet. I do not have a clue what the solutions may be—what they would even look like. They may be technological, although I don't know what magnitude of technological shift could give the help we need, as quickly as it's needed. Technology over the past century hasn't generally trended toward less consumption; more often it allies with capital rather than sustainability. That said, trends in wind and solar power are hopeful. Will they come fast enough to avert the worst?

The more radical shifts that could bring reprieve may be social rather than technological. Certainly, social shifts will play a part. Individual choices add up, especially if they are directed at those powerful enough to force the required policy changes.

On both technological and social fronts, I know what won't bring the solution: hopelessness.

So, what cause is there for hope? Most of the time, I'm an optimistic guy. Not always with reason, but I prefer it to the alternative.

Our species has shown a remarkable knack for problem solving over the millennia. And the key to our remarkable collective intelligence, our adaptability, lies in our capacity for cumulative culture.[15] We learn together, innovate together, live or die together.[16]

As we learn about culture, we've learned about the conditions in which innovation is most likely. We can culturally evolve solutions to complex problems when we allow different ideas to mingle. Diversity drives innovation.[17] This is a recurring theme that emerges from lots of different literatures, all trained on understanding innovation and collective wisdom. Solving collective problems means harnessing collective intelligence; it involves bringing people together to share their different views.[18]

We stand a more reasonable chance of collectively surviving the consequences of our actions over the last century if we can put aside differences and work together. Innovation doesn't come from sole geniuses working in well-funded isolation—no matter what well-funded and self-appointed geniuses say. It comes from the serendipitous intermingling of ideas, in the synergies produced by them. We'll greatly increase our chances of stumbling across technological and social solutions to climate catastrophe if we broaden the pool of problem solvers, as much as possible.

Because we need all hands on deck, a huge priority needs to be expanding the size and accessibility of that deck. We need to rapidly remove global barriers to participation in science. We need to hugely diversify our talent pools. We simply cannot afford to project an image of science as closed to religious believers. We cannot afford to keep science expensive and inaccessible to most.

Each young person on earth today may play a crucial role in averting collapse. Nobody—not a government official, not some tech-startup billionaire, not a preacher or teacher or science proselytizer—knows who may have the idea that spurs us collectively toward a much-needed solution. If each mind working toward our future is a ticket in a lottery, with the jackpot being global livability, then we really need to be buying as many tickets as possible. Broadening educational opportunity, leveling inequities, promoting the intermingling of people from more diverse backgrounds—especially those backgrounds historically excluded from the game of science—this is our best chance at finding much-needed solutions. In *The Panda's Thumb*, Steven Jay Gould wrote, "I am, somehow, less interested in the weight and convolutions of Einstein's brain than in the near certainty that people of equal talent have lived and died in cotton fields and sweatshops."[19] This is fundamentally the right approach to intellect and innovation, not focusing on individual successes so much as on maximizing their probability of discovery across entire populations of humans. It is our task now to make sure that every potential Albert Einstein or Marie Curie has a chance to contribute, to help save us from the worst.

Assuming, by serendipitous chance, that we are able to avert the worst that climate collapse promises to offer, the future of faith and atheism remains uncertain. Humanity may, with some new technological doodad or geegaw, fix our climate, but in doing so engage in little reflection on how we've chosen inequitable systems of wealth and power. We'll dodge the worst the climate may throw at us, without any fundamental rethinking of the human patterns that got us in this mess to begin with. If we make that choice, expect religion to still be globally dominant, much as it is today. This outcome is simply a less violently awful version of my first prediction. Don't get me wrong—I greatly prefer this version, due to its drastically lower levels of overall suffering. We might still have penguins and polar bears on the other side, and avert billions of human deaths and displacements.

But a true shift toward global secularism will only come with globally equitable allocation of safety, stability, and security. One would hope that narrowly averting climate-induced societal collapse would spur the type of collective introspection that might lead to an equitable future. But only time will tell. Assuming, that is, we make choices in the coming years to open a future where even mildly good outcomes remain globally possible.

MY VERDICT

Will religion fade away, as learned men over the centuries have predicted? Almost certainly not. Our species simply hasn't put in the work to create the type of world where religion fades. Instead, we've chosen to have pockets of unimaginable wealth (which correspondingly secularize) set against a backdrop of global insecurity, and thus faith.

I hope for the final world described above: one in which the worst disaster is somehow averted through collectively intelligent action and innovation, one in which we celebrate overcoming our close call by fundamentally reworking our world. I'm not optimistic that this outcome is probable, but I'm confident that striving to make it happen is worthwhile. Without collective striving? My first prediction seems inevitable.

Religion will never fade from humanity—it's simply too ingrained a part of human nature to disappear entirely. But, as we saw in the previous chapter, atheism can come quite easily. The futures of faith and atheism remain very much unwritten, awaiting societal choices made in the next handful of years.

CHAPTER FIFTEEN

CODA

Though sympathy can't alter facts, it can make them more bearable.
—MINA MURRAY, BRAM STOKER'S *DRACULA*

Curiosity is the hope that something wondrous waits just out of sight, for we are surrounded by a garden of miracles.
—MARJORIE LIU AND SANA TAKEDA, *MONSTRESS: INFERNO*

I write these words in a pew at St. Bartholomew the Great, in central London. London houses many wonderful churches, but this one is perhaps my favorite. St. Paul's majestic dome caps a cathedral large enough to be seen from much of the city. Westminster Abbey hosts coronations and royal weddings and entombs geniuses of history from Newton to Darwin. But St. Bart's holds an aura of less ostentatious solemnity that I find endearing. Although an atheist, I appreciate and enjoy churches, especially those with a character of antiquity like St. Bart's exudes.

One enters St. Bart's through a pleasant churchyard, off the main streets of London's busy downtown. Less than a mile from the Barbican, the brutalist monstrosity that incongruously also houses much of London's aspiring artistic genius, St. Bart's is near the former printing quarter, where Benjamin Franklin lived and worked for a spell while learning the trade.

The church itself is relatively plain from the outside, with a surprisingly elegant and spacious interior. The main chapel features a humble tile floor, interspersed with old headstones used as pavers. The lighting is natural, with sunlight today entering through the third story windows of the main hall. Pews face not toward a dais at the front, as one may perhaps be accustomed to, but toward a central aisle. Instead of the gilded golden pillars or statuary that other fine chapels hold, the stonework is plain, almost rustic in its beauty. High above, the ceiling is sturdy wood. Well decorated, well made, but not gaudy or fancy. The air is heady to breathe, tinged with incense. One can imagine the centuries of smoke that billowed through this hall, the countless people who breathed it in, seeking commune with their God and their fellow churchgoers. In here, it is majestic, tranquil, awesome, and peaceful. It feels timeless, remote from the modern bustle just outside, preserved rather than overridden by centuries of development.

St. Bartholomew's was founded in 1123. At that time, London's population was about fifteen thousand. Today, the London metropolitan area homes nearly ten million. A lot has changed, on St. Bart's watch.

Its location just a few short blocks from a former site of executions no doubt brought conflicting and complex thoughts through the door in centuries past. William Wallace, the Scottish firebrand depicted in *Braveheart*, was executed just down the street, and a monument plaque is frequently decorated with thistles and Scottish flags. Movie-depicted scenes like Wallace's execution pervade St. Bart's history, but now it occasionally features in movies itself. This marvelous church has graced the screen on several occasions—notably it was the scene of the fourth wedding in *Four Weddings and a Funeral* and marked a scene in *Avengers: Age of Ultron*. As I sit here today though, film crews and superheroes are tough to fathom. In this church, it could be 2023, or 1423. It's timeless.

This church survived the Great Fire of London in 1666. It survived the black death, although many of its then-parishioners surely didn't. It survived the Blitz in World War II, largely unscathed by the bombs that leveled much of the rest of the city. As England, and London in particular, rapidly secularized in the postwar period, St. Bart's kept calm and carried on.

Nowadays, the church isn't visited by post-execution revelers and mourners, but by an interesting mix of people. There are believers, come for service or prayer. There are sightseers, like me, who come inspired less by faith than by a more secular reverence. We come to soak in the aura of this place, to admire the craftsmanship of its construction and the artistry of its decoration. To breathe in its history.

The city has changed. The church has changed. The people have changed. But the faith animating the original construction of this church persists. Religion changes, but it carries on. I suspect these two things will always be true.

In these pages we've seen how religions persist. We've seen how religions—much like St. Bart's itself—change, and how some religions even thrive, and, by doing so, change our world. Most interestingly we've seen how, through all of these changes that religion has helped wrought, atheism has emerged.

OUR JOURNEY

At the outset, I posed two puzzles that I'd hoped the book could answer. First was the Puzzle of Faith, how our species alone became a religious one. And second was the Puzzle of Atheism, how nonbelievers can exist within our religious species.

As we saw in chapter 13, the dual inheritance approach this book developed to simultaneously answer both puzzles suggests a fundamentally different vision of atheism than that portrayed by prior generations of theories, and thus also a different vision of religion itself. It is a vision in which atheism emerges naturally, in cultural conditions that are increasingly common in many parts of the world; in which specific religions—far from emerging with little cultural prodding—are somewhat fragile cultural constructions that require maintenance and sustenance from adherents. And it is the human capacity for culture—the secret of our species' tremendous success—that enables us to be simultaneously a religious species and a species in which self-conscious and reflective atheists emerge, cognizant of beliefs about gods without partaking in them. The Puzzles of Faith and Atheism, with a single shared solution in our species' evolution as a cultural species.

THERE BUT FOR THE GRACE OF CULTURE GO YOU

In the sixteenth century, John Bradford supposedly saw a group of prisoners being led to execution and uttered, "There but for the grace of God, John Bradford." His utterance hearkens back to scripture: 1 Corinthians 15:8–10 reads, "But by the grace of God I am what I am," a reminder that much of our own existence is highly contingent. Bradford and the writer of Corinthians viewed their circumstances as contingent on God, but this book urges readers to view their own circumstances as highly contingent on millennia of cultural evolution interacting with nervous systems that are themselves the product of millions of years of genetic evolution, combining to produce the religious landscape we see in the world today, and our own place within it. The dual inheritance approach developed in these pages, to me, recommends a scientifically backed humility in how we deal with those of religious beliefs different from our own.

Religious readers—the dual inheritance approach recommends humility. To a reader in suburban Des Moines, Iowa, who is an Evangelical Christian arguing online with a Hindu in Delhi or an atheist in Denmark, I say: there but for the grace of culture go you. Very few people in the world have their own specific religious beliefs because they sampled the full global marketplace of religious ideas and then intentionally chose their current faith. It's far more likely that they adopted the faith modeled by their parents and neighbors. When interacting with people from other faiths—or no faith—this is an important reminder of humility and contingency: if your upbringings were swapped, it's likely that you'd be on the opposite side of the debate, and just as certain that you are (still) correct.

Atheist readers—the dual inheritance approach recommends humility. I've been scientifically studying atheism for a decade and a half now. I've run dozens of scientific studies trying to figure out what makes atheism tick. And across pretty much every study we've run, the conclusion has been the same: cultural learning is a better predictor of atheism than is rational sophistication, science knowledge, or any other cognitive proclivity we've tried. Cultural exposure's also the single best predictor of who ends up belonging to any specific religious tradition. As tempting as it is to view one's own atheism as a product of rigorous freethought, or brave skepticism, keep in mind that across the world most people have the religious beliefs or disbeliefs they have largely because they live in a cultural milieu conducive to those beliefs or disbeliefs. Hearkening back to chapter 3, the Rational Atheist is largely a myth! Atheists who find themselves interacting with or debating against a strongly religious individual, I urge you to remember: there but for the grace of culture go you. According to our best science, if you and your opponent swapped upbringings, you'd probably hold more or less their beliefs, and they yours. This should inject a healthy dose of humility into any debate between you and a believer, especially if you're tempted to mock their culturally inherited beliefs as products of feeble-mindedness or irrationality. If you're an atheist and you're happy about being atheist, that's great! I love it when people are at home in their own skin. But be very wary of feeling superior to others because your cultural inheritance differs from theirs.

Humans have, in all likelihood, always been religious. We've evolved minds that can easily entertain the existence of gods, of angels, of djinn, of spirits. Supernatural agents help satiate our explanatory needs, anchoring our perhaps intuitive sense that things in the world are as they are for some reason.

The gods imagined by humans are as diverse and varied as humans themselves. Gods all seem to have their moral concerns, over what people ought to be doing or avoiding. But the scale of gods' moral purview varies widely. Some gods care deeply about how things are done, but just in their localized corner of the world. Other gods can be truly universal, monitoring human thought and action everywhere and always, policing generalized moral dictates.

The religions birthed around different gods also appreciably differ. Some include ornate pageantry, extravagant displays in which people prove their faith in potentially costly ways. Martyrdom, tithing, scarification, the options for behavioral proof of faith are varied.

Among those religions with Big Gods who care widely, and rituals that enable people to display the depth of their commitment, there lies transformative potential. Not all religions share these features. But religions with these features tend to thrive. They survive, they spread, they persist across time and space. In part, these religions thrive because they help the groups that practice them. Of the countless religions that people have had throughout our species' tenure, most fizzle and fade. But religions that include beliefs and practices that promote cooperation, internal cohesion, reproduction, or missionary outreach tend to outcompete religions that don't.

Big God religions, those winners of the cultural evolutionary arms race for adherents and cohesion, spread through the globe, gradually gaining near-total market capture. Most believers today, believe in a Big God—even though most gods worshipped by humans haven't been all that Big. These Big God religions shifted people's intuitions about religion and morality, making one nigh synonymous with the other. And as Big God religions spread, they made way for greater proliferation of cooperative potential. Secular institutions arose, helping to secure and seal the cooperative gains that Big God religions helped initiate.

Where these secular institutions proved particularly successful, Big God religions became ever less necessary for securing cooperative esteem. In pockets of the world, secular structures, paired with newfound wealth and the unlocking of new fuels, created conditions where religion itself began to fade away.

First, people held their faith but ceased their public demonstrations of it. Next, cultural learners—seeing little behavioral proof that one ought to believe in this or that god—stopped believing entirely. Belief in gods, in these places, has waned. But it's possible that lingering intuitions about religion's fundamental connections to morality linger. Belief in belief persists, even as belief in gods declines in large parts of the world.

The origins of religion, the rise of Big God religions, and the eventual (albeit partial) decline of religion constitute the Puzzles of Faith and Atheism, and they share an answer that lies in our capacity for cultural learning. We learn from each other which gods to believe in; without consistency in these cues, we learn disbelief as well.

Make no mistake: religion is going nowhere. Successful religions—those that have proven victorious in cultural evolutionary competition—tend to be good at attracting new worshippers, at keeping the ones they have, and they largely do so by fulfilling people's needs in some way, or by furnishing their adherents with culturally competitive advantages. It's very much not a coincidence that some religions have thrived over the scale of centuries and millennia.

The success of religions, however, does not at all imply their inevitability. The fact that most of our species have been religious believers does not mean that atheism is unnatural, or even unlikely. It just means that our species has only recently (in cultural evolutionary scales) developed the sorts of societies in which religion loses its influence, and in which atheism becomes easy. When life becomes predictable and secure—through wealth, through social safety nets, through equitably distributed human development—religious zeal fades. And without public cultural support for given religions, atheism naturally grows.

Above all, we humans are a cultural species. Our ability to learn from each other underlies our global success, our remarkable adaptability, our capacity to colonize all ecosystems on the globe. And the ways that we culturally learn also answer both the Puzzle of Faith and the Puzzle of Atheism. Our species alone is religious. Our species alone has reflective atheists who disbelieve in gods they can easily imagine. There is grandeur in this view of faith and atheism: our species is capable of both, because we've evolved cultures that naturally sustain either.

NOTES

CHAPTER ONE

1. S. J. Gould, "Non-overlapping Magisteria," *Skeptical Inquirer* 23, no. 9 (August 1999): 55.

2. H. Fountain, "Slime Mold Proves to Be a Brainy Blob," *New York Times*, January 25, 2010.

3. Some of the themes and imagery in this opening also appear in a piece I wrote for *Big Think*: https://bigthink.com/the-well/atheism-rare-rational/.

4. D. Clingingsmith, A. I. Khwaja, and M. Kremer, "Estimating the Impact of the Hajj: Religion and Tolerance in Islam's Global Gathering," *Quarterly Journal of Economics* 124, no. 3 (2009): 1133–70.

5. J. M. Jones, "Some Americans Reluctant to Vote for Mormon, 72-Year-Old Presidential Candidates" (based on February 9–11, 2007, Gallup poll), Gallup News Service, https://news.gallup.com/poll/26611/some-americans-reluctant-vote-mormon-72year old-presidential-candidates.aspx.

6. W. M. Gervais, M. B. Najle, and N. Caluori, "The Origins of Religious Disbelief: A Dual Inheritance Approach," *Social Psychological and Personality Science* 12, no. 7 (2021): 1369–79.

7. A. Cherry-Garrard, *The Worst Journey in the World: Antarctic 1910–1913* (New York: Penguin, 2022).

8. P. Feyerabend, *Against Method: Outline of an Anarchistic Theory of Knowledge* (New York: Verso Books, 2020).

9. B. Resnick, "Animals Can Navigate by Starlight: Here's How We Know," *Vox*, June 28, 2021, https://www.vox.com/22538268/animal-navigation-starlight-emlen-planetarium-experiments.

CHAPTER TWO

1. C. Darwin, *The Descent of Man: and Selection in Relation To Sex* (London: John Murray, 1888).

2. K. Marx, "Introduction." in *A Contribution to the Critique of Hegel's Philosophy of Right*, trans. A. Jolin and J. O'Malley, ed. J. O'Malley (Cambridge: Cambridge University Press, 1970).

3. M. Inzlicht, A. M. Tullett, and M. Good, "The Need to Believe: A Neuroscience Account of Religion as a Motivated Process," *Religion, Brain and Behavior*, 1, no. 3 (2011): 192–212.

4. S. Solomon, J. Greenberg, and T. Pyszczynski, "The Cultural Animal: Twenty Years of Terror Management Theory and Research," in *Handbook of Experimental Existential*

Psychology, ed. J. Greenberg, S. L. Koole, and T. Pyszczynski (New York: The Guilford Press, 2004), 13–34.

5. K. E. Vail, Z. K. Rothschild, D. R. Weise, S. Solomon, T. Pyszczynski, and J. Greenberg, "A Terror Management Analysis of the Psychological Functions of Religion," *Personality and Social Psychology Review* 14, no. 1 (2010): 84–94.

6. P. Norris and R. Inglehart, *Sacred and Secular: Religion and Politics Worldwide* (Cambridge: Cambridge University Press, 2011).

7. Dante Alighieri. (2001). *The Inferno*. Translated by J. Ciardi. New York: Signet Classic.

8. See also the opening chapter to P. Boyer, *Religion Explained* (New York: Random House, 2008).

9. D. H. Hamer, *The God Gene: How Faith Is Hardwired Into Our Genes* (New York: Anchor, 2005).

10. M. Alper, *The "God" Part of the Brain: A Scientific Interpretation of Human Spirituality and God* (Naperville, IL: Sourcebooks, 2008).

11. T. R. Jennings, *The God-Shaped Brain: How Changing Your View of God Transforms Your Life* (Westmont, IL: Intervarsity Press, 2017).

12. M. Beauregard and D. O'Leary, *The Spiritual Brain: A Neuroscientist's Case for the Existence of the Soul* (New York: HarperOne/HarperCollins, 2007).

13. A. Newberg and M. R. Waldman, *Why We Believe What We Believe: Uncovering Our Biological Need for Meaning, Spirituality, and Truth* (New York: Simon & Schuster. 2006).

14. M. Shermer, *The Believing Brain: From Ghosts and Gods to Politics and Conspiracies—How We Construct Beliefs and Reinforce Them as Truths* (New York: Macmillan, 2011).

15. I. Dar-Nimrod and S. J. Heine, "Genetic Essentialism: On the Deceptive Determinism of DNA," *Psychological Bulletin* 137, no. 5 (2011): 800.

16. R. Dawkins, *The God Delusion* (Boston: Houghton Mifflin Company, 2006).

17. R. Dawkins, *Outgrowing God: A Beginner's Guide* (New York: Random House, 2019).

18. J. Henrich, *The Secret of Our Success: How Culture Is Driving Human Evolution, Domesticating Our Species, and Making Us Smarter* (Princeton, NJ: Princeton University Press, 2016).

19. P. J. Richerson and R. Boyd, *Not by Genes Alone: How Culture Transformed Human Evolution* (Chicago: University of Chicago Press, 2008).

20. R. Boyd and P. J. Richerson, *Culture and the Evolutionary Process* (Chicago: University of Chicago Press, 1988).

21. J. Henrich, "The Evolution of Costly Displays, Cooperation and Religion: Credibility Enhancing Displays and Their Implications for Cultural Evolution," *Evolution and Human Behavior* 30, no. 4 (2009): 244–60.

22. R. Dawkins, *The Selfish Gene* (Oxford: Oxford University Press, 2016).

23. S. A. Birch, S. A. Vauthier, and P. Bloom, "Three-and Four-Year-Olds Spontaneously Use Others' Past Performance to Guide Their Learning," *Cognition* 107, no. 3 (2008): 1018–34; E. S. Pasquini, K. H. Corriveau, M. Koenig, and P. L. Harris, "Preschoolers Monitor the Relative Accuracy of Informants," *Developmental Psychology* 43, no. 5 (2007): 1216; M. A. Sabbagh and D. A. Baldwin, "Learning Words from Knowledgeable versus Ignorant Speakers: Links between Preschoolers' Theory of Mind and Semantic Development," *Child Development* 72, no. 4 (2001): 1054–70; S. A. Birch, N. Akmal, and K. L. Frampton, "Two-Year-Olds Are Vigilant of Others' Non-Verbal Cues to Credibility," *Developmental Science* 13, no. 2 (2010): 363–69.

24. V. K. Jaswal and L. A. Neely, "Adults Don't Always Know Best: Preschoolers Use Past Reliability over Age When Learning New Words," *Psychological Science* 17, no. 9 (2006): 757–58.

25. M. Vanderborght and V. K. Jaswal, "Who Knows Best? Preschoolers Sometimes Prefer Child Informants Over Adult Informants," *Infant and Child Development: An International Journal of Research and Practice* 18, no. 1 (2009): 61–71.

26. T. Sharon and J. D. Woolley, "Do Monsters Dream? Young Children's Understanding of the Fantasy/Reality Distinction," *British Journal of Developmental Psychology* 22, no. 2 (2004): 293–310.

27. M. Taylor, *Imaginary Companions and the Children Who Create Them* (New York: Oxford University Press, 1999).

28. D. Skolnick and P. Bloom, "What Does Batman Think about SpongeBob? Children's Understanding of the Fantasy/Fantasy Distinction," *Cognition* 101, no. 1 (2006): B9–B18.

29. R. Banerjee, N. Yuill, C. Larson, K. Easton, E. Robinson, and M. Rowley, "Children's Differentiation between Beliefs about Matters of Fact and Matters of Opinion," *Developmental Psychology* 43, no. 5 (2007): 1084.

30. L. Heiphetz, E. S. Spelke, P. L. Harris, and M. R. Banaji, "The Development of Reasoning about Beliefs: Fact, Preference, and Ideology," *Journal of Experimental Social Psychology* 49, no. 3 (2013): 559–65.

31. P. L. Harris and M. A. Koenig, "Trust in Testimony: How Children Learn about Science and Religion," *Child Development* 77, no. 3 (2006): 505–24.

32. P. L. Harris, E. S. Pasquini, S. Duke, J. J. Asscher, and F. Pons, "Germs and Angels: The Role of Testimony in Young Children's Ontology," *Developmental Science* 9, no. 1 (2006): 76–96.

CHAPTER THREE

1. R. Dawkins, S. Harris, D. C. Dennett, and C. Hitchens, *The Four Horsemen: The Discussion That Sparked an Atheist Revolution*, foreword by Stephen Fry (New York: Random House, 2019).

2. J. S. B. Evans, "In Two Minds: Dual-Process Accounts of Reasoning," *Trends in Cognitive Sciences* 7, no. 10 (2003): 454–59.

3. D. Kahneman, *Thinking, Fast and Slow* (New York: Farrar, Straus and Giroux, 2017). Do yourself a favor and skip the chapter on "priming." That work hasn't held up well on further scrutiny, as Kahneman himself acknowledges.

4. W. M. Gervais and A. Norenzayan, "Analytic Thinking Promotes Religious Disbelief," *Science* 336, no. 6080 (2012): 493–96.

5. S. Frederick, "Cognitive Reflection and Decision Making," *Journal of Economic Perspectives* 19, no. 4 (2005): 25–42.

6. G. Pennycook, J. A. Cheyne, P. Seli, D. J. Koehler, and J. A. Fugelsang, "Analytic Cognitive Style Predicts Religious and Paranormal Belief," *Cognition* 123, no. 3 (2012): 335–46.

7. A. Shenhav, D. G. Rand, and J. D. Greene, "Divine Intuition: Cognitive Style Influences Belief in God," *Journal of Experimental Psychology: General* 141, no. 3 (2012): 423.

8. C. Sanchez, B. Sundermeier, K. Gray, and R. J. Calin-Jageman, "Direct Replication of Gervais and Norenzayan (2012): No Evidence That Analytic Thinking Decreases Religious Belief," *PLoS ONE*, 12, no. 2 (2017): e0172636.

9. C. F. Camerer, A. Dreber, F. Holzmeister, T. H. Ho, J. Huber, M. Johannesson, . . . and H. Wu, "Evaluating the Replicability of Social Science Experiments in *Nature* and *Science* between 2010 and 2015," *Nature Human Behaviour* 2, no. 9 (2018): 637–44.

10. S. A. Saribay, O. Yilmaz, and G. G. Körpe, "Does Intuitive Mindset Influence Belief in God? A Registered Replication of Shenhav, Rand and Greene (2012)," *Judgment and Decision Making* 15, no. 2 (2020): 193–202.

11. M. Farias, V. Van Mulukom, G. Kahane, U. Kreplin, A. Joyce, P. Soares, . . . and R. Möttönen, "Supernatural Belief Is Not Modulated by Intuitive Thinking Style or Cognitive Inhibition," *Scientific Reports* 7, no. 1 (2017): 15100.

12. G. Pennycook, R. M. Ross, D. J. Koehler, and J. A. Fugelsang, "Atheists and Agnostics Are More Reflective Than Religious Believers: Four Empirical Studies and a Meta-analysis," *PLoS ONE* 11, no. 4 (2016): e0153039.

13. W. M. Gervais, M. van Elk, D. Xygalatas, R. T. McKay, M. Aveyard, E. E. Buchtel, . . . and J. Bulbulia, "Analytic Atheism: A Cross-Culturally Weak and Fickle Phenomenon," *Judgment and Decision Making* 13, no. 3 (2018): 268–74.

14. W. M. Gervais, M. B. Najle, and N. Caluori, "The Origins of Religious Disbelief: A Dual Inheritance Approach," *Social Psychological and Personality Science* 12, no. 7 (2021): 1369–79.

CHAPTER FOUR

1. J. Bering, *The Belief Instinct: The Psychology of Souls, Destiny, and the Meaning of Life* (New York: W.W. Norton and Company, 2012).

2. J. L. Barrett, *Why Would Anyone Believe in God?* (Lanham, MD: AltaMira Press, 2004).

3. P. Boyer, *Religion Explained* (New York: Basic Books, 2001).

4. J. L. Barrett, *Born Believers: The Science of Children's Religious Belief* (New York: Simon and Schuster, 2012).

5. P. Bloom, "Religion Is Natural," *Developmental Science* 10, no. 1 (2007): 147–51.

6. S. J. Gould and R. C. Lewontin, "The Spandrels of San Marco and the Panglossian Paradigm: A Critique of the Adaptationist Programme," in *Shaping Entrepreneurship Research* (New York: Routledge, 2020), 204–21; P. W. Andrews, S. W. Gangestad, and D. Matthews, "Adaptationism: How to Carry Out an Exaptationist Program," *Behavioral and Brain Sciences* 25, no. 4 (2002): 489–504.

7. D. Johnson, *God Is Watching You: How the Fear of God Makes Us Human* (New York: Oxford University Press, 2016).

8. J. H. Barkow, L. Cosmides, and J. Tooby, eds., *The Adapted Mind: Evolutionary Psychology and the Generation of Culture* (New York: Oxford University Press, 1995).

9. P. Boyer, and H. C. Barrett, "Domain Specificity and Intuitive Ontology," in *The Handbook of Evolutionary Psychology*, ed. David M. Buss (Hoboken, NJ: John Wiley and Sons, 2015), 96–118.

10. E. S. Spelke, "Core Knowledge," *American Psychologist* 55, no. 11 (2000): 1233.

11. F. C. Keil, "The Roots of Folk Biology," *Proceedings of the National Academy of Sciences* 110, no. 40 (2013): 15857–58.

12. S. Atran, "Folk Biology and the Anthropology of Science: Cognitive Universals and Cultural Particulars," *Behavioral and Brain Sciences* 21, no. 4 (1998): 547–69.

13. H. M. Wellman, *The Child's Theory of Mind* (Cambridge, MA: MIT Press, 1992).

14. C. D. Frith and U. Frith, "The Neural Basis of Mentalizing," *Neuron* 50, no. 4 (2006): 531–34.

15. N. Epley and A. Waytz, "Mind Perception," *Handbook of Social Psychology* 1, no. 5 (2010): 498–541.

16. R. I. Dunbar and S. Shultz, "Evolution in the Social Brain," *Science* 317, no. 5843 (2007): 1344–47.

17. W. M. Gervais, "Perceiving Minds and Gods: How Mind Perception Enables, Constrains, and Is Triggered by Belief in Gods," *Perspectives on Psychological Science* 8, no. 4 (2013): 380–94.

18. M. Chudek, R. A. McNamara, S. Birch, P. Bloom, and J. Henrich, "Do Minds Switch Bodies? Dualist Interpretations across Ages and Societies," *Religion, Brain & Behavior* 8, no. 4 (2018): 354–68.

19. B. Hood, N. L. Gjersoe, and P. Bloom, "Do Children Think That Duplicating the Body Also Duplicates the Mind?," *Cognition* 125, no. 3 (2012): 466–74.

20. E. Slingerland and M. Chudek, "The Prevalence of Mind–Body Dualism in Early China," *Cognitive Science* 35, no. 5 (2011): 997–1007.

21. R. Richert and P. Harris, "The Ghost in My Body: Children's Developing Concept of the Soul," *Journal of Cognition and Culture* 6, nos. 3–4 (2006): 409–27.

22. Barrett, *Why Would Anyone Believe in God?*

23. P. Boyer and C. Ramble, "Cognitive Templates for Religious Concepts: Cross-Cultural Evidence for Recall of Counter-intuitive Representations," *Cognitive Science* 25, no. 4 (2001): 535–64.

24. A. Norenzayan, S. Atran, J. Faulkner, and M. Schaller, "Memory and Mystery: The Cultural Selection of Minimally Counterintuitive Narratives," *Cognitive Science* 30, no. 3 (2006): 531–53.

25. D. Kelemen, "Why Are Rocks Pointy? Children's Preference for Teleological Explanations of the Natural World," *Developmental Psychology* 35, no. 6 (1999): 1440.

26. D. Kelemen, "Function, Goals and Intention: Children's Teleological Reasoning about Objects," *Trends in Cognitive Sciences* 3, no. 12 (1999), 461–68.

27. T. Lombrozo, D. Kelemen, and D. Zaitchik, "Inferring Design: Evidence of a Preference for Teleological Explanations in Patients with Alzheimer's Disease," *Psychological Science* 18, no. 11 (2007): 999–1006.

28. D. Kelemen and E. Rosset, "The Human Function Compunction: Teleological Explanation in Adults," *Cognition* 111, no. 1 (2009): 138–43.

29. D. Kelemen, "Are Children 'Intuitive Theists'? Reasoning about Purpose and Design in Nature," *Psychological Science* 15, no. 5 (2004): 295–301.

30. G. E. Newman, F. C. Keil, V. A. Kuhlmeier, and K. Wynn, "Early Understandings of the Link between Agents and Order," *Proceedings of the National Academy of Sciences* 107, no. 40 (2010): 17140–45.

31. E. M. Evans, "The Emergence of Beliefs about the Origins of Species in School-Age Children," *Merrill-Palmer Quarterly* 46, no. 2 (2000): 221–54.

32. E. M. Evans, "Cognitive and Contextual Factors in the Emergence of Diverse Belief Systems: Creation versus Evolution," *Cognitive Psychology* 42, no. 3 (2001): 217–66.

33. A. K Willard, "Agency Detection Is Unnecessary in the Explanation of Religious Belief," *Religion, Brain & Behavior* 9, no. 1 (2019): 96–98.

34. A. Lisdorf, "What's HIDD'n in the HADD?," *Journal of Cognition and Culture* 7, nos. 3–4 (2007): 341–53.

35. P. Bloom, "Religion Is Natural," *Developmental Science* 10, no. 1 (2007): 147–51.

36. T. Gura, "The Evolutionary Wars in Ohio," National Center for Science Education, February 26, 2016, https://ncse.ngo/evolutionary-wars-ohio.

CHAPTER FIVE

1. C. Heyes, *Cognitive Gadgets: The Cultural Evolution of Thinking* (Cambridge, MA: Harvard University Press).

2. Royal Museums Greenwich, "How Did Inuit Oral History Help Locate HMS *Erebus* and *Terror*?," September 20, 2017, https://www.rmg.co.uk/stories/blog/how-inuit-oral-history-helped-locate-erebus-terror.

3. J. Henrich, *The Secret of Our Success: How Culture Is Driving Human Evolution, Domesticating Our Species, and Making Us Smarter* (Princeton, NJ: Princeton University Press).

4. R. Boyd, P. J. Richerson, and J. Henrich, "The Cultural Niche: Why Social Learning Is Essential for Human Adaptation," *Proceedings of the National Academy of Sciences* 108, supplement 2 (2011): 10918–25; S. Mathew and C. Perreault, "Cultural History, Not Ecological Environment, Is the Main Determinant of Human Behaviour," *Proceedings of the Royal Society B: Biological Sciences* 283, no. 1826 (2016): 20160177.

5. S. Pinker, *The Blank Slate: The Modern Denial of Human Nature* (New York: Viking, 2004); K. Popper, *Unended Quest* (London: Fontana, 1974).

6. P. J. Richerson and R. Boyd, *Not by Genes Alone: How Culture Transformed Human Evolution* (Chicago: University of Chicago Press).

7. R. Boyd and P. J. Richerson, *Culture and the Evolutionary Process* (Chicago: University of Chicago Press).

8. K. N. Lala and G. R. Brown, *Sense and Nonsense: Evolutionary Perspectives on Human Behaviour* (New York: Oxford University Press, 2011).

9. J. Henrich, R. Boyd, and P. J. Richerson, "Five Misunderstandings about Cultural Evolution." *Human Nature* 19 (2008): 119–37.

10. M. A. Kline, "How to Learn about Teaching: An Evolutionary Framework for the Study of Teaching Behavior in Humans and Other Animals," *Behavioral and Brain Sciences* 38 (2015): e31.

11. S. Okasha, *Evolution and the Levels of Selection* (Oxford: Clarendon Press).

12. Also check out R. Chvaja, "Why Did Memetics Fail? Comparative Case Study," *Perspectives on Science* 28, no. 4 (2020): 542–70.

13. M. Muthukrishna, and J. Henrich, "Innovation in the Collective Brain," *Philosophical Transactions of the Royal Society B: Biological Sciences*, 371, no. 1690 (2016): 20150192.

14. S. Blackmore and S. J. Blackmore, *The Meme Machine* (Oxford: Oxford University Press, 2000).

15. R. L. Kendal, N. J. Boogert, L. Rendell, K. N. Lala, M. Webster, and P. L. Jones, "Social Learning Strategies: Bridge-Building between Fields," *Trends in Cognitive Sciences* 22, no. 7 (2018): 651–65.

16. P. Boyer, and C. Ramble, "Cognitive Templates for Religious Concepts: Cross-Cultural Evidence for Recall of Counter-Intuitive Representations," *Cognitive Science* 25, no. 4 (2001): 535–64.

17. A. Norenzayan, S. Atran, J. Faulkner, and M. Schaller, "Memory and Mystery: The Cultural Selection of Minimally Counterintuitive Narratives," *Cognitive Science* 30, no. 3 (2006): 531–53.

18. S. Nichols, "On the Genealogy of Norms: A Case for the Role of Emotion in Cultural Evolution," *Philosophy of Science* 69, no. 2 (2002): 234–55.

19. J. Henrich, and R. Boyd, R. "The Evolution of Conformist Transmission and the Emergence of Between-Group Differences," *Evolution and Human Behavior* 19, no. 4 (1998): 215–41.

20. J. Henrich, and F. J. Gil-White, "The Evolution of Prestige: Freely Conferred Deference as a Mechanism for Enhancing the Benefits of Cultural Transmission," *Evolution and Human Behavior* 22, no. 3 (2001): 165–96.

21. J. Henrich, "The Evolution of Costly Displays, Cooperation and Religion: Credibility Enhancing Displays and Their Implications for Cultural Evolution," *Evolution and Human Behavior*, 30, no. 4 (2009): 244–60.

22. C. Heyes, "When Does Social Learning Become Cultural Learning?," *Developmental Science*, 20, no. 2 (2017): e12350.

CHAPTER SIX

1. J. Barrett, "Why Santa Claus Is Not a God," *Journal of Cognition and Culture* 8, nos. 1–2 (2008): 149–61.

2. W. M. Gervais and J. Henrich, "The Zeus Problem: Why Representational Content Biases Cannot Explain Faith in Gods," *Journal of Cognition and Culture* 10, nos. 3–4 (2010): 383–89.

3. J. Henrich and R. Boyd, "The Evolution of Conformist Transmission and the Emergence of Between-Group Differences," *Evolution and Human Behavior* 19, no. 4 (1998): 215–41.

4. J. Henrich and F. J. Gil-White, "The Evolution of Prestige: Freely Conferred Deference as a Mechanism for Enhancing the Benefits of Cultural Transmission," *Evolution and Human Behavior* 22, no. 3 (2001): 165–96.

5. S. Atran and J. Henrich, "The Evolution of Religion: How Cognitive By-Products, Adaptive Learning Heuristics, Ritual Displays, and Group Competition Generate Deep Commitments to Prosocial Religions," *Biological Theory* 5 (2010): 18–30.

6. J. Henrich, "The Evolution of Costly Displays, Cooperation and Religion: Credibility Enhancing Displays and Their Implications for Cultural Evolution," *Evolution and Human Behavior* 30, no. 4 (2009): 244–60.

7. W. M. Gervais, A. K. Willard, A. Norenzayan, and J. Henrich, "The Cultural Transmission of Faith: Why Innate Intuitions Are Necessary, but Insufficient, to Explain Religious Belief," *Religion* 41, no. 3 (2011): 389–410.

8. C. M. Mills, T. R. Goldstein, P. Kanumuru, A. J. Monroe, and N. B. Quintero, "Debunking the Santa Myth: The Process and Aftermath of Becoming Skeptical about Santa," *Developmental Psychology* 60, no. 1 (2023): 1–16.

CHAPTER SEVEN

1. C. Darwin, *The Descent of Man: And Selection in Relation to Sex* (London: John Murray, 1888).

2. P. Clarke, ed., *Encyclopedia of New Religious Movements* (New York: Routledge, 2004).

3. J. Henrich, "Cultural Group Selection, Coevolutionary Processes and Large-Scale Cooperation," *Journal of Economic Behavior & Organization* 53, no. 1 (2004): 3–35.

4. A. Norenzayan, A. F. Shariff, W. M. Gervais, A. K. Willard, R. A. McNamara, E. Slingerland, and J. Henrich, "The Cultural Evolution of Prosocial Religions," *Behavioral and Brain Sciences* 39 (2016): E1.

5. S. Pinker, "The False Allure of Group Selection," https://www.edge.org/conversation/steven_pinker-the-false-allure-of-group-selection.

6. Do this yourself with R. McElreath and R. Boyd, *Mathematical Models of Social Evolution: A Guide for the Perplexed* (Chicago: University of Chicago Press, 2008).

7. I enthusiastically recommend S. Okasha, *Evolution and the Levels of Selection* (Oxford: Clarendon Press, 2006).

8. J. Henrich, "Too Late: Models of Cultural Evolution and Group Selection Have Already Proved Useful," Edge, 2012, https://www.edge.org/conversation/the-false-allure-of-group-selection#jh.

9. D. Queller, "Two Languages, One Reality," Edge, 2012, https://www.edge.org/conversation/the-false-allure-of-group-selection#dq.

10. D. S. Wilson, "The Central Question of Group Selection," Edge, 2012, https://www.edge.org/conversation/the-false-allure-of-group-selection#dsw.

11. O. Harman, "A History of the Altruism–Morality Debate in Biology," *Behaviour* 151, nos. 2–3 (2014): 147–65.

12. N. Raihani, *The Social Instinct: How Cooperation Shaped the World* (New York: Random House, 2021).

13. V. C. Wynne-Edwards, *Animal Dispersion in Relation to Social Behaviour* (London: Oliver and Boyd, 1972).

14. K. S. DeConnick, and E. Rios, *Pretty Deadly Vol. 3: The Rat* (Portland, OR: Image Comics, 2020).

15. P. E. Smaldino, "Models Are Stupid, and We Need More of Them," in *Computational Social Psychology*, ed. R. R. Vallacher, S. J. Read, and A. Nowak (New York: Routledge, 2017), 311–31.

16. Thought provoking read here: B. Skyrms, *The Stag Hunt and the Evolution of Social Structure* (Cambridge: Cambridge University Press, 2004).

17. G. R. Price, Selection and Covariance, *Nature* 227 (1970): 520–21.

18. O. Harman, *The Price of Altruism: George Price and the Search for the Origins of Kindness* (New York: Random House, 2010).

19. For an accessible look at this concept and its applications, check out A. Rutherford, *How to Argue with a Racist: History, Science, Race and Reality* (London: Hachette UK, 2020).

20. J. Henrich and R. Boyd, "The Evolution of Conformist Transmission and the Emergence of Between-Group Differences," *Evolution and Human Behavior* 19, no. 4: 215–41.

21. M. Chudek and J. Henrich, "Culture–Gene Coevolution, Norm-Psychology and the Emergence of Human Prosociality," *Trends in Cognitive Sciences* 15, no. 5 (2011): 218–26.

22. R. Boyd and P. J. Richerson, "Punishment Allows the Evolution of Cooperation (or Anything Else) in Sizable Groups," *Ethology and Sociobiology* 13, no. 3 (1992): 171–95.

23. J. Henrich, "Cooperation, Punishment, and the Evolution of Human Institutions," *Science* 312, no. 5770 (2006): 60–61.

24. M. Muthukrishna, A. V. Bell, J. Henrich, C. M. Curtin, A. Gedranovich, J. McInerney, and B. Thue, "Beyond Western, Educated, Industrial, Rich, and Democratic

(WEIRD) Psychology: Measuring and Mapping Scales of Cultural and Psychological Distance," *Psychological Science* 31, no. 6 (2020): 678–701.

25. A. V. Bell, P. J. Richerson, and R. McElreath, "Culture Rather Than Genes Provides Greater Scope for the Evolution of Large-Scale Human Prosociality," *Proceedings of the National Academy of Sciences*, 106, no. 42 (2009): 17671–74.

26. J. Henrich, J. (2020). *The WEIRDest People in the World: How the West Became Psychologically Peculiar and Particularly Prosperous* (New York: Farrar, Straus and Giroux, 2020).

27. A. Norenzayan, *Big Gods: How Religion Transformed Cooperation and Conflict* (Princeton, NJ: Princeton University Press, 2013).

28. D. Wilson, *Darwin's Cathedral: Evolution, Religion, and the Nature of Society* (Chicago: University of Chicago Press, 2019).

29. J. Haidt, *The Righteous Mind: Why Good People Are Divided by Politics and Religion* (New York: Vintage, 2012).

30. C. J. White, M. Muthukrishna, and A. Norenzayan, "Cultural Similarity among Coreligionists within and between Countries," *Proceedings of the National Academy of Sciences* 118, no. 37 (2021): E2109650118.

31. D. Johnson, *God Is Watching You: How the Fear of God Makes Us Human* (New York: Oxford University Press, 2016).

32. Norenzayan et al., "The Cultural Evolution of Prosocial Religions," E1.

33. R. Sosis and E. R. Bressler, "Cooperation and Commune Longevity: A Test of the Costly Signaling Theory of Religion," *Cross-Cultural Research* 37, no. 2 (2003): 211–39.

34. F. L. Roes and M. Raymond, "Belief in Moralizing Gods," *Evolution and Human Behavior* 24, no. 2 (2003): 126–35.

35. B. Purzycki, *The Minds of Gods: New Horizons in the Naturalistic Study of Religion* (London: Bloomsbury, 2023).

36. B. G. Purzycki, D. N. Finkel, J. Shaver, N. Wales, A. B. Cohen, and R. Sosis, "What Does God Know? Supernatural Agents' Access to Socially Strategic and Non-strategic Information," *Cognitive Science* 36, no. 5 (2012): 846–69.

37. B. G. Purzycki, T. Bendixen, and A. D. Lightner, "Coding, Causality, and Statistical Craft: The Emergence and Evolutionary Drivers of Moralistic Supernatural Punishment Remain Unresolved," *Religion, Brain & Behavior* 13, no. 2 (2023): 207–14.

38. J. Henrich, J. Ensminger, R. McElreath, A. Barr, C. Barrett, A. Bolyanatz, . . . and J. Ziker, "Markets, Religion, Community Size, and the Evolution of Fairness and Punishment," *Science* 327, no. 5972 (2010): 1480–84.

39. M. Lang, G. Purzycki, C. L. Apicella, Q. D. Atkinson, A. Bolyanatz, E. Cohen, C. Handley et al. "Moralizing Gods, Impartiality and Religious Parochialism across 15 Societies." *Proceedings of the Royal Society B* 286, no. 1898 (2019): 20190202.

40. Q. D. Atkinson and P. Bourrat, "Beliefs about God, the Afterlife and Morality Support the Role of Supernatural Policing in Human Cooperation," *Evolution and Human Behavior* 32, no. 1 (2011): 41–49.

41. A. F. Shariff and A. Norenzayan, "God Is Watching You: Priming God Concepts Increases Prosocial Behavior in an Anonymous Economic Game," *Psychological Science* 18, no. 9 (2007): 803–9.

42. C. M. Gomes and M. E. McCullough, "The Effects of Implicit Religious Primes on Dictator Game Allocations: A Preregistered Replication Experiment," *Journal of Experimental Psychology: General* 144, no. 6 (2015): E94.

43. W. M. Gervais, S. E. Mckee, and S. Malik, "Do Religious Primes Increase Risk Taking? Evidence against 'Anticipating Divine Protection' in Two Preregistered Direct Replications of Kupor, Laurin, and Levav (2015)," *Psychological Science*, 31, no. 7 (2020): 858–64.

44. M. E. Aveyard, "A Call to Honesty: Extending Religious Priming of Moral Behavior to Middle Eastern Muslims." *PLoS ONE* 9, no. 7 (2014): E99447.

45. E. P. Duhaime, "Is the Call to Prayer a Call to Cooperate? A Field Experiment on the Impact of Religious Salience on Prosocial Behavior," *Judgment and Decision Making* 10, no. 6 (2015): 593–96.

46. R. McKay and H. Whitehouse, "Religion and Morality," *Psychological Bulletin* 141, no. 2 (2015): 447.

CHAPTER EIGHT

1. A. Cowburn, "Saudi Arabia Sentences a Man to 10 Years in Prison and 2,000 Lashes for Voicing His Atheism on Twitter," *Independent*, February 27, 2016, https://www.independent.co.uk/news/world/middle-east/saudi-arabia-sentence-man-to-10-years-in-prison-and-2-000-lashes-for-expressing-his-atheism-on-twitter-a6900056.html.

2. "Man 'Sentenced to Death for Atheism' in Saudi Arabia," *Independent*, April 26, 2017, https://www.independent.co.uk/news/world/middle-east/saudi-arabia-man-sentenced-death-atheism-ahmad-al-shamri-hafar-albatin-appeal-denied-a7703161.html.

3. E. Hossain, "Bangladesh Bloggers Face Constant Death Threats Since Government Labeled Them 'Atheist,'" *Huffpost*, May 18, 2013, https://www.huffpost.com/entry/bangladesh-bloggers-death-threats_n_3294831.

4. "Rajib Murder 'Cracked,'" BDNews 24, March 1, 2013, https://bdnews24.com/bangladesh/2013/03/02/rajib-murder-cracked.

5. RFI, https://www.rfi.fr/fr/moyen-orient/20171224-egypte-enfants-retires-mere-cause-atheisme.

6. KRQE, https://www.krqe.com/2015/09/14/court-ordered-religious-classes-raise-concerns/.

7. E. Volokh, "Discrimination against Atheists," http://www.volokh.com/posts/1125342962.shtml.

8. P. Edgell, J. Gerteis, and D. Hartmann, "Atheists as 'Other': Moral Boundaries and Cultural Membership in American Society. *American Sociological Review* 71, no. 2 (2006): 211–34.

9. H. Tajfel and J. C. Turner, "The Social Identity Theory of Intergroup Behavior," in *Political Psychology: Key Readings*, ed. J. T. Jost and J. Sidanius (New York: Psychology Press), 276–93.

10. D. T. Campbell, *Ethnocentric and Other Altruistic Motives* (Lincoln: University of Nebraska Press), 283–311.

11. W. M. Gervais and M. B. Najle, "How Many Atheists Are There?" *Social Psychological and Personality Science* 9, no. 1 (2018): 3–10.

12. A. J. Cuddy, S. T. Fiske, and P. Glick, "Warmth and Competence as Universal Dimensions of Social Perception: The Stereotype Content Model and the BIAS Map," *Advances in Experimental Social Psychology* 40 (2008): 61–149.

13. J. H. Barkow, L. Cosmides, and J. Tooby, eds., *The Adapted Mind: Evolutionary Psychology and the Generation of Culture* (Oxford: Oxford University Press).

14. C. A. Cottrell and S. L. Neuberg, "Different Emotional Reactions to Different Groups: A Sociofunctional Threat-Based Approach to 'Prejudice,'" *Journal of Personality and Social Psychology* 88, no. 5 (2002): 770.

15. M. Schaller and S. L. Neuberg, "Danger, Disease, and the Nature of Prejudice(s)," *Advances in Experimental Social Psychology* 46 (2012): 1–54.

16. W. M. Gervais, A. F. Shariff, and A. Norenzayan, "Do You Believe in Atheists? Distrust Is Central to Anti-Atheist Prejudice," *Journal of Personality and Social Psychology* 101, no. 6 (2011): 1189.

17. W. M. Gervais, "Everything Is Permitted? People Intuitively Judge Immorality as Representative of Atheists," *PLoS ONE* 9, no. 4 (2014): e92302.

18. W. M. Gervais, D. Xygalatas, R. T. McKay, R. M. Van Elk, E. E. Buchtel, M. Aveyard, . . . and J. Bulbulia, "Global Evidence of Extreme Intuitive Moral Prejudice against Atheists," *Nature Human Behaviour* 1, no. 8 (2017): 1–6.

19. J. L. Brown-Iannuzzi, S. McKee, and W. M. Gervais, "Atheist Horns and Religious Halos: Mental Representations of Atheists and Theists," *Journal of Experimental Psychology: General* 147, no. 2 (2018): 292.

20. J. W. Moon, J. A. Krems, and A. B. Cohen, "Opposition to Short-Term Mating Predicts Anti-atheist Prejudice," *Personality and Individual Differences* 165 (2020): 110136.

21. J. W. Moon, J. A. Krems, and A. B. Cohen, "Is There Anything Good about Atheists? Exploring Positive and Negative Stereotypes of the Religious and Nonreligious," *Social Psychological and Personality Science* 12, no. 8 (2021): 1505–116.

CHAPTER NINE

1. R. H. Frank, *Passions within Reason: The Strategic Role of the Emotions* (New York: W.W. Norton, 1998).

2. J. H. Tan and C. Vogel, "Religion and Trust: An Experimental Study," *Journal of Economic Psychology* 29, no. 6 (2008): 832–48.

3. S. Harris, *The End of Faith: Religion, Terror, and the Future of Reason* (New York: W.W. Norton, 2005).

4. W. James, *The Varieties of Religious Experience*, ed. M. Bradley (1902; Oxford: Oxford University Press, 2012).

5. R. Dawkins, "Religion's Misguided Missiles," *Guardian*, September 15, 2001.

6. C. Hitchens, *God Is Not Great: How Religion Poisons Everything* (Toronto: McClelland & Stewart, 2008).

7. S. Atran, *Talking to the Enemy: Violent Extremism, Sacred Values, and What It Means to Be Human* (New York: HarperCollins).

8. S. Atran, "Genesis of Suicide Terrorism," *Science,* no. 299 (2003): 1534-1539; N. Hassan, "An Arsenal of Believers." *New Yorker* 19 (2001): 1–34.

9. J. Ginges, I. Hansen, and A. Norenzayan, "Religion and Support for Suicide Attacks. *Psychological Science* 20, no. 2 (2009): 224–30.

10. J. Ginges, H. Sheikh, S. Atran, and N. Argo, "Thinking from God's Perspective Decreases Biased Valuation of the Life of a Nonbeliever," *Proceedings of the National Academy of Sciences* 113, no. 2 (2016): 316–19.

11. J. M. Smith, M. H. Pasek, A. Vishkin, K. A. Johnson, C. Shackleford, and J. Ginges, "Thinking about God Discourages Dehumanization of Religious Outgroups," *Journal of Experimental Psychology: General* 151, no. 10 (2022): 2586.

12. M. H. Pasek, C. Shackleford, J. M. Smith, A. Vishkin, A. Lehner, and J. Ginges, "God Values the Lives of My Out-Group More Than I Do: Evidence from Fiji and Israel," *Social Psychological and Personality Science* 11, no. 7 (2020): 1032–41.

13. P. Zuckerman, *Society without God* (New York: New York University Press, 2008).

14. A. F. Shariff, A. K. Willard, T. Andersen, and A. Norenzayan, "Religious Priming: A Meta-analysis with a Focus on Prosociality." *Personality and Social Psychology Review* 20, no. 1 (2016): 27–48.

15. J. Mikhail, "Universal Moral Grammar: Theory, Evidence and the Future," *Trends in Cognitive Sciences* 11, no. 4 (2007): 143–52.

16. K. Banerjee, B. Huebner, and M. Hauser, "Intuitive Moral Judgments Are Robust across Variation in Gender, Education, Politics and Religion: A Large-Scale Web-Based Study," *Journal of Cognition and Culture* 10, nos. 3–4 (2010): 253–81.

17. F. de Waal, *The Bonobo and the Atheist: In Search of Humanism among the Primates* (New York: W.W. Norton, 2013).

18. J. K. Hamlin, K. Wynn, and P. Bloom, "Social Evaluation by Preverbal Infants," *Nature* 450, no. 7169 (2007): 557–59.

19. P. Bloom, *Just Babies: The Origins of Good and Evil* (New York: Crown, 2014).

20. J. Piazza, "'If You Love Me Keep My Commandments': Religiosity Increases Preference for Rule-Based Moral Arguments," *International Journal for the Psychology of Religion* 22, no. 4 (2012): 285–302.

21. W. Hofmann, D. C. Wisneski, M. J. Brandt, and L. J. Skitka, "Morality in Everyday Life," *Science* 345, no. 6202 (2014): 1340–43.

22. J. Decety, J. M. Cowell, K. Lee, R. Mahasneh, S. Malcolm-Smith, B Selcuk, and X. Zhou, "RETRACTED: The Negative Association between Religiousness and Children's Altruism across the World," *Current Biology* 25, no. 22 (2015): 2951–55.

23. Richard Dawkins Foundation, "Far from Bolstering Generosity, a Religious Upbringing Diminishes It," November 6, 2015, https://richarddawkins.net/2015/11/far-from-bolstering-generosity-a-religious-upbringing-diminishes-it/.

24. Richard Dawkins Foundation, "Religious Upbringing Linked to Less Altruism, Study of Children Suggests," November 9, 2015, https://richarddawkins.net/2015/11/religious-upbringing-linked-to-less-altruism-study-of-children-suggests/.

25. A. F. Shariff, A. K. Willard, M. Muthukrishna, S. R. Kramer, and J. Henrich, "What Is the Association between Religious Affiliation and Children's Altruism?," *Current Biology* 26, no. 15 (2016): R699–R700.

26. Kelsey Piper, "How a Study Based on a Typo Made News Everywhere—and the Retraction Didn't," *Vox*, October 3, 2019, https://www.vox.com/future-perfect/2019/10/3/20895240/study-typo-religion-children-generosity-retraction.

CHAPTER TEN

1. T. H. Huxley, *Agnosticism* (Trench, UK: K. Paul, 1889).

2. M. Boorstein, "This Politician Isn't Sure He Believes in God, Now He's Decided to Tell People," *Washington Post*, November 9, 2017, https://www.washington

post.com/news/acts-of-faith/wp/2017/11/09/this-lawmaker-is-skeptical-that-god-exists-now-hes-finally-decided-to-tell-people/

3. A. Keysar and J. Navarro-Rivera, "A World of Atheism: Global Demographics," in *Oxford Handbook of Atheism*, ed. S. Bullivant and M. Ruse (Oxford: Oxford University Press), 553–86.

4. P. Edgell, D. Hartmann, E. Stewart, and J. Gerteis, "Atheists and Other Cultural Outsiders: Moral Boundaries and the Non-religious in the United States," *Social Forces* 95, no. 2 (2016): 607–38.

5. Wikipedia, "George Santos," https://en.wikipedia.org/wiki/George_Santos.

6. Gallup, "Religion," https://news.gallup.com/poll/1690/religion.aspx.

7. Pew Research Center, "America's Changing Religious Landscape," May 12, 2015, https://www.pewresearch.org/religion/2015/05/12/americas-changing-religious-landscape/.

8. P. Zuckerman, "Atheism: Contemporary Numbers and Patterns, in *The Cambridge Companion to Atheism*, ed. M. Martin (Cambridge: Cambridge University Press), 47–65.

9. W. Paley, *Natural Theology; or, Evidences of the Existence and Attributes of the Deity, Collected from the Appearances of Nature* (London: Lincoln and Edmands, 1829).

10. S. Kierkegaard, *Fear and Trembling* and *The Sickness unto Death* (Princeton, NJ: Princeton University Press, 2013).

11. B. Russell, *Why I Am Not a Christian: And Other Essays on Religion and Related Subjects* (London: Routledge, 2004).

12. A. J. Nederhof, "Methods of Coping with Social Desirability Bias: A Review," *European Journal of Social Psychology* 15, no. 3 (1985): 263–80.

13. A. Gabbatt, "Losing Their Religion: Why US Churches Are on the Decline," *Guardian*, January 23, 2023.

14. "Churchgoing and Belief in God Stand at Historic Lows, Despite a Megachurch Surge," The Hill, https://thehill.com/changing-america/enrichment/arts-culture/3782032-churchgoing-and-belief-in-god-stand-at-historic-lows-despite-a-megachurch-surge/.

15. D. Cox, R. P. Jones, and J. Navarro-Rivera, "I Know What You Did Last Sunday: Measuring Social Desirability Bias in Self-Reported Religious Behavior, Belief, and Identity," *Public Religion Research Institute* 2 (2014): 57–58.

16. P. S. Brenner, "The Difference between Going to Church and Going to Church," *Vox*, April 12, 2014, https://www.vox.com/2014/4/12/5601522/the-difference-between-going-to-church-and-going-to-church.

17. P. S. Brenner, "Exceptional Behavior or Exceptional Identity? Overreporting of Church Attendance in the US," *Public Opinion Quarterly* 75, no. 1 (2011): 19–41.

18. P. S. Brenner, "Identity Importance and the Overreporting of Religious Service Attendance: Multiple Imputation of Religious Attendance Using the American Time Use Study and the General Social Survey," *Journal for the Scientific Study of Religion* 50 no. 1 (2011): 103–15.

19. C. K. Hadaway, P. L. Marler, and M. Chaves, "What the Polls Don't Show: A Closer Look at US Church Attendance," *American Sociological Review* 58, no. 6 (1993): 741–52.

20. J. H. Shaver, T. A. White, P. Vakaoti, and M. Lang. "A Comparison of Self-Report, Systematic Observation and Third-Party Judgments of Church Attendance in a Rural Fijian Village," *Plos One* 16, no. 10 (2021), e0257160.

21. A. E. Jones and M. Elliott, "Examining Social Desirability in Measures of Religion and Spirituality Using the Bogus Pipeline," *Review of Religious Research* 59 (2001): 47–64.

22. D. R. Dalton, J. C. Wimbush, and C. M. Daily, "Using the Unmatched Count Technique (UCT) to Estimate Base Rates for Sensitive Behavior," *Personnel Psychology* 47, no. 4 (1994): 817–29.

23. W. M. Gervais and M. B. Najle, "How Many Atheists Are There?," *Social Psychological and Personality Science* 9, no. 1 (2018): 3–10.

CHAPTER ELEVEN

1. J. Gray, *Seven Types of Atheism* (New York: Farrar, Straus and Giroux, 2018).

2. C. F. Silver, T. J. Coleman III, R. W. Hood Jr., and J. M. Holcombe, "The Six Types of Nonbelief: A Qualitative and Quantitative Study of Type and Narrative," *Mental Health, Religion & Culture* 17, no. 10 (2014): 990–1001.

3. D. Nettle, *Personality: What Makes You the Way You Are* (Oxford: Oxford University Press, 2007).

4. L. Al-Shawaf, "Should You Trust the Myers-Briggs Personality Test?" *Areo*, March 9, 2021, https://areomagazine.com/2021/03/09/should-you-trust-the-myers-briggs-personality-test/.

5. A. Norenzayan and W. M. Gervais, "The Origins of Religious Disbelief," *Trends in Cognitive Sciences* 17, no. 1 (2013): 20–25.

6. J. Bering, *The Belief Instinct: The Psychology of Souls, Destiny, and the Meaning of Life* (New York: W.W. Norton).

7. W. M. Gervais, "Perceiving Minds and Gods: How Mind Perception Enables, Constrains, and Is Triggered by Belief in Gods," *Perspectives on Psychological Science* 8, no. 4 (2013): 380–94.

8. C. Hughes, S. R. Jaffee, F. Happé, A. Taylor, A. Caspi, and T. E. Moffitt, "Origins of Individual Differences in Theory of Mind: From Nature to Nurture?," *Child Development* 76, no. 2 (2005): 356–70; M. Taylor and S. M. Carlson, "The Relation between Individual Differences in Fantasy and Theory of Mind," *Child Development* 68, no. 3 (1997): 436–55; J. Stiller and R. I. Dunbar, "Perspective-Taking and Memory Capacity Predict Social Network Size," *Social Networks* 29, no. 1 (2007): 93–104.

9. U. Frith, "Mind Blindness and the Brain in Autism," *Neuron* 32, no. 6 (2001): 969–79; J. Dinishak and N. Akhtar, "A Critical Examination of Mindblindness as a Metaphor for Autism," *Child Development Perspectives* 7, no. 2 (2013): 110–14.

10. A. Norenzayan, W. M. Gervais, and K. H. Trzesniewski, "Mentalizing Deficits Constrain Belief in a Personal God," *PLoS ONE* 7, no. 5 (2012): e36880.

11. For a counterpoint, see I. Visuri, "Rethinking Autism, Theism, and Atheism: Bodiless Agents and Imaginary Realities," *Archive for the Psychology of Religion* 40, no. 1 (2018): 1–31.

12. D. L. Maij, F. van Harreveld, W. Gervais, Y. Schrag, C. Mohr, and M. van Elk, "Mentalizing Skills Do Not Differentiate Believers from Non-believers, but Credibility Enhancing Displays Do," *PLoS ONE* 12, no. 8 (2017): e0182764.

13. I. Hacking, *An Introduction to Probability and Inductive Logic* (Cambridge: Cambridge University Press, 2001).

14. P. Norris and R. Inglehart, *Sacred and Secular: Religion and Politics Worldwide* (Cambridge: Cambridge University Press, 2011).

15. A. L. Whitehead, L. Schnabel, and S. Perry, "Gun Control in the Crosshairs: Christian Nationalism and Opposition to Stricter Gun Laws," *Socius* 4 (2018): 1–13.

16. K. Frydl, "US Is Becoming a 'Developing Country' on Global Rankings That Measure Democracy, Inequality," The Conversation, September 15, 2022, https://theconversation.com/us-is-becoming-a-developing-country-on-global-rankings-that-measure-democracy-inequality-190486.

17. L. Schnabel, "Opiate of the Masses? Inequality, Religion, and Political Ideology in the United States," *Social Forces* 99, no. 3 (2021): 979–1012.

18. A. C. Kay, D. Gaucher, I. McGregor, and K. Nash, "Religious Belief as Compensatory Control," *Personality and Social Psychology Review* 14, no. 1 (2010): 37–48.

19. A. C. Kay, D. Gaucher, J. L. Napier, M. J. Callan, and K. Laurin, "God and the Government: Testing a Compensatory Control Mechanism for the Support of External Systems," *Journal of Personality and Social Psychology* 95, no. 1 (2008): 18.

20. W. M. Gervais and J. Henrich, "The Zeus Problem: Why Representational Content Biases Cannot Explain Faith in Gods," *Journal of Cognition and Culture* 10, nos. 3–4 (2010): 383–89.

21. W. M. Gervais, A. K. Willard, A. Norenzayan, and J. Henrich, "The Cultural Transmission of Faith: Why Innate Intuitions Are Necessary, but Insufficient, to Explain Religious Belief," *Religion* 41, no. 3 (2011): 389–410.

22. J. A. Lanman, "The Importance of Religious Displays for Belief Acquisition and Secularization," *Journal of Contemporary Religion* 27, no. 1 (2012): 49–65.

23. J. A. Lanman and M. D. Buhrmester, "Religious Actions Speak Louder Than Words: Exposure to Credibility-Enhancing Displays Predicts Theism," *Religion, Brain & Behavior* 7, no. 1 (2017): 3–16.

24. This work is currently inching its way through the publication pipeline.

25. Ditto.

26. C. Sanchez, B. Sundermeier, K. Gray, and R. J. Calin-Jageman, "Direct Replication of Gervais & Norenzayan (2012): No Evidence That Analytic Thinking Decreases Religious Belief," *PLoS ONE* 12, no. 2 (2017): E0172636.

27. W. M. Gervais, M. Van Elk, D. Xygalatas, R. T. McKay, M. Aveyard, E. E. Buchtel, . . . and J. Bulbulia, "Analytic Atheism: A Cross-Culturally Weak and Fickle Phenomenon?," *Judgment and Decision Making* 13, no. 3 (2018): 268–74.

28. P. Boyer, "Religion: Bound to Believe?," *Nature* 455, no. 7216 (2008): 1038–39.

29. W. M. Gervais, M. B. Najle, and N. Caluori, "The Origins of Religious Disbelief: A Dual Inheritance Approach," *Social Psychological and Personality Science* 12, no. 7 (2021): 1369–79.

30. A. K. Willard and L. Cingl, "Testing Theories of Secularization and Religious Belief in the Czech Republic and Slovakia," *Evolution and Human Behavior* 38, no. 5 (2017): 604–15.

CHAPTER TWELVE

1. P. Norris and R. Inglehart, *Sacred and Secular: Religion and Politics Worldwide* (Cambridge: Cambridge University Press, 2011).

2. P. Zuckerman, *Society without God* (New York: New York University Press, 2008).

3. Pew Research, "Religious Landscape Study: Belief in God by State," https://www.pewresearch.org/religion/religious-landscape-study/compare/belief-in-god/by/state/; Pew Research, "How Do European Countries Differ in Religious Commitment," December 5,

2018, https://www.pewresearch.org/short-reads/2018/12/05/how-do-european-countries-differ-in-religious-commitment/.

4. I. Puga-Gonzalez, D. Voas, L. Kiszkiel, R. J. Bacon, W. J. Wildman, K. Talmont-Kaminski, and F. L. Shults, "Modeling Fuzzy Fidelity: Using Microsimulation to Explore Age, Period, and Cohort Effects in Secularization," *Journal of Religion and Demography* 9, nos. 1–2 (2022): 111–37.

5. Joseph Brean, "Canadians' Faith in God Is 'Decoupling' from Their Attachment to Religion," *National Post*, April 6, 2023, https://nationalpost.com/news/canada/canadians-faith-in-god-religion-poll.

6. A. Acerbi, A. Mesoudi, and M. Smolla, *Individual-Based Models of Cultural Evolution: A Step-by-Step Guide Using R* (London: Routledge, 2022); P. Smaldino, *Modeling Social Behavior: Mathematical and Agent-Based Models of Social Dynamics and Cultural Evolution* (Princeton, NJ: Princeton University Press).

7. For an engaging presentation of this sort of modeling logic and interpretation, I highly recommend Cailin O'Connor, *The Origins of Unfairness: Social Categories and Cultural Evolution* (New York: Oxford University Press, 2019). The book is on a different topic than this one, but I enjoy the exposition of how models can sharpen our thinking about what is likely in our world.

8. D.Voas and S. Doebler, "Secularization in Europe: Religious Change between and within Birth Cohorts," *Religion and Society in Central and Eastern Europe* 4, no. 1 (2011): 39–62.

9. H. Turpin, *Unholy Catholic Ireland: Religious Hypocrisy, Secular Morality, and Irish Irreligion* (Stanford, CA: Stanford University Press, 2022).

10. H. Turpin, M. Andersen, and J. A. Lanman, "Creds, Cruds, and Catholic Scandals: Experimentally Examining the Effects of Religious Paragon Behavior on Co-religionist Belief," *Religion, Brain and Behavior* 9, no. 2 (2019): 143–55; H. Turpin and A. K. Willard, "Credibility Enhancing Displays, Religious Scandal and the Decline of Irish Catholic Orthodoxy," *Evolutionary Human Sciences* 4 (2022): e20.

11. J. Henrich, *The WEIRDest People in the World: How the West Became Psychologically Peculiar and Particularly Prosperous* (New York: Farrar, Straus and Giroux, 2020).

12. J. F. Schulz, D. Bahrami-Rad, J. P. Beauchamp, and J. Henrich, "The Church, Intensive Kinship, and Global Psychological Variation," *Science* 366, no. 6466 (2019): Eaau5141.

13. As with some other projects, it is making its way, intestinally, through the peer reviewed publication pipeline.

14. R. McKay and H. Whitehouse, "Religion and Morality," *Psychological Bulletin* 141, no. 2 (2015): 447.

15. C. Tamir, A. Connaughton, and A. M. Salazar, "The Global God Divide," Pew Research Center, July 20, 2020, https://www.pewresearch.org/global/2020/07/20/the-global-god-divide/.

16. W. M. Gervais, "Everything Is Permitted? People Intuitively Judge Immorality as Representative of Atheists," *PLoS ONE* 9, no. 4 (2014): E92302.

17. W. M. Gervais, D. Xygalatas, R. T. McKay, M. Van Elk, E. E. Buchtel, M. Aveyard, . . . and J. Bulbulia, "Global Evidence of Extreme Intuitive Moral Prejudice against Atheists." *Nature Human Behaviour* 1, no. 8 (2017): 0151.

18. Jonathan Evans, "Unlike Their Central and Eastern European Neighbors, Most Czechs Don't Believe in God," Pew Research Center, June 19, 2017, https://www.pewre

search.org/short-reads/2017/06/19/unlike-their-central-and-eastern-european-neighbors-most-czechs-dont-believe-in-god/.

19. J. Knobe, "Intentional Action and Side Effects in Ordinary Language," *Analysis* 63 (2003): 190–93.

CHAPTER THIRTEEN

1. P. Boyer, *Religion Explained* (New York: Random House, 2008).

2. M. Chudek, R. A. McNamara, S. Birch, P. Bloom, and J. Henrich, "Do Minds Switch Bodies? Dualist Interpretations Across Ages and Societies," *Religion, Brain and Behavior* 8, no. 4 (2018): 354–68.

3. D. Kelemen, "Are Children 'Intuitive Theists'? Reasoning about Purpose and Design in Nature," *Psychological Science* 15, no. 5 (2004): 295–301.

4. W. M. Gervais and J. Henrich, "The Zeus Problem: Why Representational Content Biases Cannot Explain Faith in Gods," *Journal of Cognition and Culture* 10, nos. 3–4 (2010): 383–89.

5. W. M. Gervais, A. K. Willard, A. Norenzayan, and J. Henrich, "The Cultural Transmission of Faith: Why Innate Intuitions Are Necessary, but Insufficient, to Explain Religious Belief," *Religion* 41, no. 3 (2011): 389–410.

6. A. Norenzayan, A. F. Shariff, W. M. Gervais, A. K. Willard, R. A. McNamara, E. Slingerland, and J. Henrich, "The Cultural Evolution of Prosocial Religions," *Behavioral and Brain Sciences* 39 (2016): E1.

7. A. Norenzayan, *Big Gods: How Religion Transformed Cooperation and Conflict* (Princeton, NJ: Princeton University Press, 2013).

8. J. L. Barrett, *Born Believers: The Science of Children's Religious Belief* (New York: Simon & Schuster, 2012).

9. P. L. Harris and M. A. Koenig, "Trust in Testimony: How Children Learn about Science and Religion," *Child Development* 77, no. 3 (2006): 505–24.

10. P. L. Harris, E. S. Pasquini, S. Duke, J. J. Asscher, and F. Pons, "Germs and Angels: The Role of Testimony in Young Children's Ontology," *Developmental Science* 9, no. 1 (2006): 76–96.

11. P. Boyer, "Religion: Bound to Believe?," *Nature* 455, no. 7216 (2008): 1038–39.

12. J. L. Barrett, *Why Would Anyone Believe in God?* (Lanham, MD: Altamira Press, 2004).

13. Barrett, *Born Believers.*

14. Boyer, "Religion: Bound to Believe?"

15. J. L. Barrett, "Counterfactuality in Counterintuitive Religious Concepts," *Behavioral and Brain Sciences* 27, no. 6 (2004): 731–32.

16. Barrett, *Why Would Anyone Believe in God?*

17. J. A. Lanman and M. D. Buhrmester, "Religious Actions Speak Louder Than Words: Exposure to Credibility-Enhancing Displays Predicts Theism," *Religion, Brain and Behavior* 7, no. 1 (2017): 3–16.

18. W. M. Gervais and A. Norenzayan, "Analytic Thinking Promotes Religious Disbelief," *Science* 336, no. 6080 (2012): 493–96.

19. C. Sanchez, B. Sundermeier, K. Gray, and R. J. Calin-Jageman, "Direct Replication of Gervais and Norenzayan (2012): No Evidence That Analytic Thinking Decreases Religious Belief," *PLoS ONE* 12, no. 2 (2012): E0172636.

20. W. M. Gervais, M. Van Elk, D. Xygalatas, R. T. McKay, M. Aveyard, E. E. Buchtel, . . . and J. Bulbulia, "Analytic Atheism: A Cross-Culturally Weak and Fickle Phenomenon?," *Judgment and Decision Making* 13, no. 3 (2018): 268–74.

21. W. M. Gervais, M. B. Najle, and N. Caluori, "The Origins of Religious Disbelief: A Dual Inheritance Approach," *Social Psychological and Personality Science* 12, no. 7 (2021): 1369–79.

22. A. K. Willard and L. Cingl, "Testing Theories of Secularization and Religious Belief in The Czech Republic and Slovakia," *Evolution and Human Behavior* 38, no. 5 (2017): 604–15.

23. J. L. Barrett, "The Relative Unnaturalness of Atheism: On Why Geertz and Markusson Are Both Right and Wrong," *Religion* 40, no. 3 (2010): 169–72.

24. J. Bering, "Atheism Is Only Skin Deep: Geertz and Markússon Rely Mistakenly on Sociodemographic Data as Meaningful Indicators of Underlying Cognition," *Religion* 40, no. 3 (2010): 166–68.

25. D. C. Dennett, *Breaking the Spell: Religion as a Natural Phenomenon* (New York: Penguin, 2006); M. Shermer, *The Believing Brain: From Spiritual Faiths to Political Convictions—How We Construct Beliefs and Reinforce Them as Truths* (London: Hachette).

26. K. N. Lala and G. R. Brown, *Sense and Nonsense: Evolutionary Perspectives on Human Behaviour* (New York: Oxford University Press, 2011).

27. R. Chvaja, "Why Did Memetics Fail? Comparative Case Study. *Perspectives on Science*, 28, no. 4 (2020): 542–70.

28. J. Henrich, S. J. Heine, and A. Norenzayan, "The WEIRDest People in the World?," *Behavioral and Brain Sciences* 33, nos. 2–3 (2010): 61–83.

29. K. Banerjee and P. Bloom, "Would Tarzan Believe in God? Conditions for the Emergence of Religious Belief," *Trends in Cognitive Sciences* 17, no. 1 (2013): 7–8.

CHAPTER FOURTEEN

1. Two short articles may pique the reader's interest: R. Stark, "Secularization, RIP," *Sociology of Religion* 60, no. 3 (1999): 249–73; R. Inglehart and P. Norris, "Why Didn't Religion Disappear? Re-examining the Secularization Thesis," in *Cultures and Globalization: Conflicts and Tensions*, ed. Helmut K. Anheier and Yudhishthir Raj Isar (Los Angeles: Sage, 2007), 253–57.

2. R. Dawkins, *Outgrowing God: A Beginner's Guide* (New York: Random House, 2019).

3. J. Preston and N. Epley, "Science and God: An Automatic Opposition between Ultimate Explanations," *Journal of Experimental Social Psychology* 45, no. 1 (2009): 238–41.

4. J. McPhetres, J. Jong, and M. Zuckerman, "Religious Americans Have Less Positive Attitudes toward Science, but This Does Not Extend to Other Cultures," *Social Psychological and Personality Science* 12, no. 4 (2021): 528–36.

5. K. R. Miller, *Only a Theory: Evolution and the Battle for America's Soul* (New York: Penguin, 2008).

6. P. Norris and R. Inglehart, *Sacred and Secular: Religion and Politics Worldwide* (Cambridge: Cambridge University Press, 2011).

7. A. K. Willard and L. Cingl, "Testing Theories of Secularization and Religious Belief in the Czech Republic and Slovakia," *Evolution and Human Behavior* 38, no. 5 (2017): 604–15.

8. D. Voas, "The Rise and Fall of Fuzzy Fidelity in Europe," *European Sociological Review* 25, no. 2 (2009): 155–68.

9. O. O. Táíwò, *Reconsidering Reparations* (New York: Oxford University Press, 2022).

10. For an eye-opening exploration: Yaryna Serkez, "Every Country Has Its Own Climate Risks. What's Yours?," *New York Times*, January 28, 2021, https://www.nytimes.com/interactive/2021/01/28/opinion/climate-change-risks-by-country.html.

11. Táíwò, *Reconsidering Reparations.*

12. G. Vince, *Nomad Century: How Climate Migration Will Shape Our World* (New York: Flatiron, 2022).

13. "Bangladesh: A Country Underwater, a Culture on the Move, Nation Resources Defense Council," September 13, 2018, https://www.nrdc.org/stories/bangladesh-country-underwater-culture-move.

14. O. O. Táíwò, *Elite Capture: How the Powerful Took Over Identity Politics (and Everything Else)* (Chicago: Haymarket Books, 2022). This is the clearest exposition I can recommend for understanding how the global game's been played, and largely already won, to the benefit of so few.

15. J. Henrich, *The Secret of Our Success: How Culture Is Driving Human Evolution, Domesticating Our Species, and Making Us Smarter* (Princeton, NJ: Princeton University Press, 2016).

16. M. Muthukrishna and J. Henrich, "Innovation in the Collective Brain," *Philosophical Transactions of the Royal Society B: Biological Sciences* 371, no. 1690 (2016): 20150192.

17. K. J. Zollman, "The Epistemic Benefit of Transient Diversity," *Erkenntnis* 72, no. 1 (2010): 17–35.

18. C. O'Connor and J. O. Weatherall, "Scientific Polarization," *European Journal for Philosophy of Science* 8 (2018): 855–75; P. E. Smaldino, C. Moser, A. Pérez Velilla, and M. Werling, "Maintaining Transient Diversity Is a General Principle for Improving Collective Problem Solving," *Perspectives on Psychological Science* (2022): 17456916231180100.

19. S. J. Gould, *The Panda's Thumb: More Reflections in Natural History* (New York: W.W. Norton, 2010).

ACKNOWLEDGMENTS

You may have noticed that this is a large book. These hundreds of pages are supported by lots of people from over the years and decades. Here's my effort to name most of them. Let's go more or less chronologically.

First, Marty and Mary Gervais, without whom this book would be biologically and intellectually impossible. We had mountains instead of church. Camping trips around the Southwest provided my first notion that different cultures were different, and religions could look very different while still fulfilling the same roles. Wouldn't have had it any other way! Thanks, then and now. Jack: I've jawed at you about this stuff a lot over the years, from downstairs in Breck to the apartment in Denver to now Maine and Vancouver and Kentucky and Colorado again. We're proud of you buddy, keep it up.

I'm indebted to many great teachers over the years, but the first who really stands out was Denise Oaks-Moffett at Summit High School. I remember her justifiably palpable disappointment at the first writing assignment we all turned in. But damn it, she taught me to write and that's made so many things easier over the years.

At the University of Denver I was a shiftless student who hopped from major to major. Hallie Ward's intro psychology class stuck, and I've been psychologizing ever since. Danny McIntosh convinced me to join the psych honors program, and thus began my research career. Over the years I've enjoyed thinking of myself as a rare third-generation psychologist of religion, of the Denver school (Spilka → McIntosh → me), even if that's a bit of a fudge because I didn't start working on religion until a couple years later. Cathy Reed and Ralph Roberts saw me from that point to grad school, providing valuable mentorship (and employment!) along the way.

At the University of British Columbia, I had a mighty mentoring triumvirate: Ara Norenzayan, Joe Henrich, and Mark Schaller. You know grad school went well when you stay in touch with and collaborate with your mentors some decade later. Thanks for all you taught, fellas. Aside from the big three mentors who appeared on most of my paperwork, there was a great group of folks whom I chatted with about various things over the grad school years. Kiley Hamlin, Jeremy Biesanz, Sue Birch, Steve Heine, Ted Slingerland, you all shaped my thinking for the better. Grad school success is only about 8 percent down to faculty. The other 92 percent? The friends and fellow students who get you through it: Damian Murray, Lara Aknin, Maciek Chudek, Aiyana Willard, Jelena Brcic, Alyssa Croft, Rita McNamara, Emma Buchtel, Will Dunlop (we miss you dearly, buddy!).

Then there are grad school friends who become family. Catherine Rawn, Russell Ball, Lesley Duncan, Brad Lauzon: we're eckshnited for the next in-person round of PWC, next time y'all are in London or we're back in Vancouver.

After UBC, seven years in Kentucky. Lexington is a hidden gem, the funnest little city you've never been to or even heard much about. The first few years there, I was one of the few junior folks in my department, so our closest friends had little to do with the university—something that I cherished. Shooting the shit or trying trick shots after soccer* matches, the street parties, just goofing around. The river trip. It was the best. The whole crew: Tony, A.J. (Eyeballface), Becca, Paul, Kate, Garland, Burke (Pinky), Thai, Matty, Angie, Emily, Price, everyone else. Our neighbors on both sides: Greg, Molly, Arnold, and Rigdon to the left, Chris and Barb to the right, front porch happy hour! We miss everyone and still plan to make good on our promise to come back for a proper sendoff one of these days. Until then, hit us up next time you're passing through London.

At the University of Kentucky, Jazmin Brown-Iannuzzi and I struck up a friendship and collaboration, without which this book would be different indeed. You'll see that name numerous times in this book. Jazi was part of a super cohort that brought much needed young blood to the department right around the same time: Rachel, Stacey, Jazi, Andrew, Liz, Dan, Christal, Lou, it was a fun bunch, and I hope you're all still well, in Lexington or since departed! Bob Lorch was on sabbatical when I interviewed, so I didn't get to meet my new department chair until on the job. Bob, thank you so much for your support and mentorship over the years! You were

* Yes, Huxley, I know it's called football. But, you see, *these people are Americans.*

always "Awesome Bob" when I was talking about my department to friends who hadn't visited. Bob's compassionate, ethical, and supportive leadership proved irreplaceable. Jonathan Golding—I miss you man. Special shout out to Christal Badour and Lou Hirsch, who, in addition to being all around fun and great people, were supportive when that's all that was needed. We have stolen your Easter party shenanigans and exported them to England. Chris Marshburn, I wish we'd overlapped for more than just a turbulent year, but we'll catch up at a conference soon!

In Kentucky, we also made friends with members of the local humanist and secular groups. They welcomed us and showed us the importance of nonreligious community, in a religious region. Clay and Stacey Maney, Dan Wu, Lauren Sherrow, Kelly and Leanna McCormick, Dan Delaney et al., I really hope you enjoy this book! I had you all in mind when writing it.

Over the years I've been fortunate to work with some fantastic students, thanks to you all. Special thanks to Nava Caluori and Maxine Najle, whose names you'll see littered throughout these pages, and for good reason! Their projects shape these chapters.

Here in London, there's the Centre for Culture and Evolution, the intellectual incubator for this book. Our dozen-plus evolutionary and cultural thinkers are a really unique bunch, and I love you all. The CCE's an oasis, it's special. Visit it! Special thanks go out to CCErs Aiyana Willard and Lora Adair, who've most dealt with my grumpiness and most cheered me through the book writing journey.

Whether we were living in Denver or Vancouver or Kentucky or New Zealand or London, Reyna Kellie was always positive and supportive. I've cherished our conversations over the years, on the topics in these pages or about the Avs, or whatever else is going on. Gracias!

Now the amorphous set of thanks to all the friends and fellow scientists near and far who I've enjoyed chatting with about atheism and culture and science over the years, you folks keep me sharp. In no particular order, some already mentioned, and with no doubt plentiful omissions: Aiyana Willard, Ara Norenzayan, Joe Henrich, Michael Muthukrishna, Rita McNamara, Joe Bulbulia, Dimitris Xygalatas, Mickey Inzlicht, Linda Skitka, Kiley Hamlin, Jazi Brown-Iannuzzi, Hugh Turpin, Ben Purzycki, Jon Lanman, Ryan McKay, Rob Ross, Gord Pennycook, Lora Adair, Jonathan Jong, Hans IJzerman, Berna Devezer, Andrew Shtulman, Paul Smaldino, Danielle

Navarro, Nicole Wen, Michelle Kline, Matt Gervais,[†] Catherine Rawn, Lesley Duncan, Cristina Moya, Alyssa Croft, Larisa Heiphetz Solomon, Nicole Wen, Quentin Atkinson, Bob Calin-Jageman, Mark Aveyard, Penny Edgell, Dave Schmitt, and everyone else.

Massive thanks also to Nick Gibson, who made space for good research on religion and atheism, and who helped us keep our jobs as we were coming up. This field is yours, Nick.

Many folks were generous enough to look through chapters, to keep me honest with my science and tolerable as regards my other nonsense. Drew, who's read it all multiple times, from back before it was anything like a book. Aiyana volunteered to read a few chapters and so I naturally sent her all the really long and complicated ones. If those heavy-lifting chapters make any sense, that's on her. Michelle Kline provided excellent feedback on the cultural evolution chapter. Hugh Turpin kept me honest on the state of Irish Catholic CRUDs. Lora told me exactly what I wanted to hear about the opening chapter ("I love it. I wanna read more of it"). Dixbik Kellielellalia was nice enough to give feedback while traversing about Europe, much appreciated! Jack Willans, thank you for reading drafts even though you'd only met me once at time of offer, I appreciate your perspective on this book.

You! Yes, you. Nobody actually reads these acknowledgments things, unless they half expect to be in them. So this one's all yours, champ: thank you for your attention to detail and commitment to digesting this entire tome. This book makes a great gift for friends and family (*hint*).

Huge thanks to my agent, Giles Anderson. My earliest proposals merited feedback tantamount to "Books . . . are you familiar with them, Will? How they work at a basic level?" My earliest proposals and pitches were poorly organized, just lengthy lists of things I knew about or had studied. If, as I sincerely hope, you enjoy this book, that's down to Giles reminding me that *books are about things*, they hold together around some center. Thanks for sticking with me past those bumpy starts, Giles. Much appreciated. While on the business side of writing a book, my editor at Prometheus, Jake Bonar, has been constantly supportive. From early enthusiasm and encouragement, to rounds of title and cover work, to feedback and hype on the

[†] We get asked a lot, and don't definitively know. Probably distant cousins of some sort, given family history and geography?

early drafts, and to inexplicably trying to convince me the Sabres are better than the Avs, it's been a fun ride . . . thank you!

A book this thick is a team win, and I'm grateful to all these folks' contributions, plus those that I've no doubt forgotten.

Last but not least, who's to say that scientists only take inspiration from science? Full disclosure: I probably read comics and novels more than I read academic journals. Fiction lets us imagine other worlds than our own—a particular world, or a possible world, or a terrible world. What and who I've read and loved of late: *Pretty Deadly*, *Monstress*, *Eight Billion Genies*, *The Sandman*, *Locke and Key*, *East of West*, *Bitter Root*, *Preacher*, *Wytches*, *Bone*, *Daytripper*, *Amulet*, Jeff Lemire and Andrea Sorrentino, Brubaker and Phillips, Emil Ferris, Tillie Walden, Emily Carroll, Kate Beaton, Gene Luen Yang, Ken Liu, Victor LaValle, Alan Moore, Rivers Solomon, Silvia Moreno-Garcia, Terry Pratchett, Ted Chiang, Sarah Gailey, Gabino Iglesias, Kazuo Ishiguro, Mariana Enriquez, Rebecca Roanhorse, Ryka Aoki, Stephen Graham Jones, Nghi Vo, Kacen Callender, and Rebecca Kuang, to name a few.

Finally, the whole time I've been doing my science and writing my book, I've been well sheltered and fed, surrounded by people who love me. I haven't had to fight particularly hard to prove I belong in this world. That's not true for everyone, but together we can make it truer. Be kind to each other, y'all.